Jack Huberman grew up in Mo[...] architecture from McGill Univers[...] where he pursued a dizzying s[...] cartoonist, illustrator, graduate student, magazine writer, freelance book editor, newspaper reporter and stock trader. He is also the author of *The Bush-Hater's Handbook – An A-Z Guide to the Most Appalling Presidency of the Past 100 Years*, also published by Granta Books.

BUSHIT!

HOW THE BUSH CREW IS WRECKING AMERICA AND ENDANGERING THE WORLD

JACK HUBERMAN

Granta Books
London

Granta Publications, 2/3 Hanover Yard,
Noel Road, London N1 8BE

First published in Great Britain by
Granta Books 2006

A CIP catalogue record for this book is
available from the British Library.

1 3 5 7 9 10 8 6 4 2

ISBN-13: 978-1-86207-843-7
ISBN-10: 1-86207-843-2

Printed and bound in Great Britain by
Bookmarque Limited, Croydon, Surrey

Contents

To Renée

INTRODUCTION

[T]hese princes . . . have done great things who have had little regard for good faith, and have been able by astuteness to confuse men's brains.

—Machiavelli, whom Karl Rove is said to reread "the way the devout study their Bibles" [1]

Conservatives are not necessarily stupid, but most stupid people are conservative.

—John Stuart Mill

The modern conservative is engaged in one of man's oldest exercises in moral philosophy: that is the search for a superior moral justification for selfishness.

—John Kenneth Galbraith

This book picks up where my *Bush-Hater's Handbook*, published in December 2003, left off. It covers the profusion of fresh Bush administration outrages since then and new information about older ones—all with the deeper, fuller understanding and loathing of Bushism that two additional years of suffering and study have produced.

The aim, again, is to provide a user-friendly, frighteningly entertaining overview of the Bushevik revolution, covering, from A to Z, all the main bases of Bush baseness, duplicity, and all-around villainy. Hardliners among us liberals and lefties insist we have no credible peace partners. This book aspires to unite "red" and "blue" readers in a mutual understanding of Bushism as a bottomless well of wickedness; to win the hearts and minds of hard-hearted, bone-headed Bushites and at the same time fill gaps in the knowledge of even the most devoted and learned Bush-hater. For those who fall somewhere in between, or are just waking from a four-year nap, this may serve as the perfect, utterly fair and balanced primer. A survey course. A big-picture book.

Red, blue, purple, avocado green, or harvest gold, you will come away convinced that this administration is indeed, as John Kerry said in an inadvertent and, alas, isolated moment of complete candor, "the most crooked, lying group [we've] ever seen": that it is an insult to our intelligence and our sense of truth and fairness; a threat to the rights and well-being of workers, consumers, women, gays, and at least six other categories of Americans; a menace to America's environmental and economic health, its social safety net, its scientific and intellectual standing, its diplomacy, credibility, and security, and its very democracy. And to a lot of people overseas.

My favorite endorsement of Kerry in 2004 came from the Crawford, Texas, *Lone Star Iconoclast*, "Bush's hometown paper," which endorsed W. in 2000. It said: "Few Americans would have voted for George W. Bush four years ago if he had promised that . . . he would: Empty the Social Security trust fund by $507 billion . . . Cut Medicare by 17 percent and reduce veterans' benefits and military pay. Eliminate overtime pay for millions of Americans and raise oil prices by 50 percent [make that 100 percent]. Give tax cuts to businesses that sent American jobs overseas . . . Give away billions of tax dollars in government contracts without competitive bids. Involve this country in a deadly and highly questionable war, and . . . [t]ake a budget surplus and turn it into the worst deficit in the history of the United States, creating a debt in just four years that will take generations to repay."

The Bush legacy will include all that, PLUS: a major erosion in middle-class living standards. More Americans in poverty. A tax system in which middle- and lower-income Americans find themselves in effectively higher brackets than many of the richest. Presidential power and secrecy increased. Constitutional checks and balances, and civil liberties, curtailed. The federal courts skewed far to the right. An emasculated press, in which the line between news and propaganda is ever more blurred. The wall between church and state so near to collapse that traffic must be rerouted.

Huge holes in our "homeland" security. An exhausted and overstretched U.S. military. Growing dependence on imported oil, which keeps us meddling in the Middle East, which drives our global popularity to new lows, which makes our exports less popular, which hurts our balance of trade, which drives down our dollar, which drives up the price of oil, which hurts our balance of trade and helps finance terrorism, which hurts our economy and increases our defense costs, which increases our debt, which drives down our dollar, which drives up the price of oil, which . . .

Dirtier air and water. Ravaged landscapes. Accelerating global warming. Mass extinctions. The decay of the Earth's orbit, finally sending the planet hurtling into the sun.

I'm glad *you* think it's funny. The fact is, America has been pulled so far out of *its* orbit—*hijacked*, rather, and flown so far off course to the right—it may never swing back, and may truly be headed for a crash.

The hijackers represent three branches of the GOP network, joined in jihad to reverse decades of progress. The dominant, business wing merely wants tax breaks, subsidies, rollbacks of environmental, consumer, and labor rules, and—oh, yeah—full control of the government. The religious and "social conservative" wing wants to impose its beliefs and values on everybody else; to drive gays back into the closet, abortion back into back alleys, and the country, intellectually, back into Darwin-knows-what century. The "neocon" wing wants an America that exercises its power aggressively and unapologetically in "America's" self-interest (mine? Yours? Exxon's?), with as much *dis*regard as possible for international law, organizations, and opinion. (What gives us this right is that we're the good guys. We *do* say so ourselves. And a military budget larger than the 25 next largest in the world combined says so.)

Under Bush, big-business interests rule as never before. Corporate executives, lawyers, and lobbyists fill almost all important administration positions, typically overseeing their own industries. Industry lobbyists not only in effect pay for but *write* the laws governing their industries. They have friendly, if not wholly owned, majorities in both houses of Congress and on the federal court benches. There are few checks left on corporate power and greed.

All now hinges on the Republicans' continuing success in persuading a certain number of middle- and working-class voters to forget that the administration sides with big business and the rich against the little guy *every* time, and to vote Against Their Own Interests. It has been remarked that, rather than create policies to reflect majorities, the Bushies seek to create majorities to support their policies. Luckily for them, pro-Republican conglomerates control the most influential news media and are not interested in biting the government hands that feed them regulatory favors—with regard, for example, to media ownership rules—or in offending their mostly pro-Republican corporate advertisers.

The Bushies, moreover, have excelled at the manipulation of emotions through symbols, slogans, and stagecraft. By staking out religious and moral values (of a kind) as its own territory, the GOP has succeeded in identifying itself in millions of Americans' minds with ~~Gop~~ God and faith and the flag and with all that is traditional, comforting, solid, simple, decent, and good. Rove knows, that is a formidable military position.

(Make no mistake—in the Bushrovian scheme of things, the Christian right's function is to provide votes, campaign contributions, volunteers, and passion—and then receive, in exchange, mostly promises, gestures, and pleasing rhetoric, while big business and the wealthy get the meat and potatoes, or rather, *filet mignon avec pommes de terre au caviar.*)

But cheer up—a little—little liberals: "Cultural" or "values" issues may be all the Repubs have left. With their credibility on national security issues damaged by revelations of their pre-9/11 neglect of terrorism, the protracted war in Iraq, and the apparent good health of Al Qaeda, the Bushies' exploitation of patriotism and fear isn't the *slam-dunk*, as it were, that it was after 9/11. A majority of Americans (57 percent, according to a CNN/*USA Today*/Gallup poll in May 2005) have decided it was not worth going to war in Iraq. As for the Bush domestic policies the war has helped distract from, most Americans have been opposed to them from the start. Poll after poll has shown an overwhelming preference for increased spending on health care, education, environmental programs, and deficit reduction over tax cuts and military spending, and overwhelming opposition to cuts in Medicare and Medicaid and to Bush's Social Security privatization scheme.

Unfortunately, according to a pair of remarkable studies in 2004, many Bush voters didn't *know* what his policies were and assumed he favored the same things they themselves did. Large majorities (versus few Kerry supporters) not only continued to believe the Bushit about Saddam's WMDs and support for Al Qaeda—even after official, well-publicized investigations concluded that neither existed—but also believed, for example, that Bush favored such multilateral agreements as the Kyoto treaty on global warming, the Comprehensive [Nuclear] Test Ban Treaty, and the International Criminal Court.

Bush has often testified about what faith has meant to him. Amen. These studies attest to the faith-based nature of his political support.

Not to dismiss "cultural issues" as mere weapons of mass distraction that help the Bush gang pick the pockets of the prayerful masses. Bush himself may be genuinely religious (or just *believe* he is—perhaps the way he believed in Saddam's WMDs, out of what the *New York Times* called a terrifying "capacity for politically motivated self-deception"). In the conservative movement, we are witnessing the gleeful revenge of people who resented and despised the social, cultural, and political developments of the 1960s, which are to the movement what the Civil War long remained to the white South. Conservatives look back to an "antebellum" time—before Vietnam and civil rights, before all this equality and liberation and criticizing of America came along. The Cheneys and Rumsfelds and Bushes seek to restore the pre-Watergate "imperial presidency," in all its glorious secrecy, unaccountability, and war-making power. For others, the nostalgia is variously for an era before the evils of legal abortion and open homosexuality were let loose, or before the supremacy of rich white Christian men was so cruelly attacked. I believe many conservatives are not just indifferent but hostile to social equality. If you don't think many Republicans wear U.S. flag pins on their lapels and Confederate flags on their hearts, you have a (Trent) Lott to learn. Check out the Confederate paraphernalia—like the "never surrendered" Confederate sword—that "mainstream" conservative outfits like the Heritage Foundation offer for sale.[2] By the way, every former Confederate state voted for Bush in 2004, while almost all the states that sided with Lincoln voted for Kerry. And of the 21 senators who declined to co-sponsor a resolution in June 2005 apologizing to the victims of lynching and their descendants for the Senate's failure to enact anti-lynching legislation, 18 were Republicans.

Bizarre as it is, a sense of being a downtrodden minority—no, worse, a downtrodden *majority*—persists, thrives in, and helps to drive the movement. Add a little religious absolutism, stir in some racially charged tax resentment (or is it fiscally charged racial resentment), and you have a potent political fuel blending fear, vengefulness, selfishness, self-righteousness, sheer us-versus-them tribalism, and the energy, glamour, and momentum of what "conservative" radicals like Tom DeLay themselves call a *revolution:* the thrilling sense that there is no law or institution, however well established, that can't be marked for destruction;

that anything is possible, everything is *sayable* again. The gag of political correctness has been removed. At times, the movement's sole object seems to be to discover how far it can go. A fanatic, wrote George Santayana, is one who redoubles his efforts just when he has forgotten his ends.

Power is, of course, quite famous for becoming an end in itself. According to former Nixon White House counsel John Dean, "the only agenda [the Bushies] had during the first term was to get a second term," and their second-term agenda is "to make sure the Republicans control the federal government (all three branches) indefinitely." And to make sure the executive branch controls the other two, Dean should have added. Ask Republican Senator Chuck Hagel (R-NE), who warned that under Bush, Congress "could become an adjunct to the executive branch," and that "Congress is the only thing that stands in the way [of] essentially a modern-day democratic dictatorship."

Apologies to readers to whom some of my information will seem overly familiar. This is not a work of journalism. I did no original research. It's basically an opinionated catalog distilled from various news and opinion sources. In dismissing the famous August 6, 2001, Presidential Daily Brief that warned Bush, "Bin Laden Determined to Attack Inside the United States," Condoleezza Rice claimed it was merely "historical" and "analytic" in nature. That's my excuse, too. In fact, as I did in *The Bush-Hater's Handbook*, I wrote in a tense I call the "past hopeful," both out of impatience for the day when the Bushies are history and in the hope that this book will still be useful then.

Indeed, consider it a protest against the news-ist equation of *not new* = *not important*. The cultural habit of boredom with yesterday's news breeds forgetfulness—Gore Vidal's "United States of Amnesia." And that breeds right-wing victories. Today's bogus terrorism warning, or Michael Jackson story, drives "yesterday's" White House scandal off the news. The Bushies of course want us to forget about their mother of all failures, the failure to prevent 9/11. And about Saddam's "huge stockpiles" of WMDs and "threat of unique urgency." And that the vast majority of Americans never wanted the radical changes being foisted on us—that Bush's election *loss* in 2000, and the narrowest reelection victory in presidential history in 2004, amount to a "mandate" as phony as "Jeff Gannon's" media credentials.

These points are, to be sure, well enshrined in the anti-Bush canon. But that's one reason I couldn't leave them out. Plus, truths, if not visited and tended to, decay into tru*isms*. Besides, when more than 40 percent of Americans (down from some 70 percent) still believe Iraq had something to do with 9/11—and 42 percent (as of June 2005) still believe Bush is doing a good job (down from 90 percent after 9/11, and the lowest for any second-term president at that point)—nothing can be taken for granted.

ABORTION AND BIRTH CONTROL

I want to thank you, especially, for the civil way that you have engaged one of America's most contentious issues.
——George W. Bush, speaking to "pro-life" activists, January 2005. Since 1982 there have been 169 bombings or arsons of abortion clinics.

In an ABC News/*Washington Post* poll in January 2003—the 30th anniversary of *Roe v. Wade*, the Supreme Court case that legalized abortion in the U.S.—57 percent, including women and men in roughly equal numbers, said abortion should be legal in all or most cases; 80 to 90 percent said abortion should be legal to save the woman's life, to preserve her health, or when the pregnancy was caused by rape or incest. Only 42 percent wanted abortions to be harder to get. Polls showed similar results year after year.

But Bush policies were not determined by polls or majorities but by special interest groups, right-wing ideologues, and a political strategy that gave religious conservatives disproportionate power. And "pro-life" zealots were impatient for Bush to push for a constitutional amendment banning abortion outright—for which he declared support in 2000. They also knew that just one or two Bush appointments to the Supreme Court would be enough to overturn *Roe*, in which case it was estimated that at least 21 states and possibly 38 would quickly outlaw abortion. "To overturn a constitutional decision that secured a fundamental personal liberty to millions of persons," wrote former Justice

Harry Blackmun, "would be unprecedented in our 200 years of constitutional history." Nor, of course, would it end abortion: Before *Roe*, thousands of American women died every year from botched, illegal abortions—as some 80,000 women around the world still do. And 43 percent of all abortions are performed in countries where abortion is illegal.

Indeed, the U.S. abortion rate *fell* about 27 percent during the Clinton years—apparently thanks to improved access to medical care, family planning services, and education—but began to climb again under Bush, as poverty, anti-abortion agitation and legislation, and the national stupidity level (NSL) increased.

Civil rights for fetuses, not for women. The right understood that radical social changes are best accomplished by increments; and "incrementalism" was the very word a delighted "pro-life" activist used in November 2003 when Bush signed into law a bill banning so-called "partial-birth abortions," an array of safe, common abortion methods used in the second or third trimester of pregnancy, normally only when there are serious health complications for the mother or fatal abnormalities in the fetus. Although these constituted fewer than 0.2 percent of abortions, the bill, the *New York Times* reported, "strikes at the heart of *Roe v. Wade* by criminalizing many midterm abortions and omitting exceptions for a mother's health." It was the first-ever federal ban on abortion procedures. A photograph of Bush signing the bill surrounded by a dozen or so middle-aged Republican men gleefully "celebrating depriving women of a medical procedure that could save their health and their lives," as one Democrat put it, spoke volumes. (Thenceforth, the

White House would be more careful to include a woman in the picture while amBushing women's rights.)

Three federal judges immediately issued restraining orders blocking enforcement of the new law; three years earlier, the Supreme Court had declared a nearly identical law unconstitutional. In an insult to the very words "civil rights," Attorney General JOHN ASHCROFT assigned the Justice Department (DOJ)'s civil rights division to enforce this law, which the courts had "essentially found . . . to violate the civil rights of millions of American women," the *Guardian* noted.

Deaths *and abortions* in the name of "life." Bush's war on reproductive rights, at home and abroad, began on his first day in the Oval Office, when he reinstated President Reagan's so-called "global gag rule" by cutting off U.S. funding for international organizations that so much as provide abortion counseling or information. Groups that lost funding, such as the United Nations Population Fund (UNFPA), provided family planning services that *prevented* abortions by preventing unwanted pregnancies. The UNFPA also aided in AIDS education, sexual violence prevention, maternal care, literacy, job training, and emergency disaster relief in 156 countries. UN officials estimated the loss of funding from the U.S. would undermine their ability to prevent 800,000 abortions and could result in the deaths of 4,700 women and 77,000 children. The global gag rule has since led to closed health clinics, dwindling medical supplies, and a *complete* cutoff of USAID funds in 16 countries.[3]

In September 2003, Bush expanded the gag rule to cover all family planning programs funded through the State Department, meaning that even more women, including refugees, would be denied basic health care services. "The upshot is that women and babies are dying in Africa" because of Bush's "idealism," wrote the *New York Times*'s Nicholas Kristof.

- One of Bush's first actions was to disband the President's Interagency Council on Women, a group appointed by Clinton to help implement the 1995 BEIJING DECLARATION ON WOMEN'S RIGHTS, which called for governments to close the gender gap in health, education, employment, and political participation and recognize women's right to "decide freely and responsibly on matters related to their sexuality . . . free of coercion, discrimination and violence." At a UN conference in February 2005, the U.S. alone, opposed by more than 100 nations, tried to amend this disgraceful declaration to state that it does "not create any new international human rights [God forbid!] [or] include the right to abortion." The move was "a preemptive strike against U.S. judges who could someday use the Beijing document as a basis for protecting abortion rights" at home, wrote Tim Grieve in *Salon.com*.
- While they pretended to champion "life," the Bushies' first budget proposal, in March 2001, sought to cut the MATERNAL AND CHILD HEALTH block grants and to freeze the HEALTHY START program, which had been shown to reduce infant mortality and morbidity.
- Out of over 200 judges nominated to the federal bench in Bush's first term, only two expressed even the slightest respect for the abortion rights granted by the laws they were supposed to uphold (see **justice**).

Embryos are "children" and "human research volunteers." After imposing crippling restrictions on STEM CELL RESEARCH to please anti-abortion fanatics (see **Compassion**), in 2002 the administration further limited vital medical research by declaring that embryos counted as human research volunteers under the protection of Health and Human Services (HHS)'s Advisory Committee on Human Research Protection.

- What is it about *birth* that instantly renders a fetus so much less worthy of **compassion**? In January 2002, in a move of breathtaking cynicism, HHS Secretary TOMMY THOMPSON, an "outspoken" abortion-rights opponent, announced that thenceforth, a fetus would be defined as a "child" for the purpose of entitling poor women to prenatal care under the State Children's Health Insurance Program (SCHIP). The administration *could* just have said it was extending prenatal care to all pregnant women—but that wouldn't have helped define abortion as murder. Which was in fact *all* this move did: SCHIP already had mechanisms to provide prenatal care; what it didn't have was *funding*—and no new funding was provided for this "expansion." Indeed, it was estimated that budget cuts would result in at least 600,000 children *losing* SCHIP coverage by 2007 and joining the 8 million American children with no health insurance coverage. *Someone* had to pay for Bush's $2-trillion-plus Tax Cuts for the Rich program.

Comparing abortion-rights supporters to terrorists.
Never mind that it was abortion-rights *opponents* who
bombed clinics and killed doctors; in declaring January 22,
the anniversary of *Roe v. Wade*, "National Sanctity of Human
Life Day" in 2002, Bush twisted and slandered that date's
meaning by declaring obscenely, "On September 11, we saw
clearly that evil exists in this world, and that it does not value
life . . . Now we are engaged in a fight against evil and tyranny
to preserve and protect life." In response to a huge demonstration against Bush policies on women's rights in Washington in April 2004, Bush adviser KAREN HUGHES likewise said,
"The fundamental issue between us and the terror network
we fight is that we value every life." Indeed? See **Iraq, Consumer Protections, Environment, Health Care**.

Dredful comparison. In a 2004 debate with Kerry, Bush,
echoing a popular right-wing equation, compared *Roe v.
Wade* to the 1857 *Dred Scott* decision upholding slavery.
That court refused to see blacks as human, the rightists said,
and the same was done to fetuses in *Roe*. As if the party of
Strom Thurmond and Trent Lott and Haley Barbour and
Charles Pickering (see **Justice**) would have opposed *Dred*
in its day.

The science of disinformation. In December 2002, the
administration altered a fact sheet on the National Cancer
Institute (NCI) Web site to suggest that abortion could cause
breast cancer, a pet scare tactic of the anti-abortionists. As
the fact sheet previously stated, the scientific evidence overwhelmingly denied any link. The administration also
removed 25 reports from its Women's Bureau Web site,

"deleting or distorting crucial information on issues from pay equity to reproductive healthcare," *Salon* reported. (Also see **Secrecy** and **Science and Truth, War on**.)

Servicewomen left to own devices. In May 2003, Congressional Republicans, with Bush's backing, rejected measures to repeal a ban on overseas servicewomen or dependants obtaining abortions at military hospitals, even if they pay for them themselves. U.S. military women risking their lives in Iraq could now risk their lives at the hands of local abortionists.

ANDAnother step . . . In December 2004, Bush signed into law the so-called ABORTION NON-DISCRIMINATION ACT (ANDA)— a domestic counterpart to the global gag rule. Actually just two sentences slipped into a 3,000-page appropriations bill by House Republicans in a closed-door session, ANDA allowed Medicare, HMOs, insurance companies, and hospitals to ignore *Roe v. Wade* and to bar doctors from providing abortion referrals or even from counseling patients about their options. "[A]n extraordinary sneak attack on women's rights," said Democratic House leader Nancy Pelosi.

Faith healers take over at FDA. In 2002, Bush named DAVID HAGER to chair the powerful Reproductive Health Drugs Advisory Committee of the Food and Drug Administration (FDA), which evaluated the safety and effectiveness of drugs used in obstetrics, gynecology, and related specialties. Two other anti-abortion zealots were appointed to the committee at the same time. Hager, an OB/GYN, was the author of *As Jesus Cared for Women: Restoring Women*

Then and Now and *The Reproduction Revolution: A Christian Appraisal of Sexuality, Reproductive Technologies and the Family*, which endorsed the medically inaccurate claim that the birth control pill causes abortion. He had spoken out against the use of condoms outside of marriage and suggested that women who suffer from premenstrual syndrome, postpartum depression, and eating disorders should seek help from reading the Bible and praying.

"As Jesus Cared for Women"? "God has called me to stand in the gap . . . regarding ethical and moral issues in our country," Hager declared. His ex-wife of 32 years, Linda Davis, saw him rather differently: She told *The Nation* in May 2005 that between 1995 and their divorce in 2002, Hager repeatedly sodomized her without her consent. "[I]t was the painful, invasive, totally nonconsensual nature of the [anal] sex that was so horrible,'" she said. (According to Davis, Hager—an OB/GYN—would say, "Oh, I didn't mean to have anal sex with you; I can't feel the difference.") Davis also alleged that Hager pressured her to let him videotape and photograph them having sex and said she let him pay her for oral and anal sex because he kept such a tight grip on the family purse strings. Such exchanges, she said, "took place almost weekly for several years."[4] (Also see **Values**.)

Plan C: Coat hanger? In May 2004, the FDA caved to pressure from anti-sex conservatives and the White House and refused to permit over-the-counter sales of EMERGENCY CONTRACEPTION (EC), aka the "morning-after birth control pill" (brand name: PLAN B)—overruling two FDA scientific panels, which had reviewed 40 studies and 15,000 pages of data and voted 23–4 that permitting the sales would be a safe and important way to, like, *prevent abortions*. In 2000, when it was only available by prescription, Plan B prevented more than 100,000 pregnancies and 51,000 abortions.[5] Doctors' groups said easier access could reduce the nation's 3 million unintended pregnancies each year by half. The abstinuts feared that increased access would encourage teenagers to be sexually active. (Like they needed encouragement.)

Satan, science overcome. It was HAGER who supplied the FDA's pretext: At its panel hearing, he repeatedly questioned whether Plan B had been adequately tested among adolescents—even though another physician on the panel called Plan B "the safest product that we have seen brought before us," and other contraceptives and scores of other drugs did not require age-group-specific testing. (In fact, the Bushies in 2002 suspended a Clinton rule that required drug companies to test their products for children!) Political fig leaf? We report, you decide: Nearly a year after the manufacturer proposed offering Plan B only to women over age 16, the FDA *still* withheld approval.

In a videotaped church sermon obtained by *The Nation*, Hager boasted that "[f]or only the second time in five decades, the FDA did not abide by its advisory committee opinion." He had argued "from a scientific perspective," but "[o]nce again, what Satan meant for evil [*science*, presumably] God turned into good." Christians such as himself were at "war" with secular medicine, he added.[6] (We repeat, see **Science and Truth, War on**.)

ABSTINENCE (A BuShiT INitiativE for No Condoms Ever) **AND AIDS PREVENTION**

Abstinence was the sole form of birth control and STD prevention the Bushies *were* willing to support. In his first term, Bush nearly tripled funding for abstinence programs—giving them the largest percentage increases for any area outside of defense and draining money from other family planning services. By 2005, the federal government had spent nearly a billion dollars on abstinence programs "that have yet to be found effective in even a single respected, peer-reviewed journal," creating and feeding "political pork" to an entire industry of right-wing organizations, said an AIDS policy expert.[7]

But what are facts? Minor inconveniences. In 2002, the administration revised fact sheets on the Centers for Disease Control Web site to suggest that studies on the effectiveness of condoms in preventing the spread of HIV and other STDs were "inconclusive" and that abstinence is the only effective path to sexual health. Also removed were an online guide to proper condom use and a list of studies that showed no rise in sexual activity among teens taught about condoms.

Among the 100-plus taxpayer-funded abstinence-only programs, some of the most popular taught teenagers that touching another person's genitals can result in pregnancy; abortion can lead to sterility and suicide; the HIV virus can be spread via sweat and tears; half the gay male teenagers in the U.S. have tested positive for HIV; a 43-day-old fetus is a "thinking person" (time to lower the age requirement for Supreme Court justices!); HIV and other STDs can "pass through" condoms; and condom use by heterosexuals fails to prevent HIV transmission up to 31 percent of the time (correct figure: 3 percent). Also that men need "admiration" and "sexual fulfillment" while women need "financial support," and that women who offer their men too much advice risk driving them away.[8] A report by Rep. Henry Waxman (D-CA) released in December 2004 found these and other assertions in 11 of the 13 most commonly used abstinence programs.

The White House took quick action: It shifted oversight of abstinence programs to a new—and abstinence-friendlier— agency within Health and Human Services (HHS), one led by an abstinence-only advocate. An HHS spokeswoman called Waxman's report "political," said it does a "disservice to our children," and repeated that abstaining from sex "is the most effective means" of preventing STDs and pregnancy.

That was indisputable, but irrelevant: 88 percent of teenagers who take "virginity pledges" eventually have premarital sex—compared to 99 percent who don't "pledge"— and then are *less likely to use condoms*, according to a Columbia and Yale University study published in March 2005. The "abstainers" were also four to six times more likely to have oral and anal sex than other virgin teens; as likely to be infected with STDs as their non-abstinent peers; but less likely to get tested for STDs or to know their STD status.[9] Texas A&M researchers reported that among Texas teens, the number who were sexually active *increased* after abstinence indoctrination, by as much as 60 percent: "[M]ost of what we've discovered shows there's no evidence the large amount of money spent is having an effect . . . These programs seem to be much more concerned about politics

than kids." [10] *No* researchers were able to document meas-
urable benefits of the abstinence-only model, the *Washington
Post* reported.

Completely **nuts.** "Now conservative Christian groups are
preparing to battle a new scourge," *The New Republic*
reported in May 2005: "Vaccines that could prevent more
than 200,000 women from dying of cervical cancer each
year." The vaccines immunize against a sexually transmitted
virus, HPV, that is responsible for the vast majority of cervical cancer cases. "But 'abstinence only' advocates love
HPV. That's because the virus can be spread by skin-to-skin
contact other than intercourse . . . Abstinence groups don't
want a vaccine to eliminate this fear factor." Young women
might see the vaccine "as a license to engage in premarital
sex," said Bridget Maher of the Family Research Council
(FRC), a powerful "Christian" lobby. "Of course, absolutely
no evidence supports Maher's claim," *The New Republic*
noted. "But there's plenty of evidence that an HPV vaccine
will prevent thousands of needless deaths. Now what was
that about a culture of life?"

You are accused of untraditional activities. In 2003, in
response to complaints from the "conservative" Traditional
Values Coalition (TVC), the National Institutes of Health
(part of HHS) phoned more than 150 scientists who were on
a TVC hit list to question the value of their NIH-funded
research on high-risk sexual behavior and related problems.
TVC had accused the scientists of "endors[ing] sexual
behavior and condom use among teens," among other
crimes. "[M]illions and millions of dollars have been flushed

down the toilet over years on this HIV, AIDS scam and sham," TVC's executive director revealed. Well, as Jerry Falwell said, "AIDS is the wrath of a just God against homosexuals." If all that NIH officials sought was information—rather than intimidation—they could just have read the grant applications, Representative Waxman noted.

Political "audits." The same was happening to nonprofit organizations that provided sex education: Those that didn't agree with the abstinuts and promoted condom use to fight AIDS were "repeatedly investigated by the government, while **faith-based** groups get a free pass," *Salon* reported. After never being audited in 18 years as a federal grantee, Advocates for Youth was audited three times in one year. A leaked HHS memo described the organization as "ardent critics of the Bush administration." San Francisco's STOP AIDS program and the Sexuality Information and Education Council were likewise subjected to sudden, multiple audits. All three groups came through "with flying colors," while a number of abstinence programs that were found guilty of misusing government money by courts were not audited.[11]

Dare not speak its name! In 2004, the National Council for Research on Women reported that pressure from ~~the Jesus police~~ right-wing groups had led scientists to stop using words like "gay," "sex worker," and "transgender" in their grant applications.

GLOBAL AIDS PREVENTION: "More politics than compassion." When Bush used his 2003 State of the Union message to pledge $15 billion over five years to fight AIDS in

15 hard-hit countries (and, pardon the cynicism, to throw a veil of humanity over his main project—**Iraq**), the U.S. appeared to be becoming more responsive to the crisis. Two years later, it was "becoming increasingly clear that the administration's embrace of the global fight against HIV/AIDS is more politics than compassion," wrote AIDS policy expert William A. Smith. "The political hijacking of HIV prevention will stand as one of the most cynical and short-sighted efforts of the Bush administration to politicize public health."

The administration purported to adopt Uganda's successful AIDS prevention program, Smith wrote, but "dumbed [it] down . . . to what has become known as the ABC model—A for abstain, B for be faithful, and C for use a condom every time you have sex," and further "distorted it to fit its own ideological agenda." The President's Emergency Plan For AIDS Relief (PEPFAR) "portrays condoms as negligible in their overall impact and asserts that abstinence and fidelity are primary and paramount." This approach, Smith noted, "could not be further from the cardinal rule that pervaded Uganda's effort: do not undermine condoms."

It was, however, consistent with the Bushies' practice of launching expensive programs that divert public funds to key political supporters. The PEPFAR law mandated that one-third of the plan's funds must be spent on abstinence programs that *do not mention* condoms. By late 2004, even more was going to such programs. The Bushies were now exporting abstinence-only programs "en masse overseas," Smith wrote, "divert[ing] substantial funding from experienced public health agencies" that take "a more comprehensive and science-based approach." For example, when the State Department announced a $10 million federal grant to combat sex trafficking in Mexico, part of the money went to Concerned Women for America (CWA), a right-wing advocacy group with no experience in this area, but whose mission "is to protect and promote Biblical values among all citizens."

BUSHISMS, THE BRAINS ISSUE, AND THE SANITY ISSUE

The best-loved Bushisms—those brilliantly imbecilic and illiterate things Bush says—are from his early period, when he was working mainly with non sequiturs and malapropisms and was beginning to find his own artistic voice, distinct from his father's, the greatest verbal surrealist and English-mangler of *his* day. The Dada influence still marks the younger Bush's early works. They include the classic, "Rarely is the question asked: Is our children learning?" and "Will the highways on the Internet become more few?" The Magrittian "I know the human being and fish can coexist peacefully." The Chagall-esque "Families is where our nation finds hope, where wings take dream." And the Yogi-Berra-esque "It's your money. You paid for it," and, "More and more of our imports are coming from overseas."

Many of the classics date from the 1999–2000 campaign period. But as artist-in-residence at the White House, Bush's unscripted public appearances grew, as he said, "more few," and his imagination seemed to ebb. As Bush himself said, "I think we agree, the past is over." Yet rumors of his artistic demise proved premature. "Poor people aren't necessarily killers" (2003) showed Bush still at the peak of his powers. In "A West Texas girl, just like me" (2004), he returned to the investigation of transgendered identities in postmodern politics—a theme he had first explored years earlier in "The most important job is not to be governor, or first lady in my case." The same year brought the definitive statement of Bushism, "Our enemies are innovative and resourceful, and so are we. They never stop thinking about new ways to harm our country and our people, and neither do we."

Critic Mark Crispin Miller rejected the early consensus that Bush's work bespoke genuine idiocy. Bush, he wrote, is "a sociopathic personality" who is "incapable of empathy. He has no trouble speaking off the cuff when . . . he's talking about violence, when he's talking about revenge . . . When he struts and thumps his chest, his syntax and grammar are fine. It's only when he leaps into the wild blue yonder of compassion, or idealism, or altruism, that he makes these hilarious mistakes . . . He's a very angry guy, a hostile guy." Citing "Fool me once, shame—shame on—you . . . [long pause] . . . Fool me—can't can't get fooled again," Miller remarked, "Bush could not say, 'Shame on me' to save his life. That's a completely alien idea to him." And "I know how hard it is to put food on your family" reveals a man who "doesn't care about people who can't put food on the table" and "can't keep his focus on things that mean nothing to him."[12] Miller's view fits the "diagnosis" by George Washington University psychiatrist Justin Frank in his book *Bush on the Couch: Inside the Mind of the President*, which described Bush as "an untreated alcoholic with paranoid and megalomaniac tendencies" and a "lifelong streak of sadism, ranging from childhood pranks (using firecrackers to explode frogs) to insulting journalists, gloating over state executions and pumping his hand gleefully before the bombing of Baghdad."

A more common view was that the Bushism was part of Bush's carefully crafted, just-plain-folks persona—that it was in fact *art*. But as Michael Tomasky wrote, referring to the Bush revealed by Bob Woodward's book *Plan of Attack*, "It's amazing how often first impressions . . . end up being exactly right . . . Woodward's account shows a man who just doesn't have the intellectual capacity to do this job."[13]

"COMPASSION"

"According to Bush's philosophy of government, America's ability to assert its will for the greater good around the world is enormous. In Toledo [Ohio]—well, there are limits."

—George Packer, the *New Yorker*

How well Bush delivered on his 2000 campaign promise of "compassionate conservativism" [*sic*] should not be judged by his record on the **economy, health care, human rights,** etc. As it is basically a **"faith-based initiative,"** one must basically have faith.

Or, if you prefer, consider the official Bush/Cheney 2004 reelection site, described by Lawrence Weschler in the *Los Angeles Times:* "Click the ['Compassion'] tab, and there you

are on the Compassion page . . . Nice big picture of Bush
merrily shooting the breeze with two black teenage girls . . .
'Click here for the Compassion Photo Album.' . . . First one
up: short-sleeved Bush, holding a black kid in his arms, a
bleacher full of black kids behind him, and he's merrily
waving to the crowd. [Next:] Bush at a Waco Habitat for
Humanity building site, his arm draped around a black
woman, his other hand tapping the shoulder of another of
the black construction volunteers. Next: Bush waving to the
Urban League . . . Bush in an African thatch-roofed school-
room . . . Why, the Compassion page even includes a photo
of him standing next to his own Secretary of State, Colin
Powell!" Where's your cynicism *now*?

As Wechsler wrote, "bracket for a moment some of the
actual facts concerning the fate of blacks and other people
of color." Actually, those who were rich received compassion galore, regardless of race, color, or creed, in the form of
huge tax cuts—while, in symbolic displays of fiscal discipline, Bush made budget cuts that hit hard at the middle
class and the poor yet scarcely dented the huge deficits he'd
created. (See **Economic Policy**.)

Examples of Bush compassion light up this entire book like,
why, a thousand points of light. Here are but a sparkling few:

- Proposed a "morally reprehensible" (not Bush's
  description—he would have had trouble with "reprehensible") 2006 BUDGET that almost literally "takes
  food from the mouths of babes and gives the proceeds
  to his millionaire friends." (See **Economic Policy**.)
- Denied the CHILD TAX CREDIT increase that upper-
  income families got to 6.5 million low-income families

with 20 million children, including 260,000 children of active military service personnel.

- Signed a bill that made it more difficult for poor and moderate-income families to use BANKRUPTCY protection, while doing nothing about predatory lending practices and while exempting schemes used by wealthy families and corrupt corporations to shelter assets from creditors. (See **Corporate**.)
- Ended his first term as the first president since Hoover, in the Great Depression, to preside over a net loss of JOBS. Meanwhile, more than 45 million Americans—a record number—lacked **health** insurance, and nearly double that number were uninsured at least part of the time.
- Put **abortion** opponents' votes and the "lives" of lab-created embryonic cells (that are discarded anyway) over those of disease sufferers by imposing crippling restrictions on funding for human embryonic STEM CELL RESEARCH, which promised to yield cures for degenerative diseases. In May 2005, Bush threatened his first veto over a bill to permit such research. Bush's 2006 budget proposal eliminated funding for a stem cell program using *non*-embryonic sources.
- Sided with big drug companies to block cheaper generic versions of key **AIDS** drugs.
- Was expected in 2005 to reward business by "revising" the FAMILY AND MEDICAL LEAVE ACT, which allowed employees up to 12 weeks of unpaid, job-protected leave to care for a seriously ill family member or a newborn or newly adopted child.
- Citing the budget deficit, cut U.S. GLOBAL FOOD AID

contributions by $100 million in December 2004, just as the *New York Times* reported that "the number of hungry in the world is rising for the first time in years and all food programs are being stretched," and UNICEF estimated that more than one billion children were growing up hungry. (See **Foreign Aid**.)

- "Streamlined" deportation procedures, which condemned many religious and political ASYLUM seekers to torture in their homelands.

Charity for millionaires. "My administration will give taxpayers new incentives to donate to charity," Bush once promised. According to the Congressional Budget Office, Bush's repeal of the ESTATE TAX, which benefited only the richest 2 percent of Americans, would result in a 6–12 percent decline in charitable giving, which the rich would otherwise have used to reduce the taxable portion of their estates.

CONSUMER, HEALTH, AND SAFETY PROTECTIONS, *ALL-OUT BUSHIST ASSAULT ON*

"What does **corporate ownership of government** mean for me?" I am often asked. It means, according to a senior director of the Consumer's Union, an administration that has "bestowed enormous benefits on the largest corporate enti-ties at the expense of consumers' safety and pocketbooks." **Environmental**, health, workplace and product safety rules "have been modified in ways that often please business and industry leaders while dismaying interest groups repre-senting consumers, workers, drivers, medical patients, the elderly and many others," wrote the *New York Times*'s Joel Brinkley, who detected "a pro-business tilt" under Bush. Most of the changes, he added, were "done through regula-tion, not law—lowering the profile of the actions" and pre-venting Congress from getting in the way.

THE FDA'S *OLD* MISSION: PROTECTING THE PUBLIC.

The administration went to court repeatedly to block law-suits by consumers who said they were injured by MEDICINES AND MEDICAL DEVICES. The Bushies contended that consumers were not entitled to damages for such injuries if the prod-ucts were approved by the FOOD AND DRUG ADMINISTRATION (FDA). In early 2005, a measure prohibiting damages in such cases was buried in Bush's proposed legislation to curb MAL-PRACTICE LAWSUITS (see **Tort Reform**)—this despite fresh studies linking the huge-selling, FDA-approved painkillers CELEBREX and VIOXX to increased risk of heart attacks and strokes and linking the antidepressant PROZAC to violent and suicidal behavior among adolescents—and despite evidence that the makers of Vioxx and Prozac had long concealed the dangers. Critics noted that damage awards served as an important deterrent to corporate and medical negligence. "The FDA is certainly not doing its job. The legal system is . . . the last line of defense" to ensure product safety, a con-sumer advocate told the *New York Times*.

- In November 2004, a public health scientist, Dr. Curt Furberg, was removed from an FDA panel studying the safety of COX-2 inhibitor drugs such as BEXTRA, Celebrex, and Vioxx because he publicly stated he thought Bextra caused heart problems and that its maker, PFIZER, knew that and was covering it up. The FDA referred to his expert opinion as "bias." "This is a routine procedure," an FDA spokeswoman said of Furberg's removal.[14] Indeed; see **Science and Truth, War on**.

- When patients successfully sued to stop ads from claiming that the antidepressant PAXIL "is non-habit forming," the administration joined the manufacturer, GLAXOSMITHKLINE, in challenging the order, claiming the restrictions "would overly deter use of a life-improving medication." The judge said the administration's arguments were unpersuasive and contrary to the public interest.

Corporate rights over states' rights. Before Bush, the government said FDA standards were only a *minimum*, and that states could provide "additional protection to consumers." The administration, in one of its serial betrayals of the conservative principle of states' rights, argued that states could *not* set more stringent rules—that FDA standards "set a ceiling as well as a floor"—even though the Supreme Court had "expressly ruled that FDA regulation does not pre-empt state law and local regulation" in all cases, a constitutional scholar noted.[15] The administration has "taken the FDA in a radical new direction, seeking to protect drug companies instead of the public," said Rep. Maurice Hinchey (D-NY).

Drug industry, FDA in secret love nest! Leading the Bush charge on behalf of the drug industry was the FDA's chief counsel, DANIEL TROY. As a top drug and tobacco industry lawyer before joining the administration, Troy repeatedly sued to limit the FDA's regulatory powers. At the FDA, he repeatedly interceded in suits on behalf of drug and medical device manufacturers.

FDA standards for chutzpah: As an industry lawyer, Troy had successfully challenged the FDA's power to regulate drug as well as tobacco advertising based on "the dramatic proposition that . . . *First Amendment free speech rights are the primary consideration.*"[16] (Emphasis added.) At the FDA, Troy then pointed to all those cases the agency had lost—*to him*—in order to justify bringing fewer enforcement actions! After he took charge, these quickly dropped from an average of seven a month to two.

- Not content to cut back on enforcement, in October 2002, the FDA *invited* the drug industry to point out any regulations regarding drug advertising that the industry felt infringed on its "free speech" rights.
- As de facto head of the agency in 2001-2002 while Bush left the commissionership vacant, Troy held at least 50 private meetings with drug manufacturers and others regulated by the FDA. *U.S. News* sought records of those meetings under the FREEDOM OF INFORMATION ACT but was told by Troy's office that there are "no minutes, no memos, no nothing."[17] (See **Secrecy**.)
- In December 2003, Troy, addressing several hundred drug industry lawyers in New York, *invited them to*

suggest lawsuits against drug companies that the FDA might get involved in on their behalf—a whole, exciting new role for the agency, whose mission was previously to protect the *public*.

- Troy argued in court briefs that lawsuits filed in state courts arguing that drug-company warnings are inadequate—the largest category of cases against drug companies—were invalid. "If Troy's legal position prevailed," a legal expert on the FDA told the *Denver Post*, "it would be catastrophic for consumers."

BLOCKING CHEAPER DRUG IMPORTS. Millions of Americans had taken to (illegally) buying their medicines from pharmacies in Canada, where the same drugs or their equivalents sold for up to 72 percent below the U.S. cost. The CBO found that legalized importation would reduce total U.S. prescription drug expenditures by about $40 billion by 2012, saving businesses money on health benefits, thereby increasing profits and tax revenues. The Bush administration sided with the drug industry, echoing its claims that Canadian drugs might not be safe, and threatening to veto any drug importation bill that didn't meet a detailed set of requirements designed to protect the industry. The threat came on the same day in December 2004 that a task force appointed by Bush conceded that drugs from Canada *were* safe.

The Bushies warned that imported drugs must "adhere to the 'gold standard' of safety and efficacy that is expected from FDA-approved drugs." That wouldn't be too hard: While Bush's task force couldn't show a single example where Americans were harmed by an imported drug, just over the previous month, Vioxx, Celebrex, Bextra, Aleve, and two other major FDA-approved drugs had been shown to pose serious unacknowledged risks to consumers.

The R&D threat to R&D. The drug industry and therefore the Bushies claimed legal importation would force the industry to reduce research and development spending, resulting in fewer new drugs. Ridiculous & Disingenuous. The drugmakers were Rolling in Dough: In 2002, *"the combined profits for the ten drug companies in the Fortune 500 ($35.9 billion) were more than the profits for all the other 490 businesses put together."*[18] (Amazement added.) "If the drug industry decided to pare back its profits by just 3 percent, Americans could have access to cheaper drugs with no impact on drug innovation," noted the Center for American Progress's *Progress Report.*

Meanwhile, the *Chicago Tribune* reported in February 2005, a Congressional investigation revealed that "the pricing system used by drug makers has resulted in over-payments by government insurers of at least $800 million annually, while patients . . . spend an extra $200 million a year." Rotten & Disgusting.

Letting drug companies gouge AIDS patients. In August 2004, the administration "refused to override patents on the AIDS drug NORVIR, effectively allowing [manufacturer ABBOTT LABORATORIES'] quintupling of the price to stand despite consumer groups' accusations of price gouging," AP reported. Advocates for the override noted that Norvir's discovery was partially funded by taxpayer dollars. "But the president has accepted more than $21,000 from Abbott executives, and the

Republican National Committee has raked in more than $440,000 in soft money from the company," the *Progress Report* noted.

FOOD SAFETY AND NUTRITION. In each election since 2000, the agribusiness, food, and tobacco industries gave GOP candidates roughly $55 million, or three to four times as much as they gave Democrats. The industries in turn grew fatter on GOP favors.

Mad cow. As of June 2005, three cases of bovine spongiform encephalopathy, or MAD COW DISEASE, had been detected in Canada and two in the U.S. The administration's response was to try to *balance public safety against cattle and meat industry interests.* A dilemma indeed, *if* your moral **values** have been eaten away by doughvine spongiform political pay-offpathy. (The livestock and meat processing industries contributed around $17.5 million to federal candidates in the 2000 to 2004 election cycles, 80 percent of it to Republicans.)

Meathead. A month after mad cow turned up in Canadian cattle in May 2003, the Agriculture Department (USDA) banned many types of Canadian beef but opposed a new law requiring meat labels indicating the country of origin. USDA's undersecretary for marketing and regulation, CHARLES LAMBERT—previously a lobbyist for the NATIONAL CATTLEMEN'S BEEF ASSOCIATION (see sidebar)—said he would bet his life and his job that mad cow could not enter the U.S. When it did so six months later, apparently from Canada, Lambert said, "I overstated my case," but failed to make good on his bet.

"A wholly owned subsidiary of America's cattlemen."
When he came to the USDA, CHARLES LAMBERT signed an
agreement stating that in his first year he would "not par-
ticipate personally and substantially in any particular
matter" involving his former employer, the NATIONAL CAT-
TLEMEN'S BEEF ASSOCIATION. "During that period he met at
least twelve times with current or former members of [the
association] and its affiliates," the *Denver Post* reported.
More than a dozen other high-ranking USDA officials
appointed under Bush also had ties to the meat industry.
The director of the Consumer Federation of America's
Food Policy Institute called the agency "a wholly owned
subsidiary of America's cattlemen." When second-term Ag
Secretary MIKE JOHANNS held "a sort of pep rally for beef" in
June 2005, the *New York Times* reported, "no consumer
groups were on a panel that declared American beef 'very,
very safe,' but [beef industry] lobbyists were."

Products preapproved. When the USDA partially resumed
Canadian beef imports in August 2003, then-Ag Secretary
ANN VENEMAN said "thorough scientific analysis" had been
done and "our experts have determined that the risk to
public health is extremely low." But "I knew in fact that we
hadn't," a senior USDA scientist told the *New York Times*
anonymously in February 2004. He said department scientists were pressured by top officials to approve food products

before their safety could be confirmed—including cattle from Mexico, where bovine tuberculosis was endemic, and fruit with fungus problems and other products from China.[19]

Ground rules ignored. Since reaffirming that Canadian ground beef remained too risky to allow in, the USDA had, under "undisclosed permits," allowed U.S. meatpackers to import 33 million pounds of Canadian ground and other "processed" beef, because the restrictions "hurt profits in both countries," the *Washington Post* reported in May 2004.

Dead cow walking. After a cow tested positive for mad cow in Washington State in December 2003, Veneman and other officials said the cow had been unable to walk, supporting their contention that only such so-called "downers" were at risk. But seven people saw the cow walking that day, according to an inspector general's report, including the veterinarian at the slaughterhouse—who nonetheless reported it as a "downer." The slaughterer charged that Ag officials had pressured the vet to change his report. After a second U.S. cow tested positive in November 2004, the USDA kept the results secret for seven months.

Better not to know? In July 2004, the USDA's inspector general reported that the department's testing plan for mad cow was seriously flawed. Rather than impose random testing, the plan made testing voluntary. Only one in 1,000 of the cattle killed in the U.S. were tested; Japan tested every cow, Europe, about one in four. The USDA did not even test all cattle condemned at slaughter with signs of brain disease. Yet as late as 2005, Ag Secretary Johanns "was discussing cutting back" testing, the *New York Times* reported. "The bottom line is that the U.S. government is afraid of putting in real food-safety testing because it would certainly find additional cases," said John Stauber, co-author of *Mad Cow U.S.A.* (How many *had* it found?)

Besides, there were better uses for the money and ways to solve the problem: In June 2005, the administration—mindful that 36 countries had banned U.S. beef imports, virtually wiping out a $3 billion export market—awarded $12 million to the U.S. Meat Export Federation to advertise its product overseas. Meanwhile, countries like Japan were threatened with trade retaliation if they did not accept U.S. beef.

De-funding safety. Bush's 2006 budget plan cut "nearly all [FDA] inspection programs, from checks on imported food to reviews of overseas plants that make prescription drugs bound for the USA," *USA Today* reported. The budget plan—which would also cut domestic food safety inspections and checks on U.S. blood banks—"could make the USA more vulnerable to counterfeit drugs or improperly made products," said an FDA adviser. Inadequate inspections of a British vaccine plant had led to its shutdown in October 2004, creating a nationwide U.S. FLU VACCINE shortage at the start of the winter flu season.

Creating a less safe cigarette. In October 2004, Congress abolished mandatory government inspection of imported tobacco to ensure it is not laced with chemicals and pesticides, such as DDT, banned in the U.S. but permitted elsewhere, *Salon* reported. U.S. tobacco companies—which increasingly relied on imported leaf—had paid for the inspection program. No other agricultural product comes into the country without some kind of inspection.

Salad dressing with a kick. In December 2004, FDA tests found an explosive rocket fuel additive in almost every sample of lettuce and milk taken in a nationwide investigation. PERCHLORATE, which leaks from military bases and defense contractor's facilities, "is known to cause regional water pollution, resulting in serious health effects," including impaired thyroid function, cancer, and severe developmental problems in children, BushGreenwatch.org reported. There were no government safety standards for perchlorate in drinking water. Industry and Pentagon scientists maintained that perchlorate was safe at levels 200 times greater than a standard proposed by the EPA. Although perchlorate's health dangers had been known for 15 years, in December 2003, the administration—concerned that a cleanup could cost billions and impair its ability to test weapons systems—ordered a further review of the EPA proposal. Perhaps Bush hadn't heard that geologists suspected the water at his Texas ranch might be perchlorated by the nearby Naval Weapons Industrial Reserve Plant. (It *had* to be something in his drinking water . . .)

Defending the obesity industry. In January 2004, Health and Human Services (HHS) issued a 28-page, line-by-line attack on a UN/World Health Organization (WHO) diet and nutrition report that (gasp!) urged people to limit their sugar consumption. "Although [HHS] framed the critique as a principled defense of scientific integrity," wrote two public health experts, "much evidence argues for another interpretation—

blatant pandering to American food companies that produce much of the world's high-calorie, high-profit sodas and snacks" (and that sweeten GOP candidates' finances).

Defending junk-food marketing. In 2004, 135 health and consumer organizations, 79 health experts and children's advocates, and 22 elected officials from 18 different countries urged the WHO to support a global ban on the marketing of junk food to children under 12. A free Twinkie if you can name a government that did *not* support the ban. In fact, the Bush administration sent a letter to the WHO "reciting arguments eerily similar to those voiced by the tobacco industry to deny a connection between smoking and cancer . . .[and] denying the effect of the heavy marketing of what it calls 'energy-dense food,'" a critic noted. [20]

WORKPLACE SAFETY, too, was amBushed!

- In 2003, the *New York Times* reported that, out of 2,197 workplace deaths caused by employers' willful violations of safety laws over the previous twenty years, the OCCUPATIONAL SAFETY AND HEALTH ADMINISTRATION (OSHA) declined to seek criminal charges in 93 percent of cases; only 81 cases ended in convictions and 16 in jail sentences. Even repeat violators and cases involving multiple deaths were rarely prosecuted. Presented with the report, Bush's OSHA administrator "made it clear that he saw no need to change either the law or OSHA's handling of these worst cases of death on the job," the *Times* noted.

- Bush's 2004 budget proposed to cut 77 enforcement and related positions from OSHA while adding two new staff members to help industry "comply with" agency rules.
- In Bush's first term, OSHA "eliminated nearly five times as many pending standards as it has completed. It has not started any major new health or safety rules, setting Bush apart from the previous three presidents . . . [and] Bush has canceled more of the unfinished regulatory work he inherited than he has completed," the *Washington Post* reported.
- In March 2003, the Mine Safety and Health Administration (MSHA) proposed a dilution of the rules protecting coal miners from black lung disease.
- In another dig at miners, the administration rolled back Clinton administration rules limiting underground diesel exhaust from mining equipment, which caused an astoundingly high rate of lung cancer deaths and cardiovascular problems among mine workers. Bush also reversed Clinton's efforts to increase MSHA's budget and hire more mine inspectors.

VEHICLE SAFETY problems: Not the public's concern. In April 2004, at the behest of auto and tire manufacturers, the National Highway Traffic Safety Administration published a regulation *forbidding public release* of industry reports, consumer complaints, and warranty-claim information about unsafe motor vehicles, saying that publicizing the information would cause "substantial competitive harm" to manufacturers. "I can't believe this information would be of much interest to the general public," said the agency's chief spokesman.[21]

ENERGY: Gouge away. During the West Coast energy crisis of 2001, when Bush's buddies at ENRON—his biggest campaign contributors—were "fleecing at least a billion dollars from consumers and laughing about it, the White House refused to support temporary price caps and pressured allies on Capitol Hill . . . to vote them down," the *American Prospect* noted. (Also read in **Energy Policy** about the doubling of oil prices from January 2001 to June 2005.)

BANKS: Let us prey. In another of the Bushies' betrayals of their own stated principles of federalism (states' rights), in January 2004, the administration issued regulations prohibiting states from enforcing their consumer protection laws against national banks—including laws against misrepresenting the terms of loans, charging exorbitant fees, paying illegal kickbacks to mortgage brokers, and other predatory and discriminatory practices. The Supreme Court had "unequivocally" affirmed the states' authority to regulate national banks, said New York Attorney General ELLIOT SPITZER. All 50 state attorneys general and all 50 state banking superintendents, along with consumer groups and Congress members of both parties, protested the new rules, which left states "powerless to protect their citizens from even the most egregious conduct engaged in by national bank or its subsidiary," Spitzer said.

A gift to banking and credit card companies came in March 2005 in the shape of Bush's BANKRUPTCY BILL, which made it more difficult for poor and moderate-income families to use bankruptcy protection, while exempting schemes used by wealthy families and corrupt corporations to shelter assets from creditors. (See **Corporate-owned Government**.)

SECURITIES AND INVESTMENT FIRMS: A Cox on all their houses. After Securities and Exchange Commission (SEC) Chairman WILLIAM DONALDSON resigned in June 2005 "under fire from business groups who complained about overzealous regulation," *USA Today* reported, Bush replaced him with Rep. CHRISTOPHER COX (R-CA), of whom a trial lawyer said, "It's hard to imagine somebody with a more nakedly deregulatory agenda." Cox:

- Opposed requiring companies to show stock-option compensation as an expense on their financial reports, as they were allowed to do on their tax returns, thereby earning enormous deductions while inflating the profits they report to shareholders.
- Sponsored legislation making it much more difficult for shareholders to win lawsuits against corporate executives who have defrauded them. Cox would even have made "forgetfulness a legitimate defense against charges of recklessness," *The New Republic* noted.
- Was expected to abandon Donaldson's effort to make it easier for shareholders (or as the *Wall Street Journal* called them, "special interests") to nominate corporate board members.

The investment industry gave $47.8 million to Republicans in the 2004 election and was the Bush campaign's largest contributor. By the way.

TELECOM: Disconnecting competition. In 2004, the administration, siding with the four regional Bell phone companies, chose not to defend Federal Communications Commission (FCC) rules aimed at promoting competition—a decision that could lead to far higher phone bills for nearly 50 million customers. The D.C. Circuit Court had decided for the Bells in a case over the fees they charge rivals for access to their networks. The White House chose not to appeal to the Supreme Court—and pressured the FCC not to either. The three Republican FCC commissioners then outvoted the two Dems to drop the case. In return for White House support, "the Bell companies pledged not to raise rates before the [November 2004] election," the *New York Times* reported.

NURSING HOMES: Letting "market forces" take care of Granny. In 2002, the administration announced a "nursing home quality initiative" which shifted the emphasis from enforcement to improving "collaboration" with nursing home operators and letting "market forces" take care of quality issues. Lo and behold, by 2004, the number of nursing homes penalized for violations of federal health and safety standards dropped by as much as 47 percent. The same period saw a sharp increase in private lawsuits alleging abuse or wrongful death of nursing home residents. In 2004, the Government Accountability Office (GAO) found that one-fifth of nursing homes had been cited for "serious deficiencies involving actual harm or immediate jeopardy to residents" and 59 percent were cited for fire safety deficiencies—even though inspectors in some areas were "asked to lighten up and not to find so many serious deficiencies," the *New York Times* reported.[22]

CORPORATE-OWNED GOVERNMENT: *THE BUSH-BUSINESS AXIS OF CORRUPTION*

> *The interest of [businessmen] is always in some respects different from, and even opposite to, that of the public . . . The proposal of any new law or regulation of commerce which comes from this order . . . ought never to be adopted, till after having been long and carefully examined . . . with the most suspicious attention. It comes from an order of men . . . who have generally an interest to deceive and even to oppress the public.*
>
> —Adam Smith, *The Wealth of Nations*

The Bushies' version of Smith's sacred text of capitalism seemed to read, "The interests of big business may be opposite to those of the public . . . but they always come first. The proposal of any new law or (de)regulation which comes from this class (our class, after all) ought always to be adopted as quickly as possible. It comes from an order of men who have generally an interest to deceive and even to oppress the public—and we're here to help them. That's what they pay us for!"

Under Bush, business executives and lobbyists occupied almost all key administration posts, and the corporate agenda *was* the Bush agenda—on **consumer** issues, **energy policy, environment, health care,** the **judiciary, labor, media, Social Security, "tort reform"**—the whole A to Z. Even Bush's **foreign policy** was in the final analysis a servant the corporate agenda—and not just with regard to oil and **war profiteering** in **Iraq:** Iraq and the "war on terror" were used to secure electoral victories and smokescreen the administration's domestic war on behalf of big business. The wars "push a lot of other issues off the page, literally and figuratively," said a policy analyst for the conservative Heritage Foundation—or as Rep. David Obey (D-WI), over on the "left," said, "all the focus on Iraq and bin Laden . . . gives the administration an opportunity to take a lot of loot out the back door without anybody noticing." **"Values"** issues were likewise exploited as weapons of mass distraction. These are essential: In a nationwide Harris poll in February 2004, 83 percent agreed that big business has too much influence on Washington. Without wrapping himself in the flag, a flight suit, and religious piety, Bush would have been toast.

"There is a simple way to understand **economic policy**-making under George W. Bush," wrote *The New Republic*. "Whichever pressure group has the strongest and most direct stake in an issue gets its way. Wealthy individuals and business owners have received large tax cuts; farmers have gotten lavish assistance; and insurance and drug companies won enormous subsidies in the Medicare prescription-drug bill. When steel firms lobbied for tariffs, Bush granted them," conservative free-trade principals be damned. "If there's a single prominent case where Bush offended a powerful corporate interest—except to benefit an even more powerful corporate interest—we have not come across it."

Big-government "conservatives." As Adam Smith would be the first to recognize, there's a big difference between free-market capitalism and CRONY CAPITALISM. "Traditional conservatives wanted to reduce, even eliminate, government and cut taxes," wrote *New York Daily News* columnist Lars

Erik Nelson in 2000. "These new conservatives want the government to continue to collect taxes—but turn the proceeds over to private industry"; to convert every government program into a generator of business profits. *Expand* Medicare with a $900 million drug benefit: That's taxpayer money that will flow to HMOs, insurance, and drug companies. (See **Health Care**.) *Spend* $3 trillion "reforming" **Social Security**—and enrich Wall Street financial firms. Collect school taxes, but give the money out in vouchers for private schools increasingly run by corporate chains. "[Using] the government's coercive powers of taxation and legislation to funnel public wealth to the private sector [is] what made Bush and Cheney rich." Nelson noted.

A wholly owned subsidiary. According to former Republican speechwriter David Brock, after the crushing defeat of Barry Goldwater in 1964, conservative business interests laid out a plan whereby they would "create and underwrite a 'movement' to front their agenda." The Bush regime and the GOP-run Congress, wrote David Sirota in the *American Prospect*, are "the culmination of industry's master plan: Take over the government and remove it as an obstacle to fleecing the average American." Ask not what the Bushies can do *for* big business; they *are* big business. In the past, wrote Sirota,

> corporate America was one of a number of players in the public-policy arena. But under the Bush administration, big business is both the player and the referee, having finally won its decades-long campaign to eliminate the boundary between executive suite and public office. No longer does the private-profit motive

compete in the legislative process with public good; profit now owns the process . . . Industry no longer needs to lobby hard for regulatory rollbacks, because many of its own lobbyists have been appointed federal regulators. Congress openly admits that business writes many of the most important pieces of legislation. The White House slaps an official seal on memos from corporate executives and labels them 'presidential policy initiatives' . . . In short, the government is now a wholly owned subsidiary of corporate America.[23]

THE BUYING OF THE GOVERNMENT. From the start, Bush's name alone drew well-heeled supporters like flies to shit. In his first Texas gubernatorial campaign, his adviser, KARL ROVE—at the time a lobbyist for PHILLIP MORRIS—made **"tort reform,"** shielding corporate wrongdoers from lawsuits, the campaign's centerpiece. And as Rove boasted, "business groups flocked to us."

Bush's "grassroots" support. As Bush broke all fundraising records in 2000, his campaign boasted that its support came from large numbers of small contributors. In fact, most "hard money"—individual contributions limited to $1,000 per candidate—came from the wealthiest 1 percent of the population. (Only around 0.1 percent of voting-age Americans gave $1,000 to any candidate in 2000.) And hard money accounted for more than 80 percent of all campaign funds even before the McCAIN-FEINGOLD bill of 2002 banned "soft money."

Besides, much of Bush's funding in 2000 was raised by

his army of "PIONEERS"—billionaire tycoons, corporate executives, and industry lobbyists, each committed to raising at least $100,000 in "bundled" $1,000 donations. The checks each Pioneer brought in were given special tracking numbers so the corporation or industry they represented could later be rewarded accordingly. More than half the Pioneers were heads of companies. They included at least 44 energy and natural resources executives. And they all knew just what they wanted in return.

The McCain-Feingold bill doubled the limit on individual contributions to a federal candidate to $2,000 (really $4,000, since primaries and general elections count separately). Sure enough, Bush's take in 2004 almost doubled, to $367 million (compared with Kerry's not-too-shabby $317 million; both figures include $75 million in federal matching funds). Bush's Pioneers were joined in 2004 by "RANGERS," each pledged to raise $200,000, who could achieve "Super Ranger" status by raising an additional $300,000 for the Republican National Committee. *Around 90 percent of Bush's Rangers and Pioneers represented big business special interests*, according to Public Citizen. This "extraordinarily organized and disciplined machine" was now twice as big as in 2000, the *Washingon Post* noted, adding, "[the fund-raisers'] real reward is entree to the White House and the upper levels of the administration." (Not just on behalf of industry, by the way: At least 17 Rangers and Pioneers were hired by foreign governments to lobby for them with the U.S. government, the *Los Angeles Times* reported.)

And the White House said unto them: *"Entrez."*

"Mi casa es su casa." Of 246 known Bush Pioneers in the 2000 campaign, the *Washington Post* reported, 104 ended up in government posts. At least two dozen received ambassadorships (compared to five of Clinton's $100,000-plus donors). Three got cabinet posts: Commerce Secretary DON EVANS, Homeland Security Secretary TOM RIDGE, and Labor Secretary ELAINE CHAO. At least 37 Pioneers were named to transition teams that helped select appointees for key regulatory positions. KEN LAY, CEO of ENRON, Bush's biggest contributor in 2000, was one of three Pioneers named to the Energy Department's transition team. Two of his picks were appointed to the five-member Federal Energy Regulatory Commission, the agency responsible for regulating (or rather, *not* regulating) Enron's business.

There were in fact 551 Bush Pioneers in 2000, but the Bush campaign—which boasted that it "set the standard for disclosure"—never released more than half the names, claiming the most successful fund-raising list in political history had been misplaced! Campaigns are required to report the names of individual donors but not of fund-raisers; thus, the Pioneers/Rangers program allowed Bush's biggest financers to accrue White House credit despite the limit on individual donations, *and* without the public knowing who they were.

Did they always get what they were after? Absolutely not! In fact, said a Bush official, "There is no preferential treatment given to anyone. Every American has access to the administration." You, me, the head of the American Petroleum Institute—everyone. True, a lobbyist-Ranger said, "I can call Karl [Rove], and I can call about half of the Cabinet, and they will either take the call or call back." But "[t]here were instances of donors being disappointed," concerned Republicans told the *Washington Post*.

PUTTING THE "RO-B" IN "PRO-BUSINESS." Okay, so the service wasn't up the standards of, say, Bolivia or Cameroon. But at least the Bushies accepted checks; no schlepping heavy briefcases. And it was certainly an improvement over Clinton. Clinton let his major donors sleep in the Lincoln Bedroom. Bush rewarded his with whole cabinet departments; subsidies, tax breaks, and regulatory rollbacks; public lands and programs, indeed, the public itself, to milk. A report by Public Citizen outlined Bush's donors and some of the favors they received:[24]

The financial industry overtook **energy** in 2004 as Bush's top source of funding. Bush's tax cut on stock dividends was the securities industry's top priority; his tax cuts saved executives themselves hundreds of thousands if not millions of dollars each per year; and the industry would be the prime beneficiary of Bush's **Social Security** privatization scheme.

Real estate developers donated $32.2 million to Bush in 2000 and 2004, and 37 of the critters were Rangers or Pioneers in 2004. The Bushies made it easier for developers to build on wetlands and "appointed crusading opponents of the Endangered Species Act to key positions at the Interior Department."

Oil and gas companies kicked in at least $15.8 million. (Why so little? Maybe they got special rates.) At least 30 energy executives, lobbyists, and lawyers got influential appointments in the Bush oil-igarchy. The Bushies opened vast areas of federal land for oil and gas exploration, sped up the awarding of drilling leases, and gave the industry tax breaks and subsidies galore.

The mining industry was good for at least $3.1 million. Mining executives and lobbyists were appointed to top Interior posts and got all kinds of OKs to rape the **environment,** such as legalization of "mountaintop removal" coal mining. Bush Pioneers helped secure the appointment of mine industry executive DAVID LAURISKI to head the so-called Mine Safety and Health Administration, where he weakened black lung and respiratory protections for miners.

Electric utilities donated nearly $6 million. The administration gutted the CLEAN AIR ACT to benefit power companies, the country's biggest air polluters. In 2000, three industry Pioneers—including ENRON CEO Ken Lay—got slots on the Energy Department transition team. They in turn made appointments such as power industry lawyer JEFFREY HOLMSTEAD for air pollution administrator at EPA, where he was instrumental in rolling back clean air standards; somewhat like naming Al Capone to head the Bureau of Alcohol, Tobacco and Firearms.

Health insurers and HMOs: The 2004 Pioneers and Rangers included the CEOs of three of the largest HMOs and several giant insurers—the chief beneficiaries of Bush's MEDICARE privatization and Health Savings Accounts schemes. (See **Health Care**.)

Professional sports teams: At least four principal owners were Rangers and Pioneers—William DeWitt (St. Louis Cardinals), Tom Hicks (Texas Rangers and Dallas Stars), Carl Lindner (Cincinnati Reds), and Alex Spanos (San Diego Chargers). Buried in the $136 billion, pork-stuffed corporate tax cut bill Bush signed in October 2004 was a GOP-sponsored measure that increased the values of professional sports franchises by tens of millions of dollars each by allowing owners to write off the entire value of their franchises over 15 years.

Lobbyists donated four times as much to Bush as to Kerry. More than 100 got high-level appointments— typically to agencies that oversee the very industries they were paid millions to lobby for—a "geometric" increase over the number of lobbyists hired by previous administrations, the *Denver Post* noted. "In at least 20 cases, those former industry advocates have helped their agencies write, shape or push for policy shifts that benefit their former industries." But there's really no cause for concern about conflicts of interest because, a White House spokesman said, "Any individual serving in the administration must abide by strict legal and ethical guidelines." In fact, said a Brookings Institution analyst, "There are so many ways around, over and under [the guidelines], they almost never work."

Crime pays. As of February 2005, the Republican Party had a six to one cash advantage over the Dems. Eight out of ten political action committees (PACs) were corporate, of which 90 percent gave most or all of their money to Repubs. (In December 2004, the Republican-dominated Federal Election Commission changed the rules to make it easier for industry association PACs to raise money.) The oil and gas industry gave 80 percent of its contributions to Repubs in 2002 and 2004. Dems enjoyed more union support, but business out-contributed labor nine to one. And in 2004, the candidate who spent the most money won in 95 percent of House races and 91 percent of Senate races. It pays to be the "pro-business" party. (Also see **K Street**.)

A FEW MEMBERS OF THE BUSH PLUTOCRACY merit a brief look:

Samuel Bodman, Energy Secretary: Former CEO, CABOT CORP (oil, gas, and chemicals).

George W. Bush, President: Legendary former Texas oilman—legendary in that his company, Arbusto, never struck oil. But as Molly Ivins noted, "Arbusto was not an oil company so much as a tax write-off company." How "Junior" was repeatedly bailed out by various family friends, bin Ladens, and other "investors" in White House connections, and how he sold his shares of HARKEN ENERGY for a tidy profit just before they tanked, is described in the unforgettably moving *Bush-Hater's Handbook.*

Andrew Card, White House Chief of Staff: Former chief lobbyist for the auto industry and for GM.

Dick Cheney, Vice President: Former CEO, HALLIBURTON, from which he continued as vice president to receive about $150,000 a year in deferred pay and to own more than 433,000 Halliburton stock options—even while his office "coordinated" the awarding to Halliburton of huge, no-bid, open-ended U.S. government contracts in **Iraq.** (See **Dick, Secrecy,** and **War Profiteering**.)

James Connaughton, Chairman, White House Council on Environmental Quality: Former legal counsel to ATLANTIC RICHFIELD and GENERAL ELECTRIC, whose pollution created more Superfund toxic waste sites than any other U.S. corporation.

Linda Fischer, Deputy Administrator, EPA: Former MONSANTO lobbyist against regulation of genetically engineered crops.

Steven Griles, first-term Deputy Interior Secretary: Top oil and gas lobbyist. After promising "to avoid any actual or apparent conflicts of interest," Griles "the poster child of the corporate influence on this administration" [25]—continued to receive $284,000 a year from his "former" firm and repeatedly intervened with the EPA on behalf of his former industry clients in order to, in his own words, "try to expedite drilling" of tens of thousands of environmentally destructive coalbed methane gas wells in the West. (See **Environment**.)

Jeffrey Holmstead, EPA administrator for air pollution programs: Former lawyer for power utilities, the country's biggest air polluters. In March 2002, the Clean Air Trust named Holmstead its "clean air villain of the month" in recognition of his achievements in gutting the CLEAN AIR ACT. In rolling back clean air standards further in January 2004, the EPA directly adopted language written by Holmstead's law firm.[26] (See **Environment**.)

William Myers, III, Solicitor, Interior Department, which controls grazing licenses on hundreds of millions of acres of federal land: Former NATIONAL CATTLEMEN'S BEEF ASSOCIATION lobbyist.

Gail Norton, Interior Secretary: Former oil and mining lobbyist and chairwoman of the Coalition of Republican Environmental Advocates, a "greenscam" front group funded by major oil and auto companies and other polluters. The interior secretary oversees the one-fifth of U.S. land that is federally owned—which Norton once called "so-called public lands" and believed should *all* be transferred into private hands and plundered for resources with minimal government interference.

Mark Rey, former timber industry lobbyist: As head of the Forest Service, scrapped forest protections to make way for clear-cutting.

Condoleezza Rice, National Security Adviser/Secretary of State: A board member of CHEVRON from 1991 to 2000. Had a Chevron tanker named after her—but then, who doesn't?

Thomas Scully, Medicare and Medicaid Administrator: Former hospital industry lobbyist. At Medicare, negotiated a settlement described as "a total sellout"[27]in a case of alleged Medicare fraud by a hospital chain he formerly represented, HCA Inc. Coauthored Bush's 2003 Medicare bill and, ten days after its enactment, returned to lobbying for drug and health companies that benefited from it. The administration granted him a "special ethics waiver" so he could negotiate with potential employers *while* he helped write the new law. (See "The Revolving Door" below, and **Health Care**.)

INAUGURAL GIFTS: Because it's never too late to say, "I care." Forget to order your legislative or regulatory services *before* the presidential election? It's not too late. Bush's January 2005 inauguration festivities—the most expensive in the nation's history—brought in at least $40 million in donations, an unprecedented 96 percent of which came from corporations. That is, in fact, the beauty of an inauguration: Corporations are barred by law from direct contributions to presidential candidates and campaigns; but with inaugural events, they can, as it were, express themselves freely.

At least 110 interests donated $100,000 or more, compared to only 14 that gave that much to Clinton's 1993 inauguration. *All* the major donors had either profited from Bush policies and/or stood to profit from his second-term agenda, the *Washington Post* reported.

BUSH'S SECOND TERM started off with a gang-bang of the public by the GOP–**K Street** gang. In February 2005, the *New York Times* reported "quick, early gains" and "heady days on Capitol Hill for business lobbyists." Three big bills worth big bucks to big business were about to be delivered, and others waited in the wings.

1. Denying legal recourse to ordinary folks. In February 2005, Bush signed a bill sharply restricting CLASS-ACTION LAW-SUITS brought against companies for fraud or negligence. (See **"Tort Reform."**)

2. A bill permitting oil drilling in the Arctic National Wildlife Refuge—an energy industry and GOP dream for years (see **Environment**)—was approved by a 51–49 Senate vote in March 2005.

3. The Bush (moral) bankruptcy bill. The same month, Bush rewarded some of his largest contributors, the banks and credit card companies, by signing a bill that made it harder for poor and moderate-income families to shield themselves from creditors by forcing many to file for bankruptcy under Chapter 13, which requires continued payments to the credit card companies, instead of Chapter 7. But according to the American Bankruptcy Institute, 96 percent of people who file Chapter 7 can't afford to pay anything more. The rise in bankruptcy filings was due not to irresponsibility, extravagance, and abuse of the laws, as the industry and its GOP shills charged: Nine out of ten bankruptcies are triggered by the loss of a job, divorce, illness and/or medical bills—which alone account for half of all bankruptcy filings. A Harvard study found that in the two years before filing for bankruptcy, 19 percent of families went without food, 40 percent had their phone service shut off, and 53 percent went without important medical care. The bankruptcy bill came "[a]t a moment when the president is proposing cuts in Medicaid and when many Americans are losing part or all of their health insurance coverage," *Washington Post* columnist E. J. Dionne noted.

Bush's laughably named "Bankruptcy Abuse Prevention and Consumer Protection Act of 2005," meanwhile, exempted schemes used by wealthy families and corrupt corporations to shelter assets from creditors, and did nothing to address credit industry practices such as luring consumers in with low introductory rates, then raising them to 30 percent or more, and aggressively targeting people the lenders know can't afford to pay off their balances—which helped the industry collect *$11.7 billion* in penalty fees in 2004. The bill was nonetheless backed by the party whose politicians "love to quote Scripture, [where] such outrageous usury was explicitly condemned," columnist Robert Scheer observed.

Big Tobacco got a $120 billion gift in June 2005 when the administration, in a suit against the tobacco companies filed by Clinton's Justice Department in 1999, decided to seek $10 billion for a stop-smoking program instead of the $130 billion (the 25-year cost of the program, or around 2.2 percent of industry revenues) originally sought. The judge presiding in the trial told the court that the sudden change perhaps "suggests that additional influences have been brought to bear." Actually, the administration had been trying to kill the suit since Bush took office. As Texas governor, Bush refused to support a state lawsuit against Big Tobacco. Philip Morris/Altria was the largest GOP contributor among consumer brand companies from 1999 to 2004.

THE REVOLVING DOOR. Serving as a corporate executive, lawyer, or lobbyist is a prerequisite for a job in the Bush administration. The purpose of serving in the Bush administration is to make connections and perform services that increase one's value in the corporate job market. Only through spiritual purification—or an eight-figure salary— can one break this karmic cycle that in the East is called *samsara*, and in the West, the "revolving door."

The Bushies didn't invent the revolving door—they merely got it working smoothly. At the end of Bush's first term, 9 of 15 cabinet members departed for, well, *greener* pastures, as did scores of lower-level appointees and retiring members of Congress. Nowhere except at the Pentagon (see below) was the door busier than between the government and the **health care** industry, through which passed at least seven officials who had helped pass that giant giveaway to drug and insurance companies known as the Bush Medicare bill. Several had made two complete round trips through the Door of Corruption.

- HHS Secretary TOMMY THOMPSON announced in December 2004 he was resigning "to get into the private sector" of the health care industry—"formally," he should have added. Thompson "has spent the last four years delivering favors to insurance, pharmaceutical and other health care corporations," the *Progress Report* noted—such as shepherding Bush's Medicare bill into law; working to prevent importation of cheaper medicines; and presiding over an FDA that allowed drugs to stay on the market for years after studies showed serious dangers. (See **Consumer**.) In an effort to elude "federal rules [that] bar top officials from actively seeking jobs while they are in office," AP reported, Thompson had hired two attorneys to "sift through job offers."

- Also taking a healthy pay raise was Rep. BILLY TAUZIN (R-LA), chairman of the House Energy and Commerce Committee, who led the fight to keep drug-price controls out of the Medicare bill. In December 2004, Tauzin left Congress to become president of the PHARMACEUTICAL AND RESEARCH MANUFACTURERS OF AMERICA for an estimated $2 million a year.

- One day after leaving the White House, the executive director of Cheney's energy task force, ANDREW LUNDQUIST, became a consultant helping companies benefit from the policy he helped devise, and was a registered lobbyist for those companies within months.

- In May 2005, JOHN ASHCROFT became the first former AG to open up a lobbying shop—to provide homeland security, "strategic consulting" and "internal investigative services" to businesses and governments. (See **War Profiteering, Corporate**.)

- In May 2005, first-term commerce secretary and best Bush buddy DON EVANS hired on as CEO of the

FINANCIAL SERVICES FORUM, a lobbying group for the country's biggest financial service firms and a key supporter of Bush's **Social Security** privatization scheme—a gold mine for financial services firms. In his "new" role, Evans said, "I will be out there applauding the president and his leadership and talking about how important it is that our entitlement plans be reformed."

Improving Bush officials' job prospects. Three weeks after the November 2004 election, the presidentially appointed OFFICE OF GOVERNMENT ETHICS scrapped the rule requiring former Cabinet secretaries and other top officials to wait a full year after leaving office before lobbying former colleagues. With a flurry of top officials announcing their departures, "[t]he timing was perfect," the *Washington Post* noted. In fact, the change was so urgent that the ethics office waived the normal requirement for a 30-day advance notice of the rule change and opportunity for public comment. Requests for the change had come from the HOMELAND SECURITY department, whose outgoing secretary, TOM RIDGE, stood to earn millions if or when he "takes his name brand to a corporation competing for the burgeoning business of domestic security."[28] (Ridge's aides cited his need to pay for college for his two children. Skyrocketing tuition costs for children of former cabinet officials are a problem Congress must address!) In April 2005, Ridge was named to the board of a military supply chain management company with more than $100 million in Pentagon contracts. Ridge "has no experience in supply chain management," the *New York Times* noted.

THE REVOLVING DOOR TO THE PENTAGON. In its first year and a half, the Bush administration named 32 former executives, paid consultants, or major shareholders of top military contractors to top policy-making positions—more than Clinton did in eight years or Bush I did in four. Go figure: While defense contractors trampled each other trying to hire former Pentagon officials, Defense Secretary RUMSFELD "made clear his preference for corporate expertise in the Pentagon," and named executives from military contractors as heads of the three services: JAMES ROCHE, secretary of the air force, from NORTHROP GRUMMAN; GORDON ENGLAND, secretary of the navy, from GENERAL DYNAMICS; and THOMAS P. WHITE, secretary of the army (first term), from ENRON. It was the first time in recent memory that heads of all three services came directly from government contractors. In addition, 13 of the 30 members of the DEFENSE POLICY BOARD, which advises the defense secretary, had ties to companies that won more than $76 billion in defense contracts in 2001 and 2002, according to the Center for Public Integrity.

Boeing: Tanking up on tax dollars. In 2003, two sitting members of the Defense Policy Board, retired Adm. DAVID JEREMIAH and retired Air Force Gen. RONALD FOGLEMAN, were hired by BOEING as lobbyists to the Pentagon while the aircraft maker was seeking a deal to lease 100 fuel-tanker planes to the air force for $20 billion—$6 billion more than it would cost to buy the planes outright. Air Force Procurement Officer DARLEEN DRUYUN took a job with Boeing that she had been offered while negotiating the deal, for which she was later sentenced to nine months in jail. Sen. JOHN McCAIN (R-AZ) accused Air Force Secretary JAMES ROCHE of conspiring to fix the bidding. Roche even called a Boeing lobbyist and told him to put pressure on another Pentagon official. "Unbelievable," "shameless," "incestuous," McCain fumed. "They have forgotten their duty to American citizens." (The air force or the Bush administration as a whole?)

Two full orbits. In 2004, Bush named EDWARD ALDRIDGE chairman of the President's Commission on Space Exploration, aka "Moon-to-Mars Commission," while Aldridge served on the board of LOCKHEED MARTIN, NASA's top contractor and the operator of the space shuttle. On joining Lockheed, Aldridge "was immediately named by [Rumsfeld] to a blue-ribbon panel studying how the Pentagon should buy weapons—including those made by Lockheed, which has received $142 billion in government contracts in the last seven years."[29] From 2001 to 2003, Aldridge was under secretary of defense for acquisition, technology, and logistics, and before that, president of McDONNELL DOUGLAS and CEO of AEROSPACE CORP.

DICK HEAD-OF-GOVERNMENT CHENEY

The Cheney-Bush administration—and that's the accurate order—has simply become more than I can stand . . . I am more fearful for the state of this nation than I have ever been—because this country is in the hands of an evil man: Dick Cheney.

—Republican former Minnesota Governor
Elmer Andersen, *Minneapolis Star-Tribune,* 10/13/04

Bush can't dump Cheney, for it is Cheney, not Rove, who is Bush's backroom brain . . . Cheney knows how to play Bush so that Cheney is absolutely no threat to him, makes him feel he is president, but Bush can't function without a script, or without Cheney. Bush is head of state; Cheney is head of government.

—Former Nixon White House counsel John Dean,
interview in *Salon,* 3/31/04

For those who regard *Bush* as to the right of Attila the Hun, it bears remembering what else made Richard B. Cheney so indispensable. In 2000, right-wing guru RICHARD VIGUERIE wrote, "Conservatives are thrilled that Bush, a centrist [!] . . . has selected a solid conservative" as his running mate—as the Christian right had demanded in return for their support. Cheney "looks like 'them' (establishment Republicans)," Viguerie added, "but he sounds like (and is) one of 'us.'" JERRY FALWELL praised the "excellent move." The *National Review* nodded, "a man of the center [!] . . . has now chosen a man of the right." Cheney, said a "well-known conservative," was "TOM DELAY with table manners." Two conservative pundits ominously called Cheney "the best veep choice . . . since Eisenhower tapped Nixon."

Cheney's remark, "Principle is okay up to a certain point, but principle doesn't do any good if you lose," was perfectly sound Nixonism. But with all due respect to Tricky Dick I, this judge gives Tricky Dick II higher scores on arrogance, imperiousness, cronyism, even secretiveness and mendacity, as well in the talent and swimsuit competitions.

"A man governed by greed." Cheney had good reason to stump around in 2004 filthily impugning John Kerry's commitment to defense and saying that if Kerry were elected, "we will get hit again" by terrorists. (See **Election**.) And it wasn't just that Kerry was a decorated Vietnam hero while Bush and Cheney were CHICKENHAWKS (Cheney received five deferments; "I had other priorities," he explained). Nor was Cheney merely deflecting attention from his central role in misleading the country on **Iraq** and botching the occupation.

"Beyond blatantly mischaracterizing Democrats' positions on defense," David Sirota and Jonathan Baskin wrote in the *American Prospect*, Cheney's "shameless attacks" in 2004 served "to distract from the vice president's own proclivity for undermining American foreign policy." As CEO of the Texas energy services and construction firm HALLIBURTON from 1995 to 2000, "Cheney was willing first to do business with countries on the U.S. government's terror list, then to travel abroad and condemn U.S. counter-terrorism policy when it got in his way. In the process, Cheney proved repeatedly he could be trusted to put Halliburton's bottom line ahead of his country's national security . . . Far from embodying lofty ideals of 'freedom' and 'democracy,' Cheney's record depicts a man governed by greed." [30]

Dick head of Halliburton. In August 2004, Halliburton paid a paltry $7.5 million to settle SEC charges that it defrauded shareholders of billions while under Cheney's management by using accounting tricks similar to ENRON's to inflate revenue. The maneuvers—which Cheney was aware of, Halliburton's new CEO told *Newsweek*—boosted the value of Halliburton's stock and earned Cheney more than $35 million when he sold his shares in 2000, right before news of the investigation caused the stock to plummet. All five of the SEC commissioners who approved the $7.5 million settlement—and who said Cheney should not be held accountable—were appointed by Bush.

Though he claimed to have severed his ties with Halliburton, Cheney as vice president continued to receive about $150,000 a year in deferred pay from the company and to own more than 433,000 Halliburton stock options—even while he helped "coordinate" the awarding to Halliburton of huge, no-bid U.S. government contracts in Iraq which became cesspools of corruption and waste. (See **War Profiteering**.)

Strong on defense (of his own power). In 2004, Cheney attacked Kerry for having "repeatedly voted against weapons systems for the military." But almost all of the cuts Kerry voted for were endorsed or originally proposed by Cheney himself. As a congressman in the 1980s, during the height of the Cold War, Cheney called for President Reagan "to hit defense [spending] . . . to reach out and take a whack at everything." As secretary of defense under Bush I, Cheney bragged that he was setting "an all-time record . . . for canceling or stopping production" of weapons and that he had "put an end to more than 100 systems" in less than three years. "Cheney was so successful at cutting weapons that the *Boston Globe* worried the Army 'will soon have virtually no major weapons in production.'"[31] He also reduced active-duty troop strength by 600,000, or 22 percent, and made deep cuts in the reserves and national guard—leaving the U.S. military stretched thin even 15 years later, most notably and disastrously in Iraq.[32]

Cheney also attacked Kerry for being "deeply irresponsible" on **intelligence** issues. Kerry's proposal to slightly reduce intelligence funding "was nothing compared to Cheney's shortsighted effort to stifle intelligence reforms in the name of retaining his own personal power," wrote Baskin and Sirota. "Some of the most important intelligence reforms proposed by the 9/11 Commission, including the creation of a director of national intelligence (DNI), might have been adopted over a decade ago if not for the opposition of the secretary of defense at the time, Dick Cheney," the Federation of American Scientists (FAS) noted.

"YOU'VE GOT TO GO WHERE THE OIL IS," said Cheney as Halliburton's CEO—and he meant *wherever* the oil is:

Iraq. As defense secretary under Bush I, Cheney was one of the architects of the post Gulf War trade embargo on Iraq. During the 2000 campaign, Cheney said he had "imposed a 'firm policy' [at Halliburton] against trading with Iraq" even if the deals were legal. Actually, on his watch, Halliburton acquired two foreign subsidiaries and used them to sell Iraq more than $73 million in oil production equipment. "Two former senior executives of the Halliburton subsidiaries say that, as far as they knew, there was no policy against doing business with Iraq. One of the executives also says . . . he is certain Cheney knew about" the Iraqi contracts, the *Washington Post* reported.[33]

Iran and Libya. In speeches overseas in 1998 and 2000, Cheney attacked U.S. trade sanctions on these two countries—which the State Department listed as state sponsors of terrorism—and complained the policy prevented U.S. firms from "invest[ing] significantly in Iran." Apparently, it didn't: By 2004, the Treasury Department was investigating Halliburton for "serious and willful violations" of the sanctions laws while Cheney was CEO. Halliburton denied performing $30–$40 million annually in oilfield service work in Iran: *That*, it said, was its Cayman Islands–registered subsidiary, Halliburton Products & Services Limited (HPSL)—which, it argued, was exempt from any U.S. embargo. In 2003, Halliburton generated about $80 million in revenue in Iran, part of Bush's "AXIS OF EVIL." In January 2005—a week before Halliburton announced it was pulling out of Iran—HPSL signed a new $30–$35 million deal to help develop Iran's natural gas fields. Cozy with the regime? One of the principals in the project's lead firm was Iran's chief international negotiator on its nuclear program. "They're still acting like the sanctions laws are a big joke," a congressional investigator told *Newsweek*, which noted that the deal "appears to suggest a far closer connection with the country's hard-line government than the firm has ever acknowledged." Halliburton also continued doing business in Libya throughout Cheney's tenure.

Burma shame. While Cheney was boss, Halliburton helped build a notorious gas pipeline in Burma whose construction and operation involved the use of forced labor, forced relocation or "depopulation" by the military of whole towns along the route, "and even murder, torture and rape," and whose revenue would prop up the brutal regime, Earth-Rights International charged. Cheney said Halliburton had not violated U.S. sanctions on Burma, which only forbade *new* U.S. investments. (Oh, okay, cool.)

During Cheney's tenure, Halliburton also did business with AZERBAIJAN, where Congress had imposed sanctions because of concerns about ethnic cleansing of Armenians—sanctions Cheney lobbied to remove; INDONESIA, whose dictator, SUHARTO, was named "most corrupt leader in modern history" by Transparency International; and NIGERIA, where Halliburton was accused of complicity with the regime's "kill and go" Mobile Police Unit in violence against villagers and protesters. But as Cheney liked to say back then, "The good Lord didn't see fit to put oil and gas only where there are democratic regimes" friendly to the U.S. (Well, if he had *God's* blessing . . .)

9/11. In May 2001, Cheney appointed Bush to appoint Cheney to take charge of a new terrorism task force, but it never met before **September 11**. Cheney was busy, damn it—he and KEN LAY were drafting national **energy policy**. (Also see **Presidential Power** and **Secrecy**.) After 9/11, Cheney played a vital role—or as Bush would say, "did a tremendous job"—in hampering inquiries into the attack.

The Iraq "steamroller." During the 2000 campaign, Cheney said the U.S. should not act like "an imperialist power, willy-nilly moving into capitals in [the Middle East], taking down governments." By 2002, Cheney had become a leading manufacturer and distributor of phony claims in favor of invading Iraq. In fact, Cheney was the "steamroller," wrote Bob Woodward. It was conventional wisdom in the intelligence community that Cheney and Rumsfeld strong-armed CIA Director George Tenet into exaggerating Iraq's WMD capacity.[34] When CIA analysts maintained there was no intelligence to support the allegation that Iraq had tried to purchase uranium in Africa, Cheney told them they were not looking hard enough. A retired senior CIA officials told a Senate panel: "This is the first time in 27 years I have ever heard of a Vice President sitting down with desk analysts and pushing them to find support for something he believes." (Or didn't believe, as the case may be.) Cheney was especially tireless in trying to link Saddam to bin Laden and even to 9/11.

Wrote Sidney Blumenthal in *Salon*, "It was Cheney who said to [UN] weapons inspector HANS BLIX . . . 'We will not hesitate to discredit you'; Cheney who personally tried to force the CIA to give credence to [Iraqi National Congress leader] AHMED CHALABI's fabricated and false evidence on WMD; Cheney who [along with Rumsfeld] undermined Secretary of State Colin Powell at every turn." And Cheney who, in late 2003, tried to shut down the Senate Select Committee on Intelligence inquiry into pre-war intelligence on Iraq— and who pressured the committee's chairman to put all the blame on the CIA and leave the White House's role out of the inquiry entirely. Cheney, wrote Blumenthal, "is the neoconservatives' godfather . . . [he has] come to stand for special interests, secrecy and political coercion."

Halliburton's extraordinary rise. In 2002, Halliburton was the Pentagon's 37th largest contractor. By 2004, it was number one, with some $18 billion in contracts for services in Iraq. In addition to an open-ended, "cost-plus" contract for army support services, Halliburton subsidiary KBR was secretly awarded a deal worth up to $7 billion to upgrade oil facilities (which, it turned out, also allowed the company to pump and distribute the oil for a time) without the competitive bidding normally required for government contracts. The results are described under **War Profiteering**.

Everything about the KBR deal was extraordinary. Bidders for government contracts are usually chosen by career civil servants rather than political appointees, to avoid any appearance of political influence. The selection of Halliburton was made by the office of Under Secretary of Defense DOUGLAS FEITH, authorized by Deputy Defense Secretary PAUL WOLFOWITZ, reviewed by Cheney's chief of staff, I. LEWIS LIBBY, and "coordinated" with the vice president's office, according to a Pentagon e-mail.[35] A former deputy defense secretary said he'd "never heard of anything like" that amount of political input on a defense contract. Sen. Patrick Leahy (D-VT) said it "totally contradicts the vice president's previous assertions" of having no involvement. Coincidentally, the KBR executive in charge of Pentagon contracts, Joe Lopez, was an aide to Cheney when he was defense secretary, and was subsequently hired by Halliburton at Cheney's suggestion.

"Fuck off"–gate. Less unusual, perhaps, was Cheney's response in the Senate after Leahy called for congressional hearings into the Halliburton matter in June 2004: "Fuck off." (Reports that it was "fuck *you*" were denied by a Cheney spokeswoman.) As president of the Senate, the vice president may not have known Senate rules prohibit profanity in the chamber—or may have felt the rules needed to be reformed. Just months later, the administration hiked the maximum penalty for broadcasting such Cheneyisms on the air from $27,500 to $500,000. (See **Free Speech**.)

Plamegate. In July 2005, suspicions were confirmed that Cheney's office was a—if not *the*—source of the possibly criminal leak of CIA operative VALERIE PLAME WILSON's identity to reporters. (See **Plamegate**.)

ECONOMIC POLICY: *TAXES, SPENDING, AND CLASS WARFARE*

This is an impressive crowd. The 'haves' and 'the have-mores.' Some people call you the 'elite.' I call you my base.
—George W. Bush at a fund-raising dinner
during the 2000 campaign

Nation's Poor Win Election For Nation's Rich
—The *Onion*, 11/10/04

It's never enough. After three rounds of big, fat tax cut for Bush's fattest-cat constituents/clients, one in each of his first three years—cuts that shifted the burden of taxation to the middle class and ran up record deficits, putting the next generation of taxpayers deeply in hock, undermining the dollar, driving up **energy** prices, and jeopardizing vital social programs as well as **homeland security** and the safety of U.S. troops, all without reviving much economic vigor or creating jobs—the Bushies just kept coming back for more. As Bush started his second term, his first priority was to make his tax cuts, which were set to expire after ten years, permanent. (Deals are made to be broken, right?) And under a new marketing slogan, far more radical changes, once dreamt of only in the philosophies of marginal right-wing theorists and crackpot candidates, were in store.

Let's review the Bushists' ten-point "economic" (i.e., political) program:

1. To shift the burden of taxation from those at the top to middle- and lower-income workers.

2. To increasingly tax only wages—*work*—and eliminate all taxes on *wealth*, on unearned or "investment" income (interest and dividends) and inheritances, on the convenient theory that private investment and savings alone produce economic growth.

3. Ultimately, to replace the graduated income tax with a flat tax or a "consumption" or sales tax, which would hit hardest at those at the bottom, who must spend most or all of their incomes. Each of these first three policies would—indeed, already had—effectively put many lower- and middle-income households into higher tax brackets than some of the wealthiest.

4. To shift the tax burden from federal to state and local taxes to prop up the myth of the Republicans as tax-cutters.

5. To eliminate taxes on **corporations**—60 percent of which already paid no income taxes, and 95 percent of which paid less than 5 percent of their incomes—and shift the burden onto households.

6. To free businesses from **consumer, health, and safety regulations,** from **environmental** responsibility, and from having to pay for harm they cause their workers and consumers. (See **"Tort Reform."**)

7. To crush what remained of organized **labor**.

8. To privatize government programs so as to funnel taxpayers' money into corporate coffers.

9. By reducing tax revenue and running up huge deficits, to "starve the beast"—force drastic cuts in social spending and, eventually, complete elimination of the major "entitlements," **Social Security**, Medicare, and Medicaid (see **Health Insurance**)—the pillars of America's social safety net (okay, so nets don't have pillars); in GOP activist GROVER NORQUIST's immortal phrase, "to get [government] down to the size where we can drown it in the bathtub."

10. To divide and conquer the Democrats, splitting their middle-class supporters off from the working class and poor on the issues of taxes, Social Security, and health care, and luring the better-off to the GOP.

Same old scam, new packaging. Bushonomics was basically the next phase of the Reaganite "supply-side" revolution—"voodoo economics," as Bush père once called it. The Bushies were, however, slicker at packaging it. And repackaging it.

It started with the budget surplus the Bushies inherited from Clinton and falsely projected into the future. It was imperative to give the surplus back to the taxpayers, said Bush; hey, "it's your money." (In his book *The President of Good and Evil*, the philosopher Peter Singer explained how remarkably untrue that slogan is by showing how our jobs and as much as 90 percent of our earnings derive from and depend on economic infrastructure provided by government.)

Next came the Bush recession, and Bush's tax cuts became "economic stimulus" and "jobs plans"—even though they went mainly to those least likely to spend their savings and help stimulate the economy—the wealthy. Next came 9/11—and Bush argued that huge tax cuts were essential to the nation's "economic security." To oppose them was unpatriotic! As House Majority Leader TOM DELAY said, "Nothing is more important in the face of a war than cutting taxes"! This was really a new one; taxes had always been *raised* to pay for wars. But for Bush's political benefit, this war was to be billed to future generations.

The richest 20 percent already owned 84 percent of the nation's private wealth before Bush came along; the top 1 percent owned 38 percent (up from 20 percent in 1983). The bottom 60 percent owned 4.7 percent. Between 1983 and 1998, the average household worth of the bottom 40 percent *declined* 76 percent, as debt increased; those at the top saw their wealth rise 42 percent.[36] Over roughly the same period, the top 20 percent enjoyed a 50 percent increase in real after-tax income, while the bottom 20 percent stagnated at around $11,000. In 2001, the top 20 percent of households "for the first time raked in more than half of all income, while the share earned by those in the middle was the lowest in nearly 50 years," the *Progress Report* noted.

Something had to be done to increase this growing inequality.

THE BUSH TAX CUTS. Bush claimed repeatedly that most of his tax cuts "went to low- and middle-income Americans." Compare and contrast:

Giveaway 2001. In Bush's first, $1.3 trillion tax cut, 38 percent of the benefits went to richest 1 percent of taxpayers. This group got benefits averaging $100,000 a year, while the bottom half (and after 2005, three-quarters) of all households were to get *less than $100*.

The bill included a phased repeal of the ESTATE TAX, which affected only the richest 2 percent of Americans, and which the right falsely described as "DOUBLE TAXATION," when in fact most of the accumulated wealth subject to estate tax represented unrealized capital gains and was never subject to income tax. By one estimate, Bush's cabinet members stood to save $5–$19 million apiece from estate tax repeal. (A hundred years earlier, steel magnate Andrew Carnegie proposed that estates be taxed 100 percent; let the sons of wealth earn their own fortunes, he thought. They have already enjoyed plenty of advantages, such as elite educations, social and business connections, and powerful family names. Haven't they, George, George, and Jeb?)

Giveaway 2002. In the Orwellianly titled Job Creation and Worker Assistance Act of 2002, the sole provision for workers was a 13-week extension of benefits for a narrowly limited segment of the unemployed—which the Democrats managed to include against the Republicans' wishes. Businesses got a depreciation tax cut worth $97 billion—seven times the amount provided for the unemployed.

Giveaway 2003: Rewarding wealth, punishing work. Bush's January 2003 "stimulus plan," popularly known as the "No Millionaire Left Behind Act," called for accelerating the 2001 tax cuts and increasing them by $727 billion—of which 70 percent would go to the richest 5 percent. Just the top 226,000 tax filers—those with income over $1 million—would receive as *much as the bottom 125 million taxpayers combined.*

The largest piece of the plan was the elimination of TAX ON STOCK DIVIDENDS, which, like the estate tax, the right falsely decried as "double taxation": In fact, most corporations whose income was supposedly taxed before stockholders received their dividends paid no income tax. This measure alone would benefit the richest 1 percent of taxpayers—those who earned more than $300,000 per year—*more than the bottom 95 percent combined.*

The plan also cut CAPITAL GAINS TAX—again, to the overwhelming benefit of the wealthy. Under Bush—the champion of traditional values—tax policy rewarded investment and inheritance, while relying on work for your income, wrote Harold Meyerson in *the American Prospect*, "turns you into a second-class citizen."

More than 60 percent of Americans at the time said more

big tax cuts were not needed. Around 400 leading economists, including ten Nobel winners, signed a statement condemning the Bush plan for being, as one said, "both *grossly* unequal *and* ineffective" as economic stimulus. What it would do, they said, is make the rich richer, raise interest rates, increase borrowing from abroad, and weaken the economy.[37] Even some Republicans were getting embarrassed about the giveaways to the rich.

Instead of paying for **Iraq** war "and its messy aftermath," *Newsweek*'s Eleanor Clift noted, Bush was making support for his tax cuts a test of patriotism: "a shameless exploitation . . . with the goal of intimidating Republican holdouts on Capitol Hill." When Senators George Voinovich (R-OH) and Olympia Snowe (R-ME) pledged to hold the tax cut to $350 billion, the shock troops at the "conservative" Club for Growth took out ads in the two senators' home states, showing each alongside a French flag while the narrator equated their opposition to the full tax cut with French opposition to the Iraq invasion. The group's press release called Voinovich a "Franco Republican." (Pistols at dawn, *monsieur*?) (See **War Profiteering, Political**.)

Honey, I shrunk the child tax credit: or, 20 million children left behind. The moderates held out. Taxes on dividends and capital gains were only cut to 15 percent, for the time being. But at $350 billion, the so-called Job and Growth Act of 2003 remained the third-largest tax cut in U.S. history. (And gave those earning more than $500,000 an average of $17,000 and those earning $40,000 an average of $320.) Yet the Bushies couldn't find $4 billion in it to provide low-income families the $400-per-child increase that higher-income taxpayers received in the CHILD TAX CREDIT, which was intended to help lower-income families. Nearly 20 million children were left out—including 260,000 children of active military service personnel, because conservatives in Congress refused to allow combat pay to be included in the credit.

Giveaway (and takeaway) 2004: The next year, the same patriots effectively raised taxes on 4 million low-income families who would see their child tax credit shrink or disappear in 2005. Fixing this inequity would have cost less than 5 percent of Bush's $146 billion 2004 tax bill. The Republicans refused—while adding three times as much in corporate tax breaks.

Damage report: In all, about 77 percent of Bush's first-term tax cuts went to the richest 20 percent of households, whose average income was above $200,000. One-third went to the top 1 percent, or those earning an average of $1.2 million a year, who received an average $78,500 tax break in 2004, according to a Congressional Budget Office (CBO) report. Bush's own tax break: $31,000. Millionaires' incomes got a 10.1 percent boost, while those of middle-income families rose 2.3 percent. Eighty percent of taxpayers saved less than $1,500; those in the bottom 20 percent got a $250 cut, and a majority saved $850 or less. In 2006, the average American worker, earning $36,000 a year (less than the millionaire's tax break) would save $600.[38]

Meanwhile, state and local taxes went up (local property taxes, which hit the middle class particularly hard, rose an average of more than 10 percent between 2001 and 2003), and the average family's housing, education, and health care costs rose by *twice* their tax saving.

As a result of Bush's tax cuts, the *share* of federal taxes paid by the wealthiest 20 percent dropped by 20 percent—four-fifths of that decline occurring in the top 1 percent of taxpayers. Those earning between $51,500 and $75,600 saw their share increase. Meanwhile, Bush refused to close tax loopholes for those earning over $200,000 a year "because he acknowledges 'the really rich people figure out how to dodge taxes anyway.'"[39] (First-hand knowledge?) According to IRS data released in 2005, among the top 2 percent of earners, the number who paid *no* federal income tax more than doubled from 2000 to 2002. More than 100,000 among this group paid less tax per dollar of income than the average taxpayer.

The Bush campaign dealt with the report by the independent, nonpartisan CBO—which was headed by a former senior economist from the Bush White House—by labeling it "the Democrat-requested report." By ignoring Social Security, Medicare, and other levies, Republicans claimed the tax cuts actually made federal income taxes more equitable, that the rich were paying more! Yet at the same time, they said tax cuts for the wealthy were overdue because lower-income households were making out so well, thanks to all the new jobs the Bush tax cuts had generated (!!) and the higher wages workers were getting (!!!). Not to make it *too* easy to dispute such assertions, in 2001 the Treasury Department had stopped releasing information on the distribution of tax cuts by income level.

Screwed as never before. Lower-income people were also to bear the brunt of the spending cuts and, indeed, tax *increases* needed to pay for Bush's GRIFTR (Greedy RIch Folks' Tax Relief) program. Bush's budgets had already raised fees, such as increased surcharges for veterans' health care, by almost $20 billion. Bush had effectively hiked taxes on millions of low-income families by lowering the value of the child tax credit. State and local taxes went up. More workers lost health insurance and pension coverage. Millions of middle-class families were getting hit for the first time by ALTERNATIVE MINIMUM TAX. And while Bush was giving a $52,000 tax cut to every millionaire in America and eliminating cleanup taxes on industrial polluters, 1.7 million Americans fell below the poverty line. As David Sirota put it in the *American Prospect*, "Average Americans are being screwed as never before."

DEFICIT ATTENTION DISORDER. Bush's tax cuts would be paid for not only by the present generation of ordinary Americans but future ones as well. In 2001, Bush inherited a federal surplus of more than $100 billion. In 2004, he could boast a record deficit of around $450 billion, of which his tax cuts accounted for more than half. It was the third consecutive deficit after four straight years of surpluses under Clinton.

"No Republican would defend him." The Bushies always blamed the deficits on things beyond their control—the recession they claimed to have inherited from Clinton but which began in March 2001, and the economic shock of 9/11. But in 2004, the CBO estimated that economic weakness accounted for only 6 percent of the deficit, which stemmed "much more from rising government spending and progressively deeper tax cuts."[40]

Federal spending grew by 33 percent in Bush's first term—at the end of which, he had yet to veto a spending bill, no matter how pork-laden. The national debt, which Bush had promised in 2000 to "pay down to a historically low level," stood at an all-time high of over $7 trillion—29 percent higher than in 2001. By 2014, Bush's fiscal policies would create $10 trillion in debt. Bush's tax cuts alone, if extended as he demanded, would cost $5.5 trillion—nearly as much debt as the U.S. government had accumulated in two centuries when Bush took office. The *New York Times*'s Nicholas Kristof noted that Bush "has excoriated the 'death tax,' as he calls the estate tax. But his profligacy will leave every American child facing a 'birth tax' [share of the debt] of about $150,000." Wrote conservative journalist Andrew Sullivan, "If a Democrat had this appalling fiscal record, no Republican would defend him."

Stunting growth. Bush's tax cuts would likely *reduce* long-term economic growth, according to the CBO, Congress's Joint Committee on Taxation, Brookings Institute and Federal Reserve economists, and others. "[H]igher deficits reduce national saving and thus result in less domestic investment (and more borrowing from overseas) . . . [and] can raise long-term interest rates. Such outcomes lower the nation's future income and standard of living," the Center on Budget and Policy Priorities (CBPP) explained quite clearly.

Our fiscal banana republic and "the decline American greatness." In 2004, the International Monetary Fund

(IMF), whose business is to monitor fiscally irresponsible and debt-ridden governments, warned that U.S. deficits were spiraling out of control, threatening to undermine Social Security and Medicare, create a currency crisis, and imperil the U.S. and global economies. U.S. Comptroller General DAVID WALKER—who had gone from conservative Democrat to Republican to independent—said 2004 may have been the most fiscally reckless year in the U.S. government's history, and called fiscal irresponsibility "the greatest threat to our future." The *Times*'s Kristof wrote that the way the administration "is putting us in hock to China"—the biggest buyer of U.S. debt—is probably a bigger risk "to our way of life and our place in the world" than Al Qaeda or the Iraq war. Warning of the "decline of American greatness," Elaine Kamarck of Harvard's Kennedy School of Government wrote that Bush's fiscal and military recklessness would undercut America's wealth and therefore also its military power for years to come.

"The [political] bottom line." The Bushies masked the true fiscal impact of their tax cuts by, among other deceptions, basing the advertised costs on the cuts expiring after ten years. But no sooner were they enacted than Bush began pushing to make them permanent. That would cost $1.8 trillion by 2014, only around one-fifth of which would go to middle-income households, which would save an average of $655 a year, while that lucky top 1 percent gained an average of $58,200, or roughly ninety times as much, according to the CBPP.

Even the *Wall Street Journal*'s editors—who were to the right of Attila the Hun *and* Milton Friedman—opposed extending the tax cuts, which would reduce economic growth by an estimated 17 percent, according to a widely cited report from *Economy.com*, and further reduce tax revenues just as baby boomers were due to start retiring, putting enormous demands on Medicare and Social Security.

But this wasn't *about* 2014. It was about buying votes and campaign contributions in 2004 and 2006. As Bushite Stephen Moore of the Club for Growth—citing "the political benefits"—told the *New Yorker*, the "bottom line" was that "nobody lost an election in the past twenty years because of budget deficits."

There was one tax cut Bush chose *not* to renew in his 2005 budget: The LOW-INCOME SAVERS CREDIT. An "above-the-line" deduction for higher EDUCATION expenses, too, was in doubt. Lest anyone accuse Bush of lack of fiscal discipline.

Nine cents on the dollar. "The tax cuts are working" remained Bush's mantra. But it really, really depended on one's definition of "working." According to *Economy.com:*[41]

- For every dollar of tax revenue lost, Bush's reduction in the tax rates provided only 59 cents of economic stimulus. The dividend and capital gains tax cuts produced 9 cents of stimulus.
- The economic bang for a buck in federal aid to state governments is $1.24, yet state aid accounted for only 3 percent of the total cost of Bush's fiscal policies.
- *The tax cuts that went to middle- and lower-income people contributed twice as much to growth as the upper-income and business breaks combined.* Yet the latter received nearly twice as much of the tax cuts.
- Most of the economic stimulus by far came not from

tax cuts but from low interest rates—which deficits eventually raise.

But as economist Lawrence Mishel wrote in the *American Prospect*, Bush's policies "were never intended to generate jobs or growth . . . they were always about cutting government revenue and shifting the tax burden away from income from investments (from the few) and onto income from labor (that's most of us)."

THE HIGH-PROFIT, LOW-WAGE, LOW-JOB-GROWTH, BUSHED ECONOMY. Bush ended his first term as the first president to preside over a net loss of jobs since Hoover, in the Great Depression. Of the 2.7 million jobs lost in 2001 to 2003, "the vast majority have been restructured out of existence," according to a Federal Reserve Bank study. Overwhelmingly, the lost jobs were in higher-paying industries; the job gains were in industries that paid 21 percent less. And an increasing proportion were part-time jobs with no health benefits. The *Washington Post* reported on "The Vanishing Middle-Class Job."

A rebound in 2004—though rather well timed for Bush politically—was the weakest on record in terms of job growth. In this, Bush's best year to date, job growth was worse than in any of the Clinton years. Eight million Americans were out of work; many more had given up looking and were no longer included in the government statistics. Real unemployment was probably close to 10 percent.

Also in Bush's first term:

• The number of Americans lacking health insurance rose to 45 million, the highest level on record and 5.2 million more than when Bush took office.

- The share of total income that goes to the bottom 20 percent of households fell to one of its lowest levels since the end of World War II. In 2003, inflation-adjusted wages fell; in 2004, actual wages fell for the first time in nearly a decade, even as corporate profits grew and the costs of housing, education, and medical care increased at double-digit rates. Many economists said wages would remain under pressure for years to come—"a most unusual development in a period of high productivity growth," one economist said.

- The number of Americans living in poverty increased by more than 10 percent to nearly 36 million (officially). In March 2004, the *New York Times* reported that the number of U.S. households facing "limited or uncertain availability of food" had risen 15 percent in four years. More and more of them were working families, and more and more lived not in inner cities but in suburban and outlying areas. The director of a food bank on suburban Long Island said demand was the greatest in her 17 years there.

But, **corporate profits were up 46 percent**—and as Labor Secretary ELAINE CHAO said in response to another lousy jobs report, "the stock market is, after all, the final arbiter, and the stock market was very strong this morning." That figured: Employers took advantage of the high unemployment, boosted by plenty of OFFSHORING of jobs, to keep wages and salaries down; and as Lawrence Mishel noted, "With fast productivity and minimal growth in wages and employment, you get big profits." Even right-wing Federal Reserve Chairman ALAN GREENSPAN acknowledged, "Most of the recent increases in productivity have been reflected in a sharp rise in [corporations'] profits," while wage and salary gains remained "quite modest," so that compared to corporate profits, wages and salaries "were at *a very low level by the standards of the past three decades.*" (Emphasis added.)

As for the "final arbiter," in Bush's first term the Dow fell 4.4 percent, the broader S&P 500 fell 15 percent, and the NASDAQ fell 23 percent. GDP underperformed the average by 2.3 percent, "giving Bush the third worst administration since Truman while besting only his father and Nixon's 2nd term."[42]

"Kerry, Kerry!" In August 2004, Bush "reacted decisively to [a] shockingly bad employment report—by quickly changing the topic to terror," the *New York Times* remarked. Traders in the Chicago pit reacted a bit differently: They reportedly began chanting, "Kerry, Kerry."

The shining vision: No taxes for the rich. The right was pushing for *zero* tax on dividends, capital gains, and corporate income. The administration, wrote John Cassidy in the *New Yorker*, appeared set on undermining the two principles on which the tax system had been based for a century: the tax burden is distributed according to the ability to pay, and capital and labor carry their fair share. If Bush's economic agenda was fully enacted, corporate profits "wouldn't be taxed at all, and labor would end up shouldering practically the entire burden of financing the federal government."

Under such a system, wrote Daniel Altman in his book

Neoconomy, "[t]he fortunate and growing minority who managed to receive all their income from stocks, bonds and other securities would pay nothing—not a dime—for America's cancer research, its international diplomacy, its military deterrent, the maintenance of the interstate highway system, the space program . . ." That could only mean tax *increases* for the majority—as Bush himself had all but acknowledged when he said his second-term tax changes would be "revenue neutral," i.e., would not reduce total tax revenues. What the wealthy saved, someone else would have to pay. This, the conservative founders of the flat-tax movement had called "an obvious mathematical law."

DIVIDE AND CONQUER! A grand—one could almost say Rovian—political strategy was at work here. "Under Bush's slogan of an '**ownership society**,'" wrote law professor Charles Tiefer in *Salon*, "using changes in Medicare, Social Security and taxes," the Republicans intend "to pit better-off and worse-off Democrats against each other, offering all-but-irresistible incentives for some to desert the others—and any progressive national coalition." The wedge, Tiefer and others predicted—the key to dismantling the whole existing tax structure—would be the Alternative Minimum Tax (AMT).

"No tax cuts for the Gore/Kerry states." AMT was originally enacted to ensure that the rich pay at least some tax, no matter how many deductions they have. But with rising incomes, cuts in the regular income tax, and inflation, millions of middle-class taxpayers were becoming subject to AMT in addition to their regular tax. But it mostly affected Democratic areas like New York and California because those were more likely to levy state and local income taxes, which taxpayers deduct from their regular income tax. AMT "performs the politically dangerous trick of surcharging Democratic areas and sparing Republican ones," wrote Tiefer. Bush's 2001 tax bill slashed the taxes that "irritate very wealthy Republicans," but did not address AMT: "No Tax Cuts for the Gore States," ran a tax journal's headline.

"Change 'Gore' to 'Kerry' or just plain 'Democratic,'" Tiefer wrote, "and the post-2005 prospect becomes alarmingly clear." The Republicans, he predicted, will "repeatedly and visibly" present Democrats in Congress with the "politically lethal dilemma" of having to vote whether to cut the AMT and make up for the lost revenue by raising taxes on the working poor (by, say, repealing the earned income tax credit)—to sell out their own states and districts or the party's base. Either way, the GOP would portray the Dems as tax increasers—while Bush kept cutting taxes for his own high-income constituency.

AMT also offered "a chance to discuss fundamental tax reform," said the former chairman of Bush's Council of Economic Advisers, Glenn Hubbard. Translation: to replace the individual income tax with a FLAT TAX or NATIONAL SALES TAX that would shift the tax burden downward dramatically.

STEALING TOWARD THE FLAT TAX. To Republicans "who understand his coded language," wrote John Cassidy,

The "red-ink" states. As AMT punished blue states while
sparing red ones, the main beneficiaries of federal spending,
too, were the supposedly anti-government, self-reliant, free-
market-loving "red" states, like Alaska, Mississippi, the
Dakotas, Alabama, Montana, and New Mexico. These "welfare
states" or "red-ink states" received up to $1.99 in federal bene-
fits, subsidies, and contracts for every federal tax dollar they
paid. The biggest losers—getting back as little as 57 cents on
the buck—were New Jersey, Connecticut, New York, California, Massachusetts, and Illinois: all blue electorally, black
and blue fiscally, and presumably green with envy toward the
red states.

"The fleecing of the blue states has increased markedly over
the past decade as Republicans tightened their hold on Washington," wrote the *Washington Post*'s Steven Pearlstein. And "it's
about to get worse." Was it coincidence, he asked, that after
voting 91 percent for Kerry, the District of Columbia got stuck
with a $12 million tab for Bush's inauguration security? Or that

when Bush invokes the "ownership society," he "is also
talking . . . about a vision that has entranced but eluded conservatives for decades: the abolition of the graduated
income tax and its replacement with a levy that is simpler,
flatter, and more favorable to rich people."

Bush first revealed this intention publicly in August 2004,
when asked about a proposal from House Speaker DENNIS
HASTERT to abolish the IRS and replace the graduated income

Cheney was still pushing tax cuts and royalty breaks for red-state oil drillers and miners, "even after **energy** prices for blue-state consumers have rocketed to record highs? . . . Or that the tax plan being cooked up by the Treasury will eliminate the deduction for state and local taxes, which just happen to be highest in blue states?" The Treasury, he might have added, had just made state *sales* tax deductible—a boon to red states with no state income tax, like Texas and Florida.

Meanwhile, the feds' **Homeland Security** funding formula awarded such obvious (and red) terrorist target areas as Wyoming and the Dakotas three times more per capita than blue New York and New Jersey—enabling, for example, Alaska's Northwest Arctic Borough, "a desolate area of 7,300 people that straddles the Arctic Circle," to stock up on decontamination tents and night vision goggles and Juneau to buy a robot for deactivating bombs while New York's police and firefighters lacked compatible radios. To the victor, Pearlstein concluded, belong the spoils.[43]

tax with a national sales tax or flat tax. "It's an interesting idea . . . that we ought to explore seriously," Bush replied. (It was "a very dumb idea," wrote conservative economist Bruce Bartlett, who served under Reagan and Bush I.) By the end of the year, Bush had appointed a commission "to explore all the ideas on the table, including a single-rate flat tax and a national sales tax," the *New York Times* noted. Translation: To start preparing the public for what was coming.

"A tremendous boon to the economic elite." Studies had shown that a sales tax would enormously benefit the wealthy and penalize middle- and lower-income people, who must spend much larger portions of their income and would therefore wind up in higher tax brackets than the rich. Indeed, the founding fathers of the flat tax wrote in 1983 that it "would be a tremendous boon to the economic elite ... it is an obvious mathematical law that lower taxes on the successful will have to be made up by higher taxes on average people."[44] (Could any words be more thrilling, to Republican ears?) So, advocates preferred to call it the more benign-sounding "consumption tax," and to approach it by stealth. "That's the hidden story of what is going on under Bush," anti-tax lobbyist STEPHEN MOORE told the *New Yorker.* "Nobody could get [a flat tax] done politically. What Bush has done, in a hidden way, is move us in baby steps toward the flat tax."

Ready for a 100 percent sales tax? A flat-tax proposal by Rep. John Linder (R-GA) in 2004 claimed that a 23 percent sales tax—really 30 percent, figuring it the normal, "tax-exclusive" way—would suffice to replace the revenues from income taxes. Linder's calculations assumed that *all* goods and services would be taxed, including, presumably, medical care, insurance, purchases of homes—all of which would instantly cost at least 30 percent more. It was "completely idiotic" to think that would ever happen, wrote Bruce Bartlett, and so "every serious economist who has ever looked at this question has concluded that a vastly higher rate would in fact be needed." Congress's Joint Committee on Taxation figured *57 percent.* A Brookings Institution estimate went much higher. You don't want to know. Anyway, 54 Congress members—all Republicans, including House

Majority Leader TOM DELAY—cosponsored Linder's completely idiotic proposal.

THE 2006 BUSH BUDGET: "Top-down class warfare in action." That's what Paul Krugman called the 2006 budget plan released in February 2005. "It may sound shrill to describe President Bush as someone who takes food from the mouths of babes and gives the proceeds to his millionaire friends," wrote Krugman, but that is almost literally what this proposal did. It would:

- Cut $45-$60 billion over ten years from MEDICAID, which provides basic health coverage to the poor.
- Terminate food stamp aid for about 300,000 people and end child care assistance to about 300,000 children in low-income working families.
- Substantially cut housing assistance for low-income families, people with disabilities (by half), and people with AIDS.
- Cut the Low-Income Home Energy Assistance program (LIHEAP), which had already fallen by 23 percent under Bush, by another 8 percent, while fuel costs were skyrocketing. (Do they rub their hands and chortle fiendishly while cutting off poor people's heat?)

There were substantial cuts for veterans' health benefits; health insurance and emergency medical services for children; the National Youth Sports Program for low-income children; state education technology grants; Safe and Drug-Free School grants; law enforcement grants to states; the Even Start literacy program and job training.

The Hope VI program to repair "severely distressed" public housing. The Lead Hazard Reduction program, to reduce children's exposure to lead poisoning. Land and Water Conservation grants. The Advanced Technology Program, which helps to finance research in medicine, engineering, and computer science. (See **Science**.) The National Science Foundation. The Centers for Disease Control. Bush had praised many of these same programs at campaign stops.

The literally hidden agenda. The plan included cuts for 2006–2009 that the White House had planned for more than a year but kept hidden until after the election: The budget tables that would normally show these cuts were "missing from the budget books" issued by the White House in 2004, the CBPP discovered.[45] Many of these cuts, too, were to programs Bush touted on the campaign trail. They included:

- SPECIAL EDUCATION FUNDING for educating children with disabilities: Bush had boasted of increasing this program's funding in 2005, while planning to cut it to $530 million below the 2004 level.
- The SECTION 8 HOUSING VOUCHER PROGRAM, the nation's principal housing assistance program for low-income, elderly, and disabled households, would be cut by 40 percent. Most of these households live below the poverty line. This would be the deepest cut in a major program for the poor since at least the early Reagan years.
- VETERANS HEALTH SERVICES would be cut by $5.7 billion, or 17 percent.
- "TITLE I" EDUCATION FUNDING for low-income and other disadvantaged children would be cut by $660 million.

- HEAD START, which provides medical, nutritional, educational, and early childhood development help for pre-school, low-income children: An estimated 62,000 children would be eliminated from the program.
- SUPPLEMENTAL NUTRITIONPROGRAM FOR WOMEN, INFANTS, AND CHILDREN (WIC): Around 450,000 low-income pregnant women and young children at nutritional risk would be cut off.
- COLLEGE GRANTS for hundreds of thousands of low-income students would be eliminated. Meanwhile, the Education Department was cracking down hard on student loan repayments, using private collectors and "power that would make a mobster envious," a bankruptcy specialist told the *Wall Street Journal*.

All these cuts, though "inspired" by concern about the deficit, would barely make a dent in it, or even pay for Bush's upper-income tax cuts—which accounted for 17 times as much of the swing from surplus to deficit as growth in discretionary spending. But perhaps they would give the right some other kind of satisfaction.

"Warped values." The budget plan in fact added $1.4 trillion to Bush's Tax Cuts for the Rich program: $1.1 trillion to make the 2001 and 2003 tax cuts permanent, $300 million in new cuts. It phased out two limits on deductions and exemptions for high-income households: Ninety-seven percent of the benefits would go to people with incomes exceeding $200,000; more than half would go to people with incomes of more than $1 million. "It so happens that the number of taxpayers with more than $1 million in annual income is about the same as the number of people who would have their food stamps cut off under the

Bush proposal," Krugman noted. "But it costs a lot more to give a millionaire a break than to put food on a low-income family's table." The plan was "like that all the way through."

A rollback of Bush's cuts to high-income rates, capital gains and dividend income taxes would save nearly twice as much as the budget's spending cuts, while costing middle-income families an average of $156.[46] Just rolling back the tax cuts above the first $200,000 in income would save enough to avoid cuts in veterans' health care, education, and environmental cleanup funding, Rep. Jan Schakowsky (D-IL) pointed out. "This is a morally reprehensible budget that clearly demonstrates President Bush's lack of compassion, misplaced priorities, and warped values," the Democrat wrote in a vicious, politically motivated attack on our president.

Warped **values—or: What the public wanted, as if that mattered.** After four years of MILITARY SPENDING increases and domestic spending cuts by Bush, the Pentagon consumed over half of the money allocated by Congress each year. Bush's 2006 budget proposed another $20 billion increase for the Pentagon (excluding the wars in Iraq and Afghanistan)—64 times his cuts in discretionary Health and Social Services spending. A University of Maryland survey the following month (March 2005) found that 65 percent of Americans favored "deep cuts in defense spending" and using the savings for energy conservation and renewables, deficit reduction, education, job training, medical research, and veterans benefits, which the Bushies were trying to slash. These "liberal" priorities were supported by Republicans in the survey nearly as much as by Democrats.[47]

According to GOP pollster Linda DiVall in December

2004, Americans supported reducing the deficit, but *would start by rolling back Bush's tax cuts* for those earning over $200,000. Next would come cutbacks for foreign aid, corporate tax breaks, the war in **Iraq,** and welfare. "Medicaid, Social Security and Medicare are the untouchables," DiVall said. Funny she should say that: The Bushies were even then drafting legislation to scale back funding for each of these programs, and targeting Social Security and Medicare for death by privatization.

Politicizing the CBO. Since 1974, when the CONGRESSIONAL BUDGET OFFICE was created to keep the White House Office of Management and Budget (OMB) honest, the CBO had "consistently issued reports disputing the rosy budgetary assessments emanating from the White House," wrote Franklin Foer in *The New Republic.* The CBO had always calculated the effects of tax cuts using neutral, "careful, consensusminded" models that conservatives derisively termed "static analysis." The right-wingers wanted the CBO to adopt their "dynamic" model—"one that assumes, as supply-siders do, that cutting top marginal tax rates will [spur] growth rates higher than any Keynesian would dare imagine possible." The conservatives succeeded, and in 2003, the CBO used dynamic scoring for the first time. Unfortunately, Foer noted, "the economy's performance over the last two years has demonstrated that the CBO's old methods predict economic performance far more accurately."[48]

CORPORATE TAX DODGING AND PORK. Around 95 percent of corporations paid less than 5 percent of their income in taxes and more than 60 percent paid no taxes at all—this at a time of rising corporate profits and "while the middle class struggles to fulfill its tax obligations," said the *Progress Report* in April 2004. The percentage of federal tax revenue paid by corporations was near record lows, partly due to increased "outsourcing" and "offshoring" of business activity and jobs overseas. The administration's policy "has been to slash taxes on investment, even as investment in corporations has less and less to do with creating jobs here at home," the *American Prospect* observed. Feast your eyes, if they can stomach it, on a porky pair of Republican bills enacted in 2004:

"A new level of sleaze." In 2001, the World Trade Organization had ruled that an annual $4 billion tax break the U.S. gave American exporters was illegal, and the European Union threatened sanctions. In 2004, the Republicans came up with a truly Republican solution for this simple problem: A bill replacing the $4 billion tax break with *$136 billion* in new tax breaks for U.S. companies.

To collect the needed votes in Congress, the election-year bill lavished billions on key districts and states. Titled, in Orwellian GOP style, the "AMERICAN JOBS CREATION ACT," it ended up providing $30 billion in tax breaks on companies' *foreign* earnings, along with "dozens of tax breaks for timber companies, oil and gas drillers, wine distributors, and manufacturers of bows and arrows," plus $9.6 billion for tobacco farmers. At the behest of engineering giant BECHTEL, which is virtually part of the GOP (or vice versa), the bill included engineering as a form of manufacturing. Chinese manufacturers of ceiling fans were exempted from $44 million in tariffs—thanks to, and *in* thanks to, Sen. ZELL MILLER (D-GA), the "Democrat" who denounced Kerry at the 2004 Republican convention: Home Depot, which sold half of all ceiling fans in the U.S., was based in Miller's Atlanta district.

There were giveaways to everyone from GENERAL ELECTRIC, EXXON MOBIL, and BOEING to fishing tackle box makers (a big producer was located in House Speaker DENNIS HASTERT's district), **NASCAR** race track owners, shopping mall developers, and foreigners winning bets at U.S. horse and dog racing tracks. "House and Senate leaders openly invited lawmakers and industry groups to draw up their own wish lists," the *New York Times* reported. It became a feeding frenzy—"a perfect storm for pork." A lobbyist involved in drafting the bill said (exulted?) it represented "a new level of sleaze."

The Bush administration immediately announced it would support the bill.

"A naked payoff . . . emblematic of Bush's presidency." House Republicans "adamantly rejected" a Senate attempt to tie the $9 billion tobacco buyout to a measure subjecting tobacco products to FDA regulation. They also rejected Democrat-sponsored measures to protect the right to overtime pay, which new Bush rules attacked; to encourage employers to make up for the pay lost by members of the reserve and national guard who are called to active duty; and to spend $250 million—a mere drop in a $136 billion "American Jobs Creation Act"—to retrain workers who lose their jobs to foreign competition. Critics like Rep. Lloyd

Doggett [D-TX] said the bill would actually "encourage corporations to ship jobs overseas. It advantages their earnings in doing that."[49] And why not? White House economist GREGORY MANKIW had declared "offshoring" to be "a good thing," "a plus for the economy in the long run."

The bill was supposed to close loopholes and crack down on schemes that turn real profits into paper losses purely to avoid taxes, costing the government tens of billions a year. The Republicans, backed by business groups, succeeded in removing or weakening those provisions, too.

It was fitting that this bill was the last one Bush signed into law before the 2004 election. It represented "the apotheosis" of his "appalling tendency" to give powerful business groups whatever they wanted, *The New Republic* said. "If anybody needs a final reminder of this administration's lack of concern for the national interest . . . this is it." The bill was "a naked payoff . . . That's why it is so emblematic of Bush's presidency."

And when it was all over, it remained uncertain whether the bill would solve the original problem; a several year "transition period" appeared to leave the U.S. technically in violation of the WTO ruling.

"The fattest legislative hog that we have ever seen." That's what Taxpayers for Common Sense called the $338 billion "OMNIBUS" SPENDING BILL Bush signed two weeks after the November 2004 election. The bill, which "virtually no one has read, and no one knows much about," was packed with exactly the kind of "pet projects" Bush vowed to cut from the budget when he first took office; four years later and $2.2 trillion deeper in debt, he had yet to veto a spending bill, however porcine.

It doesn't get much porkier than $50,000 to control wild hogs in Missouri, which this bill included, along with $1 million for a "Wild American Shrimp Initiative," $250,000 for "Asparagus Technology and Production" in Washington state, and $443,000 to develop salmon-based baby food. The bill *cut* funding for air traffic controllers, the National Science Foundation, college tuition grants, and prevention of illegal purchases of guns by kids—but "somehow, there was enough money for Mariachi music in Nevada ($25,000), a 'historic cafeteria building' in Alabama ($8 million) and the American Cotton Museum in Texas ($200,000)," the *Progress Report* noted.

While they were at it, the Republicans slipped in provisions that authorized oil drilling in the ALASKA NATIONAL WILDLIFE REFUGE, loosened environmental rules for large livestock and dairy farms, and—what's this?—*gave GOP committee chairmen access to all Americans' income tax returns?* Democrats caught that one at the last second.

ELECTION 2004: *THE CAMPAIGN, THE OUTCOME, THE "MANDATE"*

Fool me once, shame on—shame on you. Fool me—can't get fooled again.

—George W. Bush

The question of whether the 2004 vote and vote count were kosher is considered in the next section. This section assumes they were, and asks: *How* did the Bushies get a

slight majority of Americans to vote against their own interests and to forgive or forget a spectacular series of scandals
and failures, from the pre-**September 11** neglect of terrorism to the biggest of big Bush lies, **Iraq**, to Bush's record
deficits and Robin-Hood-in-reverse **economic policies**?
What did those voters believe they were voting for when
they gave four more years to the party of big money and big
business, anti-environmentalism, foreign-policy unilateralism and militarism, scientific and intellectual recidivism,
and, yes, **NASCAR** racing?

SCHMANDATE. In Bush's first term, after losing the popular vote (by half a million votes) *and* the electoral vote (had
all the Florida votes been counted), the Bushies behaved as
if they'd won in a landslide. What, then, would they make of
Bush's 2.5 percent margin of victory over Kerry in 2004—
which, if anything, represented a mandate for moderation,
bipartisanship, and *resistance* to Bush's right-wing revolution? Obviously, as Cheney said, a "mandate for change"—
and he didn't mean back toward the center.

Falling to their knees in record time. But who could
blame the Bushies for trying? After all, to most of the media,
too, the meaning of Bush's smashing, 50.8 to 48.3 percent
popular vote win was absolutely clear. MSNBC's Chris
Matthews: "To me the big story is the president's mandate."
USA Today: "Clear Mandate." *Dallas Morning News:* A
"newly minted mandate." (Why? Because this time Bush
didn't *lose* the popular vote!) And the "liberal" press? *Boston
Globe:* "[A] clear mandate to advance a conservative
agenda." CNN's Wolf Blitzer: "[H]e's got a mandate from the

American people . . . by all accounts." *Los Angeles Times*, weirdly: "Bush can claim a solid mandate of 51 percent of the vote"! Renee Montague of National Public Radio: "By any definition I think you could call this a mandate." *New York Times:* "[H]e has the real thing." As Eric Boehlert wrote in *Slate*, the *press* gave Bush his "mandate," "falling to its knees in record time."

Amid all the genuflecting, however, the *Wall Street Journal*'s Al Hunt managed to notice that Bush's win in 2004 was the narrowest for a sitting president since Woodrow Wilson in 1916. But that was by electoral college votes. Bush's 2.5 percent popular vote margin was in fact the narrowest of *any* sitting president in U.S. history (see table). And of *all* 25 presidential victors from 1904 through 2000, 21 won by wider popular vote margins than Bush in 2004, and 23 won by wider Electoral College margins.

Incumbent:	Popular vote Margin (%):	Electoral vote margin:
Franklin Roosevelt, 1936:	25	515
Calvin Coolidge, 1924:	25	246
Richard Nixon, 1972:	23	503
Ronald Reagan, 1984:	18	512
Theodore Roosevelt, 1904:	17	196
Dwight Eisenhower, 1956:	16	384
Franklin Roosevelt, 1940:	10	367
Franklin Roosevelt, 1944:	8	333
William Clinton, 1996:	8	220
Harry Truman, 1948:	4.5	114
Woodrow Wilson, 1916:	3.2	23
George W. Bush, 2004:	**2.5**	**34**

Undeterred by facts, conservative commentator Bill Kristol declared Bush's win "an even larger and clearer mandate than those won in the landslide reelection campaigns of Nixon in 1972, Reagan in 1984, and Clinton in 1996."

Bush boasted of receiving the most votes of any presidential candidate in U.S. history. This was true. He also had more people voting *against* him than any winning presidential candidate. Yes, Kerry received the second most votes in presidential history. Bush's record was merely due to the large increase in the total number of voters. Even so, only 29.5 percent of eligible voters voted for Bush.

Rumors of our death . . . Regarding the election as a whole, "the American people have spoken in deafening terms that they want Republican leadership," declared Rep. Mike Pence (R-IN). *Newsweek* concluded that the GOP "may be the majority party for the foreseeable future" and that "red-state Democrats are a diminishing breed." The "liberal" *New York Times* declared the election "the clearest confirmation yet that America is a center-right country," while Democratic strategist James Carville pronounced that "the Democratic Party died Tuesday."

Wait—reopen that coffin. The balance of governorships remained unchanged (at 28 R, 22 D). Outside of Texas, the Republicans had a net *loss* of two House seats. Most House Democrats—and all the Dem incumbents—won by margins several times larger than Bush's. The Dems' 45 of 100 Senate seats and 202 of 435 House seats were hardly small minorities. Nor could the GOP gain of four Senate seats and three House seats be described as a tectonic shift—especially considering that, as Michelle Cottle noted in *The New Republic*, the House gain was due entirely to House Majority Leader

TOM DELAY's "spending the past couple of years bending laws in order to carve up the Lone Star State into congressional districts more twisted than Bill O'Reilly's fantasy life" in order to add Republican seats. The Center for Voting and Democracy called DeLay's redistricting "the most flagrantly rigged insider's racket in decades."

Even so, there in the very heart of darkness and redness, Democrats won a third of Texas' House seats. Bush's own district in Waco, though targeted by the DeLay redistricting, went to a Dem. Dems gained seats in the state House for the first time in more than 30 years. And Dallas County elected a Democratic, Hispanic, openly gay woman as sheriff. *Manos contra la pared, Republicanos!*

"Mandate for change"? According to the largest and probably most reliable exit poll, voters in 2004 identified themselves as 37 percent Republicans, 37 percent Democrats, and 26 percent independents. An awe-inspiring 34 percent of voters identified themselves as conservative— 5 percent more than in 2000 but the same level as in 1996. The largest share of voters continued to describe themselves as moderate. Evangelical Christians made up about 23 percent of the electorate in both 2000 and 2004. On **abortion,** voters barely moved, and 62 percent supported gay marriage or civil unions, even though 11 of 11 ballot measures to ban same-sex marriage passed. "Moral **values**" was picked as the most important issue by 22 percent of voters—the same proportion as in 1996. "Rarely have election returns been so widely but wrongly—in fact, dangerously—misconstrued," the *National Journal*'s Jonathan Rauch noted. As he titled his column, "The Country Didn't Turn Right, But the GOP Did."

TOP 10 REASONS BUSH WON:

1. THE SLEAZY, LYING ATTACKS ON KERRY. Greg Sargent in the *American Prospect* rejected the view that the outcome was Kerry's fault (reason number 3 below). "The real story of this race," he wrote,

> is that . . . the Republicans ran a campaign that was sleazier, more ruthless, and more dishonest than anything in memory—by far. The key Bush attacks on Kerry were, first, that he would allow the United States' own security decisions to be vetoed by other nations; and that he would hike taxes on the middle class and small businesses. Those contentions weren't mere rhetorical distortions; they were lies. The grotesque misrepresentation of Kerry's war record, courtesy of the SWIFT BOAT veterans, was likewise based on lies . . . Yet [these assertions] either passed unchallenged by the media, or they were challenged too late—after they'd succeeded in their objective of creating, as Rove innocently put it, 'doubts about the other guy.' And the GOP got away with it, because they knew that they could count on political reporters to write about the campaign with the moral urgency of a sportswriter covering a baseball game in June. [50]

- Bush said "Kerry's approach would permit a response [to terrorism] only after America is hit." Kerry actually said, "The president always has the right, and always has had the right, for preemptive strike."

- Bush said Kerry was "against vital weapon systems during his entire career." According to Factcheck.org, Kerry had voted for 16 Pentagon funding bills and against just three, which were overall spending bills, not votes against specific weapons. (It's called *fiscal restraint*, George.)

- A Bush 2004 campaign video charged Kerry with taking "more special interest money than any other senator." Kerry actually ranked 92nd out of 100 senators in lobbyists' *and* PAC contributions—and Bush took more money from lobbyists the previous year than Kerry had in the previous 15.

Call him *Jean-François* Kerry. When Kerry blurted that many foreign leaders secretly favored him, the Bushies pretended to be outraged, wrote Molly Ivins, "as though it were not painfully obvious to every dimwit in the nation" that "foreign leaders favor anyone over Bush." The Bush campaign struck back by hinting that Kerry was . . . you know . . . "Secretary of Commerce Donald Evans has repeatedly said Kerry 'looks French.' . . . TOM DELAY begins every speech: 'As John Kerry would say, "Bonjour."' The Republican National Committee blasts out regular e-mails . . . charging . . . that he has a French cousin."[51] *Merd'arbuste!* Charge him with selling state secrets or molesting children— anything but the F-word!

2. TERRORISM, SHAMELESS EXPLOITATION OF. As a letter to *The New Republic* put it, "The presidency was lost in November because, on September 11, Bush was transformed from a mediocre golfer into a wartime president." Despite—*and* to paper over—their own negligence on terrorism, the Bushies made sure they *owned* 9/11 and the "war on terror" from the start, and implied that to oppose Bush was to help the terrorists: If Americans made "the wrong choice" on November 2, **Dick** Cheney said obscenely in a campaign speech, "then the danger is that we'll get hit again [by terrorists] in a way that will be devastating." (Some might say the "wrong choice" in this regard was Bush; see **September 11**.)

3. KERRY'S MEDIOCRITY AND TIMIDITY. Who among us never composed, in his mind, the stump speech he wished Kerry would give? Who didn't tear at his already sparse hair day after day over the issues Kerry shied away from? Who didn't wish Kerry's speeches were a bit more like his accidentally broadcast remark, "This is the most crooked . . . lying group I've ever seen"? Kerry wasted wonderful opportunities the Bush record offered—issues that cried out to be cried out. Neither Kerry nor Edwards attacked the Bushies' class warfare forcefully enough. But the real elephant in the room—the most deafeningly undiscussed subject of the campaign—was the very issue Bush had chosen as the defining one of his presidency. Bush, "with the unwitting complicity of Kerry's campaign, turned the gravest blunder of his presidency—the attacks of **September 11**—to his advantage," wrote Joseph Finder in *The New Republic*. "If Kerry loses the election, his failure to speak honestly and strongly about Bush's pre-9/11 failures will likely go down as his most significant mistake."[52]

**4. THE TIMID, TOADYING MEDIA AND CONSERVA-
TIVE MEDIA BIAS.** A few examples noted by Eric Boehlert
in *Salon* [53]:

Yellow on the yellowcake. In September, CBS's *60
Minutes* decided to delay until after the election an
investigation into the administration's use of forged
documents on uranium from Niger in making its case
for the Iraq war. A network spokesperson said at the
time, "It would be inappropriate to air the report so
close to the presidential election."

In bed on Fallujah. Less than a week after the election,
U.S. forces in Iraq launched an all-out assault on the
insurgent stronghold of Fallujah, which was expected
to involved heavy casualties (and did). Network news
departments acknowledged matter-of-factly that the
assault was postponed until after the election because
it could have hurt Bush at the polls—*and* that they
had known it all along, and had *played* along. [54]

Second-term agenda? Why do you need to know?
After the election, the media were full of reports
about Bush's "ambitious agenda"—which Bush
"rarely if ever laid out in detail during the campaign,"
NBC's David Gregory noted—and which very few
journalists pressed Bush on at the time. Bush was
wise to avoid specifics: The less voters knew about
his already unpopular *policies* . . .

Bulgegate. A week or so after the election, a *New York
Times* story led: "Now that the election is over . . . Whatever was that strange bulge in the back of President
Bush's suit jacket that was visible during the three
debates?" The rectangular bulge had inspired wide-

spread speculation that Bush was wired to receive help with his answers. But why would the *Times* examine this only "now that the election is over"?

5. IT'S THE STUPIDITY, STUPID! Following their election loss, Democrats were bombarded from within and without with admonitions that they must stop alienating all those good, pro-Bush folks out in the "heartland" by mocking them as religion-addled ignoramuses. But what else are we to make of data like this, from an amazing report[55] conducted by the University of Maryland's Program on International Policy Attitudes (PIPA) and released in October 2004:

- Even after chief U.S. weapons inspector CHARLES DUELFER concluded that **Iraq** did not have WMD or a significant WMD program, 72 percent of Bush supporters continued to believe it did, and 56 percent thought most experts—including Duelfer—believed so as well. Kerry supporters held opposite beliefs on all these points.
- Even after the 9/11 COMMISSION came to the opposite conclusions, 75 percent of Bush supporters continued to believe Iraq provided substantial support to Al Qaeda; most believed clear evidence of this had been found (63 percent) and that this was the conclusion of most experts (60 percent). "Here again, large majorities of Kerry supporters have exactly opposite perceptions." A month or so earlier, Gallup found that nearly two-thirds of Republicans still believed Saddam Hussein was personally involved in 9/11. Two-thirds of Democrats believed he was not.

Cognitive difficulties. PIPA director Steven Kull said one reason Bush supporters held these false beliefs was that "they perceive the Bush administration confirming them," i.e., the Bushit worked. And Bush supporters believed that if Iraq had *not* had WMDs or supported Al Qaeda, Bush should and would not have gone to war. For supporters "to accept that Bush "took the U.S. to war based on mistaken assumptions" creates "substantial cognitive dissonance," and leads them "to suppress awareness of unsettling information about prewar Iraq." And more:

- Only 31 percent of Bush supporters, versus 74 percent of Kerry supporters, recognized that most of the world opposed the U.S. invasion and occupation of Iraq.
- 57 percent of Bush supporters thought most of the world favored Bush's reelection. In fact, polls consistently found huge majorities in almost all countries disliking Bush and favoring Kerry.

The most delectable parts of the PIPA study revealed how confused Bush supporters were about their own candidate's positions and policies:

- Most Bush supporters believed he favored multilateral approaches to international issues—for example, that he supported the Comprehensive [Nuclear] Test Ban Treaty (69 percent), the land mine treaty (72 percent), the Kyoto treaty on global warming (51 percent), as well as labor and environmental standards in trade agreements (84 percent). After Bush denounced the International Criminal Court in the debates, the perception among his supporters that he favored it dropped—from 66 to 53 percent. Almost as many believed he opposed building a missile defense system (41 percent) as believed he favored it (44 percent). Again, Kerry supporters were much less . . . confused.

"Resistance to information." What was going on here? In all these cases, the PIPA report observed, *Bush supporters held these "liberal" positions themselves*, and therefore, apparently, assumed Bush must support them, too. The roots of Bush supporters' "resistance to information," wrote Kull, probably lay in 9/11, which "created a powerful bond between Bush and his supporters," an "idealized image" that makes it difficult for them to imagine he could have "made incorrect judgments" or that his policies could be at odds with public opinion or their own. Homage to the Bushies' **media and image control.** As one blogger wrote, "[Bush] says it on the stump all the time . . . 'People know where I stand. [They] know what I believe.' The truth is, a lot of Americans *do* know where Bush stands and what he believes . . . they're called Kerry voters."[56]

You are what you watch. An earlier PIPA report, in October 2003, found that Americans who got most of their news from FOX NEWS were three times more likely than the next nearest network to hold mistaken impressions about WMD in Iraq, Iraqi involvement in 9/11, and international support for the Iraq war. And while 80 percent of Fox viewers held at least one of the three misperceptions, "an overwhelming majority" of the NPR/PBS audience did not hold any of them. (No wonder NPR and PBS were under all-out GOP attack; see **Media**.) NPR listeners alone were better informed than those who relied on newspapers, who were in turn better informed than those who relied on any TV network for their news.[57] In fact, one would have done better on the survey by receiving no news and simply guessing than by watching Faux.

The descent of man: The flat-earth vote. To put the PIPA report into proper context: In a CBS News poll of November 2004, *only 28 percent of Bush voters said they believed humans evolved.* Only 6 percent believed in evolution unguided by a God. Bush voters were much more likely than Kerry voters to reject evolution and favor schools teaching creationism. Naturally, support for evolution (as for Kerry) was more concentrated among those with more education and those less likely to attend religious services.[58] Bush clearly owed his success in good part to this widespread American retreat to a faith-based mental world in which evidence—whether skeletons in the museum *or* in Bush's closet—is irrelevant.

6. TRIED-AND-TRUE PROPAGANDA METHODS. The Bushies had learned the propaganda lessons of history—such as one written in 1924, in German, in jail, in a furor: "The receptivity of the great masses is very limited, their intelligence is small, but their power of forgetting is enormous. [Therefore] all effective propaganda has to limit itself only to a very few points . . . slogans . . . [and] stereotyped formulas . . . and repeat them over and over." Or as W. said in 2005, "I'll probably say it three more times, see, in my line of work you gotta keep repeating things over and over and over again for the truth to sink in, to kinda catapult the propaganda."

7. INCUMBENCY. Its advantages are manifold and obvious—and since 1944, seven out of ten sitting presidents seeking reelection have won. All by much larger margins than Bush.

8. WEALTHY VOTERS. This was the group that "almost everyone has ignored" but that may have made the biggest difference, wrote Philip Klinker in *The New Republic*. For all the talk about religious voters (reason number 10), their contribution to the outcome did not change at all from 2000. By contrast, Bush's performance, while declining among voters earning less than $50,000, improved sharply among high-income voters—indeed, the higher the income, the larger the percentage Bush won. Bush's gains among the wealthiest Americans—the chief beneficiaries of his tax cuts, and the group whose share of national income increased the most since 2000—"account for a good chunk of his popular-vote margin of victory," wrote Klinker.

9. CAMPAIGN FINANCE EDGE. Bush raised a record $360 million compared to Kerry's $317 million (and Bush's then-record $193 million in 2000), and outspent Kerry $306 million to $241 million. And in close to 95 percent of all federal election races in 2004, the candidate who spent the most money won.

10. "MORAL VALUES." "By near universal agreement the morning after, these two words tell the entire story of the election," wrote the *New York Times*'s Frank Rich. Supposedly, the country had swung to the right on cultural issues. "[T]he anti-abortion, anti-gay marriage, socially conservative agenda is ascendant," gloated right-wing columnist Robert Novak. "It really is Michael Moore versus Mel Gibson."—Newt Gingrich. "'God gap' may force Dems to search souls."—*Arizona Republic*. Even many Dems bought into this as the moral of the story their party must learn or else perish. But there was, Rich wrote, only one problem with it: "It is fiction."

If my math is correct, the 22 percent of voters (the same number as in 1996) who picked "moral **values**" as their top election issue—79 percent of whom voted for Bush—left 78 percent who did *not* pick "values." And it bore an uncanny resemblance to the number who described themselves as evangelical Christians—23 percent, unchanged from 2000. There was hardly any change in support for **abortion** rights; 62 percent supported gay marriage or civil unions; and only 34 percent even described themselves as conservative.

The 20 percent who selected "economy/jobs" as their most important issue—a statistical tie with "values"—voted 80-18 against Bush. If a tiny shift in Ohio (or less GOP mischief—see **Election Reform**) had given Kerry the win, the pundits would have explained that this election was all about the economy, stupid. Headlines might have read, "Jobs Gap May Force Republicans to Search Souls," *The Nation*'s John Nichols noted. Another 15 percent chose Iraq as their top issue, far more than "education," "health care," or "taxes"—and they went 73–26 for Kerry. Shouldn't at least a few pundits have noted that? Moreover, "economy" or "Iraq" topped or tied "values" in every region of the country but the South, in whose non-battleground states the "moral" voters were highly concentrated.

And yet, the "values" debunkers went too far. A "whole

[moral values] culture" really had "sprung up," as Christian-right propagandist David Barton asserted—although whether it had "sprung up" or been *laid down* was debatable. The censorious influence of the Christian right was perceptible across the culture, from a virginity vogue among teenagers (what *was* the world coming to) to the FCC's new tape-delay requirements and tougher "decency" rules for networks (even if an estimated 99.9 percent of all indecency complaints to the FCC came from a single "e-mail factory," the conservative Parents Television Council). Only 22 percent of voters picked "moral values" as their *top* concern, but it surely mattered to many more.

The VRWC (Vast Right-Wing Conspiracy) masterminds didn't earn their mastermind licenses by being dumb. Here are some of the ways they worked the "morality" racket during the 2004 campaign:

† "Republicans Admit Mailing Campaign Literature Saying Liberals Will Ban the Bible," ran a *New York Times* headline. The mailings included images of the Bible labeled "banned" and of a gay marriage proposal labeled "allowed."

† The GOP distributed flyers in church parking lots saying John Kerry favored "anti-Christian, anti-God, antifamily" judges, same-sex marriage, and abortion.

† Evangelical imam JERRY FALWELL told CNN that Democrats were on an "anti-God, anti-Christ, anti-religion kick." Right-wing radio host Rush Limbaugh said Democrats "don't like God." (*I* don't, but among Dems as a whole, He's surprisingly popular.) And evangelist BOB JONES called Bush's reelection a

"reprieve from the agenda of paganism," telling his flock, liberals "despise you because they despise your Christ." No, we despise them for themselves.

If this was "moral values" politics, did the Dems want any part of it? "Let's be clear," wrote John Nichols:

> If the Democratic Party wants to get on the good side of the crowd that always ranks 'Moral Values' . . . as its top issue, that will require adjusting Democratic positions to be more in tune with those of the old Confederacy . . . And what are the moral values of the old Confederacy? Well . . . last week in Alabama, voters appear to have narrowly turned down a proposal to remove "Jim Crow" segregationist language from their state Constitution. . . . Democrats can either waste four years developing a doomed outreach to voters for whom 'Moral Values' means denying rights to others [and not just gays, clearly], or they can work on getting more in tune with the vast majority of voters who rank other issues as their top priorities.[59]

SWIFT BOAT SMEARERS FOR BUSH. Bush, with the help of wealthy and powerful family friends, avoided Vietnam, then shirked his relatively cushy National Guard duty—then lied about it all. But as president, he didn't hesitate to swagger around like John Wayne, dress up in a flight suit, and send more than 200,000 U.S. troops into harm's way in **Iraq** to satisfy an assortment of personal, political, and ideological obsessions. JOHN KERRY volunteered for service in Vietnam, risked his life saving one of his crew, was wounded, and came home with a Silver Star, a Bronze Star, and three Purple Hearts—then had the moral sense and courage to speak out against atrocities committed by U.S. soldiers. As former Clinton chief of staff John Podesta said, "Senator Kerry carries shrapnel in his thigh . . . [Bush] carries two fillings in his teeth from his service in the Alabama National Guard, which seems to be his only time that he showed up." Something, the Bushies realized, had to be done about this embarrassing and dangerous contrast.

So: In the crucial final months of the presidential campaign, a hastily formed group of Vietnam veterans who hate Kerry for speaking out against the war and its atrocities launches an ad campaign in which they dispute Kerry's medal citations and claim he lied to get his awards, "betrayed the men and women he served with," and "dishonored his country." He is, as their best-selling book is titled, *Unfit for Command* (brought out by right-wing Regnery Publishing three months before the election). The so-called SWIFT BOAT VETERANS FOR TRUTH (SBVT) turn out to be financed and advised by top Bush campaign funders and advisers. And, oh yes—their accusations turn out to be what one *might* call *Bushit*.

"People without decency." Former officers who served with Kerry confirmed—as did the military records—the details of his citation for "extraordinary daring and personal courage . . . in attacking a numerically superior force in the face of intense fire" from several sides. One of the Swift Boat Bushies (henceforth, Swushies) said he had made a "terrible mistake" by signing an affidavit against Kerry, saying he had "chosen to believe the other [SBVT] men," and, "I absolutely do not know first hand" about the events in question.[60] The former first lieutenant whose life Kerry saved—another episode the Swushies tried to discredit—Jim Rassmann, a Republican, wrote in the *Wall Street Journal* that SBVT were "people without decency" who are "lying" and "should hang their heads in shame."

Yet, for weeks, the "liberal" media dwelled on the Kerry/Swift Boat "issue" instead of on, say, Bush's record as president. SBVT hardly had to pay to air their ads, they were sampled so often during cable "news" programs. The lesson—that the more scandalously vicious and lying the attack, the more free media play it gets—was not lost on the Bushies (see **Social Security**, even).

Where "all low roads lead." The White House and the Bush/Cheney campaign said repeatedly they "weren't involved in any way in these ads." Guess it depended on the definitions of "involved," "way," and "weren't":

- SBVT's chief financial backer, developer BOB PERRY, was the top GOP donor in Texas, a major Bush fundraiser, and a friend of KARL ROVE for nearly 20 years. Perry provided nearly two-thirds of SBVT's initial funding.
- Sen. JOHN MCCAIN (R-AZ) was also a decorated Vietnam veteran whose military record was attacked by the Bush campaign during the 2000 primaries; and according to political analyst and recovering Republican Marshall Wittmann, "Anyone who was involved in the 2000 McCain campaign, as I was, knows exactly who is responsible for the 'Swift Boat' slime attack on

Senator Kerry—in Bush World, all low roads lead to ROVE. "[61]

- A top Bush adviser and chief outside counsel to the Bush 2004 campaign, BENJAMIN GINSBERG, acknowledged he had been advising SBVT.
- One of the SBVT leaders, KENNETH CORDIER, turned out to be a member of the Bush/Cheney veterans' steering committee, which, according to its own Web site, "serve as messengers for the President's re-election campaign." When this fact emerged, the Bush campaign said it had no idea Cordier was involved in the ads. (He appeared prominently in the ads, which ran on TV for weeks.)
- Bush-Cheney campaign headquarters in Florida was caught distributing fliers for a Swushie rally.

The Vietnam "question." Meanwhile, as Katha Pollitt wrote in *The Nation*, the commentators were "debating the 'questions' these GOP hacks have raised about Kerry's patriotism. "The Commander in Chief who avoided active service and has made such a mess of Iraq is honored as manly and decisive; the man who volunteered to serve and then protested a war few would defend today gets labeled a prevaricating shirker, unqualified to lead."

In fact, Kerry's denunciation of the Vietnam War, columnist Robert Scheer noted, was much the same as COLIN POWELL's in his autobiography. The difference "is that Powell's dissent came 20 years too late to stop the carnage."

But history's verdict on Vietnam as a tragic U.S. blunder had to be overturned for the right-wing revolution to be complete. The SBVT affair was both part of the Bush campaign and part of the campaign to rehabilitate Vietnam as a just and noble cause. The aim was more than historical: Vietnam stood for Iraq. Kerry's Vietnam protest, wrote Paul Krugman, "rings truer than ever. The young John Kerry spoke of leaders who sent others to their deaths because they wanted to seem tough." It was *that* Kerry record, not his combat record, that the Bushies were really targeting.

How were "men who assiduously avoided service in Vietnam, like **Dick Cheney** (five deferments), John Ashcroft (seven deferments) and George Bush" able to get away with questioning "the patriotism of men who risked their lives and suffered for their country: John McCain, [former Senator] Max Cleland [see **War Profiteering, Political**], and now John Kerry"? The answer, Krugman wrote,

> is that we have been living in what Roger Ebert calls 'an age of Rambo patriotism' . . . As the carnage and moral ambiguities of Vietnam faded from memory, many started to believe in the comforting clichés of action movies, in which the tough-talking hero is always virtuous and the hand-wringing types who see complexities and urge the hero to think before acting are always wrong, if not villains. After 9/11, Mr. Bush had a choice: he could deal with real threats, or he could play Rambo. He chose Rambo. Not for him the difficult, frustrating task of tracking down elusive terrorists, or the unglamorous work of protecting ports and chemical plants . . . he wanted a dramatic shootout with the bad guy . . . As a domestic political strategy, Mr. Bush's posturing worked brilliantly. As a strategy against terrorism, it has played right into Al Qaeda's hands.[62]

ELECTION REFORM, VOTING RIGHTS, AND THE ☐ FAIR OR ☐ FRAUDULENT 2004 VOTE

Given how badly the 2000 presidential election undermined millions of Americans' faith in the fairness and trustworthiness of their electoral system, it was widely expected that action would be taken to prevent such a mess from ever recurring. But the lesson drawn by the Republicans—who have shown little interest in democracy in other respects (see **Foreign Policy, Free Speech, Human Rights, Media Control, Presidential Power, Secrecy**)—was that electoral confusion was their friend, as much as were the state officials and Supreme Court justices who decided the outcome. While we were invading other countries in the name of spreading democracy, we were setting a pretty bad example for it at home, where, according to Jimmy Carter, our electoral system would not meet the minimal standards the Carter Center sets for free and fair elections abroad.

WHAT—STILL GRIPING ABOUT 2000? Absolutely! The small matter of who really won a U.S. presidential election, with all that it signifies for our democracy and all that it has led to, deserves more than the "get over it" and "move on" urged by the Republicans, the media, and many Democrats upon the tens of millions of voters who quite rightly felt disfranchised by the outcome.

So, let's review: Al Gore got 540,000 more votes than Bush; but the Electoral College vote came down to Florida—which Bush officially won by 537 votes—and in the end, to the U.S. Supreme Court, whose 5–4 ruling in *Bush v. Gore* stopped a recount sought by Gore in four Florida counties. By not seeking a statewide recount, Gore enabled the five Republican-appointed justices to absurdly invoke "equal protection" for the rights of voters in other counties. Never mind that different counties had drastically different voting methods and ballot designs to begin with—including some ridiculously bad and probably illegal ones; never mind the kind of protection that GOP state election officials—led by Secretary of State/Bush-Cheney state campaign chairwoman/ millionaire heiress KATHERINE HARRIS and her boss, a governor also named Bush—gave to tens of thousands of mostly minority Democratic voters, whom they protected from voting by a Nixrovian variety of dirty tricks.

The most thorough reexamination of the 2000 vote was the six-month-long FLORIDA BALLOTS PROJECT, sponsored by a consortium of major media organizations and carried out by the University of Chicago's National Opinion Research Center (NORC), which examined all of the more than 175,000 disputed and uncounted ballots. The study, published in November 2001, concluded that *under any standard that tabulated all disputed votes, Gore won.* The NORC study did find that under the four-county recount Gore sought in court, Bush still won—and that's the way the media spun it, in those no-questioning-the-president days following 9/11: "Florida Recounts Would Have Favored Bush" (*Washington Post*, 11/12/01). But as the same paper reported—in a box on page ten—"Full Review Favors Gore." The NORC and other studies concluded that:

- Among all votes disqualified on technicalities, *tens of thousands* more were clearly intended for Gore than for Bush.[63] The number of ballots disqualified because Gore's name was both marked *and* written in was greater than Bush's official 537-vote margin of victory. Florida law was supposed to make "voter intent" the overriding criterion. Demand that Bush resign!

- A University of Miami study found that the incidence of disqualified ballots in African-American precincts was much higher than could be explained by education or income levels or *any factors other than specific targeting of African Americans*—90 percent of whom favored Gore.

- In Republican-controlled Duval County, four times as many ballots were disqualified as in 1996. Blacks cast an estimated 60 percent of them.

- Before the election, Katherine Harris tried to purge more than 57,000 mostly black Floridians from the voter rolls as "possible" felons. The job was farmed out to a GOP-connected database firm; like everything else under the Bushies, election theft was to be privatized. Even after thousands on the list were shown to be completely innocent (in the one county that checked each name, the list turned out to be 95 percent wrong), at least 1,100 eligible voters, wrongly labeled as felons, were prevented from voting, as were another 2,900 previously convicted felons who had had their legal rights restored.[64] The *Palm Beach Post* reported that 88 percent of those purged were black. Wrongly purged votes alone probably cost Gore the election.

"Had Florida's election laws been followed, and followed consistently, it is certain that Al Gore would be in the White House today," researcher Paul Lukasiak concluded.[65] The NORC study showed "in quite dramatic and comprehensive ways how the American system of elections failed voters," wrote the *New York Times*'s John Broder. But the White House's response was "get over it," "move on," and in those early months after 9/11, the media were not inclined to question.

2004: JUST LIKE OLD TIMES (but without the paper trail). By 2004, the electoral system had only grown *less* transparent and trustworthy, thanks to advances in technology and in GOP depravity.

E-voting = W-voting? After the 2000 Floriasco, states rushed to install millions of new touch-screen voting machines, which nearly one-third of voters would use in November 2004. But as these machines produced no paper record, permitting no audits or recounts, they raised fears that now the fix would *really* be in—in so deep that no one would ever know. *Fortune* magazine declared paperless voting the worst technology of 2003. Stanford computer science professor and e-voting critic David Dill said all elections conducted on these machines "are open to question."

The Republican chairman of the U.S. Election Assistance Commission (EAC) advised not to "take seriously the conspiracy theories." Really, *so what* if Florida's Bush administration, the nation's craftiest election managers, were also the nation's most militant opponents of paper records, and in June 2004 rejected a request to allow independent audits of the state's voting machines? Governor Bush explained clearly that those seeking audits were only trying to "scar[e] people" and "undermine voters' confidence." But the fact was, without a paper trail, we *could* never know if election results were tampered with. Here, on the other hand, is what we did know:

- The two largest manufacturers of the new machines were run by Bush/GOP backers. The CEO of Ohio-based DIEBOLD INC. declared in a 2003 GOP fund-raising letter that he was "committed to helping Ohio deliver its electoral votes to the president next year." Diebold contributions since 1991 favored GOPers over Dems by 127 to 1. ELECTION SYSTEM AND SOFTWARE (ES&S) was owned by prominent conservatives in Nebraska; Sen. CHUCK HAGEL (R-NE) was its former chairman. Between them, ES&S and Diebold counted 80 percent of all votes in America. A principle investor at a third big manufacturer, Texas-based Hart InterCivic, was TOM HICKS, one of Bush's biggest fund-raisers. The three firms were rumored to be merging into one called VRWC (Vast Right-Wing Conspiracy) Inc.

- Computer scientists testified before the EAC in May 2004 that e-voting systems were "terrible and highly vulnerable to hackers." Some of the manufacturers' own programmers regarded the machines as so unreliable and full of security flaws that an election could easily be rigged. Voter group Black Box Voting claimed to have taught a chimpanzee in ten minutes to delete the "audit log" voting record from a Diebold machine. Was this what Diebold meant when it declared the machines could not be altered "by human intervention"?

- In California's March 2004 presidential primary, e-voting machines malfunctioned in more than half the precincts in San Diego County and elsewhere. Afterwards, the state banned 14,000 Diebold machines and called for a criminal investigation, alleging Diebold's use of uncertified software amounted to fraud.

- Following the 2002 Florida gubernatorial primary, which was decided by just 4,794 votes, an ACLU study found that 8 percent of touch-screen votes in Miami-Dade County had been lost. E-voting problems also plagued Broward County. The following year, almost all the electronic records of the Miami-Dade vote were lost in computer crashes, leaving no audit trail whatsoever.

- Florida officials prohibited manual recounts in counties using touch-screen machines, claiming that those machines made voting twice impossible and that no recorded vote meant the voter didn't cast one. But an analysis by the *Fort Lauderdale Sun-Sentinel* found that voters using touch-screen machines were eight times as likely to record no vote as voters using optical-scan machines, which read markings on paper ballots.

- The Republicans were so unselfish, they wanted the joys of e-voting reserved for Democrats. Even as the GOP denounced the Dems for demanding a paper trail, the Florida Republican Party in July 2004 mailed flyers to GOP voters warning that "the new electronic voting machines do not have a paper ballot to verify your vote in case of a recount," and urging them to use absentee ballots.

Faith-based voting. Hacking into the machines might be easy; getting information out of the manufacturers that could verify their security was not. David Dill told journalist Ronnie Dugger: "You ask about the hardware. 'Secret.' The software? 'Secret.' What's the cryptography? 'Can't tell you . . .' Federal testing procedures? 'Secret'! Results of the tests? 'Secret'! Basically we are required to have blind faith." One expert said, "The secrecy of the ballot has been turned into the secrecy of the vote count." Echoing the faith-based theme, a California election official, asked how he *knew* a new paperless machine would count the vote correctly, answered, "Because it has been federally certified! . . . It's really a matter of trust."

HAVAnother four years, Mr. Bush! The 2002 Help America Vote Act (HAVA), which was supposed to fix the election problems revealed in 2000, only making things worse, Dugger wrote. Under HAVA, the new Election Assistance Commission (EAC) was charged with scrutinizing the security of and setting standards for voting technology. But Bush delayed appointing a commissioner for nearly a year, and EAC didn't conduct its first hearing until six months before the 2004 election. In June 2004, EAC approved $861 million for states to buy computerized machines (hear Diebold's cash registers ring) for which no standards had been set. Meanwhile, EAC itself was so underfunded that it had just seven full-time staffers and would be forced, *Salon* reported, "to abandon or delay much of its intended mission"—for example, reliable testing of voting machines. What was advertised as "federal testing," Dugger noted, was actually conducted secretively by three private companies paid by the manufacturers themselves and using voluntary and obsolete standards. Bottom line: Oversight of these systems remained "illusory," the California Voter Foundation told *Salon*.

TRADITIONAL (ANALOG) ELECTION MISCHIEF.

The landmark Voting Rights Act of 1965 ensured African-Americans equal access to the polls—in theory:

Hey, if it worked once . . . In 2004, as in 2000, the Bush crew running Florida hired a GOP-friendly company, Accenture, to prepare a list of felons to be stricken from the voter rolls. They refused to make the list public until a judge ordered it—whereupon its 47,000 supposed felons were found to include 2,100 citizens who had had their voting rights restored, and, odder still, thousands of blacks, but almost no Hispanics, who in Florida tend to vote Republican. State officials first denied there was a problem, then insisted it was an honest mistake. In fact, state computer experts had warned Governor Bush repeatedly the "mistake" would result automatically from the method they were using.[66] "This governor [is] essentially trying to rig the election for George Bush," said Rep. Robert Wexler (D-FL).

Block the vote. In July 2004, a Republican state legislator in Michigan, John Pappageorge, told a suburban county GOP meeting, "If we do not suppress the Detroit vote, we're going to have a tough time in this election." Everyone knew what he meant: 83 percent of Detroit's population is black. Pappageorge would not at first apologize for the statement—nor did his party condemn it—and when he finally offered a sorry-if-anyone-took-offense "apology," he reiterated that the Detroit vote needed to be kept down![67] Apparently, his crowd no longer remembered or cared that such voter suppression efforts were both racist and criminal.

Jim Crow lives. Pappageorge was only blurting out what was actually going on in key states. In Orlando, Florida, "armed state police officers went into the homes of elderly black voters to question them as part of a so-called criminal investigation involving absentee ballots," the *New York Times* reported. In Kentucky, a Republican county chairman announced plans to place "vote challengers" in Democratic precincts on Election Day. Black GOP officials protested that African American precincts were being targeted. In Texas, a Republican district attorney threatened to arrest students at the majority black Prairie View A&M University if they tried to vote in the county in which the school was located. In fact, students can vote in their college town if they designate it as their home address.

A report by People for the American Way (PFAW) and the NAACP recounted how the voter-suppression tactics targeting minorities in 2004 had been practiced and perfected by the Republicans over more than two decades, in the guise of "ballot security" and "voter integrity" initiatives. At least three times, beginning in 1981, "these initiatives were successfully challenged in federal courts as illegal attempts to suppress voter participation based on race." And each time, the GOP went right back to them.

The poll taxes, literacy tests, and physical violence of the Jim Crow era have disappeared, the report noted. "Today, more subtle, cynical and creative tactics have taken their place." And in our age, Republicans have taken the place of the Southern Democrats as masters of these black arts. "President Bush could put a stop to it," wrote the *New York Times*'s Bob Herbert, "but so far he's chosen not to."

Preemptive strike. The Justice Department didn't remain entirely passive. In the final months of the campaign, AG ASHCROFT jumped into the fray—launching investigations of new voter registrations in poor and minority neighborhoods, where the GOP alleged voter fraud. "Republicans seem to have begun laying the groundwork for an argument . . . in the case of a contested Kerry win, that Democrats stole the election," wrote Clay Risen in *The New Republic*. A related move was to charge Dems with "reverse voter intimidation," such as in a claim by Florida Republicans that roving bands of "Kerry thugs" were harassing early Republican voters.

"The hanging chads of 2004." PROVISIONAL BALLOTS, required nationally for the first time in 2004, were supposed to prevent what happened in 2000, when some 1.5 million legally eligible voters were turned away from the polls because of clerical errors or other problems. A voter, if challenged, might now cast a provisional ballot that election officials would decide later whether to accept or reject. Enough provisional ballots were expected as to perhaps decide the winner—and they were thought to favor Democrats. So when Democrats went to court claiming the rules adopted in battleground Michigan for counting these ballots were too strict, which side do you suppose the Justice Department jumped in on?

Election Day blues (for "blue" voters, mostly). "The story of today has been voting machine failure," said a voting rights advocate on Election Day. The nonpartisan Verified Voting Foundation and other groups counted more than 30,000 "incidents" across the country, of which nearly 900 involved "significant" e-voting problems. Serious problems were documented in at least a dozen states, including machine breakdowns (42 in New Orleans alone, 28 in Philadelphia) that created long waits at the polls. In Carteret County, NC, 4,438 e-votes disappeared, apparently due to overloaded computer memories. In North Carolina, Ohio, Nebraska, and Washington, double counting or undercounting of thousands of ballots was discovered. In Franklin County, Indiana, the *Boston Globe* reported, "a tabulator credited about 600 straight-ticket Democratic votes to Libertarian Party candidates." In Broward County, Florida, "multiple misrecordings" occurred when votes for Kerry on touch-screens appeared as Bush votes. (There was, however, "at least one account of a Bush vote going to Kerry.")[68] In Volusia Country, Florida—where in 2000, a faulty memory card deducted 16,022 votes from Gore's total—there were, what do you know, memory card problems in six precincts. A University of California study claimed that "irregularities associated with electronic voting machines" may have awarded Bush 130,000 excess votes in Florida. How many "irregularities" around the country were *not* detected?

Machine-related irregularities weren't the only kind. According to PFAW, "men in dark suits" and "law enforcement insignia" intimidated voters waiting in line in Philadelphia. In Ohio, Michigan, and Arizona, automated phone calls directed African-American voters to the wrong polling places and/or reminded them to vote on November 3. (Election Day was November 2.) In Tucson, the calls were reportedly traced back to the local Republican Party.[69] (As opposed to who—MoveOn.org?)

"THE FLORIDA OF 2004" was not, as many predicted, Florida. OHIO was the state that decided the outcome (officially, by 118,000 votes, or 2.2 percent)—and where voting problems were most numerous, most of them occurring in Democratic-leaning precincts—and where I believe the election was stolen by a combination of tactics that resulted in large-scale disfranchisement of Ohio voters, as reported in the press and detailed in a report by Democrats on the House Judiciary Committee led by Rep. John Conyers (D-OH).[70]

And the 2004 Katherine Harris Award for worst performance as an impartial election supervisor goes to . . . Ohio Secretary of State KEN BLACKWELL. Like the GOP heroine of 2000, Blackwell oversaw the election while also serving as state co-chairman of the Bush/Cheney campaign. But Blackwell, wrote journalist Greg Palast, made Harris "look like Thomas Jefferson." A former Justice Department attorney told *The New Republic*, "He's doing everything he can to suppress the vote in Ohio." How? By:

- Ruling that voter registration cards would be accepted only on heavy card-stock paper, which may have resulted in thousands of new voters not being registered in time.
- Refusing to replace or fix old voting machines that

produced high rates of spoiled ballots and that Blackwell conceded were concentrated in black areas.

- Barring provisional ballots cast in the right county but the wrong precinct from being counted. Some of these voters may have just moved down the street. According to the Conyers Report, this decision "departed from past Ohio law on provisional ballots" and disfranchised "tens, if not hundreds, of thousands of voters, again predominantly minority and Democratic voters."

- Ordering that people be banned from casting provisional ballots if they had applied for absentee ballots, even if those had not arrived. A judge blocked the order, but too late, and thousands more voters, particularly seniors, were turned away.

- Tagging voters as felons and purging them from the rolls—à la K. Harrison, 2000.

After the election, Blackwell sent out a letter to Republicans (on secretary of state stationery) saying, "Thank you for helping deliver the great Buckeye State for George W. Bush. Without your enthusiasm, generous support and vote, I'm afraid the President would have lost. And an unapologetic liberal Democrat named John Kerry would have won. Thankfully, you and I stopped that disaster from happening."

The other VRA (Vote-stopping Republican Army). Thousands of Republicans were deployed at polls in Democratic areas around Ohio on Election Day to challenge "fraudulent" (i.e., *black*) voters—defying a court ban on the GOP's challenge lists as a violation of the VOTING RIGHTS ACT (VRA).

"The tactic was very much the same as that used by the allies of the White Citizens Councils and Bull Conners in the early '60s," wrote Greg Palast—"targeted and unequal application of picayune registration and voting requirements." The challengers succeeded in intimidating some voters, causing long lines that drove away many others, and shunting an astonishing 155,000 to provisional ballots, "where their votes would be vulnerable to the partisan predation of GOP Secretary of State Blackwell," *Salon* noted.

Engineered shortages of voting machines in minority neighborhoods led to long lines that disfranchised perhaps thousands of predominantly Democratic voters, according to the Conyers Report. In Columbus, despite a 25 percent increase in voter turnout, 29 percent of precincts had fewer machines than in 2000. Machines were added in Republican precincts and taken away in Democratic ones, leaving the latter with half as many as officials knew were needed. Lines at some polls were ten hours long. In Columbus alone, up to 15,000 people who couldn't afford to wait left without voting. The Board of Elections director—who formerly headed the county GOP—held back 125 machines at the opening of the polls and never deployed an additional 68, even as desperate poll workers called his office about the shortages and "while thousands of inner city voters stood in the rain, were told their cars would be towed, and were then forced to vote in five minutes or less" on one of the longest ballots in history, with 35 separate ballot choices and 11 extensively worded issue questions.[71]

In the same county, at least 77 machines malfunctioned. Bush's famous luck seemed to make even random technical glitches favor him: One machine registered 4,258 votes for Bush in a precinct where only 638 people voted. In Youngstown, 25 e-voting machines transferred an unknown number of Kerry votes to Bush. In Mercer County, machines recorded thousands of ballots as showing no vote for president. Similar problems occurred in other states.[72]

The company that created and maintained the vote-counting software in dozens of Ohio counties, Triad GSI, allegedly gave officials "cheat sheets" on how to equalize machine and hand counts so as to avoid the requirement of a county-wide hand count. Conyers and a county prosecutor asked the FBI to investigate "likely illegal election tampering."

The bottom line: Over 250,000 Ohio ballots went uncounted as either "spoiled" or provisional ballots. Over 93,000 were discarded as "spoiled" by punch-card machine error—overwhelmingly in African-American precincts, according to an ACLU analysis. Add together Kerry's likely gain from those votes, the Democratic voters directed to the wrong polling places or foiled by long lines or wrongly purged from the rolls, plus a few, or a few thousand, e-votes lost here or transferred to Bush there, and they could easily have exceeded Bush's official 118,457-vote margin—giving Ohio's 20 electoral votes, and the election, to Kerry.

If U.S. officials like Secretary of State Colin Powell and Sen. Richard Lugar (R-IN) who declared the November 2004 election in Ukraine fraudulent "applied the same standards in Ohio," wrote economist James K. Galbraith, "then our own presidential election certainly was stolen." Were the "irregularities" in Ohio enough to change the outcome? "No one can say.

But [wrote Galbraith] the same is true in Kiev. And there, allegations by the defeated opposition are taken in good faith, and are quite enough to satisfy . . . the government of the United States. So . . . Why has our election, with all its thuggery, been forgotten just three weeks after it occurred? [Because] our press, like that in 'Putin's Russia,' follows [government direction]. Our political leaders, if one could call them that, stay silent . . . terrified of being mocked and bullied by the press. [And] in Ohio, pissed-off voters are well behaved . . . In Kiev, by contrast, hundreds of thousands of demonstrators are on the streets.[73]

ENERGY POLICY

If you were King, or Il Duce, what would you include in a national energy policy?
>—E-mail from top aide to Energy Secretary Spencer
>Abraham to a natural gas industry lobbyist, 3/18/01

From Bush's inauguration as oilman-in-chief in January 2001 to April 2005, the price of oil and the price most Americans paid for gasoline more than doubled, despite—or because of—Bush's no-conservation, drill-drill-drill energy policy, and despite a generally weak global economy. Energy companies reaped as much as $80 billion in additional profits from the price rise.

The chief culprit, according to many economists, was Bush's huge budget and trade deficits (see **Economic Policy**), which drove down the dollar. In addition, the liberation of **Iraq,** which was supposed to liberate its vast oil reserves, instead disrupted its oil exports—and added to the U.S. budget deficit. And in "an extreme change in energy policy," the administration added 40 million barrels of oil to the Strategic Petroleum Reserves in 2002—"in a strong market, with a tight supply of oil, [which pushed] gasoline prices to their highest levels in twelve years."[74] A conservative Cato Institute economist estimated the move added $10 to the price of a barrel of oil.[75]

But then, Bush's energy policy had less to do with solving America's energy problems than with rewarding energy and auto industry cronies and donors by refusing to increase vehicle fuel efficiency standards and by permitting, indeed encouraging and subsidizing, oil and gas drilling in every last remaining area of the country not already open to drilling—including, if not *especially*, environmentally sensitive and scenic areas whose contribution to energy needs would be negligible.

The lesson many Americans took from 9/11 was that the U.S. should reduce its dependence on fossil fuels and redouble its efforts to conserve energy and develop alternative sources, or we would remain dependent on, and allied with, corrupt, backward, and hated regimes like the Saudis that sponsored Islamic extremism.

According to the Bushies, the lesson of 9/11 was that we needed to lavish subsidies and tax breaks on oil and gas companies and permit drilling in the ARCTIC NATIONAL WILDLIFE REFUGE. The Bush Energy Department itself estimated that ANWR would at its peak produce no more than 600,000–900,000 barrels a day—at most 2 percent of U.S. consumption, and barely a dent in the 11 million barrels the U.S. imported. All the economically recoverable oil in ANWR would supply the U.S.'s oil needs for less than six months. According the Bushies, the U.S., which consumed 25 percent of global oil production but had only 3 percent of the world's known oil reserves, could drill its way to reduced dependency on imports. (See **Environment** and **War Profiteering, Political**.)

"Instead of taking a strong stand to make America energy independent," wrote author Thom Hartmann,

> Bush kisses a Saudi crown prince [Abdullah, visiting in April 2005], then holds hands with him . . . Our young men and women are daily dying in Iraq . . . And we live in fear that another 15 Saudis may hijack more planes to fly into our nation's capitol or into nuclear power plants. Meanwhile, Bush brings us an energy bill that includes $8 billion in welfare payments to the oil business, just as the nation's oil companies report the highest profits in the entire history of the industry. Americans struggle to pay for gasoline, while the Bush administration refuses to increase fleet efficiency standards, stop the $100,000 tax break for buying Hummers, or maintain and build Amtrak.[76]

The Bush energy plan was essentially the wish list drawn by energy industry insiders meeting behind closed doors with fellow industry insider **Dick** Cheney's White House ENERGY TASK FORCE in early 2001. (See **Secrecy**.) The task force met/conferred/conspired with 27 oil and gas industry representatives, 17 from nuclear power and uranium mining,

16 from electric power, 7 from coal—and 1 from the renewable-energy sector. Environmental groups were given three days to submit input in writing.

The resulting plan included $33 billion in tax breaks and subsidies for the oil, coal, and nuclear power industries; opening ANWR to drilling; the building of 1,300 new coal-fired power plants (over half of America's power already came from burning highly polluting coal); and rolling back regulations limiting pollution caused by power plants and by coal mining—but no significant support for renewable energy and conservation (r&c) (Bush's first budget slashed funding for such initiatives by a third) or for public transportation; and no significant increase in vehicle efficiency standards, which by 2004 had fallen to their lowest level since 1980.

Taking the "conserve" out of "conservative." Gasoline alone amounted to half of U.S. oil consumption. Increasing so-called Corporate Average Fuel Economy (CAFE) standards for new passenger vehicles by just three miles per gallon, the EPA calculated, would save five times as much oil per day as ANWR was likely to provide. Raising the standard to 40 miles per gallon, which was already feasible, would save more oil than the U.S. imported from the Persian Gulf *and* could extract from ANWR combined; cut **global-warming** carbon dioxide pollution by 600 million metric tons; and save vehicle owners over $2,000 in fuel over the life of their vehicles. "But with the White House headed by two oilmen," wrote David Sirota in the *American Prospect*, "industry nonsense substitutes for public policy." So:

- In 2002, the White House joined with the auto industry to block a bipartisan Senate proposal to increase CAFE standards by up to 50 percent by 2015.

- The same year, the administration sued California for imposing a higher fuel efficiency standard than required under federal law. "For those keeping score," Arianna Huffington wrote, "the Bush administration is in favor of states' rights when the states want to weaken federal safety standards of any kind, and against states' rights when the states want stronger measures."

- Bush's February 2003 budget plan increased by 50 percent or more the "HUMMER DEDUCTION" for buyers of the biggest, most gas-guzzling SUVs—making almost the full price of a $100,000 monster tax deductible: a gift to the auto industry and to wealthy yahoos.

On the renewables and conservation front:

- Bush's first budget cut the Energy Department (DOE)'s r&c programs by up to 50 percent. These programs had saved consumers and businesses $30 billion.[77] Adding i. to i., the White House then dipped into the DOE's remaining r&c funds to pay for the printing of 10,000 copies of Bush's industry-friendly energy plan.

- Bush opposed a Democrat-supported measure requiring utilities to generate a mere 10 percent of their electricity from renewable energy sources by 2010. Wind energy alone, with existing technology, could supply 20 percent of America's electricity, while the sunlight the Earth receives in 30 minutes is equivalent to all the power consumed globally in one year.

• While insisting we needed more drilling, drilling, drilling, Bush never once asked Americans to conserve.

The great giveaway. It took four years, but in July 2005, Congress gave Bush an energy bill packed with $14.5 billion in tax breaks and incentives of which nearly $9 billion was for oil, gas, coal, and electricity producers. (How much "incentive" did they need with oil above $60 a barrel? The day before, EXXON MOBIL reported a 32 percent jump in profits.) Less than $5 billion went to r&c programs. The final version of the bill dropped a requirement for the federal government to find ways to cut U.S. oil demand and improve vehicle fuel mileage. The bill would also "revive the nuclear power industry by encouraging companies to build the first new plants since the Three Mile Island accident in 1979," Reuters reported. "This bill keeps the oil, coal and nuclear industry firmly in the driver's seat," said the U.S. Public Interest Research Group. Up to $1.5 billion—or fully 10 percent of the bill—went to deep-water drilling research "that would benefit an energy consortium based in House Majority Leader Tom DeLay's Texas district," Reuters noted. The measure was added to the bill at the last minute, giving conference committee members no opportunity to examine it.

"No Mullah Left Behind." In February 2005, the *Wall Street Journal* reported that the mullahs in Iran were so flush with cash thanks to soaring oil prices, they felt free to shun Western investors and Western opinion and to pursue their nuclear program. This, wrote the *New York Times*'s Thomas Friedman, "is a perfect example of the Bush energy policy at work, and the Bush energy policy is: 'No Mullah Left Behind.'" By refusing to reduce oil consumption and dependence, "the Bush team is . . . generating huge windfall profits for Saudi Arabia, Iran, and Sudan," where the oil money ends up financing anti-Western extremism. Cheney and the rest of the "oil crowd" had dismissed advocates of conservation and alternative energies as naive, Friedman noted. "Well, what would you call a Bush energy policy that keeps America dependent on a medieval monarchy . . . where corruption is rampant . . . where we have asked all Americans to leave and where the education system is so narrow that its own people are decrying it as a factory for extremism?" Lowering our energy consumption and embracing a gasoline tax "would buy reform in some of the worst regimes in the world, from Tehran to Moscow.

It would reduce the chances that the U.S. and China are going to have a global struggle over oil—which is where we are heading. It would help us to strengthen the dollar and reduce the current account deficit by importing less crude. It would reduce climate change more than anything in Kyoto . . . significantly improve America's standing in the world by making us good global citizens . . . shrink the budget deficit . . . reduce our dependence on the Saudis so we could tell them the truth. (Addicts never tell the truth to their pushers.) . . . Most important, making energy independence our generation's moon shot could help inspire more young people to go into science and engineering . . . But no, President Bush has a better project: borrowing another trillion dollars [to fund **Social Security** privatization], which will make us that much more dependent on countries like China and Saudi Arabia that hold our debt . . . The president's priorities are totally nuts.[78]

ENVIRONMENT

I expect the Bush administration will go down in history as the greatest disaster for public health and the environment in the history of the United States.

—Sen. Jim Jeffords (I-VT; R-VT until Bush drove him
to defect), ranking minority member
on the Environment and Public Works Committee

Let's be generous and call it a "flip-flop": In his speech accepting the GOP presidential nomination in August 2000, Bush said, "We're learning to protect the natural world around us. We will continue this progress, and we will not turn back." Let author Bill McKibben, writing in 2004, supply the "flop":

For more than three years now, day after day and week after week, a small circle of political appointees at the EPA, the Forest Service, the Interior Department, and the Department of Agriculture have proceeded methodically to wreck the system of environmental oversight that dates back to the Nixon administration. Apart from their silence on global warming, they have overturned rule after regulation, largely ceased enforcement actions concerning pollution of the atmosphere and water, and reined in inspectors. Their work is . . . institutionalized corruption: a steady payback to the logging, mining, corporate farming, fossil fuel, and other industries that contributed heavily to put Bush in power.[79]

The silence of the media lambs. The Bushies' anti-environmentalism was broadly opposed by the public. In poll after poll, by ratios of better than two to one, those surveyed opposed the GOP Holy Grail of oil drilling in the ARCTIC NATIONAL WILDLIFE REFUGE and said environmental protection was more important than **energy** production.[80] Not surprisingly, Bush officials "have relied more on less-visible administrative action than on legislation to advance their agenda," the *New York Times* noted.

Where was the **media**? On covering environmental stories, the media conglomerates "have abandoned any notion of civic responsibility," wrote environmental attorney Robert F. Kennedy, Jr.:

Ocean fisheries have dropped to 10 percent of their 1950s levels, the earth is warming, the ice caps and glaciers are melting . . . Asthma rates in this country are doubling every five years. Industrial polluters have made most of the country's fish too poisonous to eat. The world is now experiencing extinctions of species at a rate that rivals the disappearance of the dinosaurs. Nearly 3 billion people lack sufficient fresh water for basic needs, and over 1 billion are threatened with starvation from desertification . . . [and] our president is engaged in the radical destruction of 30 years of environmental law. [Yet] Of the 15,000 minutes of network news that aired [in 2002], only 4 percent was devoted to the environment, and many of those minutes were consumed by human-interest stories—whales trapped in sea ice or a tiger that escaped from the zoo.[81]

The Bushies did do exactly four commendable things: Upheld the Clinton decision to order GENERAL ELECTRIC to clean up the cancer-causing PCBs the company dumped into the Hudson River, upheld a Clinton decision to limit diesel emissions, pledged to clean up abandoned urban industrial sites (although, as so often with Bush, *pledging* and *paying* were different things), and increased grants for private landowners to conserve animal habitats (which congressional Republicans promptly proposed cutting by 70 percent).

But let's not lose our heads or our cynicism. Perhaps the White House only hoped to obscure the rest of its environmental record. Consider that record, by way of the four elements (Earth first, of course):

EARTH: **Land management, national parks, wilderness and wildlife.** In their first term, the Bushies:

- Put the INTERIOR DEPARTMENT, which manages 436 millions acres of public land and vast water resources, under the control of energy, mining, and timber lobbyists and fanatic anti-environmentalists like Interior Secretary GALE NORTON and Deputy Secretary J. STEVEN GRILES.

- Increased the number of permits granted for oil and gas drilling on public land by more than 50 percent in 2004 alone. Gave the green light in January 2005 to the drilling of 225 oil and gas wells on OTERO MESA, New Mexico, a rare desert grassland. More than 85 percent of public comments on the issue—from ranchers, property rights advocates, hunters, and conservationists alike—opposed any drilling, the *Los Angeles Times* reported.

- Scrapped the phase-out of SNOWMOBILES in Yellowstone and Grand Teton national parks and decided to allow up to 720 a day in Yellowstone, regardless of public opinion: "This is not about majority votes," the park's superintendent said like a true Bushie. A former superintendent said, "If the administration goes through with this, it will mark a new low in its pattern of ignoring science to benefit a special interest at the public's expense." The decision was "hailed" (try "made") by the International Snowmobile Manufacturers Association.[82]

- Reinstated the 1872 MINING LAW, which prevented the federal government from blocking mining on public land, whatever the environmental damage (for example, the leakage of acid and heavy metals into streams caused by gold mining).

- Legalized "MOUNTAINTOP REMOVAL" coal mining, a catastrophic method that had already devastated large areas in Appalachia, destroyed 380,000 acres of forest, buried or damaged more than 1,200 miles of streams, put thousands of coal miners out of work, and endangered public health and safety with clouds of coal dust, contaminated water, and life-threatening floods.

- Repealed Clinton's "ROADLESS RULE," a key regulation protecting 60 million acres of national forest from logging and development.

- Allowed logging companies to pillage federal land in the name of forest-fire prevention, under the cynically titled "HEALTHY FORESTS" initiative.

- Removed anti-logging protection from the TONGASS NATIONAL FORREST in Alaska, the nation's only temperate rain forest, where, before the "roadless rule," clearcutting had already destroyed a half million acres of old-growth trees.

- OK'd the largest timber sale on U.S. public lands in modern history. The so-called BISCUIT PROJECT, on 20,000 acres of old-growth forest in the Siskiyou National Forest in southern Oregon, would allow enough cutting to fill 74,000 log trucks; "endanger roadless areas, ancient forest reserves, wild and scenic rivers and salmon runs"; and cost taxpayers millions of dollars for road building, BushGreenwatch.org reported.

- Into Congress's huge omnibus spending bill of November 2004, slippery Repubs slipped measures exempting pesticide users from Endangered Species Act rules, authorizing oil drilling in the Yukon Flats National Wildlife Refuge in Alaska, allowing commercial fish hatcheries in protected wilderness areas, exempting large livestock and dairy farms from Superfund laws on toxic pollutants, lifting the wilderness designation from Georgia's Cumberland Island National Seashore, and prohibiting any judicial review or citizens' appeal of the "Biscuit" project (previous item).

"Teddy Roosevelt's imprint on 21st-century America is enormous because he preserved wild spaces for future generations," wrote the *New York Times*'s Kristof, "while Mr. Bush's 22nd-century legacy may be the permanent scarring of those same spaces."

"No more wilderness." That, verbatim, is what the GOP-run state of Utah demanded—and got—from the Bush administration in 2003: The renunciation of 30 years of federal authority to protect wilderness areas—not only in Utah but nationwide. As part of a sham, prearranged court settlement with the state, the Interior Department opened 2.6 million acres of spectacularly scenic Utah land to oil and gas exploration—and claimed "that under applicable law the Interior Department is barred—forever—from identifying and protecting wild land the way it has for nearly 30 years," the *Los Angeles Times* reported. The department also repudiated its own right to give interim protection to proposed wilderness areas, so that henceforth, by time Congress considered including such areas in the national wilderness system, development might already have destroyed their wilderness character. Environmental groups challenged the agreement as an illegal backroom deal between Interior Secretary Norton and then-Utah governor MIKE LEAVITT—whom Bush appointed to head the EPA four months later. Meanwhile, the Bushies barreled ahead, so to speak, with approvals of oil and gas drilling in previously proposed wilderness areas.

The holy war on ANWR. From day one, the Bushies crusaded with crusader zeal to liberate Alaska's ARCTIC NATIONAL WILDLIFE REFUGE for oil and gas drilling. More than 100 wildlife and bird species relied on ANWR, including caribou, polar and grizzly bears, wolves, musk oxen, and artic foxes. They all deserved to die.

The Bushies could never muster the Senate votes for ANWR in Bush's first term, but finally oiled it through with a 51–49 vote in March 2005 by slipping it into a budget resolution, which, unlike an energy bill, cannot be filibustered.

In claiming that only 2,000 of the refuge's 1.9 million acres would be affected, the Bushies omitted all the new roads that would link the widely scattered facilities, and counted only the ground on which pipeline supporting posts would rest—not the ground under the pipelines!

Critics said ANWR oil would barely dent U.S. dependence on imports—in fact, it was *exported*—whereas a mere one-mile-per-gallon increase in fuel efficiency would save 500,000 barrels of oil per day—roughly as much as ANWR would likely produce at its peak. For the right, ANWR was perhaps not even *about* energy but about defeating the environmental movement *every* time, crushing its spirit, dancing on its grave in oily cowboy boots.

The endangered Endangered Species Act. The 30-year-old ESA was surely more hated on the right than even the law permitting labor unions. In Bush's first term, the administration abandoned legal protections for dozens of endangered species and millions of acres of habitat across the country. It protected only 31 new endangered and threatened species, compared with 521 under Clinton and 234 under Bush I—and every species listed under King George II was the result of a court order, petition, or settlement, Amanda Griscom Little noted in *Salon*. To cripple environmentalists' ability to bring such lawsuits, the Bushies set about dismantling the ESA itself. They argued that less than 1 percent of the 1,200-some species listed in the past three decades have recovered; the patients are still sick, so let's demolish the hospital. (Compare **Social Security** "reform": The program will run into financial difficulties—so, siphon off its funds!)

- The first assault was on the ESA's most powerful tool, the CRITICAL HABITAT provision, which limited development in areas deemed vital for species' survival. The proposed Critical Habitat Reform Act (beware Bush "reform"!) would delay designations of critical habitats and limit their size to the amount of territory currently inhabited by an ailing species, effectively *preventing* it from rebounding, environmentalists said.

- A second priority was to replace regulations and penalties for landowners who destroy habitat with voluntary programs and incentives to preserve; all carrot, no stick. "It's like saying we shouldn't regulate child molesters [but instead] reward them for not doing crimes," an environmental attorney told *Grist* magazine.

- The administration proposed requiring data on endangered species listings to be "peer reviewed" by outside panels selected by the interior secretary instead of by Fish and Wildlife Service biologists, who tended to care about, you know, fish and wildlife. When she was Attorney General of Colorado, Interior Secretary Norton filed a legal brief arguing that species that survive only within a single state should not be protected under the ESA. (Such losers did not deserve to survive. Who said the Bushies were anti-Darwinist?) That would have removed 1,051 species, or 77 percent of all those currently listed.[83]

- In December 2004, Congress repealed the ban on the slaughter of wild horses that had roamed the West for centuries. They could now be sold and butchered like animals for meat if they could find no other buyers. Ranchers complained the horses were eating up forage needed for their cattle.

Government's top wildlife protector sees bright side of species extinctions. They aren't afraid to question orthodoxy, grant them that. In November 2003, Assistant Secretary of Interior CRAIG MANSON who oversaw the National Park System and the Fish and Wildlife Service, told interviewers, "I don't think we know enough about how the world works to say" that "the loss of species in and of itself is inherently bad." He elaborated: "The orthodoxy" that "every species has a place in the ecosystem . . . sort of flies in the face of Darwinian science." (Apparently, "creationism" is just for schoolchildren; in the grownup world, reality—i.e., business, red in tooth and claw—must rule.) Manson also said extinctions "may be natural . . . [not] human-caused." What about all the studies showing the rate of extinction directly correlates to industrial development and population growth, and that more species have been lost in the last several decades than in the last several millennia combined? "It is a logical fallacy to suggest that because two things happen concurrently that they are necessarily related." [84] Perhaps the extinctions were causing the industrial development. We don't know.

"Bush to shift toxic cleanups to taxpayers." That 2002 *New York Times* headline captured the toxic essence of Bushism. The SUPERFUND was founded in 1980 to pay for the cleanup of toxic waste sites, under the slogan "the polluter pays." Under the Bush regime, taxpayers would pay while polluters went off scot-free. When the special tax on industry that funded the Superfund expired in 1995, President Clinton tried—twice—to reinstate it, but the Republican masters in the House refused, on behalf of *their* masters in the oil and chemical industries. In 2002, Bush stated explicitly he would not reinstate the tax. By 2004, all of the fund's money came from individual taxpayers, none from corporations. Meanwhile—even as the number of sites needing cleanup increasing by an average of 28 daily—the fund had dwindled by more than 99 percent, resulting in fewer sites being cleaned up: around 40 in 2002 and 2003, compared to 80 in each of Clinton's last four years. In December 2004, the fund's administrator warned that the listing of new sites for cleanups might have to be halted.

"The nation's largest polluter by far, the Department of Defense, took full advantage of the Bush regime. The DOD, which controls 28 million acres of U.S. land, had 140 toxic waste sites on the Superfund priorities list—more than any other entity in the U.S.—and was responsible for 28,500 potentially contaminated sites across the country and for contaminating billions of gallons of drinking water with residues from munitions testing, rocket fuel, etc. (See **Consumer Protections**.)

In Bush's first term, the Pentagon won exemptions from the Endangered Species Act, the Migratory Bird Treaty Act, and the Marine Mammal Protection Act. In the second term, the administration sought DOD exemptions from the Clean Air Act and the two key toxic waste laws. In 2004, a new Pentagon policy proposal eliminated the department's previous commitment to "reducing risk to human health and the environment" and complying with civil regulations.

The administration was covering up radioactive contamination of air, water, and soil around the former ROCKY FLATS nuclear weapons plant site near Denver, according to a former FBI agent who led the 1989 raid on the plant that uncovered the contamination. He and others sued the Justice Department in February 2005 for release of the information, prompted by the feds' decision to turn Rocky Flats into a wildlife refuge (see the rare five-legged antelope?), possibly including hiking and horseback riding trails (no lighting needed after dark!).[85] In January 2005, Bush told the *Wall Street Journal* that "nuclear power answers a lot of our issues. It certainly answers the environmental issue." (See the July 2005 **energy** bill.)

WATER. In their first term, the Bushies:

- Relaxed the rules on developing WETLANDS and shrank the total wetlands area the federal government could regulate by at least 40 percent.
- Opened vast areas of the West to COALBED METHANE natural gas drilling, which wastes huge quantities of groundwater and pollutes surrounding streams.
- Diverted away 56 percent of the LAND AND WATER CONSERVATION FUND funding.
- Blocked a bipartisan House bill to help states pay to clean up WATER SUPPLIES.

- Proposed "relaxing" regulations on toxic SELENIUM discharged into waterways by mining operations and coal-burning power plants. Relax: Selenium only causes kidney, liver, circulatory and nervous system damage.

- Approved large-scale development on FLORIDA'S ROOKERY BAY, which opponents said would destroy critical wetlands and pollute the bay. The developers, the Collier family, were major GOP and JEB BUSH campaign donors. In 2002, the (George) Bush administration paid the Colliers $120 million for drilling rights to prevent oil exploration on their land in Big Cypress National Preserve—rights which the National Park Service had valued at $5–$20 million.[86] The deal specified that the Colliers could claim the value at much *more* than $120 million and deduct the difference as a charitable contribution. Governor Bush said he hoped the purchase would win him pro-environmental votes in that fall's election.

- Bought back more than $115 million worth of OFF-SHORE DRILLING RIGHTS sought by Florida but not those sought by California, where the GOP had no political hopes. In fact, the administration went to court to prevent California from strengthening its power to block offshore drilling. The conservatives: champions of states' rights.

- Removed up to 90 percent of the "critical habitat" protection for endangered PACIFIC SALMON and steelhead trout in December 2004. A lawsuit against the government by the National Association of Homebuilders, along with timber and agribusiness groups, was just the excuse the administration had been looking for. This was but the Bushmen's latest act of antisalmonism.

- Announced a plan in May 2004 to count hatchery-raised fish that are released into the wild as wild fish. This would enable them to take the wild salmon off the endangered species list. (Only one in five Pacific salmon were still spawned in the wild.) Biologists— including the government's—said the new policy was "akin to counting animals in a zoo ... By this reasoning, river or forest habitats of a rare species will never be protected"; "no credible scientist believes" that hatchery fish, which lack the genetic diversity of wild fish, would help restore salmon runs.[87] The scheme appeared to be have been, yes, *spawned* by the National Marine Fisheries Service (NMFS) legal adviser, who was formerly the timber industry's top lawyer trying to overturn fish and wildlife protections.

- Rewrote Clean Water Act rules (illegally, critics said) in February 2004 to allow power plants and other industrial facilities to continue using older and cheaper cooling systems that kill fish by the millions. These "once-through" cooling systems, used by 52 percent of U.S. power plants, rival the fishing industry in the number of fish and shellfish killed every year, BushGreenwatch.org noted. New York's Indian Point Nuclear Power Plant alone sucks in twice as much Hudson River water as New York City's entire daily water consumption.

AIR: **Supplying America's oxygen for over 3 million millennia.** The CLEAN AIR ACT (CAA) had dramatically reduced air pollution since it was enacted in 1970, under that liberal (compared to Bush), Richard Nixon. In its place, the Bushies proposed legislation titled, as if by the Father of Lies, the CLEAR SKIES ACT, which was conceived and largely written by the coal, power, and oil refining industries and backed by phony data the White House pressured the EPA to produce. "Clear Skies" aimed to replace CAA rules with weaker ones and make compliance voluntary. In January 2005, the National Academy of Sciences concluded that Clear Skies "would actually weaken air quality standards . . . putting millions of Americans at greater risk from air pollution." "Clear Skies" failed for two years to get through the Senate, but following the 2004 elections it was reintroduced with "the full weight of the White House" behind it, Bush assured a power industry lobbyist. Meanwhile, the Bushies had already revised or suspended enforcement of key CAA rules, replacing them with "Clear Skies" policies. These would:

- **Reduce, and delay by 10–15 years, the cuts in power plants' sulfur, nitrogen, and mercury pollution** required by the CAA. "Clear Skies" would permit up to 100 percent more SULFUR DIOXIDE emissions, 50 percent more NITROGEN OXIDE, and seven times as much MERCURY, which causes brain and nerve damage and is especially dangerous to children and pregnant women.
- **Substitute politics for science: "Work backward."** An EPA finding that 8 percent of women have blood mercury levels high enough to cause damage to unborn children was suppressed by the agency until leaked by an insider.[88] In February 2005, the EPA's inspector general said the White House pressured the agency to ignore scientific evidence on mercury and

"back the approach preferred by industry," the *Washington Post* reported. EPA scientists were given a target number and told to "work backward" and "find ways to justify it." It took the scientists three separate tries before the results were fully cooked.

- **Permit "pollution trading."** Even Bush's lowered targets would likely never be reached because instead of making polluters reduce emissions, his plan allowed them to buy "rights" to pollute from cleaner industries. This "cap-and-trade" system might produce no overall reductions, and would do nothing to prevent, indeed could cause, high local concentrations or "hot spots."

- **Let dirty power plants keep polluting.** A CAA provision called NEW SOURCE REVIEW (NSR) required the oldest and dirtiest power plants to install pollution-reducing equipment when the plants are expanded. For decades, many had evaded that expense. As a result, dozens of plants were spewing out pollutants far in excess of current legal limits, much of which got blown from plants in the Midwest to the Northeast, causing acid rain along with respiratory and heart ailments and, by the EPA's own data, some 10,800 premature deaths annually—24,000 according to Clear the Air. In May 2001, the administration suspended NSR enforcement and leaked its plans to scrap the rules. This undermined its own legal actions (begun under Clinton) against the operators of 50 of the country's dirtiest plants—actions the Bushies finally abandoned altogether. "The power companies were on the verge of signing agreements . . . which would have delivered one of the greatest advances in clean air in the nation's history," the *New York Times Magazine* noted. "Then George W. Bush took office."

- **Leave states helpless against "interstate" pollution** by blocking them from petitioning the EPA to take action against out-of-state polluters, such as the Midwestern power plants that pollute the air of "blue," eastern states. The change was opposed by state governors, including Republicans like New York's George Pataki and California's Arnold Schwarzenegger, who reminded the Senate that "states do de majority of de work to carry out [the CAA's] mandates and all dose tings" (Arnoldisms added).

- **Block states from enacting regulations that are tougher than federal ones.**

- **Repeal smog and soot regulations** and allow violations to continue for another 17 years.

- **Break a Bush campaign pledge to regulate carbon dioxide,** the main contributor to **global warming.**

Written by corporate lobbyists. In April 2001, "a top utility industry lobbyist told coal industry representatives . . . that he and his colleagues had a plan (now known as 'Clear Skies') for the White House to allow coal plants to emit more pollution for much longer than allowed under the Clean Air Act," but which provided Bush with, in the lobbyist's words, "a fig leaf." [89]

Subsidies to pollute. In April 2003, eight power companies reviewed the Bushies' first draft of Clear Skies and submitted a wish list of "essential" changes. And behold, their wishes were fulfilled. For example, the initial plan would have given the proceeds from industry purchases of "emissions allowances" ("rights" to pollute) back to taxpayers. The utilities lobbyists wanted—and got—the proceeds to go into a largely unregulated industry slush fund, ostensibly to develop pollution control technologies. "In sum," NRDC reported, the law *"would pay industry to comply with pre-existing laws—at the taxpayers expense."*

Leave the science to the lawyers! In March 2004, EPA staffers told the *Los Angeles Times* they were told "not to undertake the normal scientific and economic studies" on mercury pollution. Instead, the White House adopted a proposal using at least a dozen passages written by lawyers representing power utilities—one of whom now headed EPA's air pollution division. EPA veterans said they could not "recall another instance when the agency's technical experts were cut out of developing a major regulatory proposal." (See **Science, War on.**)

Hey, they paid for it. The corporate owners of the nation's 50 most polluting power plants were (a) major Bush/GOP donors and (b) among those most involved in writing Bush pollution policy, according to a study conducted in 2004 by the Environmental Integrity Project and Public Citizen. These firms, along with their trade associations and lobbyists, got to meet at least 17 times with Cheney's energy "task force." Electric utility executives or lobbyists were given the posts of deputy EPA administrator; assistant EPA administrator in charge of air pollution policy; counsel to EPA's Office of Air and Radiation; assistant energy secretary; and assistant attorney general for Environment and Natural Resources. The latter was put in charge of all government lawsuits against coal-fired power plants.

IN OTHER FOUL SCHEMES, the Bushites:

- **Gave giant processors of pigs, cows, and chickens amnesty from prosecution for Clean Air Act violations.** The 575 billion pounds of animal manure these companies generate annually produces airborne toxic pollutants that are linked to a wide range of respiratory problems, especially in children.
- **Revised CAA rules governing fine-particle pollution** to exempt 1,000 industrial boiler and plywood manufacturing plants. The EPA's own data showed that the new boiler exemptions alone would save industry about $170 million a year but trigger ten times as much in public health costs and *result in over 17,000 asthma attacks, 20,000 cases of upper respiratory problems in children, and 200 premature deaths each year,* according to the Environmental Integrity Project. On the cancer risk from formaldehyde used in plywood manufacture, the White House substituted chemical industry data for government studies showing a cancer risk 10,000 times higher.[90]
- **Un-banned the ozone-destroying toxic pesticide methyl bromide** (MB), which was originally developed as a nerve gas during World War II and can cause prostate cancer, fetal defects, and respiratory and central nervous system failure. Under the Montreal Protocol on ozone protection, the U.S. had agreed to ban MB entirely by 2005. Instead, the Bushies granted "critical-use exemptions" until 2007 to 56 industry groups, including the golf course industry, whose "critical use" is to keep their greens pretty.

FIRE: Please hold while we transfer you to **Global Warming.**

"FAITH-BASED INITIATIVE," WHATEVER HAPPENED TO THE

Bush's plan to expand government funding of religious organizations, ostensibly to provide social and charitable services, was supposed to be the heart of his **compassionate** "conservativism." There proved to be very little heart. After the first head of the new White House Office of Faith-Based and Community Initiatives, JOHN DIIULIO, quit in August 2001, he made it clear that the person really in charge was political commissar KARL ROVE, whose main concern was to keep religious-conservative voters placated. The result, DiIulio said, was "a virtual absence as yet of any policy accomplishments that might, to a fair-minded nonpartisan, count as flesh on the bones of so-called compassionate conservatism." [91]

"Getting out-Jesused." Actually, the administration did increase "faith-based" funding—while *un*funding *non*-religious organizations. Result: No increase in *compassion*—only in the violation of CHURCH-STATE SEPARATION. In March 2004, the White House "faith-based" office announced that it had awarded more than $1.1 billion to religious charities—a sizable increase over 2003, "largely at the expense of nonsectarian groups that had previously received federal grants," the *American Prospect* reported. "I'm not getting out-Jesused for money ever again," said the director of a veterans' shelter who was denied a federal grant because he hadn't checked off a box that asked if the shelter was "faith-based," while some groups that got funding, he said, "previously weren't even aware of veterans." (After he re-registered as "faith-based," his federal funding nearly tripled.)

FOREIGN AID:
EN-DARKENED SELF-INTEREST

By December 2004, the **Iraq** war had cost $144 billion, but the U.S. had spent only $2 billion (out of $24 billion pledged) on reconstruction. What kind of foreign aid could be expected for countries where the Bushies had less to prove?

¢ As a percentage of GDP, the U.S., at 0.16 percent, was the stingiest of all foreign aid givers; the best, Norway and Denmark, gave more than five times as much. The European Union gave three times as much as the U.S.—and as Andrew O'Hehir noted in *Salon*, when it came time for the U.S. "to twist arms on the UN Security Council over the vote to authorize military action" in Iraq, most of the poorer nations on the council "proved more amenable to lobbying from the French and Germans than from the British and Americans."

¢ In 2002, Bush announced the creation of the Millennium Challenge Account (MCA) to promote development in poor countries, and pledged $5 billion in the first two years. When the time came, he requested only $3.8 billion, which Congress cut to $2.5 billion. As of January 2005, not a single dollar had been dispensed.

¢ In 2004, Congress cut U.S. funding for the Global Fund to Fight **AIDS**, Tuberculosis and Malaria by almost $200 million, and the White House blocked $88 billion for the fund, claiming other nations were not doing their fair share. In fact, Europe contributed over 50 percent of the fund's total contributions while the U.S., with an equal share of the global economy, would contribute less than one-third.[92]

¢ In December 2004, the administration reduced its contributions to global food aid programs by as much as $100 million, even as "the number of hungry in the world is rising for the first time in years and all food programs are being stretched," the *New York Times* reported. That month, UNICEF reported that more than a billion children were growing up hungry and unhealthy and around 29,000 children under five were dying from mostly preventable diseases every day.

¢ Bush refused to commit to Tony Blair's plan to double global aid for Africa by 2010—to which EU leaders agreed unanimously—or to increase foreign aid to 0.7 percent of GDP, as EU members including Britain,

Tsunami disaster: "Wonderful opportunity." The earthquake and tsunamis that killed perhaps 300,000 and left 1.1 million homeless in Southern Asia in December 2004 may not have been the fault of the Bush administration, but it did take Bush four days to make a public statement about it, and the publicized $15 million that Bush initially pledged in *eventual* aid was so stingy, the administration was embarrassed into upping it to two days later to $35 million—which was little more than half of what was pledged by superpower Spain, and 1/150th of the $5 billion the UN said was needed, and 1/4,500[th] of the amount we had spent on the war in Iraq. The amount Bush requested eventually rose to $950 million. CONDOLEEZZA RICE condoled by calling the disaster "a wonderful opportunity" for the U.S. to show its compassion, one that "has paid great dividends for us."[93]

France, Germany, and Italy had agreed to do. "It doesn't fit our budgetary process," Bush said. (U.S. government aid to Africa was roughly 1 percent of the defense budget.) Under worldwide scrutiny in the lead-up to the July 2005 G-8 summit, Bush "tried to fool the press . . . [and] to 'unveil' a plan to spend $674 million more in emergency aid"—funds "that Congress had already approved for needy countries," the *Progress Report* noted. Bush then pledged to double aid to Africa by 2010, but made it clear that the extra cash would only go "to those countries willing to undergo political and economic reform," the BBC noted. (Meaning, without doubt, *Bush*onomic reform; see **Foreign Policy**.)

But there was reason for skepticism, beyond Bush's record of pledging and reneging: In May 2005, the UN reported that of the $6.7 billion in aid pledged globally, just $2.5 billion had so far been actually committed or paid. It also remained to be seen how much U.S. aid would be funneled through **"faith-based"** groups. American evangelicals posing as humanitarian aid workers and bringing emergency supplies of Jesus and faith-healing quickly descended on tsunami-stricken villages in India, Sri Lanka, and Indonesia, angering the mostly Hindu, Buddhist, and Muslim residents. In southern India, a group of missionaries allegedly refused Hindu villagers aid unless they converted to Christianity.[94] Aceh Province, Indonesia is "ripe for Jesus!!" exulted the Web site of a Waco, Texas-based group that dispatched 75 soulnappers to tsunami areas to persuade people to "come to Christ."[95]

FOREIGN POLICY, INTERNATIONAL RELATIONS, AND THE "BUSH DOCTRINE"

[I]n the book of Revelation 19, [Jesus] is depicted bearing a 'sharp sword' and smiting nations, ruling them with 'a rod of iron.' Moreover, the Song of Victory in Exodus 15 hails God as a God of war . . .

—Jerry Falwell, "God is Pro-War"[96]

Actually, it's a lot of fun to fight . . . It's fun to shoot some people.

—Marine Lt. Gen. James N. Mattis, Feb. 2005. Defense Secretary Rumsfeld declined to comment on the comment, lest he sound, you know, liberal, pacifistic, or sane.

"Let's begin with the obvious," *The New Republic* remarked upon the promotion of National Security Adviser CONDOLEEZZA RICE to Secretary of State in January 2005.

The last four years can hardly be described as a resounding foreign policy triumph. **Iraq** . . . seems well on its way to becoming a gangster's paradise engulfed by civil war. The Bush administration presided over the Abu Ghraib scandal [see **Human Rights**] and then tried to cover up the culpability of top officials. Meanwhile, it has turned a blind eye to [nuclear] proliferation in North Korea and Iran, [making] the dreaded nexus of terrorists and weapons of mass destruction more dangerous than before. It has also alienated much of Europe, as well as allies across the globe. Faced with these failures, you would think [Bush might] retire the architects of these debacles . . . But the Bush administration . . . doesn't punish incompetence. Instead, it rewards it with extensions of tenure and promotions, so long as the incompetents prove their absolute loyalty.[97]

Almost to a man, "the architects of these debacles" had been members of the PROJECT FOR THE NEW AMERICAN CENTURY—a group of right-wingers formed in 1997 that included such former Reagan and future Bush officials as DICK CHENEY, DONALD RUMSFELD, deputy defense secretary/World Bank president PAUL WOLFOWITZ, Deputy Secretary of State RICHARD ARMITAGE, Undersecretary of State JOHN BOLTON, Cheney Chief of Staff I. LEWIS LIBBY, and National Security Council Senior Director and convicted IRAN-CONTRA figure ELLIOTT ABRAMS. The group advocated, not to put too fine a point on it, unilateral U.S. military *expansion*, unchallenged global hegemony, and "preemption" rather than containment of rivals. When the Project's core ideas were laid out in 1991 in a planning document drafted by Wolfowitz—then undersecretary of defense for policy—the Bush I administration rejected his plan as too radical.

A report issued by the Project in 2000 became the blueprint for the "Bush doctrine." It called for the repudiation of the ANTI-BALLISTIC MISSILE (ABM) TREATY (done in 2001) and the building of a MISSILE DEFENSE system (under way); huge military spending increases (done and done); the development of a new generation of small NUCLEAR WEAPONS for actual battlefield use (okayed by Congress in 2002); and "a network of 'deployment bases' or 'forward operating bases' to increase the reach of current and future forces," as well as "a more permanent [U.S.] role in [Persian] Gulf regional security" for which "the unresolved conflict with Iraq *provides the immediate justification*" (emphasis added). Longer term, it warned, Iran posed "as large a threat to U.S. interests" as Iraq.

Putting the "reign" and "polic(e)" in "foreign policy." In 2000, candidate Bush said the U.S. "must be humble . . . in how we treat nations that are figuring out how to chart their own course . . . If we're an arrogant nation, they'll resent us." And within two years, King George had:

- Announced his "new" national security doctrine, calling for permanent U.S. military supremacy and reserving the right to attack "preemptively" any country the president labeled a threat—a policy that "overturns 500 years of international practice and law," said former Reagan official Clyde Prestowitz, author of a book about Bush foreign policy titled *Rogue Nation.*
- Rejected, undermined, and/or violated more international treaties than any previous administration, including the ABM Treaty; the nuclear weapons Comprehensive Test Ban Treaty; the Biological and Toxin Weapons Convention; the International Criminal Court; the Land Mine Treaty; the UN Agreement to Curb the International Flow of Illicit Small Arms; the Geneva Conventions on torture; the Kyoto treaty on global warming; the International Plan for Cleaner Energy; OECD talks on offshore tax and money-laundering

havens; World Trade Organization rules; UN resolutions for an end to the illegal U.S. embargo on CUBA; the UN Convention on the Elimination of All Forms of Discrimination against Women; the UN Convention on the Rights of the Child; and the UN International Covenant on Economic, Social and Cultural Rights.

- Prepared to invade **Iraq,** without UN authorization— "a defiance of international law far graver than Saddam Hussein's non-compliance with UN weapons inspectors," wrote the *Guardian's* George Monbiot, who added: "There is something almost comical about the prospect of George Bush waging war on another nation [Iraq] because that nation has defied international law."

- Turned the international sympathy and goodwill toward the U.S. that followed 9/11 into unprecedented opposition, fear, and hatred. Canonical, even trite, but true (CTBT).

Learning from Genghis Khan. When Bush formalized his "doctrine" in a National Security Strategy report in September 2002, critics warned of opening a Pandora's box. Rep. Lloyd Doggett (D-TX) wrote that "America will now attack first with preemptive strikes in what could spiral into wars without end, because other countries will likely copy this model . . . This is a formula for international anarchy, not domestic security." Parts of the paper sounded "like a pronouncement that the Roman Empire or Napoleon might have produced," according to a *New York Times* editorial. Indeed, in the summer of 2001, Donald Rumsfeld's office had sponsored a study of ancient empires—Alexander the

Great's, the Romans, the Mongols—to determine how they had maintained their dominance. World domination used to be feared as the Soviets' ambition. "There's a name for the kind of regime in which the cops rule, answering only to themselves," wrote Hendrik Hertzberg in the *New Yorker*. "It's called a police state."

Besides, military power alone could not win the "war on terror." The 9/11 attack was planned and carried out by a few dozen men for around one-fortieth the cost of a single tank. Missile defenses could not stop suicide bombers or suitcase bombs. That would take (shudder) close *international cooperation* on intelligence, customs, and immigration controls. "It is better to be feared than loved," wrote Machiavelli. But Machiavelli "was wrong," wrote Fareed Zakaria in the *New Yorker*. "The Soviet Union was feared by its allies; the United States was loved, or at least, liked. Look who's still around."

FREEDOM AND DEMOCRACY. *Daily Show* host Jon Stewart, reporting on how many times Bush used the words "freedom" and "liberty" in his January 2005 inaugural address: "Final score: Freedom 27, Liberty 15. It was a noble effort for Liberty, which as you know has been playing hurt since the Patriot Act."

Bush's speech invoked "freedom" more than 1.5 times per minute, but included almost no specifics, not a single mention of any country—or of the war in Iraq. The administration, noted Stephen Walt of Harvard's Kennedy School of Government, "has pressed for freedom and democracy at the rhetorical level but has only pushed the countries that it doesn't like: Iraq being the most extreme example," followed by Syria and Iran. The Bushies meanwhile continued to coddle, praise, pay off, and/or do business with authoritarian regimes, human rights abusers, and/or sponsors of Islamist extremism, from Egypt, Saudi Arabia, and Kuwait to Russia and "communist" China, where the U.S. had $35 billion in investments.

The rewards in many cases were for cooperation against terrorism. As the *American Prospect*'s Matthew Yglesias noted, Bush was all too willing to help secular tyrants link their local "problems"—Putin's war in Chechnya, China's in Sinkiang—to our war on terrorism: "In the end, this is precisely the response bin Laden would hope to see"—its effect is to encourage Chechens and Muslim Uighurs in Sinkiang to buy into bin Laden's claim that their struggles are his as well.

Another reason countries like Saudi Arabia and Egypt were not pressured to democratize was because democracy there, as Walt noted, "might not run in a pro-American direction." And of course, we were wedded to the Saudis et al. by Bush's no-conservation **energy policy**, which, as the *New York Times*'s Thomas Friedman noted, was "generating huge windfall profits for Saudi Arabia, Iran and Sudan, where the cash is used to insulate the regimes from any pressure to open up their economies, liberate their women or modernize their schools," and where it ends up financing Islamist extremism.

Finally, for domestic propaganda purposes, the Bushies needed an international bad guy or three—not more; a clear-cut "axis of evil"; white hats and black hats only. Mustn't make the "message" too *complicated.*

- In RUSSIA, the *Progress Report* noted, Bush "stood idly by as his 'straightforward and trustworthy' friend

Vladimir Putin eliminated political competition, canceled checks and balances, and muzzled the press." Condoleezza Rice's policy toward opponents of the war in Iraq was summarized as "punish France, ignore Germany, and forgive Russia." (Rice, by the way, was a director of CHEVRON from 1991 to 2000, while it— along with **Dick** Cheney's HALLIBURTON—was accused of working with NIGERIA's "kill 'n' go" Mobile Police. While Rice chaired Chevron's Public Policy Committee, whose stated purpose was to monitor "domestic and foreign social, political and environmental issues," Nigerian soldiers in Chevron helicopters and boats destroyed villages and shot peaceful protestors at a Chevron oil platform.)

- PAKISTAN, despite serious human rights violations, continued to receive hundreds of millions of dollars in U.S. aid and was granted "major non-NATO ally" status, elevating it "into the highest ranks of friendship with America," Yglesias noted. Pakistani President Pervez Musharraf, a general who seized power in 1999, reneged in 2004 on his promise to return the country to even nominal civilian rule.
- The release of the 2004 Arab Human Development Report, which dealt with problems in achieving democracy, was delayed for months because the White House objected to portions in the prologue that criticized the U.S. invasion of Iraq. (Bush's new Censorship for Freedom Program?)
- Funding for the FREEDOM SUPPORT ACT, which was signed into law by Bush I to promote democracy overseas, was cut by nearly half from 2002 to 2005.

- In 2004, the GOP-led House voted to cut a promised increase in funding to promote democracy in the Middle East from $40 million to $1 million. Total U.S. expenditures in 2002 on public diplomacy for the entire Muslim world were $150 million—"about two hours of the defense budget," the *Progress Report* noted.

- In 2003, the White House led the charge to eliminate RADIO FREE EUROPE, "one of the cheapest, most effective and most popular tools of U.S. public diplomacy." [98]

- In August 2004, the administration indicated support for a major expansion of Israeli settlements in the occupied WEST BANK, a blow to Palestinian aspirations for independence, to Israeli and Palestinian moderates, and to the U.S.-backed "road map" peace plan.

- CHINA "has intensified its crackdown against Falun Gong practitioners and sought to undermine democracy in Hong Kong while Bush has done nothing," the *American Prospect* reported. President Hu Jintao "has presided over a steady crackdown on dissent, the news media, religion, Internet commentary and think tanks. China now imprisons far more journalists than any other country." [99]

- In Central Asia, Bush "entered into new alliances with a variety of tyrannical regimes—most notably UZBEKISTAN—that use counterterrorism as a pretext for suppressing freedom of religion and cracking down on political dissent." [100] Uzbekistan's dictator, Islam Karimov, "a former Communist apparatchik turned pro-Western kleptocrat . . . has tortured and killed his way to the top of the heap of the world's human rights abusers. His medieval regime notoriously suffocates prisoners with chlorine-filled gas masks and has boiled at least two opponents in cauldrons of water."[101] This ally against, you know, *terrorism* continued to receive millions in U.S. military and economic aid, and in turn permitted U.S. use of an Uzbeki airbase. After at least 700 protesters, including women and children, were shot and killed by Karimov's U.S.-trained and -equipped security forces in May 2005, Bush said, "We want to know fully what took place." A month later, U.S. and Russian defense officials teamed up to block a NATO investigation. Upsetting Karimov "would have an impact on [NATO's] activities" in the country, a Pentagon spokesman explained.

- In VENEZUELA, White House support for the illegitimate regime that ousted authoritarian President Hugo Chavez in a 2002 military coup backfired; Chavez won a referendum to retain power in 2004 by portraying the vote as a U.S. attempt to replace him with a puppet regime. Leftist, anti-U.S., anti-free-market, anti-free-trade leaders were in power or on the rise in Brazil, Argentina, Mexico, and elsewhere in Latin America. "Not long ago, the growing alienation of Latin America [from the U.S.] would have been considered a major foreign policy setback," wrote the *New York Times*'s Paul Krugman; but with Bush, "we've defined disaster down."

- In BOLIVIA, months after the Bush administration refused a plea in 2003 for emergency help to quell unrest stemming in part from the U.S. drug eradication program, the president was toppled by a drug cartel. According to a bipartisan U.S. commission, "Bolivia is a typical case of U.S. inattention" where, for a paltry amount of money, we could have avoided a costly security risk in the future.

Soothing Sudan. The administration's response to the genocide conducted by Sudanese government forces and allied militia in DARFUR, Sudan, ranged from lackadaisical to shameful. "Mr. Bush has said almost nothing about Darfur this year," the *New York Times* reported in June 2005. *Almost* nothing: In April, Nicholas Kristof noted, the White House was "roused from its stupor of indifference" on Darfur to kill the bipartisan Darfur Accountability Act, which called for $90 million in U.S. assistance to protect Darfur civilians, sanctions against the Sudanese regime, and a military no-fly zone to help stop the ongoing genocide. The act had been passed unanimously by the Senate.

The administration, the *Los Angeles Times* reported, "has forged a close intelligence partnership with Sudan, which has helped Washington's war on terrorism"—even though Sudan remained on the U.S. list of state *sponsors of* terrorism. During what the *American Prospect* called his "appeasement tour" of Sudan in April 2005, Deputy Secretary of State ROBERT ZOELLICK "gave an astonishingly low estimate of 60,000 to 160,000 people" killed in Darfur, defying "even the most conservative claims." The Coalition for International Justice estimated nearly 400,000. Zoellick also refused to endorse Colin Powell's verdict of "genocide."

Qoddling Qaddafi. "Has America Sold Out The Libyans?" *The New Republic* asked. Bush rewarded Libyan dictator MUAMMAR QADDAFI handsomely for renouncing his nonconventional weapons programs (for which Bush falsely credited his invasion of **Iraq**): In 2004, the U.S., pledging normalized relations, removed a decades-old travel ban and relaxed trade sanctions, whereupon U.S. businessmen, "many from the same oil companies that have lavishly funded Bush's campaigns," *The New Republic* noted, flocked to Libya. EXXON MOBIL clinched a deal for Libyan oil; CHEVRON TEXACO was close. Meanwhile, Libya remained "among the least free countries in the world. Torture is routine. People have been held incommunicado for decades without trial and killed arbitrarily. Restrictions on press freedom . . . 'are unparalleled almost anywhere else in the world.'" Moreover, Libyan dissidents said Qaddafi financed militants operating in Saudi Arabia and, allegedly, a plot to assassinate Saudi Crown Prince Abdullah. Bush's coddling of Qaddafi might have been a signal that the U.S. "will accept a disarmed North Korea that continues to starve its people or a disarmed Iran that continues to jail and kill its dissidents."[102] The reputed architect of the Libyan deal? Bush's appointee for UN ambassador, JOHN BOLTON (see below).

Democracy on the Iraqi casualty list? The political will to promote democracy abroad was—along with preemptive wars, unilateralism, and regime change—among "the ideas that died in Iraq," casualties of "a war whose promoters claimed [it] was waged in democracy's name," wrote *Foreign Policy* editor Moisés Naím in August 2004. "With more than 900 American soldiers dead, 10,000 coalition troops wounded, a military price tag of more than $90 billion," the main reason for going to war "dismissed as a 'massive intelligence failure,'" and "the strong likelihood that rabidly anti-American fundamentalists could come to power in free and fair elections" in Iraq and other Muslim countries, the "unspeakable, politically incorrect conclusion creeping into many influential minds in Washington is that the Middle East is 'incurable'; peace, prosperity, and political freedom are goals out of reach." Indeed, "American politicians increasingly see the promotion of democracy abroad as a threat" to stability and security.[103]

"Please don't support us." The mess-o-potamia likewise lent credibility to "the assertions of local authoritarians that their iron rule is the only thing preventing chaos," according to the *American Prospect*'s Matthew Yglesias. "Meanwhile, while freedom is eroded, Arab reformers find themselves discredited by association with an ever more loathed United States." "In every Arab country that I have been to in the last two years," Fareed Zakaria attested in *Newsweek*, "the liberals, reformers and businessmen say, 'Please don't support us. American support today is the kiss of death.'"[104] In IRAN, for example, reformists and dissidents seen as U.S.-backed were crushed, and a hard-line Islamist was elected president by a landslide in June 2005.

Exporting Bushonomics. What the Bushites seemed eager to export was not democracy so much as their radically pro-business, help-the-rich **economics**. Bush's 2002 National Security Strategy document said the U.S. should pressure other countries to adopt "lower marginal tax rates" and "pro-growth legal and regulatory policies." Tax cuts were the right of the rich regardless of race, creed, or nationality. The right to pollute belonged to *all* corporations. Freedom to produce and sell, the document said explicitly, "is real freedom." As "distinct, presumably, from the secondary, not quite real freedoms of thought, conscience, and expression," wrote Hendrik Herzberg in the *New Yorker*.

On the tabula rasa of occupied **Iraq** (and in the town of Tabula Rasa, formerly Fallujah), the Bushies sought to create a prototype Bushite state, free of any meddling by Democrats or democracy. The U.S. occupation authorities quickly replaced Iraq's progressive tax structure with a flat tax, slashed tariffs, threw Iraqi industry wide open to foreign investors, and "privatized everything in sight," Paul Krugman noted, adding: "A number of people, including Jay Garner, the first U.S. administrator of Iraq, think that the Bush administration shunned early elections . . . so it could impose economic policies that no elected Iraqi government would have approved." These moves "reinforc[ed] the sense of many Iraqis that we came as occupiers, not liberators." (See **War Profiteering, Corporate**.)

AMERICA'S DOWNFALL IN WORLD OPINION. For America's diplomacy and prestige—and by extension, its economic wellbeing and security—the Bush administration might best be called a disaster. The day after 9/11, the headline in Paris's *Le Monde* proclaimed, *"Nous sommes tous Americains."* The Iraq invasion, along with other Bush policies, quickly put an end to that kind of sentiment.

In Australia, Britain, Canada, France, Japan, Spain, and South Korea, "a majority of voters share a rejection of the

Iraq invasion, contempt for the Bush administration [and], a growing hostility to the U.S.," according to a poll in October 2004.[105] Even in Britain, our closest ally on Iraq, 73 percent said the U.S. wields an excessive influence on international affairs and a majority believed "that U.S. democracy is no longer a model for others." In a Canadian poll in November, nearly eight out of ten said Bush runs "a rogue nation," and most adults under 35 believed America had become "a force for evil in the world."[106]

Naturally, it was even worse in Muslim countries. A March 2004 Pew poll found Osama bin Laden "rated favorably" by 55 percent in Jordan, 65 percent in Pakistan, and 45 percent in Morocco, while "a clear majority" in those three countries said suicide bombings against Americans in Iraq were justified. In Saudi Arabia and Egypt, two key U.S. allies, a Zogby poll found 94 percent and 98 percent holding an "unfavorable" view of the U.S. In relatively moderate Morocco, wrote pollster Craig Charney, the press "contains pages of articles that salute 'the untamable rebels'" fighting the U.S. in Iraq.

On the diplomatic front, other nations were "joining to resist U.S. unilateralism and exacting a higher price," said the Nixon Center's vice president. The resistance, the *New York Times* noted, "has forced the administration to rethink its plans for security in Iraq and for persuading North Korea to abandon its nuclear weapons program," on which South Korea and Japan sided with China against the U.S. hard-line policy.

NATO "has been slow to meet its commitments for personnel and resources in Afghanistan." Meanwhile, the UN refused to extend to U.S. troops immunity from prosecution by the International Criminal Court.

Tear in the war on terror. A "growing rift between American counterterrorism officials and their counterparts in Europe"[107] was dramatized in June 2005, when an Italian judge ordered the arrest of 13 CIA agents on charges of kidnapping a terrorism suspect from Milan to Egypt for "questioning." The abduction "undermin[ed] an entire operation against his terrorist network," said a senior Italian investigator. The prosecutor who sought the warrants—and who in the past was accused of *right*-wing bias—said the war on terrorism must be conducted "in accordance with international laws and the rights of the defendant. Otherwise, we are giving victory to the terrorists."

Military commanders and diplomats against Bush. "[N]ot many people [overseas] agree with us, or like us or are prepared to work with us," said Richard Lugar, the Republican chairman of the Senate Foreign Relations committee. No one better appreciated this than diplomats themselves. A "rising star in foreign service" confided "that on a scale of 0-to-10, colleagues in the service would give a 9.5 grade to [outgoing Secretary of State] COLIN POWELL and a grade of 2 to the Bush administration," wrote former White House aide David Gergen. In June 2004, a group of former senior diplomatic officials and retired military commanders called DIPLOMATS AND MILITARY COMMANDERS FOR CHANGE issued a statement saying Bush had damaged U.S. security and calling on Americans to defeat him in November. Many signatories were former Reagan and Bush I officials, and many had voted for W. in 2000. They included a former chairman of the Joint Chiefs of Staff, a former head of U.S. Central

Command, a former CIA director, "and a decorated array of former ambassadors and assistant secretaries of state and defense," the *Washington Post* noted. (Also see **Republicans Against Bush**.)

"Makes Clinton look like a genius": Bushism vs. Realism. Some of Bush's harshest critics were representatives of the so-called REALIST SCHOOL of international relations—most of them conservatives—who held that the U.S. should go to war only when its vital national-security interests are at stake. In 2003, a group of realists, libertarians, and traditional conservatives formed the Coalition for a Realistic Foreign Policy, which declared that "the move toward empire" in the name of the war on terrorism "must be halted immediately . . . because it subverts the freedoms and liberties of citizens at home while simultaneously thwarting the will of people abroad."[108] The University of Chicago's JOHN MEARSHEIMER, a leading realist who voted for Bush in 2000, said, "the more time goes by, the more Bush makes Clinton look like a genius in both domestic and foreign policy." Fellow realist STEVEN WALT said Kerry "understands much better" that the U.S., "despite its preponderance of power, can operate most effectively when it operates with substantial international legitimacy and support." *The American Conservative* magazine said the administration's "go-it-alone hubris" and "sledgehammer diplomacy" have led to a "fiasco" in Iraq, and that the neocons' "incessant warmongering" had led the U.S. "into an extremely perilous situation, perhaps the most dangerous in its history."

Foreign affairs de-laid. The U.S. public got it: In an August 2004 Pew Center poll, 67 percent said the U.S. was "less respected" in the world than ten years earlier. And we're literally less loved, according to the satirical *Onion*, which reported the direst diplomatic impact of all: "REPORT: U.S. FOREIGN POLICY HURTING AMERICAN STUDENTS' CHANCES OF GETTING LAID ABROAD." But, for $25—for real—American travelers could simply order the "Going Canadian" kit, including maple-leaf-emblazoned T-shirt and luggage patch and *How to Speak Canadian, Eh?* guidebook.

"Brand America" losing market share. Bush foreign policy exacted an economic price as well as a, well, social one. *The New Republic*'s Clay Risen reported how, in overseas marketing, U.S. corporations began to conceal their products' American-ness, which had become a liability. An October 2004 poll by market-research firm Global Market Insite (GMI) found "a consistent direct correlation between how closely international consumers associate companies with the U.S. and the likelihood they'll avoid purchasing their brands in the near future." Such sentiment "gained new energy" after the November 2004 election. "American multinational companies will need to mount a valiant effort to distance themselves from the image of the U.S. federal government and its unpopular foreign policies or risk continued brand erosion and ongoing boycotting," GMI declared.[109]

Powell out, Rice in. First-term Secretary of State COLIN POWELL was a voice of relative reason and occasional opposition to the neocons on the Bush foreign policy team, whom he reportedly described as "fucking crazies."[110] With his ouster after the 2004 election "instead of the more-deserving Rumsfeld," wrote Robert Scheer, and with "the ravaging of the CIA [see **Intelligence**] . . . the coup of the neoconservatives is complete."

"CONDI" RICE, Powell's replacement in the most important cabinet post, was described by experts as "one of the weakest National Security Advisers in recent history."[111] In October 2003, Bush appointed Rice to head the "Iraq Stabilization Group," with authority to manage postwar Iraq. Seven months later, the *Washington Post* reported, the group had become "a metaphor for an Iraq policy that is adrift." It was not publicly mentioned again by the White House.

No matter. Rice was utterly devoted to "a boss whose sentences she can finish, and who trusts her totally to carry out his wishes"; she was "unlikely to have any agenda but Mr. Bush's," said the *New York Times*. Her only qualification, said Gloria Steinem, "is that she's obedient." In 2004, the never-married Rice began a sentence, "As I was telling my husb—[pause]—as I was telling President Bush . . ."[112]

Indeed, where national security advisers were once expected to remain objective and above the political fray, Rice set new standards by stumping for Bush in the 2004 campaign. Rice's appointment "should leave no doubt about where this administration is headed—full steam in the same perilous direction," said *The New Republic*.

Lying in State. The administration's already shattered credibility overseas had experts at home and abroad "shaking their heads in disbelief" at Rice's appointment, Bill Moyers noted. Rice was among the administration's chief disinformation pushers in the push for war in **Iraq**—claiming, for example, that the aluminum tubes Iraq purchased "are only really suited for nuclear weapons programs" when she knew the government's foremost nuclear experts had declared that argument "unpersuasive" because the tubes were "poorly suited" for that use. And when that became public, Rice denied having known "the nature of the dispute"— which was, after all, only "the mother of all intelligence disagreements" about the government's single best piece of evidence about its single most serious claim about Iraqi WMDs.[113] Rice also made dozens of literally incredible statements about the administration's pre-**September 11** attention to terrorist threats while she testified under oath before the 9/11 Commission.

Joining Rice at State was her protégé, ROBERT JOSEPH—the national security official widely believed to be behind Bush's fraudulent claim that Iraq sought to purchase uranium from Niger. His new job: undersecretary of state for arms control. Joseph, a proponent of preemptive war and NUCLEAR *COUNTER-PROLIFERATION* rather than nonproliferation, would be in charge of arms negotiations with Iran and North Korea.

UN-bashing—long a favorite sport of right-wing U.S. politicians and demagogs who would abide *no* check on U.S. power, *no* limitation on U.S. prerogatives—became all but official policy under Bush. In 2001 alone, the U.S. opposed UN agreements on small-arms traffic, trade with Cuba, and women's and children's rights, and was ejected from the UN Human Rights Commission for failure to pay UN dues and for opposing resolutions supporting the basic human right to adequate food, lower-cost access to AIDS drugs, and a moratorium on the death penalty. It was all downhill after that. On Iraq—where, as it turned out, the UN had ably supervised the elimination of Saddam Hussein's WMDs years before—"the UN inspectors got it all right, while the top American military, political and intelligence leaders got it all wrong," Robert Scheer sneered. For decades, he reminded, the UN had also undertaken hundreds of largely thankless humanitarian, arms control, and peacekeeping missions that "have certainly helped save countless lives and arguably prevented a third world war." The UN "deserves an apology."

What it got, in 2004, was a hyped-up right-wing frenzy over abuses of the UN-Iraq oil-for-food program; a Texas Republican Party platform calling for the U.S. to leave the UN; and (speakin' of boltin'):

John "Does Not Play Well With Others" Bolton. In August 2005, Bush bypassed the Senate and, in a recess appointment, installed a leading UN-hater, Undersecretary of State for Arms Control JOHN BOLTON, to be UN ambassador. In 1994 Bolton said, *"There's no such thing as the United Nations"*; the international community "can only be led by the only remaining superpower, which is the United States"; and, *"if the UN secretariat building in New York lost ten stories, it wouldn't make a bit of difference."* (What did he have in mind, flying a jetliner into it?) In other displays of finesse, in 1999 Bolton called for full diplomatic recognition of Taiwan, dismissing the "fantasy" that China would respond with force. In July 2003, the State Department removed him from its delegation after he called North Korea's tyrannical dictator a "tyrannical dictator" at the start of delicate disarmament talks. In 2003, he told the media that after defeating Iraq, the U.S. would "deal with" Iran, Syria, and North Korea, and that in the case of Iran, "all options are on the table." Bolton also tried to fire intelligence analysts who wouldn't stretch the truth on Iraqi weapons programs, and led an administration effort to oust Mohamed El Baradei as head of the International Atomic Energy Agency for being *right* on Iraq's alleged nuclear program.

"What message are we sending to the world community [with Bolton's nomination]?" asked Republican Senator George Voinovich. (The two-word answer?) Noting Bolton's "utter failure" in nuclear antiproliferation efforts with North Korea and Iran, the *New York Times*'s Thomas Friedman added, "no one can miss the teacher's note at the bottom of his report card: 'Does not play well with others who disagree with him' . . . why would you appoint him to be ambassador at an institution he has nothing but contempt for to do a job he has no apparent skills for?" Why, precisely because, as Maureen Dowd noted, "In Bush 43's Washington, bristling and bullying are the cardinal virtues."

Wolfowitz at the World American Bank. That same month, Dowd noted, Bush named *two* "unilateralist hawks who specialize in blowing off the globe"—Bolton and Paul Wolfowitz— "to run global institutions that epitomize multilateralism. (Wolfie's biggest qualification to run the World Bank? His prediction that Iraqi reconstruction would pay for itself with Iraqi oil revenues.)" Other items on "Wolfie's" resume: Supporting for decades "the strong and remarkable leadership" of

Indonesian dictator Suharto, who was accused of genocide and murder of his own citizens and named "most corrupt leader in modern history" by Transparency International; pressuring U.S. intelligence agencies to produce false links between Saddam Hussein and 9/11; attacking Gen. Eric Shinseki's troop estimates for Iraq as "wildly off the mark," thus helping produce severe shortages of troops and equipment and many excess casualties; and "reportedly approving the harsh interrogation methods that led to abuse and torture in U.S. prisons."[114] His role in attempting to impose radical free-market economics on Iraq "is likely to make countries distrust any economic advice Mr. Wolfowitz might give," wrote Paul Krugman. The Wolfowitz nomination "has broken the myth that this is the World Bank—it's the American Bank," said Moisés Naím. "He's a man of good experiences" [*sic*], said Bush.

FREE SPEECH, DISSENT, AND PRESS FREEDOM

It's a fantastic thing to come to a country where people are free to express their views.
— George W. Bush in London, November 2003,
commenting on anti-Bush demonstrations

The Wall Street Journal *is like* Pravda . . . *You don't want to underestimate the importance of the Leninist model . . . They [the American right] don't tolerate dissent.*
— Conservative political scientist John Mearsheimer

The $8,000 in taxpayer funds that AG JOHN ASHCROFT spent on curtains to cover up the semi-nude statue "Spirit of Justice" in the Justice Department (DOJ) lobby in 2002 was worth every penny (even if a dollar bill or two would have done the job; just one breast showed—a mere toga malfunction): Covering up one boob helped expose another.

But boobs *can* be dangerous. With no terrorist threats to worry about, apparently, the Ashcroft DOJ kept its focus firmly on hunting down domestic political activists and on the even greater threats from homosexuality and "indecency." Under Ashcroft's boss, the boob-in-chief, a blanket of repression and censorship—thin but effective enough, and smelling of, yes, fascism—spread over the government, the media, workplaces, schools, churches, and public places. The repression ranged from violent police actions against protesters to subtler but no less insidious forms of intimidation and self-censorship. The Bushies, "who have botched everything, question the patriotism and the honesty of those who dare stand up to use their First Amendment [free speech] rights" to challenge them, said Sen. Patrick Leahy (D-VT). "With the crew we have in charge right now," he added, "we would not be able to ratify the Bill of Rights."

Hail, universally beloved Leader. At Bush-Cheney rallies during the 2004 campaign, attendees were carefully screened and dissenters and would-be hecklers were turned away to prevent even a peep of protest from offending the king's ears or, God forbid, being picked up and broadcast by the media to blemish the image of the universally beloved Leader. "Bush's admission policy can leave the impression that the president has strong support wherever he goes," AP reported. So? Would Mussolini, Castro, or Saddam Hussein have done any different? Most bi-czar of all, people with pro-Bush signs were permitted to line the path of Bush's motor-cades while police cleared away those with anti-Bush signs and herded them to officially designated "free-speech zones" far away (what does that make the rest of America?), arresting anyone who resisted or strayed.

At a Cheney speech near Albuquerque, New Mexico, people were refused tickets unless they signed a pledge to endorse Bush. When Bush spoke at a Las Vegas union hall, "the campaign used its usual ticket distribution policy to pack the hall with backers," AP noted. "The crowd roared its approval throughout the speech," while the few union mem-bers admitted "sat silently in the back rows." Bush's visit to Beaverton, Oregon was billed "as a chance for ordinary citi-zens to pose questions to the president." In fact, the cam-paign filled the school gymnasium "with 2,000 passionate Bush backers." Most of Kerry's events were open to the public—hecklers included; but for Bush, "dissent is never a problem," AP noted. "When the time came to 'Ask President Bush' Friday, none of his 16 questioners challenged him on his policies. Several did not ask questions at all, but simply voiced their support: 'Mr. President, as a child, how can I help you get votes?' 'My husband and my twins and I pray for you daily.'" (Also see **Media and Image Control**.)

Protest = terrorism. What's that you say? In America, at least protesters aren't dragged off to jail and beaten? Per-haps not . . . ours are more likely to be beaten on the spot, tear-gassed, or similarly entertained by the police. Since 9/11, wrote Michelle Goldberg in *Salon*, "protest in America has increasingly come to resemble that in countries such as Egypt, where demonstrations are allowed only within tightly controlled spaces and riot police rush in at the first hint of spontaneity or disorder." In April 2003, police in Oakland, California opened fire with wooden pellets on a peaceful crowd of anti-Iraq-war protesters after the California Anti-Terrorism Information Center issued a bulletin about the potential for terrorist violence at the event. A spokesman for the center told the press, "if you have a protest group protesting a war [against] international terrorism . . . [y]ou can almost argue that *a protest against that is a terrorist act.*" After 9/11, Attorney General ASHCROFT issued *his* great dictum: "To those who scare peace-loving people with phantoms of lost liberty"—i.e., critics of his USA PATRIOT ACT—"my message is this: Your tactics only aid terrorists." The right has conflated dissent with terrorism or treason ever since. (See **War Profiteering, Political**.)

The Miami Model. The same equation governed in Miami in November 2003 during a summit meeting for the proposed FREE TRADE AREA OF THE AMERICAS (FTAA), which Florida Governor JEB BUSH "was vowing to hand his brother . . . even if that meant keeping thousands from exercising their right to protest," wrote Naomi Klein in the *Toronto Globe & Mail.* Tens of thousands of union members, senior citizens, farmers, and environmentalists were met by 2,500 riot police backed up by armored vehicles and tanks. Peaceful demonstrators, reporters, and clearly identified legal observers alike were attacked, unprovoked, by police, beaten with clubs, shot in the back with rubber bullets, pepper-sprayed in the face, and hauled off to jail by the hundreds. "Organizations were infiltrated by undercover officers who then used stun guns on activists . . . dozens of young faces were smashed into concrete and beaten bloody with batons; human rights activists had guns pointed at their heads at military style checkpoints," Klein reported. Seventeen buses full of senior citizens were prevented from joining permitted marches. Police blocked access to the portable toilets. After being arrested, handcuffed, and pepper-sprayed in the eyes while obeying police orders, a young woman from the environmentalist Sierra Student Coalition was strip-searched in jail by four male officers, denied medical treatment for her injuries, and left naked, the Sierra Club reported. As he was being charged, an attorney with the National Lawyers Guild overheard officers debating, "What will get him disbarred?"[115]

Bringing the war home. "The FTAA Summit in Miami represents the official homecoming of the 'war on terror,'" wrote Klein. Miami Mayor Manny Diaz boasted, "This should be a model for homeland defense." Indeed, this "security" was paid for with $8.5 million specially appropriated within Bush's $87 billion funding bill for the war in **Iraq**. But "more was borrowed from the Iraq invasion than just money," Klein noted. Police invited reporters to "embed" with them in armored vehicles and helicopters. "As in Iraq, most reporters embraced their role as pseudo soldiers with unsettling zeal . . . Meanwhile, independent journalists who dared to do their jobs and film the police violence up close were actively targeted. 'She's not with us,' one officer told another as they grabbed . . . a correspondent with Pacifica Radio . . . [who] was hauled away and charged." [116]

In order for the "MIAMI MODEL," as it became known, to work, wrote Klein, "the police first had to establish a connection between legitimate activists and dangerous terrorists." Enter Miami Police Chief JOHN TIMONEY . . . who repeatedly classified FTAA opponents as "outsiders coming in to terrorize and vandalize our city." At the governor's behest, police were reportedly "briefed" on the supposed desirability of the FTAA itself. "We'll try to do as many arrests as we can," said Timoney, who had been hired as Miami police chief after employing similar tactics at the 2000 Republican Convention in Philadelphia, where police infiltrated activist groups and made mass preemptive arrests.

The Miami Model was copied by police forces across the country. Law enforcement officials from Georgia, which was getting ready for the G-8 economic summit in June 2004, and New York, which was preparing for the Republican National Convention (RNC) in August, traveled to Miami during the free-trade summit to learn tactics. The director of Georgia's Department of Homeland Security said, "We need to do much the same as they did [in Miami]." Shortly *before* the G-8 summit, Georgia's Republican governor declared a state of emergency, citing a danger from "unlawful assemblages," and "call[ed] out the National Guard, flooding the streets with soldiers in full camouflage," Michelle Goldberg reported in *Salon*.

In New York, groups that applied for permits to hold marches during the RNC were stalled in some cases for more than a year. Meanwhile, the only protesters permitted to gather next to Madison Square Garden were some anti-abortion Christians; *anti*-Bush protesters were banished to sites far from the convention and sealed off in pens flanked by solid walls of police. The director of strategic communications at U.S. Central Command in Doha, Qatar was brought in to head up media operations for the convention.

At a rally in South Carolina, an activist was arrested for trespassing after he held up a "No blood for oil" sign amid a crowd of Bush supporters. In New Jersey, when Laura Bush mentioned the troops, a woman whose 24-year-old son was killed in Iraq yelled out, "When are yours going to serve?" She was arrested for trespassing. In West Virginia, two protesters were arrested for wearing "Love America, Hate Bush" T-shirts to a Bush rally that was supposedly open to the public. Welcome to Bush's America.

Pro-Bush employers played their part in the new order. In two of dozens of examples around the country, a West Virginia man was fired from his job at an advertising and design company because he heckled Bush at a local rally, and an Alabama woman lost her factory job after her employer saw a Kerry bumper sticker on her car. Schools across the country also acted against students for displaying anti-Bush messages.

The knock on the door. Let no one accuse the feds of neglecting the "war on terror." In November 2003, the *New York Times* reported on a leaked FBI memo revealing "a coordinated, nationwide effort to collect intelligence" on the antiwar movement. The memo singled out such terrorist activities as nonviolence training, videotaping of police actions, and Internet organizing. The FBI also advised local law enforcement officials to report any "suspicious activity" at protests to its *counterterrorism* squads.

In February 2004, federal prosecutors subpoenaed Drake University in Iowa for records on the sponsor of a campus antiwar forum. In advance of the 2004 RNC, the FBI questioned potential political demonstrators across the country, and their friends and families. In Colorado, where police kept files on some 3,000 people and 200 groups involved in previous protests, FBI agents visited three groups of activists. Some who were informed they were targets of a domestic terrorism investigation scrapped plans to attend protests. When an internal FBI complaint charged that such "preemptive" activity infringed on protected speech, the DOJ's Office of Legal Policy—the same office that in June 2004 authorized the use of torture against terrorism suspects (see **Human Rights**)—gave its blessing to the tactics, citing "the public interest in maintaining safety and order." "The knock on the door from government investigators asking about political activities is the stuff of totalitarian regimes," said an editorial in the radical, left-wing *New York Times*.

"Imagine." In February 2005, the DOJ disclosed that over the previous few years, the FBI had collected at least 1,173 pages of documents on the AMERICAN CIVIL LIBERTIES UNION (ACLU), which engages only in legal activities, and 2,383 pages on GREENPEACE, which had led acts of civil disobedience, along with smaller files on other groups. The disclosures were a result of a lawsuit by the ACLU, which said FBI records on dozens of protest groups could total tens of thousands of pages. In a memo on UNITED FOR PEACE AND JUSTICE, which organized massive protests against the Iraq war, FBI counterterrorism personnel saw fit to quote from a statement the group put out: "Imagine: A million people on the street, representing the diversity of New York, and the multiplicity of this nation . . . everyone who is maligned by

Bush's malicious agenda—on the street—en masse."[117] Nothing to kill or die for? Frightening indeed.

CENSORSHIP AND THE MEDIA (Also see **Plamegate and Press Freedom**.)

A swift kick in the Stern. In 2004, the Federal Communications Commission (FCC) fined Clear Channel Communications $27,500 (then the maximum) for each of 18 incidents of "indecent material" by radio host HOWARD STERN. Stern was no raunchier than he'd been for years; he had, however, cleaned up his political act and turned against Bush.

Why not the death penalty? In February 2005, new AG ALBERTO GONZALES declared the aggressive prosecution of obscenity cases as one of his top priorities. That month, the administration backed a House measure approving an increase in the maximum FCC fine for broadcasting "indecency" to $500,000. "Bono saying 'fucking brilliant' on the air would carry the exact same penalty as illegally testing pesticides on human subjects," *Rolling Stone* noted. "And for the price of Janet Jackson's 'wardrobe malfunction' during the Super Bowl, you could cause the wrongful death of an elderly patient in a nursing home and still have enough money left to create dangerous mishaps at two nuclear reactors." (More like four: The biggest fine levied by the Nuclear Regulatory Commission in 2004 was $60,000.) "Free expression and First Amendment rights are the real target of this legislation," said Rep. Bernie Sanders (I-VT).

Iraq: What's the *good* news? Throughout the war, the administration chided the media for focusing on the negative instead of on the brighter side of war and occupation. (The Pentagon pointed the way by banning media coverage of returning coffins of U.S. troops.) The media generally fell in line. In April 2004, when ABC's *Nightline*, as a tribute, aired the names and faces of the 500 U.S. troops killed in Iraq to date (as ABC had done for all who died on 9/11), the right-wing Sinclair Broadcast Group, a major owner of TV stations, ordered its ABC affiliates not to broadcast the program, saying it was "motivated by a political agenda designed to undermine the efforts of the United States in Iraq" and was "contrary to public interest."

Who's flushing now? In May 2005, *Newsweek* reported that U.S. interrogators at Guantanamo Bay let Muslim prisoners know who was in charge by flushing a Koran down a toilet. The story relied on a source who later said he could not confirm it. The ensuing uproar in the media and among the Bushies—not over the alleged desecrations (19, in fact), which the White House denied (U.S. interrogators "treat the Koran with great care and respect") but over the *story*, which was blamed for riots and 17 deaths in Afghanistan—led the magazine to retract it, even though the chairman of the Joint Chiefs of Staff and Afghanistan's president both said the riots were unrelated to it. Two weeks later came a Pentagon report—largely ignored by the media—confirming five desecrations of the Koran at Guantanamo.

Bush bigot busts Buster the bunny. In January 2005, new Education Secretary MARGARET SPELLINGS, on her second day on the job, condemned an episode of the Public Broadcasting Service children's series *Postcards from Buster.* In the dangerous episode, Buster the cartoon bunny visits 11-year-old Emma and her two mommies on a farm in Vermont. Although the show's creator said his intention was to "validat[e] children who are seldom validated," the episode's focus was in fact on making maple syrup. Spellings rebuked PBS for exposing the nation's children to "such lifestyles" and warned that the show—along with any others that displease the Bush regime—could lose its federal grant (which happened to state, "Diversity will be incorporated into the fabric of the series to help children understand and respect differences"). This "at a time when one in three gay teens is threatened with a weapon while at school," the *Progress Report* noted. PBS decided not to distribute the episode nationally.

Making public broadcasting more "balanced" (as in "Fair and"). "Conservatives" were winning their long campaign to stamp out public broadcasting's legacy of liberalism and tolerance. Bushites seized the top executive positions at the Corporation for Public Broadcasting (CPB), which funded PBS and National Public Radio. The CPB's new, Republican chairman, KENNETH TOMLINSON, picked a former co-chairwoman of the Republican National Committee to be the CPB's new president, and secretly hired a researcher who worked for 20 years at a journalism center founded by the American Conservative Union to monitor BILL MOYERS' liberal public affairs program *Now* and report on the political leanings of the guests. The political spy characterized a segment on financial waste at the Pentagon as "anti-Defense," and Republican senator Chuck Hagel as a "liberal" because he questioned Bush policy on Iraq. The show—the *only* widely broadcast, clearly liberal public affairs show in an ocean of conservative ones—was cut from an hour to a half-hour, while conservative shows hosted by Tucker Carlson and *Wall Street Journal* editors were added. In June 2005, the House Appropriations Committee voted to cut PBS's funding by 25 percent, for starters; a GOP-sponsored bill sought to eliminate it entirely. Those measures were defeated. With PBS's programming shifted rightward, perhaps its funding was safe.

Inclusion "too controversial." In December 2004, CBS and NBC, caving to right-wing pressure, decided that a TV ad in which the United Church of Christ shows its openness to all people regardless of race, sexual orientation, etc., was "too controversial" to air. CBS actually cited the Bush administration's effort to ban same-sex marriage as the basis for their decision.

Literature: "Dig a big hole." State and local officials were often in the vanguard, as it were, of the backwardness movement. In 2004, Alabama state legislator GERALD ALLEN introduced a bill to ban funds for any books "that recognize or promote homosexuality as an acceptable lifestyle." If the bill passed, Allen acknowledged, novels with gay protagonists and college textbooks that suggest homosexuality is natural would have to be removed from library shelves and destroyed. But don't start screaming "book-burning": "I guess we dig a big hole and dump them in and bury them,"

Allen said. His bill would also ban books describing hetero-
sexual acts prohibited by Alabama's sexual misconduct laws.
"Half the books in the library could end up being banned," the
Montgomery city library director told the *Birmingham
News.* "It's all based on how one interprets the material."

A few days after Allen's proposed legislation hit the
news, Bush invited this *state legislator* to the White House.
"Did Karl [Rove] want pointers on how he could bring
Allen's bill to the big leagues?" a blogger wondered.

Academic freedom. By early 2005, versions of an academic
"bill of rights" designed to restrict what university professors could say in their classrooms, bar them from "persist-
ently" discussing controversial issues, and halt liberal
"pollution" on campus had been introduced by conservatives in the House of Representatives, six or seven state leg-
islatures, and university systems in at least 20 states. The
sponsor of such a bill in Ohio, state Senator Larry Mumper,
explained that "80 percent or so of [professors] are Democrats, liberals or socialists or card-carrying Communists" who
are "anti-American" and who bully and attempt to indoctri-
nate students. (How did Mumper know about this liberal
reign of terror? He had researched for months and had heard
of a student who said she was discriminated against because
she supported Bush.)[118]

Blacks benefited from slavery? Teach us more. Most of
these proposals were based on an "Academic Bill of Rights"
drafted and promoted by right-wing activist DAVID HOROWITZ,
who claimed college campuses were a "hostile environment" for conservatives and accused professors of pushing

a political agenda and peddling "propaganda not facts."
Unlike Horowitz himself, who (though refreshingly free of
academic credentials) "freely compared American liberals
to Islamic terrorists" and "made a habit out of accusing his
detractors of racism,"[119] such as when a black historian
questioned Horowitz's claim that blacks benefited from
slavery and owed a "debt" to white America.

Meanwhile, not only did most colleges already have rules
ensuring free expression—it was increasingly the conservative movement that set the agenda on campuses. "A dozen
right-wing institutions now spend $38 million annually
pushing their agenda to students," the *Progress Report* noted.
"Conservative foundations channel tens of millions more for
academic programs" which "buff an intellectual sheen over
conservative ideology." The ultra-conservative Leadership
Institute claimed to have trained more than 40,000 college
students to become "conservative leaders." Horowitz's own
Students for Academic Freedom had chapters on 135 campuses. Such groups had no progressive counterpart.

Prefer suicide *encouragement*, perhaps? In February
2005, the mental health division of Health and Human Services, by threatening to cut funding, coerced the organizers
of a federally funded conference to delete the words "gay,"
"lesbian," "bisexual," and "transgender" from the title of
workshop *about* "Suicide Prevention Among Gay/Les-
bian/Bisexual/Transgender Individuals" (whose suicide risk
is two to three times higher than the average).[120]

GLOBAL WARMING

Some *good* news for a change: December 2004 brought hope that Republicans might pack up their golf clubs and their denial of global warming and move to Antarctica, where scientists reported that grass was flourishing for the first time, "forming turf where there were once ice-sheets and glaciers," as the continent warmed "to temperatures unseen for 10,000 years," the *London Times* reported.

Back in Washington, the glacier of right-wing denial remained solid. The Bushies still refused even to use the euphemism "climate change," let alone "global warming." Bush climate policy continued to be dictated by the big polluters and big Bush contributors in the fossil fuels, electric power, and auto industries: The policy was that there wasn't enough scientific agreement on the reality of global warming or its cause to justify mandatory limits on carbon dioxide (CO_2) and other "greenhouse gas" emissions from the burning of fossil fuels—especially by coal-burning power plants—which climate scientists all but unanimously agreed was the principle cause of global warming.

Atmospheric CO_2 was now higher than at any time in the past 400,000 years and probably the last 20 million. The 1990s were the warmest decade of the last 2,000 years. Global average temperature was increasing at a faster rate than at any time in 10,000 years. As the Bushies fiddled (with the facts), pieces of the Antarctic ice shelf the size of Delaware were breaking off and melting into the sea. Ice shelves as large as Texas were in trouble. (If only Texas itself would break off and float away.) "Climate change in Antarctica is a warning of the globally catastrophic changes that will follow unless we act now," said a scientist with the British Antarctic Survey. In August 2004, California scientists reported that by the end of the century, temperatures could rise by 15F degrees, creating a climate like that of Death Valley in inland cities and reducing the snow pack in the Sierra Nevada by up to 90 percent, disrupting much of the state's water supplies and imperiling its agriculture.

A worldwide climate-modeling study published in January 2005 in the journal *Nature* found that global warming might be twice as catastrophic as previously thought. At latitudes such as northern Europe's, average temperature could rise more than 35F degrees. Such increases were unprecedented in the Earth's geological record, and "would melt most of the polar icecaps and mountain glaciers, raising sea levels by more than 20 feet," Britain's *Independent* reported.

But as environmental lawyer Robert F. Kennedy Jr. said, "You're talking about a president who says that the jury is out on evolution . . . These people are flat-earthers."

Bush kicked off his first term by reneging on his campaign promise to regulate CO_2 emissions, and by pulling the U.S.—by far the world's biggest greenhouse gas emitter—out of the KYOTO TREATY on global warming, which aimed at modest CO_2 reductions, and which 165 other nations signed in October 2001. The White House maintained that the 7 percent reduction in greenhouse emissions the U.S. had committed to under Kyoto would have been a prescription for economic disaster. As though flooded coasts, parched farmlands, and more frequent hurricanes *wouldn't* be; the insurance company Swiss Re estimated that "climate change" cost $70 billion in 2004 alone.

The Bushies would go no further than to "call for" small, *voluntary* reductions that would not reduce total emissions (which continued to grow with industrial activity) but only slightly slow the increase—and only if companies complied, which few showed any interest in doing.

In February 2005, when Kyoto took effect, Bush's CLEAR SKIES plan had just been reintroduced in the Senate by the right-wing nut case JAMES INHOFE (R-OK), who vowed that CO_2 "certainly will not be part of [it]," adding that global warming is "the second-largest hoax ever played on the American people, after the separation of church and state."[121] (See **Election**, **Iraq** . . .)

"Eradicating" global warming. The White House *was* truly committed, however, to reducing emissions of *information* about global warming, which might raise public temperatures regarding Bush policy.

- In 2000, the Intergovernmental Panel on Climate Change (IPCC) reaffirmed that fossil fuels use was causing potentially disastrous global warming. In 2001, Bush—determined to hear the *right* answer—asked the National Academy of Sciences (NAS) to review the IPCC's findings. The NAS confirmed them with overwhelming support. White House response? The question needed more study! Moreover, at the urging of EXXON, the Bushies orchestrated the replacement of the IPCC chair, an eminent and outspoken climate scientist, with, fittingly enough, an economist.[122]

- In September 2002, the administration deleted the section on global warming from the annual federal report on air pollution. In June 2003, AP reported, the EPA scrapped a report on climate change after the White House demanded such extensive censorship that, according to an EPA staff memorandum, the report would embarrass the agency because it "no longer accurately represents scientific consensus on climate change."

- In February 2004, word got out about a secret Pentagon report stating that climate change over the next 20 years could pose a global threat vastly greater than terrorism—causing floods, droughts, famines, rioting, and wars over food, water, and fuel. The White House suppressed the report for four months. "You've got a president who says global warming is a hoax, and across the Potomac River you've got a Pentagon preparing for climate wars," said a Greenpeace spokesman.
- In 2004, Bush cut the climate change research budget of the National Oceanic and Atmospheric Administration by $9.2 million, terminating funding for research on abrupt climate change and on health and human aspects of climate change.
- In October 2004, the director of the NASA Goddard Institute for Space Studies, a top climate expert, said the administration "risked disaster" by ignoring evidence on global warming and discouraging scientists from discussing it. During a presentation he gave in 2003 on the dangers of human-caused climate change, he recalled, NASA's administrator—a Bush appointee from the Office of Management and Budget, with no background in science but close ties to Cheney—interrupted and

said there was not enough evidence even to discuss the subject.[123]

- In 2004, the administration worked to prevent an upcoming eight-nation report from recommending policies to curb global warming, and resisted "even mild language that would endorse the report's scientific findings," the *Washington Post* reported. The Arctic Climate Impact Assessment, produced by more than 300 scientists, showed regional temperature increases ten times the global average over the past century, "with worse to come if we don't cut emissions," an observer said.

- At an international conference on global warming in Buenos Aires in December 2004, the U.S. delegation blocked efforts to begin more substantive discussions; opposed further use of the term "climate change," arguing instead for "climate variability"; declared that "science tells us that we cannot say with any certainty what constitutes a dangerous level of warming"; insisted that "there shall be no written or oral report" from any seminars; and said the Kyoto accord was "not based on science."

- At the same conference, the U.S. backed Saudi Arabia's demand that compensation be included for oil-producing countries for any reduction in their revenues resulting from efforts to reduce greenhouse emissions.

- At the Bush administration's behest, the introductory statement "Our world is warming" was removed from the joint statement on global warming by the G-8 industrial nations in July 2005. The White House also requested that the statement "avoid the term 'targets.'"

- In June 2005, leaked White House documents showed that a White House official "who once led the oil industry's fight against limits on greenhouse gases" repeatedly edited government climate reports to play down links between greenhouse emissions and global warming, the *New York Times* reported. PHILIP COONEY, chief of staff for the White House Council on Environmental Quality, had no scientific training, but was a former oil lobbyist and "climate team leader" at the American Petroleum Institute. Cooney resigned after the doctored reports became public ("completely unrelated," said the White House). Five days later, EXXON MOBIL announced he was joining the firm.

HEALTH CARE AND HEALTH PROFITEERING *(Disclosure: Written by a former Canadian spoiled and corrupted by socialized medicine.)*

This section is not even *about* (yawn) health care, in the final a., but about Rovian politics on a grand scale; about partisan extremism and corporate greed; cruelty and deception; love, passion and betrayal; co-payments and, yes, deductibles.

Here, as throughout the Bush agenda, genuine crises were exploited and nonexistent ones invented to advance the right's time-honored goals of (a) dismantling the social safety net; (b) privatizing government programs and dividing the spoils among the GOP's corporate donors; and (c) destroying, by dividing and conquering, the Democrats' political base. *Health care* as such was quite literally not the issue. Indeed, every Bush health care "solution" (invariably privatization, subsidies to business, and upper-income tax breaks) promised to make the problem worse. Some basics:

Republicans want major cutbacks in programs like Medicare and Medicaid that benefit elderly, poor, and disabled Americans as well as children in order to fill the huge budget deficits created largely by Bush's TCFR (tax cuts for the rich).

Americans are overwhelmingly (93 percent) against Medicare and Medicaid cuts, according to GOP pollster Linda DiVall. (To reduce the Bush deficit, the largest number of survey respondents—59 percent—favored rolling back Bush's tax cuts for those earning over $200,000.)[124]

Lack of health insurance causes roughly 18,000 deaths each year in the U.S. and costs the economy $65-$130 billion, according to the Institute of Medicine.

The U.S. is the only wealthy, industrialized country that does not provide government-sponsored health coverage for all citizens; yet—or as a result—it spends far more per capita on health care.

In Bush's first term, the number of the uninsured rose by 5 million, to 45 million, or about one in six Americans. Those who were uninsured for some portion of the previous two years numbered *82 million* in 2004, an increase of 7 million over 2003. Eleven percent of all children and 19 percent of poor children were uninsured, as states cut back on children's health programs. Even among the employed, 35 percent of Hispanic adults were uninsured, 18 percent of blacks, and 11 percent of whites. TEXAS led the nation in the number of uninsured, as in so many other backwardness indicators.[125]

The cost of health insurance rose five times faster than wages in 2004, to around $10,000 for a family of four, up 11 percent from 2003. It was the fourth straight year of double-digit increases.

Consumers were paying more even as overall health care spending slowed, the *Progress Report* noted. In 2003, growth in out-of-pocket spending on health care accelerated by 7.6 percent, while overall spending grew more slowly than in seven years. Why? More people went without insurance, plus:

- Prescription drug prices rose an average of 7.4 percent, or more than three times the inflation rate. Medicines accounted for almost one-quarter of all out-of-pocket spending, compared with 17 percent in 1998.
- Employers transferred more costs to employees. From 2000 to 2004, employees' share increased by over 60 percent. In all, 5 million fewer jobs provided insurance in 2004 than in 2001.
- The number of employers that provide health benefits to retirees dropped from 66 percent in 1988 to 36 percent. More and more employers said they planned to end retiree health coverage.

- *Even as insurance premiums rose, health spending by insurers slowed.* They were just keeping more for themselves—and earning record profits. In short:

EVERYTHING YOU WERE TAUGHT ABOUT PRIVATE VS. "SOCIALIZED" MEDICINE IS WRONG! Private good, government bad, "socialized medicine" *disaster,* the private health care industry and its GOP shills keep telling us. Yet *almost two-thirds of Americans would prefer a government-run program providing universal coverage,* according to an ABC News poll in 2003. A Commonwealth Fund survey in 2004 showed that compared to people in "socialized" Canada, Britain, Australia, and New Zealand, "Americans report higher out-of-pocket spending and are most likely to say they did not see a doctor when sick, did not get recommended tests or follow-up care, or went without prescription medicines because of cost."[126] Americans face longer wait times to see doctors—exactly what the right claims about government-run systems—and have more trouble getting care on evenings or weekends.[127] Not surprisingly, the U.S. "has lower life expectancy than 20 other nations, near-epidemics of preventable conditions, and its infant mortality rate actually rose in 2002 for the first time in 40 years," the *Progress Report* noted.

While getting worse results, the U.S. spends roughly 75 percent more per capita on health care than other advanced countries. Why? Because, wrote economist Paul Krugman, private insurers and HMOs "spend much more on administrative expenses, as opposed to actual medical treatment, than public agencies," largely in efforts to avoid covering high-risk patients.

Business leaders seem to get it: In Canada, Krugman noted, "respectable business executives are ardent defenders of 'socialized medicine,'" and have "urged Canadians to bear in mind [its] 'economic contribution . . . to the competitiveness of Canadian businesses.'" Ask General Motors what health care is costing U.S. corporations. But:

Bush's health-care-industry donors "are winning big from the existing system," wrote David Sirota in the *American Prospect.* HMO profits increased 52 percent in 2003 alone, "meaning an extra $2.3 billion was pilfered from American consumers. These are the same companies that since 2000 gave at least $13 million to President Bush and key Republicans in Congress, and who have seven former or current executives in the president's 'Pioneer' club (those who gave him $100,000 or more)." Those contributions bought policies that increasingly remove the government from the market and leave consumers at the mercy of profiteers.

MURDERING MEDICARE. For the Bushies, the demand to do something about skyrocketing drug prices, especially for seniors, was the opportunity to begin breaking up Medicare, the federal program that provides health coverage for 41 million senior and disabled citizens—and in the process, reward major Bush/GOP donors. The MEDICARE MODERNIZATION ACT (MMA) of 2003, though initially an enormous *expansion* of Medicare (the White House was careful to conceal just how enormous), would be the wedge to split the program and its beneficiaries in two—haves and have-nots; public and privatized systems—only one of which was intended to survive. For starters, the MMA:

- Gave Bush political credit for creating a MEDICARE DRUG BENEFIT, even though it covered less than a fourth of the total drug costs of the elderly and disabled and *reduced* drug benefits for millions covered by both Medicare and Medicaid.

- *Explicitly prohibited the government from negotiating with drug makers on prices*, as other large-scale purchasers do—a provision opposed by 80 percent of Americans but worth $139 billion to the drug industry over eight years. Not that there's any connection, but since 2000, the drug industry had contributed more than $70 million to candidates, 70 percent of it to Republicans.

- *Gave more in subsidies to private industry than to help seniors pay for medicines*, including $46 billion to insurance companies to offer the drug benefit, and incentives to seniors to switch from Medicare to private plans. The private insurers would remain free to accept only the healthiest customers, leaving the sickest, costliest and, usually, poorest behind in traditional Medicare, which would become increasingly vulnerable to political pressure for its termination.

- Paid corporations $89 billion to "discourage" them from cutting retirees' drug benefits—but provided the subsidy even if they do. Many were indeed "taking the money and running," said the *Progress Report*. The Congressional Budget Office (CBO) estimated that over 20 percent of retirees with good drug coverage *would lose it as a result of the MMA*. But some corporations "are expected to post big earnings gains for 2003 or 2004" thanks to the subsidies, the *Wall Street Journal* noted. Many of these corporations belonged to the "Employers' Coalition on Medicare," which collectively gave Bush and the GOP more than $47 million since 2000.

- Was the single largest factor in the Medicare trust fund's sudden and rapid deterioration.

Making poorer seniors pay for richer ones' private plans. Premiums paid by Medicare patients rose 56 percent from 2001 to 2004. In September 2004, the day after Bush pledged to help seniors on Medicare, Medicare announced a 17 percent premium increase—the largest in its history. Costs of Bush's Medicare bill—such as subsidies to HMOs and incentives for seniors to switch to them—accounted directly for 57 percent of that increase;[128] many seniors were helping subsidize private plans they themselves could not afford. By 2006, Medicare premiums would eat up 37 percent of the average senior's Social Security income.

Medicare and the VRWC (vast Rovian wicked conspiracy). Under Bush's **"ownership society"** slogan, wrote author and law professor Charles Tiefer in *Salon*, the Republicans intend to use changes in Medicare, **Social Security,** and taxes "to pit better-off and worse-off Democrats against each other, offering all-but-irresistible incentives for some to desert the others." The strategy would "constantly impale Democrats on the dilemma of abandoning their poorer, sicker, older and minority groups, or seeing their better-off, healthier and younger members lured off to the other party," and ultimately threaten the viability of the Democratic Party itself.

Fixing the fight. The MMA set up a rigged competition between private plans and traditional Medicare. It was called the "PREMIUM SUPPORT DEMONSTRATION PROJECT." Beginning in six metropolitan areas, in any area where traditional Medicare costs were higher than average medical costs, Medicare beneficiaries would be hit with premium increases of up to 30 percent—or, they could move to a private plan. As private plans routinely "cherry-pick" the healthiest beneficiaries, Medicare would, again, get stuck with the oldest, sickest, and poorest patients, driving up its costs, forcing premiums up, and sending even more of the healthier and wealthier to private plans. "The harsh consequences," wrote Tiefer, "would be imposed on seniors who, for geographic and other reasons (for example, they live in Democratic voting states, they are working poor), Republicans see no reason to spare." In fact, the proponents' goal was to expand "Premium Support" to the entire country. Once that happens,

> the whole senior population would be split into two antagonistic camps. The sicker and poorer group . . . in traditional Medicare . . . would suffer increasing underfunding. However, the healthier and wealthier group of seniors moving into Bush's private plans would be well taught to identify their interest with the Bush-supporting private insurers." In every election thereafter, Republicans would label the Democrats "as draconian tax increasers (who would also be implicitly stigmatized as defending minorities).

Bush, wrote Tiefer, "stands on the threshold of his great dream . . . of a nation in which key former Democratic coalitions lose large and important groups that have an investment in a government that serves the common good."[129]

Taking the PAN out of C-SPAN. The MMA was enacted with extraordinary underhandedness even for the GOP, whose leaders rammed the bill through the House by a single vote, late at night, holding the debate open for an unprecedented three hours (it's typically 15 minutes) while they threatened and attempted to bribe wavering Repubs. Meanwhile, the C-SPAN TV camera—which is controlled by the House leadership—instead of panning back and forth as usual, was kept locked onto the empty, Democratic side of the chamber. House Majority Leader TOM DELAY was later censured by the House Ethics Committee for attempting to bribe one representative for his vote.

Scullyduggery. While the bill was being debated, Medicare Administrator (and former health industry lobbyist) THOMAS SCULLY, violating federal law, threatened to fire Medicare's actuary if he revealed the true cost—later revealed to be nearly double what the White House promised. The Bushies then illegally used taxpayer funds to tout the Medicare law in ads disguised as fake news reports. (See **Media**.) Ten days after the MMA's passage, Scully returned to lobbying for drug and health companies that benefited from it. By December 2004, 14 former senior Bush officials were lobbying for the drug industry.

Another gift to HMOs, employers, and the rich. Bush's main second-term health care initiative—part of his

"ownership society" canoodle—was a $25 billion expansion of HEALTH SAVINGS ACCOUNTS (HSAs), into which funds individuals deduct from their income tax could be deposited and used to pay health expenses. The accounts would be tied to insurance plans with high deductibles. (In the Bushies' view, Americans consumed *too much* health care; higher costs for consumers were not the problem but the solution.)

But this "market-based solution" really created no incentive to economize, critics said, because most medical spending occurs during high-cost episodes, when it greatly exceeds any likely deductible. Patients would, however, have an incentive to skimp on cheap preventive care, wrote Jonathan Chait in *The New Republic*—and as a result "end up suffering (and, more to the point, paying) far more later on." A study in January 2005 found that patients with high-deductible plans were far more likely to not fill a prescription or show up for a medical test, and to rack up medical debt, than those with more traditional health plans. Another study found that widespread adoption of HSAs could more than triple the deductibles workers must pay in company health plans. "[I]n reality, the accounts are nothing more than tax incentives for employers and HMOs to terminate their existing coverage, raise deductibles and premiums, and make more money," wrote David Sirota.

HSA's were just another tax shelter for the wealthy, who would benefit most, at the expense of everyone else, according to Paul Krugman: The higher your tax bracket, the bigger your HSA deduction—i.e., the more the government contributes toward your health insurance. If you don't earn enough to pay income taxes, you get nothing. Economist Jonathan Gruber calculated that about 87 percent of HSAs would be purchased by those who already have health insurance. Meanwhile, paying out so much more for the "haves" would undermine the program's ability to cover the *uninsured*, whose numbers would as a result grow by some 350,000, Gruber estimated.

Moreover, insurance "is supposed to spread risk," Jonathan Chait noted. "But HSAs would encourage the well-off and the healthy to pull out of group plans; the more that do so, the higher the rates rise for the sicker folks remaining, leading more people to drop out. That's the vicious cycle that has driven up both insurance costs and the number of uninsured."[130]

MEDICAID "REFORM": "To balance the federal budget off the backs of the poorest people in the country** is simply unacceptable," said Republican Governor MIKE HUCKABEE of Arkansas about Bush's Medicaid scheme. But to the Bushies, the 42 million poor, disabled, and elderly Americans and millions of children covered by Medicaid, the nation's largest health insurance program, were an obvious target for cutbacks to help pay for Bush's TCFR program. Besides, there was ideology to think of, and this was a big government program for the poor—one that didn't even foist religion on them.

Draconian? *Draculian*. Throughout Bush's first term, financially strapped states were forced to cut Medicaid payments and benefits; this just when the numbers of the unemployed, uninsured, and poor—and consequently,

Medicaid enrollments—were rising. The state cuts automatically led to cuts in federal matching funds.

In 2003, the White House, smelling blood, proposed a Faustian bargain: States could have additional federal funds up to 2010, but after that their federal aid would be reduced *below* current levels by the same amount; in fact, by 2013, they would receive billions less than under existing law, and not enough to keep up with increasing costs. The federal aid would also be converted to a capped "block grant"; it would no longer increase along with Medicaid enrolments when the economy weakens and people lose jobs and health insurance. This would swell the ranks of the uninsured, but achieve the cherished GOP goal of destroying Medicaid as an "entitlement" program.

The block grant scheme was pushed back into Bush's second term, but was far from dead. (Bush plans never die; though appearing dead, they awaken after dark, in secret congressional conferences and late-night legislative sessions. Only a stake through the heart . . .)

Patient's sick? Kill him. Much as with **Social Security**, Medicaid's financial strains (and Bush's huge deficits) provided the pretext to claim the program wasn't sustainable and, well, cut its funding. In February 2005, Bush's 2006 budget proposal called for federal spending on Medicaid to be cut by $45-$60 billion over the next decade, and for cuts in payments for prescription drugs and more "flexibility" on benefits. Medicaid "is not financially sustainable," new HHS Secretary MICHAEL LEAVITT asserted. (They never say that about, say, military spending, do they?) Fraud and mismanagement were rampant in Medicaid, the Bushies also alleged. The truth? Think you can *handle* the truth? Medicaid costs were both lower than, and growing less than half as fast as, private health insurance on a per-person basis. And less than 0.07 percent of Medicaid spending in 2003 was attributable to fraud, according to the Centers for Medicare and Medicaid Services.

"HOMELAND" INSECURITY: *"MORE VULNERABLE THAN EVER"*

"[We are] taking every possible step to protect our country from danger," said Bush repeatedly after **September 11.** "We'll spend what's needed to protect the homeland." They weren't. They didn't. He lied. Three and a half years after 9/11, the *New York Times* reported,

> The nation's chemical plants are still a horrific accident waiting to happen. Nuclear material that could be made into a 'dirty bomb,' or even a nuclear device, and set off in an American city remains too accessible to terrorists. Critical tasks, from inspecting shipping containers to upgrading defenses against biological weapons, are being done poorly or not at all . . . The Bush administration and Congress have been reluctant to provide the necessary money—even while they are furiously reducing revenue with tax cuts. The funds that are available are often misdirected. And Washington has caved to pressure from interest groups, like the chemical industry, that have fought

increased security measures. Most of all, the government has failed to lay out a broad strategy for making the nation more secure.[131]

Or as outgoing AG JOHN ASHCROFT announced in November 2004, "The objective of securing the safety of Americans" from terror "has been achieved."

After 9/11, the administration lost no time losing time:

- In October 2001, the White House cut an FBI emergency request for $1.5 billion for counterterrorism by nearly two-thirds, to $531 million. Result: 50–100 percent cuts in improvements in computer networking, foreign language intercepts, cyber-security, and information-sharing capabilities—the very weaknesses that permitted 9/11.
- In November 2001, Bush flatly refused a bipartisan delegation's plea for about $10 billion for top-security priorities like ports and nuclear sites.
- In December 2001, budget amendments that would have increased FBI funding "failed under the threat of a Bush veto if [Congress's] package exceeded $20 billion," the *Washington Post* reported.
- Despite numerous reports in 2002 highlighting homeland security deficiencies, in February 2003 Bush proposed to essentially freeze funding. When Senate Democrats proposed adding $1.75 billion for air cargo screening, port and transportation security, and first responders (police, fire, and emergency medical personnel), the package was defeated on a mostly party-line vote.

- Bush opposed the creation of a DEPARTMENT OF HOME-
LAND SECURITY (DHS) for as long as he could, delaying
its launch until February 2003. TOM RIDGE, Bush's
appointee to head DHS, had said, "I'd probably rec-
ommend that [Bush] veto" any bill to create such a
department. In 2004, the GAO concluded the administration was underfunding DHS (by at least $14 billion,
many experts said) and not adequately protecting
America.
- In December 2003, the GOP-led GILMORE COMMISSION on
domestic readiness said momentum for security had
"waned," and blamed the government for inspiring
complacency.
- DHS's former inspector, CLARK KENT ERVIN (whose parents were reportedly *Superman* fans), warned in 2004
that the department "is a dysfunctional, poorly managed bureaucracy that has failed to plug serious holes
in the nation's safety net," and said department officials "have wasted millions of dollars because of
'chaotic and disorganized' accounting practices" and
"lavish spending on social occasions and employee
bonuses," *USA Today* reported. The White House
decided not to renominate Ervin—who was regarded
as an "aggressive overseer" and "a standout among
inspectors general"—when his one-year recess
appointment expired in December 2004. No explanation was given.

Why this stubborn, persistent neglect of a president's
highest priority—defending the country's security? As *The
Nation*'s David Corn noted, perhaps more than 90 percent of

America's crucial infrastructure was in the hands of commercial interests. And the administration "has made it very clear it is not interested in regulation" of business, said former national security official Dr. Stephen Flynn of the Council on Foreign Relations. The Bushies' view, Flynn told Corn, is that homeland security "costs too much money and involves too much government, so we have to go straight to the source . . . But we'll never succeed at eliminating these problems at the source . . . It's a fool's game."

Airport screening. In 2003, Congressional Republicans forced the elimination of up to 10,000 airport screeners, or more than 18 percent of the federal force. During tests in November 2003, undercover investigators were able to sneak explosives, guns, and knives past security screeners at 15 airports. Government reports in 2004 and 2005 concluded that airport security remained no better than before 9/11. As of late 2004, only eight of the nation's 440 commercial airports had the new baggage-screening machines already in use in places like the White House. Installing them at all the airports would cost $5 billion (or less than 3 percent of the cost to date of the Iraq war); Bush requested one-twentieth that amount for screening equipment in 2004.

Air cargo. The Transportation Security Administration (TSA) estimated the chance of terrorists planning to place a bomb in the cargo of a U.S. passenger plane at 35 to 65 percent.[132] In 2003, the Senate—pressured by the aviation industry and the White House—blocked a Democrat-sponsored amendment requiring screening of cargo shipped on passenger planes, 95 percent of which still went unscreened in 2004.

Air marshals. In July 2003, one day before the DHS issued a hijacking warning, the TSA asked Congress for permission to reduce its air marshal program by 20 percent. TSA also told air marshals to cancel long flights requiring hotel stays due to "monetary considerations." Perhaps it *was* best not to leave them unsupervised overnight: In the previous year, federal air marshals tested positive for alcohol or drugs while on duty, lost their weapons, and falsified information.

Bioterror defense. In the winter of 2004–2005, the U.S. proved unprepared to supply flu vaccine, let alone cope with biowar agents such as anthrax or plague bacteria. A Pentagon report commissioned following the fall 2001 anthrax letter attacks, completed in April 2002, and released (heavily censored) only in March 2004 concluded that the nation remained woefully ill-prepared to detect and respond to bioterrorism.

Borders. In December 2004, former DHS inspector general Ervin told *USA Today* that immigration and customs investigators were hampered in their efforts to track down illegal immigrants because they often lacked gas money for their cars. In March 2004, DHS announced a hiring freeze for two of its three front-line units, Customs and Border Protection and Immigration and Customs Enforcement. The third, the Citizenship and Immigration Service, already had a freeze in effect.

- Suspected terrorists had long been entering the U.S. from Canada. In 2003, only 1,000 border agents patrolled the 5,000-mile-long U.S.-Canadian border, compared to 9,500 patrolling the 2,000-mile Mexican border. Extensive portions of the northern border also remained devoid of any physical security, electronic monitoring, or aerial surveillance. Canadian intelligence acknowledged that Al Qaeda maintained cells and personnel in Canada with "the capability and conviction" to carry out attacks.[133]

- Because of underfunding, the Border Patrol still lacked technology for quick, automated checks of fingerprints against FBI files, leaving the U.S. "vulnerable to infiltration by known criminals and terrorists," the *New York Times* noted. In 2005, immigration officials still did not have a workable system for tracking visitors' arrivals and departures.

- In a test of the nation's passport processing system in June 2005, the names of more than 30 wanted criminals, including nine murder suspects and one person on the FBI's most-wanted list, did not trigger any warnings. Passport applications were not routinely checked against lists of criminals and suspected terrorists. A former State Department security official said "he was asked by his bosses to terminate investigations into more than 400 cases" involving documents forged by crime rings, the *New York Times* reported, "because the department did not have enough staff to complete the inquiries." Enjoy your $300 (or $50,000) Bush tax cut.

Chemical plants. The army surgeon general ranked potential attacks on chemical plants second only to bioterrorism as the top homeland security threat. An attack on any one of 823 plants and sites could endanger more than a million people; 15,000 other chemical sites were possible targets. Yet three and a half years after 9/11, security at these sites remained porous to nonexistent, and there was still no federal plan to improve it. The industry, and therefore the White House, opposed anything more than "voluntary regulations"—which were not deemed acceptable for airports or nuclear plants. (Asked about the policy, an aide to Tom Ridge replied that on 9/11 *"it was not chemical plants that were blown up"!* That's all we wanted, an explanation.)

First responders. Less than a year after 9/11, Bush threatened to veto increased funding for first responders. In 2003, the Council on Foreign Relations reported that the U.S. "is drastically underfunding local emergency responders and remains dangerously unprepared to handle a catastrophic attack." Most public health labs lacked the personnel or equipment to respond to a chemical or biological attack. Most fire departments were understaffed and underequipped, while cuts in federal aid to police departments were pushing them "to the breaking point."

Bush heard the alarm and responded: His 2005 budget *cut* aid to state and local law enforcement by 32 percent; cut grants for fire departments to purchase equipment by $250 million; provided no funding for the Staffing for Adequate Fire and Emergency Response (SAFER) program; eliminated funding to help emergency medical personnel prepare for radiological and other terrorist attacks; eliminated grants meant to redress the inability of police and firefighters' radios to communicate with each other on 9/11; and cut $97 million from the Community Oriented Policing Services (COPS) program—Clinton's 1996 crime bill—which sought to put 100,000 police officers on the streets. Overall, the budget cut first responder funding by $1.57 billion, or 32 percent.[134]

Hazardous Waste Transport. This refers not to Air Force One but to the millions of tons of highly toxic chemicals and nuclear waste that are shipped by railroad and truck, much of it through or near densely populated areas, where a crash involving a tanker car carrying chlorine, for example, could kill 100,000 people in 30 minutes. Regulation of such transport "remains woefully inadequate," the *New York Times* reported in February 2005.

Intelligence Sharing. One of the main purposes of creating the DHS was to remedy the disastrous pre-9/11 failures in intelligence sharing between the FBI, CIA, and other agencies by coordinating it through one agency. Instead, an intelligence source told *National Journal*, "that whole effort has been gutted" by the White House's creation of two competing entities, the CIA's Terrorist Threat Integration Center and the FBI's Terrorist Screening Center, whose responsibilities "overlap with, duplicate, or even trump" those of DHS. "We now have more agencies and organizations in the counter-terrorism game than ever before," the GOP-controlled Senate Appropriations Committee complained in 2004.

They hate us for our miniature golf? Three years after 9/11, the comprehensive, reliable terrorist watch list that Bush had called "a priority" still had not been created. Neither had a national fingerprint database or a comprehensive list of potential terrorist targets. (The list in progress was described as "a haphazard compilation that includes water parks and miniature golf courses but omits some major sites in need of security.") DHS's inspector general blamed a lack of "leadership and oversight."

Nuclear Materials. Fears of terrorist attack with a nuclear device or a more easily made "dirty bomb," were well founded: Bin Laden declared acquisition of nuclear weapons to be a religious duty. There had been at least 18 thefts worldwide of highly enriched uranium and plutonium. Yet the administration chose to spend hundreds of billions of dollars to go after WMDs that weren't there, but only $1 billion a year to secure loose, and real, nuclear materials, in countries of the former Soviet Union in particular. Bush's 2005 budget *cut* roughly 9 percent from programs for that purpose. P.S.: In late 2004 **Dick**'s firm, Halliburton, lost track of a 185-pound container of radioactive material—the kind used in dirty bombs—that it was importing and failed to report the loss for four months, in violation of federal regulations.[135]

Nuclear Power Plants. Bush's 2005 budget provided no specific resources for improving security at the country's 104 nuclear power plants, many of which are near major population centers.

Ports. "For all the concern about safety at the nation's airports," the *Los Angeles Times* noted, the ports "may now present an even greater threat. Since Sept. 11, they have received far less security funding than airports, yet they continue to process far more cargo—more than 9.5 million containers a year," of which only about 2 percent were inspected. "For the cost of two F-22 fighter jets and three days of combat in Iraq, the nation's ports could be secured against terror," said Stephen Flynn, a terrorism expert and retired coast guard commander. Well, tell Bush. In 2003, port authorities and the coast guard pleaded for $1 billion to improve port security and said $7.5 billion was needed over ten years. The administration promised $300 million. It then cut port security grants from $125 million in 2004 to $46 million in 2005. Meanwhile, it lavished billions on MISSILE DEFENSE, even though the CIA had said the U.S. was more likely to be attacked with a WMD smuggled into the country aboard a ship than one delivered by a ballistic missile, which it called one of the *least* likely forms of attack.

Postal security. The U.S. Postal Service (USPS) sought $779 million in 2005 for biodetection technology to safeguard against anthrax and ricin attacks through the mail, as in fall 2001. They didn't get it, because the White House didn't *get it.* (Bush's proposed USPS budget: $37 million.)

Rail security. Bush's 2005 budget allocation for rail security was $100 million, "equal to what the U.S. spends on eight typical hours in Iraq, far short of the billions experts say are needed," the *Progress Report* noted.

Kerik: Bush's unerring instincts. As blogger Josh Marshall observed, in December 2004, the White House named former New York City Police Commissioner and Correction Commissioner BERNARD KERIK to replace Ridge as DHS secretary apparently despite knowing that: (1) In 1998 a warrant was issued for Kerik's arrest in connection to unpaid bills on his condo. (2) While in office he accepted thousands of dollars in illegal gifts, including from an allegedly mob-connected city contractor whom he had recommended. (3) After leaving his police commissioner's job, Kerik joined the board of stun gun manufacturer Taser—a NYC and DHS supplier—and received more than $6 million in stock options. He sold the stock shortly before a report came out on Taser-related deaths. (4) While correction commissioner, Kerik carried on two simultaneous extramarital affairs, one of them with a subordinate. (5) He was expelled from Saudi Arabia in 1984 amid allegations that he used his position as security investigator for a hospital complex to spy on women with whom the hospital administrator was romantically involved, among other abuses. (6) In May 2003, Kerik went to Iraq to take charge of security and train an Iraqi police force. He returned home just two months later—and within days of the first large-scale terrorist attacks. His abrupt departure was never explained.[136] Perhaps he had finished creating security in Iraq?

The nomination was withdrawn *only*, the White House insisted, because Kerik may have employed an illegal alien as a nanny. Oh: The man in charge of vetting Kerik's background was White House counsel ALBERTO GONZALES, whom Bush was about to name Attorney General.

HUMAN RIGHTS AND PRISONER "ABUSE"

The United States is committed to the world-wide elimination of torture and we are leading this fight by example.

—George W. Bush, 6/26/03

Because we acted, Saddam's torture chambers are closed.
—George W. Bush, May 2004

That very week in May 2004, around the world, photographs of prisoners hooded and attached to electrodes, lying naked on the floor, threatened with dogs and forced into mock-sexual positions by grinning U.S. soldiers at ABU GHRAIB prison in **Iraq** became symbolic of U.S. foreign policy and human rights policy, thanks to the incompetence and immorality of top Bush officials. Here was the U.S. meting out treatment to prisoners that was worthy of the tyranny we were purportedly fighting to banish, and that violated U.S. and international law. The images "shocked us into remembering that real obscenity is distinct from the revelation of Janet Jackson's right breast" (see **Values**), wrote the *New York Times*'s Frank Rich. The U.S. "has been humiliated to a point where government officials could not release this year's international human rights report," the *Times* noted, "for fear of being scoffed at by the rest of the world."

Like every other Bush scandal, this one soon faded from America's consciousness, but the damage to America's honor and moral standing was done. "The big winners," wrote *The Nation*'s Katha Pollitt, "as with so many steps taken by this Administration for our supposed protection . . . are Islamists and Al Qaeda."

"Heads will roll for this," you said? No, no, just *tails*.

The Bushies' lies about Abu Ghraib began the moment CBS broadcast the sickening photos (which the network withheld for two weeks at the request of the chairman of the joint chiefs of staff, and only aired when the *New Yorker* was about to run a report). Contrary to their repeated claims, the "abuse"—which the International Red Cross described less nicely as "torture"—was widespread across U.S. prisons in Iraq, Afghanistan, Cuba, and elsewhere, not "an exceptional, isolated" case, as DONALD RUMSFELD called it. Top White House and Pentagon officials knew of it long before it became public—indeed, had sanctioned and encouraged it—then tried to cover up their responsibility by putting all the blame on a few low-ranking soldiers and blocking any independent investigation. The abuses were in fact rooted in the most fundamental Bush doctrines, which arrogated virtually unlimited **presidential power**. The Bushies either didn't know or care what Sen. John McCain (R-AZ), a former prisoner-of-war, knew and said: "The thing that separates us from the enemy [or doesn't] is our respect for human rights."

Rumsfeld *was* appalled by the *photos*: "People are running around with digital cameras and taking these unbelievable photographs and then passing them off, against the law, to the media, to our surprise," he complained. As comedian Jon Stewart put it: "If I've said it once, I've said it a thousand times—we've got to find these weapons of mass documentation." The always amazing Sen. JAMES INHOFE (R-OK) confessed he was "more outraged by the outrage" than by the treatment of prisoners.

"The rule more than the exception." Over the following months, dozens of well-documented incidents of torture came to light from all over what America-haters called the U.S. gulag. Prisoners in Iraq were beaten, strangled, burned, forced to masturbate while wearing panties over their heads, and sodomized with a toilet plunger. ("Abuse"?) Their wives and mothers were threatened. In August 2004, an investigation by Scotland's *Sunday Herald* alleged that coalition forces were holding more than 100 children as young as ten in jails across Iraq, where they were being subjected to rape and torture.[137] Detainees at the U.S. base in GUANTANAMO BAY, CUBA, were shocked with electric guns, left in very hot or cold rooms, prevented from sleeping, given forced enemas, and chained in fetal positions on bare floors for up to 24 hours with no food or water and left to soil themselves. In AFGHANISTAN, two prisoners who died in U.S. custody in December 2002 "were chained to the ceiling, kicked and beaten by American soldiers in sustained assaults [over a five-day period] that caused their deaths," according to army reports. The reports "also make clear that the abuse . . . went far beyond the two killings," confirming previous Human Rights Watch reports that "scores of other detainees were beaten at Bagram and Kandahar bases [in Afghanistan] from early 2002 on" and that abuse was "the rule more than the exception."[138]

Crimes against humanity. The Geneva Conventions explicitly prohibit mistreatment of prisoners of war or civilians detained in a war, *regardless of the circumstances;* breaches of these rules are war crimes. The abuses of U.S. detainees might rise to the level of crimes against humanity, a Yale legal expert told the *New York Times.*

By March 2005, the army was investigating 308 allegations

of torture or other mistreatment of detainees, including 68 deaths. Of these, at least 26 were possible criminal homicides connected with interrogations—only one of which occurred at Abu Ghraib. Another nine Iraqi detainees had died in Marine Corps custody. Between 35,000 and 100,000 Iraqi civilians whom Bush's war liberated from life might also be said to have had their human rights violated. In a study by Physicians for Human Rights in May 2004, 7 percent of Iraqis surveyed reported attempting suicide in the previous year (a rate 437 times the global average) and 27 percent reported seriously contemplating it—"this in a society that places a tremendous stigma on suicide," the *American Prospect* noted. *Almost half of all households* "had someone who was tortured, disappeared, or abused," the study's author said.

Shocked, shocked! The White House claimed senior officials were unaware of the abuses until the Abu Ghraib photos were aired. In fact, the International Red Cross, Amnesty International, Human Rights Watch, and Human Rights First had all complained for months to senior U.S. officials, including the head of the occupation authority, PAUL BREMER, and National Security Adviser CONDOLEEZZA RICE. "Unfortunately," an Amnesty spokeswoman said of the Bushies, "we have not gotten the impression they've dealt with these issues very seriously."

"Methodically and carefully planned." The Abu Ghraib scandal did not put an end to such practices. A Red Cross report based on a June 2004 visit to Guantanamo suggested that conditions there, which were widely thought to be much better than at Abu Ghraib, were worse. Some detainees had been held there without charges for three years, under the Bush policy that denied them Constitutional or Geneva Convention protections just by naming them "enemy combatants" rather than prisoners of war. Tactics used at "Gitmo" included "humiliating acts, solitary confinement, temperature extremes, use of forced positions as well as beatings," according to the report. Doctors and medical workers allegedly helped interrogators by instructing them on thresholds of pain and on prisoners' particular weaknesses and by providing access to their medical files— a "flagrant violation of medical ethics" and of the Geneva Conventions. "The construction of such a system . . . cannot be considered other than *an intentional system of cruel, unusual and degrading treatment and a form of torture*," the Red Cross concluded (emphasis added). The Defense Department (DOD) dismissed the charges as a "point of view" not shared by the White House.

The report belied the notion that the Abu Ghraib "abuses" had resulted merely from the poor training and insufficient numbers of guards, the unexpectedly large number of prisoners due to the "unexpected" (in fact, widely predicted) insurgency, and general wartime disorder: Guantanamo was properly staffed and supervised, "methodically and carefully planned," legal expert Leila Sadat noted in *Salon*. "All of this looks pretty clearly like a deliberate policy." Guantanamo, she said, "has come to symbolize [internationally] this attempt by the U.S. to set up law-free zones."[139]

"Special operating procedures." In fact, "Gitmo" was apparently the model for Abu Ghraib. In 2003, Army MAJ.

GEN. GEOFFREY MILLER, who then ran the Guantanamo prison complex, headed a team that visited Iraq and suggested "special operating procedures" (oh, the antiseptic bureaucratese from which flow atrocities!) in which military prison guards would be "an enabler for interrogation." This led to orders to Abu Ghraib guards to "soften up" inmates by depriving them of sleep and subjecting them to pain and humiliation—to create "physical and mental conditions for favorable interrogation," in the words of Maj. Gen. Antonio Taguba, who conducted an inquiry. The TAGUBA REPORT, completed in May 2004, cited "numerous incidents of sadistic, blatant and wanton criminal abuses" at Abu Ghraib between October and December 2003—and estimated that more than 60 percent of the detainees were civilians "of no intelligence value." Taguba also reported that military commanders eased the rules four times in 2003 to permit guards to use "lethal force" on prisoners. Guess who was sent to Iraq *after* these revelations to overhaul the prison system? Maj. Gen. Geoffrey Miller!

None of these reports prevented "Rumsfeld" (gratuitous sneer quotes) from testifying that he "cannot conceive" that the Abu Ghraib guards thought their actions were condoned or encouraged.

FBI agents witnessed torture and made it widely known to top officials, according to FBI memoranda obtained by the ACLU. One June 2004 memo describing "serious physical abuses of civilian detainees" in Iraq was addressed to FBI director ROBERT MUELLER and other senior bureau officials and was labeled "Urgent." Another, written by an FBI counterterrorism expert at Guantanamo to the army's chief law enforcement officer in July 2004, "said FBI officials complained about the pattern of abusive techniques to top DOD attorneys in January 2003, and it appeared that nothing was done," AP reported. Another "suggested President Bush personally signed off on some, more harsh interrogation techniques in an executive order."[140] Agents said they saw military interrogators both in Iraq and at Guantanamo pose as FBI agents while abusing detainees so that if the stories ever got out, the FBI would be blamed, not the DOD.[141]

Defense personnel in Iraq who complained about abuses were threatened and harassed by special forces who allegedly took part in them. The special forces also ordered defense personnel "not to talk to anyone" in the U.S. about what they saw, said one memo written by the Defense Intelligence Agency chief, who complained to his Pentagon bosses about the harassment.[142]

These techniques had not produced any useful intelligence, but *had* destroyed any chance of prosecuting the individuals because the coerced evidence would be thrown out in court, FBI memos said. "The only thing that torture guarantees is pain," a retired FBI agent who taught interrogation techniques to the military told AP.

FOLLOW THE MEMOS: "No limits." But a trail of secret White House, Pentagon, and Justice Department (DOJ) memos that came to light after May 2004 connected Abu Ghraib more directly to top officials who drafted the underlying Bush policies.

The most basic of these policy decisions was that in the name of the "war on terror," the administration could do anything it wanted. Just two weeks after **September 11**, *Newsweek* reported, a secret DOJ memo to the White House made the unprecedented assertion that there were effectively "no limits" on the president's authority to wage war "against terrorist organizations or the States that harbor or support them, whether or not they can be linked to the specific terrorist incidents of Sept. 11." That kind of set the tone.

Geneva found "quaint." (Not the town.) In January 2002, White House counsel and future AG ALBERTO GONZALES advised Bush in a memo that Al Qaeda and Taliban suspects could be exempted from the Third Geneva Convention ban on torture and coercion, which he described as "obsolete" and "quaint." As critics noted, enemies might adopt similar policies, label *our* soldiers "unlawful combatants" or even "terrorists," and exempt *them* from Geneva protections. The move, wrote Secretary of State COLIN POWELL in a counter-memo, "will reverse over a century of U.S. policy and practice"; have "immediate adverse consequences for our conduct of foreign policy"; "undermine public support among critical allies, making military cooperation more difficult to sustain; [and cause] legal problems with extradition" of terror suspects to the U.S. Gonzales's advice prevailed.

- In July 2002, Gonzales and other government lawyers met to discuss what interrogation techniques the U.S. might get away with. Among those discussed were mock burials and "waterboarding," or making a suspect think he's drowning. The lawyers "discussed in great detail how to legally justify such methods."[143]

The "torture memo." In August 2002, the DOJ, under Gonzales's supervision, drafted a memo advising Bush that the president's powers "were so expansive that he and his surrogates were not bound by congressional laws or international treaties proscribing torture," *Newsweek* reported. The memo said torture "may be justified" and that only "the pain accompanying serious physical injury, such as organ failure, impairment of bodily function, or even death" constitute torture—mere "cruel, inhuman or degrading" treatment does not. The memo shocked military lawyers (Judge Advocates General). "Every flag JAG lodged complaints," a senior Pentagon official told the *Washington Post*. "It's really unprecedented," one JAG said. "Once you start telling people it's okay to break the law, there's no telling where they might stop." The memo was signed by the head of the DOJ's Office of Legal Counsel, JAY BYBEE, whom Bush later named an appellate judge. Although the White House repudiated the memo, its rules remained in effect.

The August 2002 memo became the basis for new DOD guidelines for "exceptional interrogations," as they were called in a March 2003 Pentagon report ordered by von Rumsfeld. The report said domestic and international prohibitions against torture were "inapplicable" to interrogations undertaken under the president's authority, and/or at Guantanamo. Pentagon lawyers "examined at least 35 interrogation techniques, and Rumsfeld later approved using 24 of them in a classified directive" in April 2003, the *Washington Post* reported. "The Pentagon has refused to make public the 24 interrogation procedures."

International expertise. The military farmed out interrogation work to unaccountable private contractors, including Serbian mercenaries and confessed members of South African pro-apartheid death squads[144]—just another part of the Bushies' fanatic drive to privatize war *and* peace. That "inexplicable chain of shifted responsibility violated not just any sort of common sense, but also military rules," the *New York Times* commented.

"Zero tolerance—except for . . . and . . . and . . ." After promising a "no tolerance" policy on torture in the wake of Abu Ghraib, the White House succeeded in removing from the December 2004 **intelligence** reform bill—after it passed a 96–2 Senate vote—restrictions on intelligence officers participating in torture and requirements for the CIA and Pentagon to report to Congress about the methods they were using. Shortly after, Gonzales told senators that CIA officials and other nonmilitary personnel "fall outside the bounds of a 2002 directive issued by President Bush that pledged the humane treatment of prisoners in American custody" and that a separate Congressional ban on cruel, unusual, and inhumane treatment has "a limited reach."

Investigating themselves. The Abu Ghraib scandal brought administration promises of "a full investigation and corrective actions." But "as anyone who'd watched the proceedings of the 9/11 Commission could have predicted," wrote Ron Reagan, "what followed was the usual administration strategy of stonewalling, obstruction, and obfuscation." The investigations were mostly in-house Pentagon probes, which don't require sworn testimony and don't have subpoena power; and all were limited in scope. No military intelligence personnel were charged, even though they allegedly gave the orders. No investigation of the roles of top authorities in the U.S. Central Command or at the Pentagon was authorized. The Taguba report, though widely praised, did not investigate military intelligence, nor did Taguba interview officers above the level of brigade commander. The commander of U.S. forces in Iraq, LT. GEN. RICARDO SANCHEZ, who ordered the inquiry—and who the former supervisor of U.S. prisons in Iraq said should share the blame for Abu Ghraib—was not interviewed.

"I really doubt whether the Defense Department can investigate itself, because there's a possibility the secretary himself authorized certain actions," a retired four-star army general told the *Washington Post*. "This cries out for an out-side commission." The administration didn't think so, nor did the congressional GOP leaders. By March 2005, eight low-ranking soldiers had been convicted of crimes in the deaths of prisoners in U.S. custody. Most ended up receiving only "nonjudicial punishments," which carry a maximum of 30 days confinement.

Punishment by promotion. In the fine old Bush tradition of punishing truth tellers, rewarding failure and abuse of power, and *never* admitting to a mistake, LT. GEN. SANCHEZ, who approved harsh interrogation methods and authorized the presence of attack dogs during interrogations, was promptly promoted to four-star general—a move that a conservative Cato Institute scholar called "one more thumb in the eye of the Iraqis and the Arab world." MAJ. GEN. GEOFFREY MILLER, who was "credited" with bringing Guantanamo's methods to

Abu Ghraib, was made senior commander in charge of detention operations in Iraq. MAJ. GEN. BARBARA FAST, the highest-ranking intelligence officer tied to the Abu Ghraib scandal, was put in charge of the U.S. Army's main interrogation training facility at Fort Huachuca, Arizona. Cheney or Rove or Bush picked ALBERTO GONZALES, the White House's legal justifier of human rights abuses, to be the nation's top law enforcement officer. DONALD RUMSFELD, whose failure to anticipate and prepare for the insurgency in Iraq led to the overflowing and understaffed prisons—and who said he offered to resign three times—was kept on. As were Cheney and Bush, on whom ultimate responsibility for the unnecessary and illegal war and its mismanagement rested.

Above the law. In June 2004, following a Supreme Court ruling that the detainees at Guantanamo had the right to challenge their detentions in the U.S. court system, the Pentagon established MILITARY TRIBUNALS to review their cases. In January 2005, D.C. District Court Judge Joyce Hens Green ruled that these tribunals failed to comply with the Supreme Court ruling by, among things, allowing the introduction of testimony obtained under torture and denying them the right to a lawyer. Prisoners, she wrote, were entitled to the protection of the U.S. Constitution and the Geneva Convention *even during the war on terror, which "cannot negate the existence of the most basic fundamental rights for which the people of this country have fought and died for well over 200 years."* Nothing, she noted, authorizes the president "to rule by fiat that an entire group of fighters" fell outside the Third Geneva Convention. The administration appealed the decision.

Handover of torture. Torture remained routine in Iraqi jails after an Iraqi interim government took over in June 2004. International police advisors, mostly Americans, had turned a blind eye to Iraqi abuse, according to a Human Rights Watch report in January 2005, which also cited arbitrary arrest and other violations of the rights of political opponents by Iraq's intelligence service, as well as improper treatment of child detainees. "The people of Iraq were promised something better than this" after Saddam Hussein, a spokeswoman said.

Outsourcing torture. Under the broad authority of a secret directive signed by Bush within days of 9/11, the *Washington Post* reported, the CIA quietly began seeking "secure locations abroad where it could detain and interrogate captives without risk of discovery, and without having to give them access to legal proceedings," while concealing them from the Red Cross and other authorities. "It's not rendering to justice, it's kidnapping," a CIA officer who was involved in the practice told the *New York Times*. The bureaucratic term was "EXTRAORDINARY RENDITION"—defined by an unnamed intelligence official as: "We don't kick the s— out of them. We send them to other countries so they can kick the s— out of them."[145] Countries where they have even fewer scruples about their methods and no free press to complain about them, and from which the prisoners would never escape to tell about their U.S. captivity; countries like Egypt, Pakistan, Yemen, Saudi Arabia, Jordan, Syria—each of which had long been condemned by the State Department for widespread and habitual use of torture.

Former prisoners claimed that after their transfers, they

were "beaten, shackled, humiliated, subjected to electric shocks, and otherwise mistreated during their long detention in foreign prisons before being released without being charged."[146] The *New York Times* cited "a half-dozen current and former government officials" who said the administration was "turning a blind eye to torture."

The UN Convention Against Torture, which the U.S. signed, bars states from sending anyone to a country "where there are substantial grounds for believing that he would be in danger of being subjected to torture." But after Abu Ghraib, the administration only stepped up efforts to "legalize" the practice:

- In March 2004, a secret DOJ memo authorized the CIA to transfer prisoners, including civilians, out of Iraq for interrogation. According to the Geneva Convention, such transfers are "a grave breach" of the treaty—and thus, according to a cautionary footnote in the DOJ memo itself, a "war crime" under U.S. federal law.

- During his confirmation hearings in January 2005, ALBERTO GONZALES told Congress the U.S. would not "transfer individuals to countries where we believe they *likely* will be tortured" (emphasis added). Two months later, Gonzales—now safely confirmed as AG—changed his wording to "countries where *we believe or we know* that they're *going to be* tortured"—opening up "wide, wide wiggle room," *Salon* noted.

- In March 2005, the Pentagon asked the State Department to help it ship hundreds of Guantanamo detainees to Saudi Arabia, Yemen, and Afghanistan. The Pentagon had already acknowledged transferring 62 Guantanamo prisoners to Pakistan, Morocco, Saudi Arabia, and Kuwait—all of which the State Department had identified as practicing torture in their prisons.

Throwing away the keys. In January 2005 the *Washington Post* reported that the administration was preparing plans for LIFETIME DETENTION for "hundreds of people now in military and CIA custody whom the government does not have enough evidence to charge in courts" or in a military tribunal, and whom "the government believes have no more intelligence to share." So: Not enough evidence to be charged + no intelligence to share = lifetime imprisonment.

U.S. prisons. Because you don't have to be a terror suspect to be treated like one. "Physical and sexual abuse of prisoners, similar to what has been uncovered in Iraq, takes place in American prisons with little public knowledge or concern," the *New York Times* reported in May 2004. Corrections experts said some of the worst abuses occurred in TEXAS, "whose prisons were under a federal consent decree during much of the time President Bush was governor because of crowding and violence by guards against inmates," and because guards had been "allowing inmate gang leaders to buy and sell other inmates as slaves for sex."[147]

Made in the USA. The man Ashcroft picked in 2003 to rebuild Iraq's jails after the U.S. invasion, reopen ABU GHRAIB, and train its guards was private prison company executive LANE MCCOTTER. (Foreign readers: Yes, we let private companies run prisons for profit—which can be maximized by, for example, skimping on inmates' food.) Ashcroft may have known of McCotter because at the time, one of his jails was under investigation by the DOJ for unsafe conditions and lack of medical care for inmates. Previously, McCotter had resigned under pressure as director of the Utah Department of Corrections in 1997 after an inmate who suffered from schizophrenia "died while shackled to a restraining chair for 16 hours . . . naked the whole time."[148] Perhaps when they offered to put McCotter in charge "of Iraq," he thought they said "of a *rack*."

HURRICANE KATRINA

Neither the Bush administration's pre-**September 11** neglect of terrorism, nor its shocking, post-9/11 underfunding of **homeland security**, nor its disastrous lack of security preparations for post-invasion **Iraq** quite brought home the Bushies' profound lack of interest in basic government functions and urgent domestic needs—except the urgent need for upper-income tax cuts—in time for voters to run Bush out of town in 2004.

With Hurricane Katrina in August–September 2005—the worst "natural" disaster in the U.S. since at least the 1906 San Francisco earthquake—the truth may have finally sunk in: If it doesn't benefit big business, big contributors, the wealthy, or other key special interest groups, if it's merely about helping those most in need, it simply isn't on the Bush agenda. From the lack of preparation for the hurricane to the slow and bungled response, the utterly unqualified political cronies who were in charge, and the instant awarding of no-bid reconstruction contracts to the usual handful of politically connected firms (see **War Profiteering**), the disaster *was* the Bush administration writ, well, not so small.

Hitherto—despite 9/11, Iraq, staggering budget deficits, huge job losses, and growing poverty and inequality—and despite years of preaching personal responsibility—Bush still couldn't think of a single mistake he had made as president. Three weeks after Katrina struck, with the death toll rising past 800 and hundreds of thousands left homeless and jobless, Bush "took responsibility" for the first time in his presidency for something that had gone wrong. Yet even now, he remained as deceptive and weasely as ever. "*To the extent* the federal government didn't fully do its job right," he said (emphasis added)—as though that "extent" was debatable—"I take responsibility." (Meaning what, exactly? Not, alas, his resignation.) And, just as with his missing WMDs in Iraq, Bush promised to "*find out* what went wrong"—as though that had nothing to do with years of Republican, anti-government government—"and what went right," as though much of anything did:

Contract on America. In 1995, the Republicans, led by Newt Gingrich, did away with the congressional Office of Technology Assessment (OTA), which developed federal plans for flood management.

Wetlands destruction. The Gulf Coast wetlands form a natural buffer that slows hurricanes down as they approach from sea. After taking office in 2001, Bush reneged on his promise to uphold the "no net loss" wetland policy his father initiated. In 2003, he rolled back Clinton wetland policies and ordered federal agencies to stop protecting as many as 20 million acres of wetlands from developers.

Hot air, hot water. Bush also reneged on his 2000 campaign promise to regulate carbon dioxide emissions, the main human cause of **global warming,** and, just a week before Katrina, "released new CAFE standards that actually encourage automakers to produce bigger, less fuel efficient vehicles, while preventing states from taking strong, progressive action to reverse global warming."[149] (See **Energy**.) According to a recent Massachusetts Institute of Technology analysis, a 50 percent increase in the duration and intensity of major storms in the Atlantic and Pacific since the 1970s is "closely linked to increases in the average temperatures of the ocean surface" which "correspond to increases in global average atmospheric temperatures during the same period."

"Nobody could have predicted" terrorists would use hijacked airplanes as missiles, Bush and Rice lied after **September 11**. And now, four days after Katrina hit the Gulf Coast and drowned New Orleans, Bush claimed nobody had expected the levees to fail. In fact, there had been repeated warnings about exactly that risk. In 2001, the Federal Emergency Management Agency (FEMA) ranked a major hurricane strike on New Orleans as "among the three likeliest, most catastrophic disasters facing this country," directly behind a terrorist strike on New York City. "The New Orleans hurricane scenario may be the deadliest of all," the *Houston Chronicle* wrote. "New Orleans was the No.1 disaster we were talking about," a former FEMA official said.

You're on your own now, people. In 2001, Bush's first FEMA director, JOE ALLBAUGH—a corporate consultant and Bush's campaign manager in 2000—told Congress: "It is not the role of the federal government to tell a community what it needs to do to protect its citizens and infrastructure. . . . [W]e are asking that [the states] take a more appropriate degree of fiscal responsibility to protect themselves. . . . Federal disaster assistance may have evolved into . . . an oversized entitlement program."

FEMA's ~~Bushit~~ horseshit leadership. The Bush administration quickly set about stripping FEMA of power, money, and competent staff. Bush "chose to make FEMA a dumping ground for unqualified cronies—a sure sign that he wanted to hasten the degradation of an agency that conservative Republicans have long considered an evil of big government," the *New York Times* noted.

Allbaugh's replacement (and college roommate), MICHAEL BROWN, spent the previous 11 years as commissioner of judges and stewards for the International Arabian Horse Association (from which he had been canned "after a spate of lawsuits over alleged supervision failures," the *Boston Herald* reported). The number two and three FEMA officials had been Bush campaign "advance men"—event planners and press flaks. FEMA's "upper ranks are mostly staffed with people who share two traits," wrote Bloomberg News: "loyalty to [Bush] and little or no background in emergency management." So as the administration's failed response to Katrina became evident, "[it wasn't] really all that surprising that the officials who run FEMA are stressing that all-important emergency response function: the public relations campaign," the *Times* commented. When Brown finally got around to asking Homeland Security for extra workers for Katrina, he said he wanted them to "convey a positive image of disaster operations to government officials, community organizations and the general public."

After Brown was sacked/scapegoated, a *Times* headline read, "THE REPLACEMENT: PICK AS ACTING FEMA LEADER HAS DISASTER RELIEF EXPERIENCE." Under Bush, that *was* newsworthy.

Fatal budget cuts. Bush cut federal flood control spending for southeastern Louisiana from $69 million in 2001 to $36.5 million in 2005, while federal hurricane protection for the New Orleans area in the U.S. Army Corps of Engineers' budget dropped from $14.25 million in 2002 to $5.7 million. Louisiana representatives begged Congress in 2005 for funds to defend Louisiana's coast, "only to be opposed by the White House," the *New Orleans Times-Picayune* reported.

In 2002, the chief of the Army Corps of Engineers resigned, "reportedly under threat of being fired, after he criticized the administration's proposed cuts in the corps' budget, including flood-control spending."[150] After 2003, the corps "sharply slowed its flood-control work, including work on sinking levees," due to the budgetary pressures of the war in Iraq and federal tax cuts. Federal budget cuts in

Bush on vacation (what else is new), and out of touch.
Thursday, August 25—the day Katrina hit Florida—Bush, on
vacation, as usual, at his Crawford, Texas, ranch, defended
his vacation habits, saying, "I've got a life to live, and will do
so." On Day 6, he "thank[ed] all the folks at the federal level
and the state level and the local level who have taken this
storm seriously," and praised FEMA chief Michael Brown's
efforts: "Brownie, you're doing a heckuva job." (A White
House spokesperson later denied Bush was on vacation,
claiming he was in Crawford "due to the renovation of the
West Wing of the White House.") It was Day 7, and more than
two days after the hurricane hit the Gulf Coast, before Bush
flew back to Washington to deal with the emergency—the
PR emergency, that is. He gave a speech in which he
"advised the public that anybody who wanted to help should
send cash, grinned, and promised that everything would
work out in the end," the *Times* commented. As hundreds
among the thousands stranded in New Orleans—most of
them poor and black—died for lack of water, medical care,
or timely rescues, "nothing about the president's demeanor
yesterday—which seemed casual to the point of careless-
ness—suggested that he understood the depth of the current
crisis." (Perhaps inability to understand distress was a
family trait: First Mother Barbara Bush remarked about the
Katrina refugees sheltered in the Houston Astrodome that
"so many . . . you know, were underprivileged anyway. So
this is working very well for them.")

An F to U, W. As the disaster engulfed New Orleans and
large swaths of coastal Louisiana, Mississippi, and Alabama,
the Bushies' first order of business was *political* damage

control: Warning against the "blame game" and "finger-pointing," while pointing their own fingers at *state* and *local* officials. Meanwhile, many on the right blamed New Orleans's poor for not saving themselves.

But even Bush backer Newt Gingrich was left wondering, "if we can't respond faster than this to an event we saw coming across the gulf for days, then why do we think we're prepared to respond to a nuclear or biological attack?" Sen. David Vitter (R-LA) gave the federal response to the disaster a grade of F.

As usual following one of his administration's f-ups, Bush promised an investigation—*by* the administration, *of* the administration. "We have learned through bitter experience...that when this administration begins an internal investigation, it means a whitewash in which no one important is held accountable and no real change occurs," the *Times* commented, citing Abu Ghraib. (See **Human Rights**.)

INTELLIGENCE "REFORM"

To the Bushies, a problem or crisis was but an opportunity to expand their power and further their hard-right agenda. Such was the urgent need for intelligence reform that became obvious on **September 11** and with regard to pre-war "intelligence" on **Iraq.**

The Bushies responded by filling top posts in the intelligence services—where political independence and the ability to "speak truth to power" was a vital matter of national security—with loyal Bush aides and partisan zealots (just as they did all over the executive branch; see **Presidential Power**). Their mission: To scapegoat the CIA for 9/11; to punish and purge anyone who had resisted White House pressure to deliver "intelligence" justifying an invasion of Iraq, or who warned of the consequences; to stop embarrassing leaks on these and other matters; to expand Defense Secretary RUMSFELD's and his neocon crew's control over the entire intelligence apparatus—in defiance of the 9/11 COMMISSION's recommendations; to boldly go . . . oh, never mind.

Policing and politicizing the CIA. In Bush's first term, CIA analysts were wont to produce, and sometimes leak, unwanted findings (such as: long-range missiles, despite the Bushite fixation on MISSILE DEFENSE, were among the least likely forms of terrorist attack). Many complained anonymously to the media of pressure to produce slanted intelligence on Iraq. The agency allowed MICHAEL SCHEUER, who headed its bin Laden unit for three years, to publish (anonymously) a book critical of the administration's conduct of the war on terrorism. GEORGE TENET resigned as director of central intelligence (DCI) the same month the National Intelligence Council, the DCI's think tank, warned that Iraq could collapse into civil war. In January 2005, the *Washington Post* headlined, *"Iraq New Terror Breeding Ground; War Created Haven, CIA Advisers Report."* *That* kind of reporting had to stop.

Enter PORTER GOSS, a Republican congressman and Bush campaign adviser, as Tenet's replacement in August 2004. "The White House has ordered the new CIA director . . . to purge the agency of officers believed to have been disloyal to President Bush or of leaking damaging information to the media about the conduct of the Iraq war and the hunt for Osama bin Laden," *Newsday* reported. Goss "was given instructions . . . to get rid of those soft leakers and liberal Democrats," as the White House saw the agency.[151]

"I am not qualified." Goss "auditioned for his current job by doing political hackwork for the president," wrote Fred Kaplan in *Slate*. In June 2003, Rep. Goss (R-FL), writing for the Bush-Cheney campaign, had attacked Kerry on national security and praised Bush's "historic achievements" and "remarkable progress" in fighting terrorism. When reports emerged about **Plamegate**, Goss dismissed them as "wild and unsubstantiated." "Somebody sends me a blue dress and some DNA, I'll have an investigation," he added, not wasting an opportunity to Clinton-bash. "As chairman of a House oversight committee and as a former CIA case officer himself," wrote Kaplan, "Goss should have been dismayed that a White House aide might have exposed the identity of an undercover agent as an act of political retaliation against the agent's spouse." This was clearly the man to "reform" the CIA. Yet, such modesty: In a March 2004 interview for the movie *Fahrenheit 9/11*, Goss said, "I couldn't get a job with CIA today. I am not qualified."[152]

"Contrarian voices" Portered out. Upon taking charge in September 2004, "Goss launched a concerted effort to bottle up contrarian voices inside the CIA," wrote Thomas Powers. He quickly got rid of the two highest officials of the clandestine service, the CIA's most powerful division. He began placing inexperienced political operatives in powerful positions, and gave them "wide latitude in running the agency," the *Wall Street Journal* reported. In an internal memo "to clarify beyond doubt the rules of the road," Goss wrote, he told CIA staff their job is to "support the administration and its policies in our work . . . As agency employees we do not identify with, support or champion opposition to the administration or its policies."[153] Heil to the chief.

New director, new cover-up. By June 2004, the CIA's inspector general had completed a reportedly "devastating" report on responsibility for 9/11. Acting CIA director John McLaughlin sat on it; Goss came in, and he too refused to release it to Congress. "Everyone feels it will be better if this hits the fan after the election," an official told *Newsweek*.

Caving to Rumsfeld. As the 9/11 Commission was completing its final report in July 2004, a Bush aide said: "We're going to focus on all the recommendations . . . The president said he wants this on a fast track." Meanwhile, Homeland Security Secretary TOM RIDGE signaled the administration's opposition to the idea of a new intelligence chief—one of the report's chief recommendations. (Such is the Bush division of lie-bor.)

Even after agreeing in principle to appoint an intelligence director, Bush opposed giving him/her control over the budgets and personnel of the CIA and other intelligence agencies—which Kean said "the position has to have . . . Otherwise it's not going to be much better than what we have now." Democrats said Rumsfeld was blocking a bill to implement the 9/11 Commission's recommendations "because he does not want to diminish the Pentagon's overwhelming control over intelligence agencies' budgets," AP reported.

No blood for intelligence! Rumsfeld was in fact seeking to expand the Pentagon's—*his*—control over intelligence by some startling new means. A new Pentagon plan, the *New York Times* reported in December 2004, included "the idea of 'fighting for intelligence,' or *commencing combat operations chiefly to obtain intelligence*" (emphasis added). Intelligence officials said the plan would "open the way to more clandestine military operations." Calling the plan "utter madness," the *New York Times*'s Bob Herbert wrote that the administration, "like a hardheaded adolescent, has learned little or nothing" from what resulted the last time Rumsfeld tried to force himself into the intelligence business: "A boutique CIA in the bowels of the Pentagon" that fabricated a link between Iraq and Al Qaeda that Rumsfeld was not getting from the CIA.

Winning Muslim hearts and minds—or, onward, jihadis for Jesus. Leading the team drafting the new Pentagon plan was Deputy Undersecretary of Defense LT. GEN. WILLIAM BOYKIN, who in 2003 told Christian groups that Muslims worship "an idol," Islamists hate the U.S. "because we're a Christian nation" (so much for the Constitution), terrorists "will only be defeated if we come against them in the name of Jesus," and—referring to a Muslim Somali warlord—"I knew my God was bigger than his"—a claim for which Boykin provided no concrete evidence. Instead of transferring him to the Salvation Army, Rumsfeld left him in charge of decisions involving conflict with Muslims, saying only that Boykin "has an outstanding record" and that "[t]here are a lot of things that are said . . .we are free people and that's the wonderful thing about our country."[154] Even complete idiots are free to remain in high office.

IRAQ

Robert M. Sapolsky, a noted primatologist and neuroscientist at Stanford University, has . . . observed that when assaulted by another adult male baboon, the first reaction is to find someone nearby who is smaller and weaker and make them pay.

—Harold Williamson, dissidentvoice.org

The real reason for this war, which was never stated, was that after 9/11 America needed to hit someone in the Arab-Muslim world. Afghanistan wasn't enough . . .Smashing Saudi Arabia or Syria would have been fine. But we hit Saddam for one simple reason: because we could.

—Thomas Friedman, *The New York Times*

The "Mission Accomplished" banner beneath which the heroically flight-suited Bush declared an end to major combat in Iraq in May 2003 cannot be waved in the Bushies' faces often enough. Two years later, *The New Republic* observed, Iraq seemed "well on its way to becoming a gangster's paradise engulfed by civil war." Rival militias controlled their own territories—including whole sections of Baghdad. Iraqis and "coalition" soldiers were being killed daily, often by the dozens—with twice as many Iraqi civilians killed by U.S. forces than by insurgents.[155] War-related deaths of Iraqis exceeded 100,000.[156] Nearly 1,600 U.S. troops had been killed. The insurgency—which Bush still described as "a handful of folks who fear freedom," "terrorists" all—had grown to some 200,000 fighters, supported by many more ordinary Iraqis who evidently preferred their own tyrant to any foreign (especially American), uninvited liberator, or who found the cure worse than the disease of Saddam; and supported, too, by millions of Muslims around the world. Neither the WMDs nor the WMD programs over which the war was supposedly prosecuted had ever been found. (U.S. forces did manage to *lose* at least one vast weapons stockpile, probably to the insurgents.)

And the Bushies continued to lie, mislead, or maintain silence about every one of these facts. Typically enough, Bush's opening statement at a January 2005 news conference left out any mention of 31 U.S. soldiers killed the night before in a helicopter crash in Iraq, the largest loss of American lives in a single incident since the war began. In his inaugural address that month, the Denier-in-Chief never once mentioned the word *Iraq*. Bush "and his equally tone-deaf supporters" then spent the next few days "partying hard while Americans, Iraqis and others continued to suffer and die," wrote the *New York Times*'s Bob Herbert. The Black Tie and Boots Ball was held on the same day that 26 people were killed in five terrorist bombings in Baghdad. The tens of millions spent on the inaugural festivities, Herbert rudely suggested, "would have been better spent on body armor for under-equipped troops."

"Never mind the chaos that reigns in Baghdad," wrote *Newsweek*'s Eleanor Clift a year into the war—"Bush is strutting the country with a triumphalism that would make Dwight Eisenhower blush." By January 2005, the administration had in effect declared victory at least five times: Upon the fall of Baghdad; the "Mission Accomplished" banner on board the USS *Abraham Lincoln* (which the White House later lied about and said the sailors had put up); the capture of Saddam

Hussein; the "transfer of sovereignty" to an interim/puppet Iraqi government in June 2004; and the Iraqi election of January 2005. Each of these events, it was suggested, would bring an end to the killing. Each only succeeded in reducing news coverage of it and obscuring the fact that we were bogged down (see the **"Q"** word). Critics like Brent Scowcroft, national security adviser under Bush I, foresaw the elections deepening the conflict between Shiites and Sunnis and warned of civil war. It seemed, in any event, a good bet that Iraq would end up a Shiite quasi-theocracy closely allied with, and resembling, Iran—the country long at the top of the U.S. list of states sponsoring terrorism.

As for the rest of the Muslim world, the war handed Al Qaeda "precisely what it wanted and needed," said former White House counterterrorism chief RICHARD CLARKE— "proof that America was at war with Islam, that we were the new Crusaders come to occupy Muslim land." For their part, "competing big powers Russia, China and the European Union are not exactly displeased to contemplate, from a distance, Bush and the neo-cons' clumsy attempts to replicate the British post–World War I empire in the Middle East," wrote *Asia Times*'s Pepe Escobar.

Bush's mantra that the world is better off without Saddam Hussein was less undeniable than it sounded. But perhaps chanting it helped him drown out the reports of gunfire and explosions. In January 2005, Bush reportedly asked outgoing Secretary of State COLIN POWELL for his views on Iraq. "We're losing," Powell said. Bush then asked him to leave. Attempts to brief Bush on various grim realities were personally rebuffed; Bush actually said he did not want to hear "bad news."[157]

Meanwhile, as columnist Robert Scheer wrote, the "screwballs" were "failing upward": Those most responsible for misleading the country into war and for the disastrous lack of planning for and mismanagement of "post-war" Iraq were still in office—or, like National Security Adviser CONDOLEEZZA RICE and Deputy Secretary of Defense PAUL WOLFOWITZ, had been promoted—while the few voices of caution or dissent, those who had tried to tell Bush the truth, like Powell and Clarke and top CIA analysts like Michael Scheuer, were out. Defense Secretary RUMSFELT, who was directly responsible for the insufficient troop levels and therefore at least indirectly for ABU GHRAIB (see **Human Rights**), and who callously waved off the shortages of protective gear that were getting his soldiers killed ("you go to war with the army you have"), was doing "a spectacular job," Bush repeated thrice daily. White House counsel ALBERTO GONZALES, Bush's legal adviser on okaying torture, was named Attorney General. National Security Council official ROBERT JOSEPH, who was widely believed to be behind Bush's notorious claim that Iraq sought to purchase uranium from Niger, was named—what else?—undersecretary of state for arms control. "That's the backward nature of this beast," wrote the *New York Times*'s Maureen Dowd: "Deceive, you're golden; tell the truth, you're gone."

BUT WHAT MADE THE WAR WRONG wasn't the delinquent planning, management blunders, and resulting chaos, the prisoner "abuses," or the 237 lies and deceptions the Bushies sold the war with, according to a report released by Rep. Henry Waxman (D-CA) in March 2004 (which only counted "misleading statements" by Bush, Cheney, Rumsfeld, Powell, and Rice—none by Wolfowitz, White House Press Secretary Ari Fleischer, or other mis-leading Bushies). Ends *can* justify means. But even if things were to turn out well in Iraq, our invasion would remain wrong—morally and legally. There was not a sufficient threat from, humanitarian crisis in, or certainty of bringing democracy and stability to Iraq or its neighbors to justify the near certainty of many thousands of casualties, a huge cost in treasure, severe damage to our international relations and credibility, and increased terrorist recruiting. Bush had no moral right to gamble so much for so little reason and on such long odds—let alone for his real reasons, which you shall learn presently. We also cannot be sure regime change in Iraq would not have come about *without* war.

"A CRIME OF AGGRESSION UNDER INTERNATIONAL LAW." When it comes to America's God-given right to kick whoever's ass we feel like, the right wing likes to dismiss questions of legality as "legalism." But the legal prohibition of war, a group of international jurists wrote, is "one of the great achievements of the twentieth century"—and it was one of many the Bushies appeared eager to reverse. A statement by three international law groups said a U.S. attack on Iraq would be "a fundamental breach of international law [that] would seriously threaten the integrity of the international legal order" and "return us to an international order based on imperial ambition and coercive force."[158] Just as the "Bush doctrine" intended! (See **Foreign Policy**.)

The UN Charter permits military force only in self-defense or when authorized by the UN Security Council. Neither condition was met in Iraq. The war was, according to the Charter, "a crime against peace," "a crime of aggression under international law"—and therefore also a violation of the U.S. Constitution, which makes our treaties part of "the supreme law of the land."[159]

Opening the door to anarchy. The Bushies claimed to be enforcing UN resolutions calling on Iraq to disarm. But the UN Charter gives no country the power to unilaterally enforce UN resolutions; this can be authorized only by the Security Council after determining that there has been a material breach of its resolution and that all nonmilitary means of enforcement have been exhausted. By the Bushies' logic, other Security Council members could claim the right to invade other UN member states that are in violation of Security Council resolutions. "For example, Russia could claim the right to invade Israel, France could claim the right to invade Turkey, and Great Britain could claim the right to invade Morocco," wrote legal scholar Stephen Zunes in *Foreign Policy in Focus*. "The U.S. insistence on the right to attack unilaterally . . . would open the door to international anarchy."

Contrary to the Bushies' assertions, no Security Council resolution authorized use of force against Iraq beyond its expulsion from Kuwait in 1991. Resolution 1441 in 2002 only stipulated "serious consequences" if Iraq did not comply with disarmament requirements—instead of "all necessary means," which is the recognized UN euphemism for military force. The Bushies implicitly acknowledged this by seeking a further resolution. In refusing it, the Security Council made clear that weapons inspections should be allowed to continue before military action could be authorized.

The Bushies invoked self-defense against Iraq's alleged

WMDs as their main reason for war. Even if there had been a real threat, the UN Charter, according to some authorities, permits use of force in self-defense only as an *urgent necessity* in response to an *imminent* attack, and where there is *no practicable alternative*. Others state flatly, "'preventive self-defense' is not admissible under international law."[160] As one critic noted, "Nazi leaders offered the same defense at the Nuremberg Tribunal. Rejecting the claim, the Tribunal found the Nazis guilty of the crime of aggression."[161]

Certainly, no UN resolution authorized the use of force against Iraq to bring about regime change, which the UN Charter prohibits. Nor was there a legal basis for war for humanitarian reasons. "It's easy to see why. Such a principle would give powerful nations carte blanche to declare a 'humanitarian emergency' and impose their will on weaker countries," wrote blogger Robin Miller. When Vietnam invaded Cambodia in 1978 to overthrow the Khmer Rouge—which was even more brutal than the regime of Saddam Hussein—the U.S. condemned the action before the UN as an act of aggression and a violation of international law. When Britain, France, and Israel invaded Egypt in 1956 in an attempt to overthrow the Nasser regime, the Eisenhower administration challenged them before the UN "and insisted that international law and the UN Charter must be upheld by all nations."[162]

"Yes, but . . . but . . . 9/11!" Which came first, the chickenhawk or the egg? September 11, fears of terrorists with WMDs, or the decision for war? What, in short, were the motives?

According to many critics, the Bushies were blinded in

their drive to war by ideology, hubris, and/or stupidity. Harvard's Stephen Walt, one of many **foreign policy** "realist" conservatives who opposed the war, said the case for the invasion was "empty," a "combination of bad history, inconsistent logic, wishful thinking, and old news."[163] The war, wrote the *New York Times*'s Bob Herbert, "was the result of powerful government figures imposing their dangerous fantasies on the world"—fantasies about WMDs, links between Al Qaeda and Saddam, "throngs of Iraqis hurling kisses and garlands at the invading Americans, and the spread of American-style democracy throughout the Middle East."

But it is scarcely credible that the Bushies believed their own public assertions about Saddam's WMDs and terrorist links—there is too much evidence to the contrary—still less that they were acting out of a humanitarian desire to liberate the Iraqis from tyranny: Too many members of this same crew—including Rumsfeld, Cheney, and Bush père— were too willing during the Reagan years, when it served their purposes, to overlook, indeed aid and abet, Saddam's use of chemical weapons—a crime they now cited as a justification for the war to oust him. And they were more than willing to do profitable business with more or less evil dictatorships, including Saddam's.

Never mind the DOWNING STREET MEMO that surfaced in May 2005, indicating that the White House had decided on war by July 2002 and was looking to fix "the intelligence and facts" to justify it. The evidence will show that Bush and much of his defense team came into office in 2001 already bent on attacking Iraq; that before **September 11**, Iraq distracted them from real terrorist threats; and that after 9/11,

Iraq was not the "central battlefield" in, but the central distraction from, the "war on terror." The invasion of Iraq "was not preemption; it was . . . an avaricious, premeditated, unprovoked war against a foe who posed no immediate threat . . . There is nothing that bin Laden could have hoped for more," wrote 23-year CIA veteran Michael Scheuer in *Imperial Hubris: Why the West Is Losing the War on Terrorism*—a book the CIA vetted and allowed Scheuer to publish anonymously in June 2004.

The administration "no doubt had its real reasons" for invading, wrote Ron Reagan, the former president's son. "They've simply chosen not to share them with the American public." But we have. One through five are the more, shall we say, Rovian, motives. (After all, according to Bob Woodward, Bush made the decision to go to war without consulting Cheney, Rumsfeld, or Powell. "I could tell what they thought," said the omniscient leader. So who did that leave to tell him what *he* thought?)

Memorize this list, then destroy it:

1. "If I have a chance to invade . . ." To build Bush's image as a war leader—in the public's eyes and his own. According to his ghostwriter for a planned autobiography, Mickey Herskowitz, Bush was thinking about invading Iraq in 1999, when he told Herskowitz: "One of the keys to being seen as a great leader is to be seen as a commander in chief," and, "My father had all this political capital built up when he drove the Iraqis out of Kuwait and he wasted it . . . If I have a chance to invade . . . if I had that much capital, I'm not going to waste it. I'm going to get everything passed that I want to get passed and I'm going to have a successful presidency." "Herskowitz said that Bush expressed frustration at a lifetime as an underachiever in the shadow of an accomplished father. In aggressive military action, he saw the opportunity to emerge from his father's shadow."[164] (And to avenge him? "After all, this [Saddam] is the guy who tried to kill my dad," said Junior in 2002.)

2. The baboon motive, if you will: To appear, after 9/11, to be waging the "war on terror" aggressively, and to satisfy the public's supposed desire for vengeance, by attacking an enemy we could *find*—"a target more suited [than Al Qaeda] to the mindset of U.S. leaders and military capabilities," wrote *Foreign Policy* editor Moisés Naím.

3. Weapon of mass distraction. To ensure that the "war on terrorism"—or indeed, anything *but* Bush's domestic policies—remained the issue going into the 2002 midterm elections. "There's a big question hanging over President Bush's Iraq policy," said CNN's Bill Schneider that September. "Why now? Why, more than 11 years after the Gulf War, is it suddenly so urgent for the U.S. to go after Saddam Hussein?" Why *exactly* then? Because, as White House chief of staff ANDREW CARD told the *New York Times*, "[f]rom a marketing point of view, you don't introduce new products in August"!

4. To present the Dems with the dilemma of either standing behind Bush on Iraq—further elevating his stature—or appearing weak on defense in the wake of 9/11.

5. 2004. To give Bush a triumphant victory on which to ride into the 2004 election.

6. The neocons' agenda—to expand America's global military supremacy and its position in the Middle East in particular, whether to secure oil sources, buttress Israel (the road to peace in Jerusalem lay through Baghdad, said Wolfowitz), or reduce strategic and oil dependence on Saudi Arabia. An "almost unnoticed, but huge" reason, Wolfowitz said, was that occupation of Iraq would allow a withdrawal of U.S. troops from Saudi Arabia, where their presence inspired many Muslims' fury. Interesting assumptions: U.S. forces' presence in Iraq (a) would *not* infuriate Muslims, and (b) was to be more or less permanent.

7. Vietnam. To turn back the clock in foreign (as in domestic) affairs and eradicate the "Vietnam syndrome," America's post-Nam wariness of military adventures; to reestablish America's "right" and *appetite* to go to war; to remilitarize America in armaments, policy, and spirit—if only because this was the opposite of what liberals wanted and the hated 1960s represented.

8. Power grab. To reclaim executive branch powers, particularly war-making powers, lost to (or rather, *recovered by*) Congress after Vietnam. "When they talk about reversing the impact of Vietnam, which Rumsfeld has alluded to on a number of occasions," said James Lindsay of the Council on Foreign Relations, "they are not simply talking about reestablishing American power abroad. They are talking about reestablishing **presidential power** here at home."[165]

9 (or 81/2). Fun. To fully exercise and enjoy the power a president and his crew are entitled to, which in their case could only mean moving great armies, kicking some ass, and marking their territory (the world).

THE PRE-OCCUPATION: "Find me a way." According to Bob Woodward's legendary account in his 2004 book *Plan of Attack*, after CIA director GEORGE TENET briefed Bush on Iraq's WMDs in December 2002, Bush was unimpressed: "This is the best we've got?" Yet Tenet's famous two words— it was a "slam dunk" case—were enough to reassure Bush, who made the final decision for war two weeks later.

No wonder the White House promoted Woodward's book—and no wonder the media played up this scene above all: It portrayed Bush as seeking after the truth, but ultimately as the victim of Tenet's faulty intelligence. The book also portrayed **Dick** Cheney as the "steamrolling force" for war.

But on closer reading, it was not so much Tenet's *evidence* Bush was worried about. As Woodward wrote, the "*presentation* was a flop. *In terms of marketing* [emphasis added] . . . the charts didn't work, the photos were not gripping . . ." This—or the possibility Woodward was fed Bushit (his "sources" were, after all, Bush, Rice, et al.)—seems the only way to reconcile his account with the fact that the Bushies had already been sounding the alarm about Iraqi WMDs for months; and with the Downing Street memo; and with insider accounts that show the Bushies hell-bent on "doing" Iraq— not Al Qaeda—from day one . . . indeed, much earlier:

- In 3 BB (1998 AD), eight future Bush officials, including Rumsfeld and Wolfowitz, coauthored a letter urging President Clinton to begin "implementing a strategy for removing Saddam's regime from power."

- On Richard Clarke's recommendation, Bush's top advisers met during his second week in office to discuss the Al Qaeda threat—or so Clarke expected. In fact, "the meeting had nothing to do with bin Laden. . . . 'They thought there was something more urgent [Clarke said]. It was Iraq.'"[166] From the very beginning, former Treasury Secretary PAUL O'NEILL recalled in the book *The Price of Loyalty*, "we were building the case against Hussein and looking at how we could take him out . . . It was all about [Bush saying] 'Go find me a way to do this.'"

- At a National Security Council meeting in May 2001, Tenet told Bush it was still only speculation whether Saddam had WMDs or was even starting a program to build them. "That wouldn't change, and I read those CIA reports for two years," O'Neill recalled. Meanwhile, Tenet stressed again and again, before and after 9/11, that *Al Qaeda* was "the most immediate and serious threat."

- When Wolfowitz finally convened a top-level meeting to discuss terrorism in April 2001, *Newsweek* reported, he "rebuffed Clarke's effort to focus on Al Qaeda. According to Clarke, Wolfowitz said, 'Who cares about *a little terrorist in Afghanistan?*'" The real threat, he insisted, was Saddam's state-sponsored terrorism.[167]

You furnish the pictures. I'll furnish the war. In *Newsweek*'s pithy description, "It was the day after 9/11, and President Bush, like many Americans, was looking for someone to bomb." No, not just anyone. Right after the attacks, Bush said, "I believe Iraq was involved" and Iraq "probably was behind this"—"despite having no proof and being told that was not the case," the *Progress Report* noted. Next day, according to Clarke, Bush pulled him aside and ordered, "See if Saddam did this. See if he's linked in any way." Clarke was "incredulous." "But, Mr. President, Al Qaeda did this," he recalled saying. "I know, I know, but—see if Saddam was involved. Just look." Six days later, Clarke "turned in a classified memo concluding that there was no evidence of Iraqi complicity in 9/11—nor any relationship between Iraq and Al Qaeda. The memo, says Clarke, was buried by an administration that was determined to get Iraq, sooner or later."[168]

Like invading Mexico. According to CBS News, *five hours* after the 9/11 attacks, "Rumsfeld was telling his aides to come up with plans for striking Iraq." At a principals' meeting soon after, he argued that Afghanistan, home to Al Qaeda's training camps, did not offer "enough good targets . . . We should do Iraq." Clarke wrote that he thought Rumsfeld was joking: "Having been attacked by al Qaeda, for us now to go bombing Iraq in response would be like our invading Mexico after the Japanese attacked us at Pearl Harbor."

The defense secretary was presumably made to understand that Afghanistan had to be dealt with first. But, wrote Ron Reagan, "the Taliban was a mere appetizer; Saddam was the entrée. (Or who knows? The soup course?)"

Creating Osama bin Hussein. From the start, the CIA had not been giving the administration's warmongers the "intelligence" they wanted connecting Saddam to terrorists. So, within a month of 9/11, Rumsfeld created "a boutique C.I.A. in the bowels of the Pentagon," as the *New York Times* put it, run by Under Secretary of Defense for Policy DOUGLAS FEITH, who was closely connected to and probably selected by Defense Policy Board chairman and Iraq überhawk RICHARD PERLE. Feith and Perle had signed a 1996 paper calling for the overthrow of Saddam to enhance Israel's security.

The new office, the COUNTER TERRORISM EVALUATION GROUP, "essentially fabricated a link" between Hussein and bin Laden—"a link used to justify the Iraq invasion," according to the *New York Times*. (The other office Feith oversaw, the OFFICE OF SPECIAL PLANS, "probably wrought even worse damage," *Slate* noted. "Its job was postwar planning.") A former Middle East analyst for the Defense Intelligence Agency (DIA) told the *Times*, "they brought in people who were not intelligence professionals, people brought in because they thought like them. They knew what answers they were going to get." Feith's office, the *Los Angeles Times* reported, was "constantly 'stovepiping' intelligence directly to Cheney and the White House in order to circumvent official channels"—i.e., the CIA. By September 2002, Cheney was going around claiming "new information has come to light" that Saddam's regime may have supported Al Qaeda.

The one reason they could agree on. "There was little proof that Mr. Hussein was working on terror plots with Mr. bin Laden, a religious extremist who viewed the Baghdad regime as a corrupt, secular enemy," the *New York Times* noted. But, as a senior CIA official said, "if you work hard enough . . . you can link just about anybody to anybody else."[169] Still, because of CIA and DIA skepticism, the Bushies were unable to reach a consensus on the terrorist link—so, "[f]or bureaucratic reasons," as Wolfowitz later said, they settled on WMDs as their story, "because it was the one reason everyone could agree on."

Mushrooming cloud of deception. Beginning in September 2002, "[j]ust like that," wrote Ron Reagan, a country "whose economy had been reduced to shambles by international sanctions," whose military was less than half the size it had been during the first Gulf War, that was hemmed in by no-fly zones and constant aerial and satellite surveillance, and whose WMDs and capacity to produce them had been destroyed or seriously degraded,

> became, in Mr. Bush's words, 'a threat of unique urgency' to the most powerful nation on earth. Fanciful but terrifying scenarios were introduced: Unmanned aircraft, drones, had been built for missions targeting the U.S., Bush told the nation . . . 'We don't want the smoking gun to be a mushroom cloud,' [Rice] deadpanned . . . And, Bush maintained, 'Iraq could decide on any given day to provide a biological or chemical weapon to [terrorists].' We 'know' Iraq possesses such weapons, Rumsfeld and Cheney assured us. We even 'know' where they are hidden. After several months of this mumbo jumbo, 70 percent of Americans had embraced the fantasy that Saddam destroyed the World Trade Center.[170]

Reality check. Cheney never gave up "his mad assertion that Saddam was somehow at the nexus of a worldwide terror network," as Reagan put it. Was Iraq involved in the 9/11 plot? "We don't know," Cheney invariably answered. (Was Barbara Bush involved? Barbra Streisand? *We don't know.*) THE 9/11 COMMISSION REPORT, completed June 2004, was less uncertain. It found:

- No evidence that bin Laden and Saddam "ever developed into a collaborative operational relationship" or "cooperated . . . in developing or carrying out any attacks." Iraq apparently rejected bin Laden's requests to provide space for training camps and to help Al Qaeda acquire weapons; and a senior associate said bin Laden vetoed the idea of working with Saddam's corrupt and "godless" regime.
- No evidence Iraq provided Al Qaeda with chemical and biological weapons training—contrary to specific claims by Bush and Cheney.
- Evidence disproving Cheney's frequent allegations of an April 2001 meeting in Prague between 9/11 ringleader Mohammed Atta and a member of the Iraqi intelligence bureau. (Evidence such as, Atta was elsewhere.)
- As the *New York Times* summarized, "Number of possible Al Qaeda associates known to have been in Iraq in recent years: one, Abu Musab al-Zarqawi." (Bush, even now, called Zarqawi "the best evidence" of an Al Qaeda link. True! And as Tenet had told the Senate, Zarqawi did not work with the Hussein regime. By Bush's logic, the presence of Al Qaeda operatives in the U.S. would indicate a Bush–bin Laden collaboration.)

The commission's Republican chairman, THOMAS KEAN, said, "We believe . . . that there were a lot more active [Al Qaeda] contacts, frankly, with Iran and with Pakistan" than with Iraq. "No serious intelligence analyst believed the connection existed," a *New York Times* editorial noted. "Mr. Bush had been told just that . . . There are two unpleasant alternatives: either Mr. Bush knew he was not telling the truth, or he has *a capacity for politically motivated self-deception* that is terrifying in the post-9/11 world." (Emphasis added.)

Cheney's response to the commission's report? Saddam, he repeated, had "long-established ties with Al Qaeda."

WMD (Weapons Myth Debunked). In October 2004, chief U.S. weapons inspector CHARLES DUELFER released a report concluding that at the time of the invasion, March 2003, Iraq had no WMD stockpiles and no program to produce them; Iraq's WMD program was essentially destroyed in 1991, and Saddam ended Iraq's nuclear program around the same time. After that, Iraq's "ability to reconstitute a nuclear weapons program progressively decayed." The CIA's National Intelligence Estimate on Iraq had concluded the same thing—six months before the invasion. Iraq did try to retain the capability to resume WMD production at some time in the future (though without any formal strategy or plan), Duelfer concluded—*primarily for defense against Iran.*

Bush's response to the Duelfer report: "[Saddam] was a threat . . . and America and the world are safer for our actions." John Kerry's: "Mr. President, the American people . . . deserve facts that represent reality, not carefully polished arguments and points that are simply calculated to align with a preconceived conception."

In January 2005, U.S. inspectors called off the search for WMDs. Bush had long since been reduced to babbling about WMD "program-related activities," and had switched to "freedom" and "democracy" as the *real* rationale for the war. (For more evidence of the Bushies' commitment to freedom and democracy, see **Election Reform**, **Foreign Policy**, **Free Speech**, **Human Rights**, **Presidential Power**, and **Secrecy**.)

"I would not send troops into Rwanda."—GWB. Much like his WMDs, Saddam's mass killings were a thing of the past: They had mainly occurred in 1988, against the Kurds, and in 1991, "when Hussein suppressed the post-Gulf War uprisings that President George H.W. Bush had encouraged but not supported," wrote *The Nation*'s David Corn. According to a January 2004 Human Rights Watch report, "Brutal as Saddam Hussein's reign had been, the scope of the Iraqi government's killing in March 2003 *was not of the exceptional and dire magnitude that would justify humanitarian intervention.*" (Emphasis added.)

Not that the U.S. was much in the habit of intervening against brutal dictatorships. During the 2000 campaign, Bush said: *"We should not send our troops to stop ethnic cleansing and genocide outside our strategic interests . . . I would not send [U.S.] troops into Rwanda."* (This did not stop the Bushies from invoking Rwanda as part of its justification for invading Iraq, or from trashing the UN as "irrelevant" for its failure to take action on Rwanda.) Indeed, we were more in the habit of installing, arming, and/or doing business with brutal dictators—including, of course, Saddam, as **Dick** and Donald well knew.

The de-imminization program. By January 2004, the White House was heatedly denying ever having called Iraq an "imminent threat." "Those were not words we used," said Bush spokesman Scott McClellan. Journalist Andrew Sullivan raged, "No member of the administration used the term 'imminent threat' . . . No one." *National Review* online editor Jonah Goldberg: There was not "a shred of proof" any Bushie "ever once said [Iraq] posed an 'imminent' threat" to the U.S. True! They called it "immediate," "urgent," and "mortal"—and said "absolutely" when *asked* if Iraq was an imminent threat.

(Emphases added:) Reporter: "[W]e said that these weapons were a direct and imminent threat to the United States? Isn't that true?" White House press secretary Ari Fleischer: *"Absolutely."* "Ari, the President has been saying that the threat from Iraq is *imminent*, that we have to act now . . ." Fleischer: "Yes." "[I]s he (Saddam) an *imminent threat* to U.S. interests, either in that part of the world or to Americans right here at home?" White House communications director Dan Bartlett: "Well, of *course* he is." Bush spokesman Scott McClellan, on helping arm Turkey against

Peace deal? Not interested. On the eve of the invasion, Bush said, "Should Saddam Hussein choose confrontation, the American people can know that every measure has been taken to avoid war." "Everything humanly possible," said Rumsfeld.

LS. (Lying scum.) In the last weeks before the invasion, top Iraqi officials, using back-channel connections to the Bush administration, attempted to avert war by reasserting

Iraq: "This is about an *imminent threat*." Rumsfeld: "Some have argued that the nuclear threat from Iraq is not *imminent* . . . I would not be so certain . . ." and, "No terrorist state poses *a greater or more immediate threat* . . ." Bush: "Facing *clear evidence of peril*," blah, blah, blah. A "threat of *unique urgency*." A "*real and dangerous* threat." A "*grave threat*."

But never, not once, okay, did a Bushie say these words: "Iraq poses an imminent threat."

To those who've lost a loved one in Iraq: Lighten up! During his speech at the annual White House Correspondents' dinner in March 2004, Bush showed how seriously he took his prewar claims and the resulting carnage. He gave a hilarious slide show of himself performing a little pantomime of searching for WMDs behind his office furniture: "Nope, no weapons over there," he narrated. "Maybe under here . . ." We on the humorless "left" feigned righteous anger, but could scarcely contain our glee over this latest foe paw. (Mustn't get *too* French.)

they no longer had WMDs and by offering to (a) let American troops and experts come and search; (b) turn over a suspect in the 1993 World Trade Center bombing; (c) support Washington's plan for an Israeli-Palestinian settlement; (d) give U.S. energy companies preferential rights to Iraqi oil; even to (e) hold UN-supervised elections—everything, one would think, the U.S. could ask for. The overtures were rebuffed. The go-between, a Lebanese-American businessman, met in London with top Pentagon adviser RICHARD PERLE, who later called the Iraqi proposal "quite astonishing" and said he sought, but was denied, CIA authorization to meet with the Iraqis. "The message was, 'Tell them that we will see them in Baghdad,'" Perle told the *New York Times*. It was in fact one of a number of back-channel overtures the Iraqis made, a senior U.S. intelligence official said. But by then, as noted in *Slate*, "the Bush administration had pretty much cocked and aimed its invasion cannon."

Premature evacuation: Running from the war on Al Qaeda. Before the invasion, critics argued it would divert military, intelligence, and diplomatic resources away from the war on terrorism. In fact, it already had.

- As early as February 2002, while chaos, warlords, and Al Qaeda supporters still ruled over most of Afghanistan, about 10,000 U.S. special operations forces, along with spy aircraft and light infantry, were siphoned off to prepare for war in Iraq. Troops from the Fifth Special Forces Group who specialize in the Middle East were replaced by "troops with expertise in Spanish cultures," *USA Today* reported. (Electing a geographically challenged president will have consequences.)
- According to Bob Woodward, in the summer of 2002, $700 million was diverted without Congress's knowledge—and probably illegally—from the war in Afghanistan to develop a war plan for Iraq.
- The CIA, meanwhile, "was stretched badly in its

capacity to collect, translate and analyze information coming from Afghanistan," *USA Today* reported. Iraq, a former Pentagon official noted, "has been a real diversion from the longer struggle against jihadists," especially in the intelligence field. A former member of the National Security Council staff told the *Los Angeles Times*, "The criticism does not seem out of line with many of the conversations I have had with officers in every branch of the military."

- The 9/11 Commission Report warned that if Iraq "becomes a failed state, it will go to the top of the list of places that are breeding grounds for attacks against Americans at home. Similarly, if we are paying insufficient attention to Afghanistan, the rule of the Taliban . . . may re-emerge and its countryside could once again offer refuge to Al Qaeda." No sooner said . . .

- Richard Clarke said on NBC's *Meet the Press* in March 2004 that if bin Laden was caught that year, "it's two years too late . . .because during those two years when forces were diverted to Iraq . . . Al Qaeda has metamorphosized into a hydra-headed organization with cells that are operating autonomously," like, apparently, the cells that carried out the bombings in Madrid that month and in London in July 2005.

The cost in treasure. In 2002, Bush's chief economic advisor, Lawrence Lindsey, told the press the war would cost $100-$200 billion. He was axed a couple of months later. The administration's chief warmongers insisted the war would cost the U.S. less than $60 billion.

By August 2005, it had already cost more than $200 billion.

And years of U.S. occupation and reconstruction still lay ahead. Estimates of the eventual cost exceeded $700 billion. The bulk of the costs were for maintaining the forces—and no sizeable reduction in troop levels looked likely anytime soon.

According to the Defense Department, the cost of simply *containing* Saddam Hussein over 12 years was $30 billion.[171]

Did we mention the White House refused to include the cost of the war in its budget deficit calculations? The Bushies "seem always to exist in a fantasy realm" in which "you can start wars without having to deal with the consequences," wrote the *New York Times*'s Bob Herbert. "You don't even have to pay for them. You can put them on a credit card."

Where was it all going? Somehow, out of at least $119 billion the U.S. spent on the Iraq war by September 2004, only $1 billion had been spent on reconstruction; the rest went to fighting the insurgency. "It's beyond pitiful, it's beyond embarrassing. It is now in the zone of dangerous," said Senator Chuck Hagel (R-NE). (Also see **War Profiteering**.)

Oil prices, meanwhile—which war supporters predicted would come down thanks to postwar upgrades in Iraqi oil production—were rising to all-time highs. "The U.S.-led invasion has resulted in the loss of an average of 2 million barrels a day of Iraqi oil from world markets," *USA Today* noted in October 2004. Instead of Iraq becoming "America's private gasoline-pumping station, the world has lost Iraq's oil."

Sacrificing homeland security. Forget education, housing, transportation, debt reduction, etc.—Bush wasn't going to fund those anyway. But the $200 billion spent in Iraq as of August 2005 could have paid for a long list of urgent but severely underfunded **homeland security** initiatives—and there'd still be money left over for eliminating nuclear weapons and technology to keep nukes out of terrorist hands; increasing foreign aid and diplomacy to help win "hearts and minds" away from extremism and terrorism; helping countries like Afghanistan improve security, foster democracy, and eliminate the drug trade that funds terrorists; and beefing up our armed services to track and fight terrorists. ("All of the services are complaining that Iraq and associated costs with Iraq are eating their lunch," a defense analyst told *Salon*.)

"Weapons of mass salvation." Columbia University economist Jeffrey Sachs criticized the administration for focusing too much on weapons of mass destruction while ignoring what he called "weapons of mass salvation," such as the Global Fund to Fight **AIDS**, Tuberculosis and Malaria. Sachs determined in 2004 that one-eighth the amount spent or committed to date for Iraq, if spent on health, could save about 8 million lives each year in poor countries, or roughly 22,000 (nearly seven 9/11s) every day—which would also help stabilize unstable regions and thus aid in the fight against terrorism.[172] For the same money, millions could be saved or tens of thousands could be killed. Decisions, decisions.

THE HUMAN COST: "Relax, celebrate victory." That was the title of an op-ed piece in *USA Today* by Pentagon adviser RICHARD PERLE on May 2, 2003, about five weeks after the start of the war. From then on, the insurgency grew steadily. An average of 73 U.S. troops a month were killed from July 2004 to June 2005, by which time there were more than 1,750 U.S. dead and at least 12,750 wounded.

"We love war." In April 2004, PAUL WOLFOWITZ was asked at a House subcommittee hearing how many U.S. troops had died to date in Iraq. "It's approximately 500, of which—I can get the exact numbers—approximately 350 are combat deaths," he answered. The correct numbers were 722 and 521. But why should the number-two man at the Pentagon be expected to remember "how many young Americans had been sacrificed on the altar of his ideology," Ron Reagan asked? After all, as right-wing guru MICHAEL LEDEEN—holder of the Freedom Chair at the right-wing American Enterprise Institute and a figure often quoted by Wolfowitz, Cheney, and Rumsfeld—told a forum in March 2003, "the level of casualties is secondary" because "we are a warlike people . . . we love war."[173] Previously, he had written that "the only way to achieve peace is through total war" "[t]he sparing of civilian lives cannot be the total war's first priority";[174] and, "Every ten years or so, the United States needs to pick up some small crappy little country and throw it against the wall, just to show the world we mean business."[175] Ledeen's daughter was appointed Coalition Provisional Authority (CPA) adviser to the Iraqi Ministry of Finance, where *important* numbers were counted.

"We're not going to have any casualties." Even more out of touch with the reality of war was the commander in chief—surprising, given his Vietnam-era military service in the jungles and dental chairs of Texas and

Alabama. In October 2004, televangelist PAT ROBERTSON said on CNN that just before the war, Bush told him, "We're not going to have any casualties." When Tim Russert asked Bush if he was "surprised by the level and intensity of resistance," Bush answered, "No." Which man of God lied *this* time?

Out of sight, out of mind: The great American flag-draped- coffin **blackout.** Lest the sight of coffins returning from Iraq weaken public support for the war, on the eve of the invasion the administration banned ceremonies for, and news coverage of, dead soldiers' homecomings on all military bases.

Presidents Carter, Reagan, Bush I, and Clinton—followed by cameras—had attended elaborate ceremonies for returning remains of soldiers. Bush junior wouldn't attend soldiers' funerals. He did, however, use *live* soldiers again and again as props, backdrops, and photo ops to help him play the heroic commander in chief—he who never completed the specially arranged National Guard service that kept him out of Vietnam and who lied ever afterwards about it.

Underreporting casualties. Another 15,000–30,000 U.S. casualties remained un-covered by the media and uncounted by the government: troops who had suffered so-called "non-battle" injuries and diseases, which included injuries in accidents while on patrol or avoiding gunfire. None of these were included in official, published casualty reports, even though 80 percent were serious enough that the soldiers never returned to their units.[176]

Stay safe—join the U.S. Army. In June 2003, Rumsfeld used a preposterous statistical sleight to suggest that U.S. troops in Iraq were safer than residents of Washington, D.C.: He compared the 42 U.S. troops that had just been killed in Iraq in one month to the "215 murders a month" that *all of Baghdad* would have if its per capita murder rate were that of (much smaller) inner-city Washington. But the number of U.S. *troops* in Iraq was only one-fortieth the population of Baghdad, and one-quarter that of D.C. A soldier in Iraq was in fact nearly eight times as likely as a D.C. resident to be killed.

"We don't do [Iraqi] body counts." A Baghdad civilian, meanwhile, was more than twice as likely to be shot to death than a D.C. resident. Baghdad was "in the midst of an unprecedented crime wave," AP reported in August 2003. Gun deaths were running not at 215 a month but 470—compared to *10* before the U.S. invasion. Part of the problem, Iraqis said, was U.S. soldiers and contractors "opening fire randomly when they feel threatened." Many other Iraqis died of normally nonfatal injuries and ill-nesses because so many hospitals were damaged, over-flowing, and short of supplies. Many more were sickened, injured, or killed by the myriad health effects of the lack of electricity, safe drinking water and food; and general mayhem. A November 2004 report by the UK physicians' group Medact said the health of the Iraqi people had "dra-matically deteriorated since the 2003 invasion, [leading] to many thousands of deaths and injuries and high levels of illness." Also contributing were abuses in military prisons and detention camps (where the U.S. puppet

Prime Minister IYAD ALLAWI had earned the sobriquet "Saddam without a mustache," and was rumored to execute prisoners personally.)

"Change the channel." If U.S. casualties were to be pushed out of sight and mind, what would be done with obviously less important Iraqi ones? The U.S. military refused to release any estimates: Asked about Iraqi casualties, Gen. TOMMY FRANKS, then head of Central Command, said, "We don't do body counts." BRIG. GEN. VINCENT BROOKS of CentCom said, "It *just is not worth* trying to characterize by numbers." (Emphasis added.) BRIG. GEN. MARK KIMMITT'S simple and practical advice to Iraqis seeing TV images of civilians killed: "Change the channel." In December 2003, the CPA ordered the Iraqi Health Ministry to stop documenting civilian war casualties.[177] The ministry stopped releasing casualty figures the following year. To "gain the invasion's acceptance among the American people," wrote the *Boston Globe*'s Derrick Jackson, Bush "had to dehumanize innocent civilians to the point where if we slaughtered some of them, they were not worth our time."

"The numbers are really very low," said the U.S. administrator in Iraq, PAUL BREMER, of Iraqi casualties. According to a study published by the medical journal *The Lancet* in October 2004, the war had so far killed *nearly 100,000* Iraqis.[178] Most of those deaths by far were due to violence, especially "coalition" air strikes, which accounted for *95 percent* of deaths by acts of violence. Most of those killed by "coalition" forces were women and children. And the figures excluded Fallujah, where the coalition's devastating siege in

December 2004 would have "boosted the numbers unnaturally." Infant mortality also rose significantly, said the researchers, who were from Johns Hopkins and Columbia universities and Al-Mustansiriya University in Baghdad.

Dying to elect Bush. University of Michigan professor Juan Cole, a specialist in Shiite Islam, told Nancy Youssef of the *Detroit Free Press* that the administration was "trying to keep U.S. military casualties to a minimum in the run-up to the U.S. elections" by using airstrikes instead of ground forces, despite all the Iraqi casualties this entailed, adding that widespread casualties had lost the U.S. the Iraqis' "hearts and minds a long time ago."

Afraid of the Americans, not the fighters. In September 2004, the Iraqi Health Ministry released statistics showing that *operations by U.S. and coalition forces and Iraqi police were killing twice as many Iraqis—most of them civilians—as attacks by insurgents.* Many Iraqi deaths were never reported, so the actual numbers were likely significantly higher. Nancy Youssef recounted stories of Iraqi families killed by U.S. soldiers at checkpoints because they didn't stop fast enough, or shot from helicopters while sleeping on their roofs to escape the heat. Many blamed the coalition for allowing security to disintegrate and terrorism to flourish, Youssef wrote. But a Health Ministry official told her, "[E]veryone is afraid of the Americans, not the fighters. And they should be." Other Iraqis said, "The Americans keep criticizing Saddam for the mass graves. How many graves are the Americans making in Iraq?"[179] Some people just don't appreciate being liberated.

A godsend for bin Laden. In a March 2004 Pew poll in four other Muslim countries, large majorities rated bin Laden favorably and said suicide bombings against Americans and other Westerners in Iraq were justified. "In the face of what is seen as continued Western aggression," wrote Ian Buruma in the *New York Times*, "it is harder for Muslims in any country to take a strong stand against fellow Muslims for fear of being branded as traitors." Members of Indonesia's Liberal Islamic Network, which promoted moderate Islam, told Buruma that after the invasion of Iraq, they were seen as American stooges. The war "becomes a new justification for the fundamentalist attitude toward America or the West. Everything we've been working for—democracy, freedom of thought—all seems in vain," one member said.

In February 2004—a month after Bush said in his State of the Union speech that the world was "a better and safer place" as a result of the overthrow of Saddam Hussein—George Tenet told Congress the world was "equally, if not more . . . fraught with dangers for American interests" compared to a year earlier. And while Bush continued trumpeting about "freedom on the march," a classified National Intelligence Estimate in July 2004 said the possible outcomes for Iraq ranged from tenuous stability at best to civil war. Those views seemed to bear out former national security adviser Zbigniew Brzezinski's assessment of the war as "a moral, political and military failure."

Liberation by the numbers. Unless otherwise indicated, the following data come from the Brookings Institution's IRAQ INDEX:

- Approximate U.S. troop fatalities per month on average, mid-2003: 40. Early 2005: 80.
- Number of insurgents, 2003: 5,000. September 2004: 20,000. January 2005: 200,000, Iraq's intelligence chief told Agence France-Presse—more than the number of U.S. troops in Iraq. (Number according to Bush: "A handful.")
- Attacks on coalition forces, November 2003: 700. August 2004: 2,700.
- Attacks on Iraqi oil facilities, July 2003: 2. December 2004: 30.
- Iraqi civilians killed per month on average, mid-2003: 50. Late 2004/early 2005: 450.
- Average hours of electricity per day, nationwide, February 2004: 13. January 2005: 9.
- Percentage of Iraqis who viewed American-led forces as liberators: 2. (*New York Times*, June 2004.)

JUSTICE AND THE JUDICIARY: PACKING THE COURTS WITH REACTIONARY EXTREMISTS

Given what this administration has done both in Congress and the presidency, the courts are now our last hope. If Bush is elected and guts the court, all hope is lost for everybody.
—Rep. Jim McDermott (D-WA), July 2004

The Index cited other poll results:

- Do you favor U.S. forces withdrawing either immediately or after an elected government is in place? Shiite Arabs: 69 percent. Sunni Arabs: 82 percent. (January 2005.)
- Do you believe the abuse of prisoners at Abu Ghraib represents fewer than 100 people or that all Americans behave this way? All Americans: 54 percent. (May 2004.)
- Do you believe the insurgent attacks are legitimate form of resistance? Sunnis: 53 percent. (Shiite percent not provided.) (January 2005.)
- The insurgents believe national dignity requires the attacks—Totally or partially true: 68 percent. Not true: 13 percent. (May 2004.)
- The coalition invasion of Iraq has done more harm than good: 46 percent. More good than harm: 33 percent. (April 2004.)

Nothing Bush did would affect the country more lastingly and drastically than his nominations of judges to lifetime seats on federal benches—and nowhere was the hijacking of America by big business and religious special interests more starkly evident than in the kinds of judges he picked. As a former Reagan official told the *Washington Post*, "Everyone on the right agreed in 2000 that judicial nominations were the single most important reason to be for Bush."

And the right's goal was to pack the courts with far-right-wing zealots ready and eager to reverse decades of progress on environmental and consumer protections, women's rights, privacy rights, civil and voting rights, and religious freedom— judges whose views were, as the *New York Times* said, "out of whack with those of the vast majority of Americans." More than 200 such judges were appointed in Bush's first term. In his second, he was expected to name as many as four justices to the Supreme Court—to which the right looked to overturn *Roe v. Wade* (which was just one Court vote away—see **Abortion**) and much, much more; perhaps—you never know—even decide a future presidential **election**.

Five BIG lies. The most monstrous of the right's lies about judicial nominations was that *they* wanted to keep politics out of the process and appoint judges that were neutral and non-ideological—while the "left" wanted "activist" judges who would use their bench to *make* law in keeping with their own left-wing-commie-terrorist ideas and values. In fact, virtually all of Bush's nominees were chosen precisely for their judicial activism. (Let alone that single most spectacular case of judicial activism in U.S. history—the Supreme Court decision in *Bush v. Gore*, whose obvious political motivation and lack of legal precedent shocked most legal scholars.) The *Progress Report* advised the right "to get in touch with reality": "Presidents have always taken ideology into account" in nominating judges, "and the Senate has always reserved the right to withhold its consent on the same grounds. Why? Because they understand that a judge's ideological views are a major factor in how they make decisions." Senators "should give explicit consideration to a nominee's ideology." Actually, only the Democrats needed this advice.

Lie number two was that the federal courts were liberal. Before Bush even got started, judges appointed by Republican presidents controlled 7 of the country's 13 circuit (appeals) courts, and by the end of his first term were on their way to forming a majority on all of them. The Supreme Court had in recent years struck down laws that prohibited the carrying of guns near school grounds, that permitted state employees to challenge discrimination based on age and disability, and that permitted victims of sexual assault to sue their attackers. It refused in January 2005 to hear a challenge to a Florida law prohibiting gays and lesbians from adopting children. On June 28, 2005, the court put in a good day's work for the right by permitting displays of the Ten Commandments on government property; preserving cable companies' monopoly over high-speed Internet access over their systems; and refusing to interfere in the administration's attack on press freedom by refusing to hear appeals from two reporters facing jail for refusing to reveal confidential sources to the **Plamegate** investigators.

Lie number three was the charge of "obstructionism" by Democrats. In Bush's first term, the Senate confirmed 201, or 95 percent, of his 211 nominees that were brought up for a floor vote—a higher number and percentage than Papa Bush's (77 percent) or than in Clinton's or Reagan's first term (81 percent, 88 percent). Democratic filibusters blocked only seven Bush nominees. Another three filibusterees withdrew. Okay, call it ten, total. (Eighteen Bush nominees never made it out of the Judiciary Committee, many of them while the committee was under Republican control.) Republicans had blocked confirmation votes on more than 60 of Clinton's nominees, including nearly half his

Circuit Court nominees—and (or rather, because) *they* weren't Bible-thumping, *Roe*-dissing, pro-business radicals like Bush's. But the Democrats' relative handful was enough for the right to keep up a non-stop "obstructionism" shriek. And Bush renominated (and in some cases re-renominated) every one of them.

Lie number four was the claim of a vacancies crisis on the federal courts that demanded faster approval of Bush's nominees. By May 2003, federal court vacancies were already at their lowest level in 13 years. By the end of Bush's first term, the judiciary was 95 percent full—the lowest vacancy level since the Reagan era.

Lie number five was the implication that the Senate's job was merely to rubber-stamp the president's judicial nominations, no questions asked. The Framers "clearly wanted to avoid vesting too much power on this issue in the President," Sen. Ted Kennedy (D-MA) noted. "By requiring the President and the Senate to share the responsibility of appointing federal judges, the Framers created one of the most important checks and balances in the Constitution and laid a solid foundation for the independence of the Judiciary."

From "advise and consent" to rubber stamp. "Republican hypocrisy here is especially impressive," wrote Michael Kinsley in *Slate*. When Clinton was appointing judges, the senior Judiciary Committee Republican, Senator ORRIN HATCH, called for "more diligent and extensive . . . questioning of nominees' jurisprudential views." Under Bush, Hatch—the committee's chairman through 2004— "says Democrats have no right to demand any such thing."

When Senate confirmation of MIGUEL ESTRADA, Bush's nominee for a seat on the D.C. Circuit (a seat open only because Republicans had blocked a Clinton nominee), got stuck in a Democratic filibuster in 2003 because neither he nor the White House would provide any information about his judicial views, Republicans were "hoarse with rage that Democratic senators want to know what someone thinks before making him or her a judge," Kinsley noted. Naturally, they also accused the Democrats of being anti-Hispanic. (Estrada, who eventually withdrew his nomination, was described by his former superior in the Solicitor General's office as a "right-wing ideologue" who "couldn't be trusted to state the law in a fair, neutral way."[180])

To minimize the Senate's constitutional interference in His Majesty's appointments, in January 2003, Hatch's Judiciary Committee began scheduling nominees' hearings in bunches, reviewing more nominees in two weeks than the committee had in six months or more under Clinton—preventing Senators from reviewing each nominee with any care and "ushering in an era of conveyor-belt confirmations" of Bush nominees, the *New York Times* commented.

In early 2004, Bush used RECESS APPOINTMENTS to bypass Senate approval and install two of his most . . . outstanding appellate court nominees, WILLIAM PRYOR (see below) and CHARLES PICKERING [see sidebar, page 286], for one-year terms. *Republican* officials described the moves as examples of Bush's "determination to expand executive power at the expense of the legislative branch," the *Washington Post* noted. (Including non-judicial appointments, Bush made 110 recess appointments in his first term—nearly as many as Clinton did in two terms.) Bush appointed Pryor during a ten-day recess (including only five business days).

According to the most widely cited legal opinion, used even by the Reagan and Bush I Justice Departments, "an adjournment for 5 or even 10 days" did not "constitute the recess intended by the Constitution." Indeed, it was unclear whether the Constitution intended the president's recess appointment power to apply to judicial nominees at all. The purpose of giving judges lifetime tenure was to insulate them from political pressure; Pryor and Pickering would know that every decision they made could affect their chances of permanent appointment.

Charles Pickering (Fifth Circuit—TX, LA, MS). As a Mississippi state senator, Pickering fought for decades against racial integration, and cast several votes to block full extension of voting rights to African-Americans. In around 700 opinions as a district court judge, he never once ruled for the plaintiff in a claim of gender discrimination, and almost always dismissed claims or granted summary judgment in cases involving racial discrimination. He lectured defendants on the need to embrace religious belief and declared that the Bible should be "recognized as the absolute authority by which all conduct of man is judged." Pickering was "not exactly known for his scholarly acumen," either, Michael Crowley observed in *The New Republic*: "He has been reversed 26 times—15 of them for rulings that departed from 'well-settled principles of law.'" And this "good man" (as Bush called Pickering and every other one of his nominees, women included) was rejected twice by the Senate. What better proof that the filibuster had to go?

Repeat offenders. In February 2005, Bush—who must *always* win or he'll take his ball and go home—renominated 20 candidates who failed to be confirmed during his first term, including all seven of his filibustered Circuit Court nominees. Never had so many judges the Senate refused to confirm been renominated. But how could Bush *not* renominate candidates like these? Consider:

Janice Rogers "war in the streets" Brown (D.C. Circuit, second in influence only to the Supreme Court). "One of the most unapologetically ideological nominees of either party in many years."—*Washington Post.* "Far out of the mainstream of accepted legal principles.'"—*Atlanta Journal-Constitution.* Her views, if adopted, "would signal the death-knell for a vast range of health labor, and environmental standards" enacted during the last century.—*Progress Report.* Brown (like *every* Bush nominee) opposed abortion rights; supported sharp limits on corporate liability; absolutely opposed affirmative action; suggested (despite being black) "that racially discriminatory speech in the workplace, even when it rises to the level of illegal harassment, is protected by the First Amendment" (several Supreme Court precedents found just the opposite); and portrayed government in general as . . . well, thus spoke a possible Bush pick for the Supreme Court: "Where government moves in . . . [t]he result is: families under siege; war in the streets . . . the loss of civility and the triumph of deceit . . . [and] a debased, debauched culture which finds moral depravity entertaining and virtue contemptible." *"Today's senior citizens blithely cannibalize their grandchildren* because they have a right to get as much 'free' stuff as the political system will permit them to extract." (Emphasis added.) The New Deal—which brought us Social Security, the minimum wage, and fair labor laws—*"marks the triumph of our own socialist revolution."* Now if we could just get the seven-year-olds back into the factories . . .

William "Geneva contravention" Haynes (Fourth Circuit—MD, VA, WV, NC, SC). As Defense Department general counsel, was a principal author of the administration's policies that Geneva Convention protections do not apply to "enemy combatants," the president is not bound by laws prohibiting torture, and U.S. citizens can be detained without counsel or judicial review—a policy the Supreme Court rejected. Was responsible for legal standards for military personnel "which failed to prevent and may have actually helped produce torture and mistreatment of U.S. detainees in Iraq, Guantanamo Bay, and elsewhere," according to PFAW.

William "carte blanche" Myers (Ninth Circuit, covering nine western states and three-fourths of all federal lands; the most significant appeals court for environmental precedents). Longtime lobbyist for ranching, mining, and timber interests. Energetically fought Clinton's "Roadless Policy," designed to protect public lands from development. Argued that the Clean Water Act, Endangered Species Act (ESA), and federal protection of wetlands are unconstitutional. As Bush's Interior Department solicitor, helped weaken the ESA. Attempted to change Interior regulations to allow a 1,600-acre, open pit gold mine to be established in the California Desert Conservation Area and on Quechan Indian lands. After a mining company was caught mining public land in California, Myers quietly tried to have the land given to the company for free. Left the Interior Department amid a departmental investigation into whether he gave illegal favors to a politically connected Wyoming rancher who enjoyed "virtually carte blanche authority to violate federal grazing laws," said the *Progress Report.* Was the first judicial nominee ever opposed by the conservative National Wildlife Federation in its 68-year history. Was never a judge, and not a single member of the American Bar Association's judicial screening committee rated him "well qualified." "Myers's chief qualification for the job rests not in his legal acumen but in the fact that his anti-environmental views match those of the president," said the *Arizona Daily Star.*

Priscilla "to-the-right-of-the-right" Owen (Fifth Circuit—TX, LA, MS). Among the most extreme right-wing judicial activists—indeed a regular dissenter—on the Texas Supreme Court, which is "made up mostly of other conservative Republicans," noted the *Houston Chronicle*, which cited Owen's "distinct bias against consumers and in favor of large corporations." Among her decisions, allowed ENRON to avoid paying millions in school taxes by allowing it an accounting advantage that an appellate court had deemed unfair and unconstitutional. AG ALBERTO GONZALES, then Owen's colleague on the court, repeatedly criticized her for ignoring the law—such as in a case where Owen would have effectively rewritten the law to protect manufacturers of products that cause injury—and described another of her decisions as "an unconscionable case of judicial activism."

William "abomination" Pryor (recess appointee, Eleventh Circuit—AL, FL, GA). As Alabama attorney general, called

Roe v. Wade "the worst abomination of constitutional law in our history" and defended restrictions on abortion with no (constitutionally required) exception to protect the health of the pregnant woman. "[B]elieves it is constitutional to imprison gay men and lesbians for expressing their sexuality in the privacy of their own homes."[181] On the Circuit Court bench, cast a vote that prevented the court from rehearing a challenge to the Florida law prohibiting gays and lesbians from adopting children—"the only such statute in the country, and . . .the only categorical adoption ban on the state's books," the *New York Times*'s Linda Greenhouse noted. Florida took adoption applications even from would-be adoptive parents with a history of drug abuse or domestic violence. The state senator who sponsored the adoption measure said "its purpose was to send a message to the gay community that 'we're really tired of you' and 'we wish you'd go back into the closet.'"[182]

Nuclear war. The 200-year-old Senate filibuster rule, whereby 41 or more senators could prevent debate from ending, was designed to ensure bipartisan consultation and prevent a narrow majority from abusing its power. Senate Republicans—prolific filibusterers when they were in the minority—now called judicial filibusters unconstitutional. The issue reached its crisis over Bush's renominated candidates in early 2005, when the Republicans threatened to deploy the "nuclear option" (or as they called it, "constitutional option") and eliminate judicial filibusters. "It is like a banana republic," said Sen. Charles Schumer (D-NY), "just steamrollering over the rules by decree." In an independent poll, only 40 percent of Americans supported the rule change.[183]

A "compromise" was reached by seven Democratic and seven Republican senators in May 2005 which the Dems proclaimed a victory. It would essentially let them keep the judicial filibuster as long as they never used it. Except in "extraordinary circumstances"—which the Repubs made clear meant basically never, or else it would be right back to the nuclear option. In fact, many Republicans warned "that they were already eager to challenge the agreement by pushing forward contested candidates," the *New York Times* reported. The Repubs also said the deal made it harder for Dems to filibuster Bush's Supreme Court nominees—which everyone regarded as the real issue, for which the lower court fights were merely a proxy.

Meanwhile, the deal let three of Bush's most, well, *extraordinary* nominees—PRISCILLA OWEN, JANICE ROGERS BROWN, and WILLIAM PRYOR—go to the Senate floor for a filibuster-free, "up-or-down" vote, where all three were confirmed. And that part of the deal—unlike the filibuster part—could *not* be reversed any time one side wanted. "This deal is more of a capitulation than a compromise," said Rep. Melvin Watt (D-NC), chairman of the Congressional Black Caucus.

Assaulting and battering judicial independence. The judiciary, like Congress (and the rest of the world, for that matter), was expected to bow before the White House—not act, as per the Constitution, as a check and balance. (See **Presidential Power**.) "ASHCROFT CONDEMNS JUDGES WHO QUESTION BUSH," ran an AP headline when, in his first remarks following his long-overdue "resignation" as AG in November 2004, Ashcroft said federal judges were jeopardizing national security during war by issuing rulings contradictory to Bush policies. (He was angry over recent court rejections of the administration's positions that the Geneva Conventions do not apply to terrorism suspects and that they may be held indefinitely without access to lawyers; see **Human Rights**.)

In March 2005, after 19 different state and federal judges ruled that the feeding tube could be removed from a severely brain-damaged Florida woman, TERRI SCHIAVO, Bush allies like TOM DELAY and brothers like Jeb tore savagely into the judges. DeLay said, evangelical gangster-style, "the time will come for the men responsible for this to answer for their behavior." A few days later, in "a moment that was horrifying even by the rock-bottom standards of the campaign that Republican zealots are conducting against the nation's judiciary," the *New York Times* commented, Judiciary Committee member JOHN CORNYN (R-TX) stood up in the Senate chamber "and excuse[d] murderous violence against judges," saying recent courthouse violence might be explained by the frustration that "builds up" about judges who "are making political decisions." In those violent incidents, a career criminal had killed a judge in his courtroom while trying to shoot his way out of a trial, and a deranged man, furious that a judge had dismissed a lawsuit, executed her mother and husband. No, no—just decent, ordinary Americans driven mad by liberal judges.

"Trying to intimidate judges used to be a crime, not a bombastic cudgel for cynical politicians," said the *New York Times*. "Through public attacks, proposed legislation and even the threat of impeachment, ideologues are trying to bully judges into following their political line. Mr. DeLay and his allies have moved beyond ordinary criticism to undermining the separation of powers, not to mention the rule of law."

On the legislative front, the Republicans—those great defenders of the sanctity of marriage and of private rights against big government—pushed through a bill designed to keep Schiavo alive—against her husband's will and, he said, her own. Bush cut short a vacation (compare his response to the terrorism briefing a week before **September 11**) to rush back to Washington and sign it. Seventy-six percent of Americans polled disapproved of the GOPpies' intervention.

Another GOP resolution declared that *international law should not be taken into account* in interpreting the Constitution (which makes all treaties signed by the U.S. "the law of the land")—something the Supreme Court had just done in striking down the DEATH PENALTY for offenders younger than 18. And during a controversy in 2004 over the display of the Ten Commandments in an Alabama courthouse, Repubs introduced a bill to bar the federal courts from applying the First Amendment when officials violate church-state separation. "[U]nhappy with some rulings of the judiciary," the *New York Times* observed, Republicans "are trying to write it out of its constitutional role."

Supreme Court ScaThology. Bush said he wanted to nominate Supreme Court justices "in the mold of Justice [ANTONIN] SCALIA or Justice [CLARENCE] THOMAS." Lawyer and author Adam Cohen described an America under a ScaTho-lagized Supreme Court: "Abortion might be a crime in most states. Gay people could be thrown in prison for having sex in their homes. States might be free to become mini-theocracies, endorsing Christianity and using tax money to help spread the gospel. The Constitution might no longer protect inmates from being brutalized by prison guards. Family and medical leave and environmental protections could disappear." Hysteria? Hyperbole? Hypoglycemia? Hardly. All based on ScaThomas's written opinions.[184]

John "mystery man" Roberts. Justice SANDRA DAY O'CONNOR, the Supreme Court's independent-minded swing vote throughout her tenure, resigned in July 2005. Bush's nominee to replace her—and then to replace William Rehnquist as Chief Justice after his death in August—was rightwing lawyer and corporate lobbyist John Roberts, who was first appointed a judge in 2003. "Little was known" about Roberts, the media said—and the White House tried to keep it that way by withholding files of cases he worked on as deputy solicitor general. Alas, enough was known. Roberts had:[185]

- Urged the Supreme Court to overturn *Roe v. Wade;* won a case that stopped some doctors from even discussing **abortion**; and "weighed in on behalf of Operation Rescue, a violent anti-abortion group."
- Argued in favor of officially sponsored school prayer before the Supreme Court, which rejected his argument.
- Suggested the Endangered Species Act was unconstitutional.
- "Opposed clean air rules and worked to help coal companies strip mine mountaintops."

- Wrote papers supporting "far-right legal theories about 'takings' which would make it almost impossible for the government to enforce most environmental legislation."
- "Worked to keep Congress from defending parts of the Voting Rights Act."
- Argued American POWs tortured in Iraq during the Gulf War should not be able to pursue claims in federal courts.

K STREET PROJECT:
TOWARD ONE-PARTY RULE

In 1995, TOM DELAY (R-TX), then House Majority Whip, joined with right-wing revolutionary GROVER NORQUIST in creating the notorious "K STREET PROJECT," whose purpose was to cut the Dems off from the **corporate** lobbying community—centered on Washington's K Street—and convert it, with its hundreds of millions of dollars in political money and tens of thousands of jobs, into a Republican political machine.

It was made clear to lobbyists that they could not do business with, contribute to, or employ Democrats if they hoped to advance their agendas in the newly GOP-controlled House. Those who needed a warning were invited into DeLay's office and shown their place on a "friendly" or "unfriendly" list of donors to each party, complete with amounts given. "If you want to play in our revolution, you have to live by our rules," DeLay told the press. (Evidently living by DeLay's rules—while violating those of the United States—in December 2004, VIACOM, parent company of CBS, advertised for a lobbyist as follows: "Must be a male with Republican stripes."[186])

After 2001, the operation was headed by Sen. RICK SANTORUM (R-PA) and Rep. ROY BLUNT (R-MO), DeLay's handpicked successor as House Whip, who divorced his first wife to marry an ALTRIA lobbyist in 2003. (Blunt's lobbyist son Andrew's clients included Altria-owned Philip Morris and Kraft Foods and part-owned Miller Brewing, and Altria was Blunt's largest campaign contributor.) Santorum and Blunt held weekly meetings with top Republican lobbyists to help fill top lobbying positions with Republicans. Soon, "Republican lobbyist" became a redundancy. "The corporate lobbyists who once ran the show . . . are being replaced by party activists who are loyal first and foremost to the GOP [not their corporation or industry]," wrote Nicholas Confessore in *Washington Monthly.* "Through them, Republican leaders can now marshal armies of lobbyists, lawyers, and public relations experts—not to mention enormous amounts of money—to meet the party's goals." By May 2005, the *Washington Post* reported, the GOP House leadership had used its "K Street lobbying arm" to win "more than 50 consecutive [legislative] victories . . . without a single defeat" by "delegating authority" to lobbyists to "help negotiate deals" with individual House members.[187]

This new machine "could usher in a new era of one-party government," wrote Confessore: More and more K Street money helps Republicans win larger and larger majorities in Congress. The larger the Republican majority, the less reason K Street has to hire or contribute to Democrats, "slowly starving them of the means by which to challenge GOP rule." It's a beautiful thing.

LABOR: *THE WAR ON WORKERS' RIGHTS AND WAGES*

Bush wasted no time earning such accolades from union leaders as, "almost seems to have a mission to attack working people" and "a nightmare for workers" whose policies are "nothing short of a declaration of war."

In just its first six months, the **corporate-owned** Bush White House nominated a host of anti-labor lawyers for key government posts and issued a barrage of executive orders and rule changes that directly attacked unions and wiped out a decade's worth of progress on workplace regulations. The first major bill Bush signed as president was a repeal of workplace safety standards.

His first term ended in similar style. Among 15 or 20 anti-labor rulings in just the last few months of 2004, the Republican majority on the presidentially appointed NATIONAL LABOR RELATIONS BOARD (NLRB):

- Gave companies greater flexibility to lock out workers in labor disputes.
- Made it more difficult for temporary workers to unionize.
- Made it more difficult for unions to obtain financial information from companies during contract talks.
- Ruled that graduate students working as teaching assistants do not have the right to unionize at private universities.
- Denied nonunion employees the right to have a co-worker present when managers call them in for investigative or disciplinary meetings.

- Upheld a company's decision to fire a worker who had asked a colleague to testify to support her claim of sexual harassment by a manager.

The labor board's Bush-appointed chairman said he "wouldn't characterize [the rulings] as pro-business or pro-union. I'd like to say they're pro-employee." Labor relations experts said the rulings were "so hostile to unions and to collective bargaining that they run counter to the goals of the National Labor Relations Act," the 1935 law that gave Americans the right to form unions.[188]

In other labor-bashing moves, the administration:

- Passed new rules allowing companies to cut off 8 million workers from OVERTIME PAY. Why? Because, anti-Labor Secretary ELAINE CHAO explained, employers were spending $2 billion a year on "needless litigation" by workers trying to receive the pay they were promised. Her department also *offered employers suggestions on how they could avoid paying legally mandated overtime*—such as cutting hourly wages to compensate.
- Proposed to make it easier for companies to convert traditional PENSION PLANS to "cash balance" plans—which can cost older workers tens of thousands of dollars in benefits—despite a federal court ruling that such benefit reductions were illegal.
- Proposed regulations to help companies avoid AGE-DISCRIMINATION lawsuits from workers forced into these plans.

- Allowed companies to cut or eliminate their retirees' DRUG COVERAGE without losing out on a new tax subsidy under Bush's Medicare bill. The provision's major backers were such major Bush donors as Lucent Technologies, General Motors, Dow Chemical, and SBC Communications.

Speaking of labor, while U.S. workers enjoyed the fewest vacation days in the industrialized world, Bush by one estimate spent 42 percent of his first six months in office on vacation. Then he took a month-long vacation.

Wal-nut. In 2004, **Dick** Cheney declared that WAL-MART "exemplifies some of the very best qualities in our country—hard work, the spirit of enterprise, fair dealing, and integrity." That's funny, because Wal-Mart paid poverty-level wages, regularly violated environmental and labor laws, and provided "such paltry health care benefits that many of its workers are forced to rely on public assistance."[189] Over 100 charges had been lodged against Wal-Mart—America's largest private employer (1.1 million)—for such labor law violations as firing workers who attempted to organize a union, locking workers into workplaces, and doctoring employees' time records to further reduce their miserable wages. Cheney's answer to such problems? "Litigation reform" to limit workers' ability to fight back.

MEDIA AND IMAGE CONTROL: *PROPAGANDA, DISINFORMATION AND INTIMIDATION*

> *The real axis of evil in America is the brilliance of our marketing and the stupidity of our people. Bush has $180 million to spend. With that amount of money, he can convince people to drink paint. And he probably will.*
>
> —Bill Maher

> *If President Bush said that the Earth was flat, news headlines would read, "Opinions Differ on Shape of the Earth."*
>
> —*New York Times* columnist Paul Krugman

Among the Bush administration's many superlatives (most secretive, most duplicitous, most bellicose, most beholden to big money) must be reckoned its famously flawless image and "message" management. "This administration is the most disciplined ever to operate in the modern media world," wrote *Newsweek*'s Eleanor Clift. "They repeat their message over and over, and the cable-news cameras transmit the images and the words unfiltered . . . [giving them] an unmatched megaphone. If we had state-run television, would it be any different?"

In fact, it would; people weren't as easily fooled by Soviet TV. The Bushies were well served by a *semblance* of an independent and critical press—in which what little criticism there was was effectively drowned out by an army of right-wing flacks and Democrat-baiters, and by the daily deluge of dreck, the semi-pornographic celebrity trials and other tabloid "news."

Exhibit A is of course the GOP News Network, aka FOX, the most widely watched news network, which is owned by right-wing tycoon Rupert Murdoch and run by former Nixon media maven Roger Ailes. With its cable channel 35 TV stations and 200 affiliates, and its partnership with right-wing CLEAR CHANNEL COMMUNICATIONS' 1,200 radio stations, all pouring well-coordinated innuendo on Dems and liberals 24/7 from behind a sham of independence, "fairness" and "balance"—Fox is the most formidable propaganda arm any right-wing regime could ask for. Yet the other networks, precisely by being less obvious, by remaining at best *neutral* in the face of outrage after Bush outrage, rendered perhaps even better service to the White House. For their part, the corporate-owned media, perennially seeking government favors such as repeal of media ownership rules, could not ask for friendlier regulators than Bush's, and weren't eager to make enemies out of so vindictive a crew as Bush's— whose party also happened to be supported by most of their corporate advertisers.

Watch what you say: Cowing and containing the press. The press learned right from the start that it was hard enough to get answers out of the Bush White House if they thought you were on their side. If they didn't, you were denied presidential interviews, like the *Los Angeles Times*, or banned from the campaign plane, like the *New York Times*, or banished to a back row and to silence at Bush's rare press conferences. The press learned, if you will, that "all Americans . . . need to watch what they say, watch what they do," as then-White House press secretary ARI FLEISCHER warned in 2001 in response to a remark by comedian/commentator Bill Maher.

When Bush told reporters they could help him "explain to people why I make the decisions I make," he indicated how he saw the media's role: as extension of White House communications office; just another loyal subordinate.

Indeed, the Bushies' vision went far beyond "discipline" and staying "on message" and scrupulously keeping Bush away from unscripted events and real questions. It was about shutting out the real news media and filling the vacuum with *manufactured* news; destroying the very distinction between real and unreal; conquering and ruling not only Congress and the courts and the news media—the whole system of checks and balances—but their ultimate adversary, truth itself.

The "liberal" media. The Bushies regarded the media (apart from Fox News) as hopelessly liberal and hostile (or pretended to, to keep up the pressure and *preempt* any liberalism). Let's go debunking. The watchdog group Media Matters for America inventoried all guests who appeared on Fox, CNN, and MSNBC during their January 20, 2005, inauguration coverage. Including only those whose party or political affiliation was generally known, the group reported that Republican and conservative commentators outnumbered Democrats and progressives 19–7 on Fox, 13–2 on MSNBC, and 10–1 on CNN (popularly known around the right-wing blogosphere as the Communist News Network—even if its senior political analyst, BILL SCHNEIDER, though billed by CNN as a nonpartisan political analyst, *was* a resident scholar at the right-wing American Enterprise Institute). Moreover, the rare Democrat or progressive usually appeared opposite conservatives, whereas most Republican and conservative guests appeared solo or alongside fellow conservatives.[190]

Plame-Rove-gate and the silence of the media lambs. On July 6, 2005, as word spread that it was KARL ROVE who, perhaps criminally, leaked the identity of CIA agent VALERIE PLAME to *Time* magazine's Matt Cooper—and if so, may have perjured himself before the grand jury investigating the matter—not a single member of the press corps aboard Air Force One on the way to the G-8 summit in Scotland saw fit to ask White House spokesman SCOTT MCCLELLAN about it.[191]

Downplaying "Downing Street." Equally revealing was the *non*-revealing by the U.S. media of the "DOWNING STREET MEMO"—the minutes of a July 2002 meeting in which British Prime Minister Tony Blair and his advisers learned of a White House effort to fix "the intelligence and facts" to justify the invasion of **Iraq**, while publicly insisting for eight more months that war was the last option. The memo, which was leaked to the London *Sunday Times* and published on May 1, 2005, also said there was "little discussion in Washington of the aftermath after military action."

Newsworthy? Relevant to the situation in Iraq? Just a wee bit *scandalous*? The memo caused an enormous stir in the UK and other countries—yet in the 19 daily White House briefings that followed, it "was the subject of only 2 out of the approximately 940 questions asked by the White House press corps," the *New York Times*'s Frank Rich noted. It took more than a month for any U.S. news network to address the story or for any reporter to ask Bush about it publicly. (Bush's reply? All together now: "The world is better off without Saddam Hussein in power.") The "liberal" *New York Times*, *Washington Post*, and National Public Radio all "missed" the story. From May 1 to June 6, it "received approximately 20 mentions on CNN, Fox News, MSNBC, ABC, CBS, NBC and PBS *combined*," Eric Boehlert reported in *Salon*. Meanwhile, "the same outlets found time to mention 263 times the tabloid controversy that erupted [around] a photograph showing Saddam Hussein in his underwear." David Brock of Media Matters for America told Boehlert: "This is where all the work conservatives and the administration have done in terms of bullying the press, making it less willing to write confrontational pieces—this is where it's paid off."

"Screw you." *American Journalism Review* editor Lori Robertson attributed the Bushies' success in "message management" to a number of factors: a Republican-controlled Congress "less likely to speak ill of the White House"; after 9/11, a docile Democratic opposition and reduced access to the president, ostensibly for security reasons ("The logic of security knows no limits," as *Newsweek*'s Howard Fineman remarked); and with the proliferation of the media, the White House no longer had to cooperate with the big three networks, media historian Douglas Brinkley noted—it could say, "Screw you, we'll give the exclusive to Fox." (And it sometimes did. See pg 321.)

Shutting out the press. At the end of his first term, Bush had given only 17 press conferences (six of which were in election year 2004), compared to the 44 and 84 that Clinton and Bush I respectively had given at that point. Apart from two or three election debates every four years, press conferences are the only times a president publicly faces questions. And as veteran White House correspondent Helen Thomas told *Salon*, "If he doesn't answer questions, there's no accountability. He can rule by edict—which he is very much doing these days."

Not that a Bush press conference was worth much, except as a study in evasion, duplicity, media control, and media toadying. On March 6, 2003, on the eve of the Iraq invasion, Bush gave a prime-time news conference—his second since taking office more than two years earlier—to explain his decision for war. The press corps was summoned into the East Room in pairs, "as if we were in grammar school," one reporter told *USA Today*. No reporter known to ask hard or critical questions was called on for questions, and for the first time, no follow-up questions were taken. Helen Thomas, an outspoken liberal, was banished from her time-honored place in the front row and not called upon by the president for the first time in memory. As Bush repeatedly said Saddam Hussein possessed "weapons of mass terror" and posed a "direct threat" to the U.S., the press corps "lobbed softballs at Bush, refusing to challenge the president for his reasons to lead the country into an unprovoked and globally-opposed war," wrote Lori Robertson. The *New York Times*'s Elizabeth Bumiller's sorry explanation was, "It's frightening to stand up there . . . asking the president of the United States a question when the country is about to go to war . . . nobody wanted to get into an argument with the president at this very serious time."

Gradually, however, the press went from "going along" to not going at all. In May 2005, so few reporters turned up at a

Bush "question-and-answer session" with Afghan president Hamid Karzai that the White House was forced to pack the room with interns. Referring to reporters at such staged White House functions as "props," one reporter told the *Washington Times*, "Since we can't ask questions, why schlep over there?"[192]

Meanwhile, the White House's "stonewall approach" to the press was setting the tone for the whole federal government. National security correspondent David Wood called it "distressing . . . to see it spread elsewhere to what I had thought of as a nonpolitical place, like the military." The people's right to know about the "the people's business," Wood remarked, was "pretty much gone."[193] (Also see **Secrecy**.)

This White House didn't like to let news *in*, either. Securing his reputation as the most insulated and out-of-touch U.S. president, Bush boasted that he rarely read news stories ("the most objective sources I have are people on my staff who tell me what's happening in the world"). "[T]hey don't want any contrary opinion or fact to shake their faith in the essential excellence of their policies," wrote the *New York Times*'s Maureen Dowd. Bush's intent, no doubt, was also to strike a populist pose and to discredit the press as just too liberal and elitist to bother with.

MANUFACTURING CONSENT. (Gravest apologies for the use of a Chomsky phrase, but it is so perfectly apt.)

1. Mythologizing the Leader. The networks' fawning coverage of the president at times approached the leader-worship of totalitarian states. Contributing mightily to this effect was the White House's Riefenstahlian production and direction of Bush's televised appearances, with their carefully screened, cheering crowds, ranks of uniformed soldiers and schoolchildren, and slogan-emblazoned backdrops. Bush's image makers—a small army of veteran network TV experts headed by a former Fox News producer—posed the Great Leader in front of Mount Rushmore, shamelessly aligning his face with the other four presidents'. (Perhaps if Republicans like GROVER NORQUIST weren't already lobbying to add *Reagan's* face to the monument . . . but wait, perhaps there's room for both!) The apotheosis of Bush stagecraft was his heroically flight-suited landing on board the aircraft carrier USS *Abraham Lincoln* in May 2003 to declare, as that famous banner read, "Mission Accomplished" in Iraq. "Try to imagine Ted Kennedy landing that navy jet on the deck of that aircraft carrier," taunted TOM DELAY. Bush of course hadn't *landed* it—he'd lost his pilot's rating in 1972 after failing to report for a medical exam while AWOL from his National Guard service; and Kennedy might not have *lied* that the expensive jet landing was necessary because the ship was too far from shore for a helicopter landing—but never mind: "The image of George Bush as a noble and infallible warrior in the service of his nation must be fanatically maintained," wrote Ron Reagan, "because behind the image lies . . . nothing?"

2. Phony-baloney photo-ops. Again and again, Bush posed with police, fire, school, hospital, and housing officials to take credit for their federal funding—which his administration was busy cutting or eliminating. (See **Economic Policy.**) On a wreath-laying visit to Martin Luther King, Jr.'s tomb in Atlanta in 2004 to observe King's birthday (and, just while in town, appear at a $2,000-a-person fund-raiser), Bush was loudly booed by protesters: "Bush's policies contradict everything Dr. King stood for," one critic said. On King's birthday the previous year, said a former King colleague, Bush had "initiated plans to gut affirmative action." Those irony-meisters, the Secret Service, citing security for the president, told organizers of a civil rights symposium in a nearby church that they would have to cut it short.

3. See no dissent, hear no dissent; above all, *broadcast* no dissent. The boos Bush endured in Atlanta were a rare exception. At Bush and Cheney campaign appearances, potential protesters weren't allowed anywhere near the events; at some, people were required to sign a loyalty oath to be let in, lest any peep of protest or anti-Bush sign or T-shirt be caught by the cameras. (See **Free Speech**.)

ALL THE NEWS THAT'S COUNTERFEIT TO PRINT. Not content with *cowing* reporters, the Bushies took to *buying* them—or just making them up. By early 2005, the count of "reporters" and columnists the Bush administration paid with taxpayers' money to write propaganda disguised as independent journalism had reached six, which may only have scratched the surface.

"In Washington, I'm Karen Ryan reporting." So ended a news report about Medicare changes broadcast on 40 TV stations around the country in early 2004. "The new law, say officials, will simply offer people with Medicare more ways to make their health coverage more affordable," Ryan reported. What Ryan never "reported," as all but the most miserably ignorant of you know, was that she was not a reporter but a contract employee playing a reporter in a "video news release" produced by the Bush administration. (A Spanish version featured "Alberto Garcia reporting.") It was part of a $12 million, taxpayer-funded ad campaign touting Bush's new Medicare bill, which 71 percent of seniors opposed as a sweetheart deal for drug companies. (See **Health Insurance**.) Ryan, whose past assignments included plugging FluMist and Excedrin in infomercials, was "if nothing else consistent in her journalistic patrons," Frank Rich remarked.

The ad was fake *and* illegal: In May 2004, the GAO said that besides being "not strictly factual," the fake news report violated the law against using taxpayer money for "covert propaganda." The administration defended its use of what a spokesman chillingly called "modern public information tools." The money appeared to have been taken from the Medicare trust fund. The media firm that placed the ads was headed by Bush contributor ALEX CASTELLANOS, who also created anti-Kerry attack ads for Bush's 2004 campaign and worked for healthcare companies to get the Medicare bill passed. In all, the administration, at a time of ballooning budget deficits, spent $250 million in public funds on PR for its policies during its first term—twice as much as the Clintonites had during the previous term—the largest portion of which ($97 million) was spent to produce the fake reports.

The drug videos: Just say no to honesty. In a similar vein—pardon the expression—the Bushies produced and distributed fake TV news segments about the effects of drug use among young people. They were broadcast by nearly 300 TV stations before the GAO declared them illegal; like the Medicare videos, they didn't identify the government as the source. Even if the message was worthwhile, the interesting thing was the Bushies' *preference* for doing it the devious, conniving, illegal, Bushie way.

No Bribe Left Behind. Next in the unfolding payola scandal came ARMSTRONG WILLIAMS, a prominent, conservative black media figure to whom the administration secretly paid $240,000 in taxpayer funds to promote Bush's NO CHILD LEFT BEHIND ACT on his nationally syndicated TV show, to interview the education secretary, and to encourage other journalists to tout NCLB as well—all while posing as an independent journalist. Armstrong's payoffs, which began in 2003, came out of around $1 million the Education Department paid PR firm KETCHUM COMMUNICATIONS to promote NCLB—while the states and schools that had to *implement* it went so underfunded, some couldn't afford textbooks. By January 2005, when the Williams story came out, the administration had paid Ketchum nearly $100 million in taxpayer funds. How much of that might have been used to buy other "journalists" remained to be discovered. But Williams told *The Nation,* "[t]his happens all the time . . . There are others." The department contracted with at least six other PR and media firms, one of which was "to develop short syndicated newspaper articles for national distribution," the *New York Times* reported. At least Williams admitted to having done something wrong—unlike the Bush officials who cooked up these payola schemes and defended them as "permissible" and "appropriate."

Unholy matrimony. Next case: MAGGIE GALLAGHER and MICHAEL McMANUS, conservative journalists paid by the administration to promote Bush's plans to spend $300 million of public money to encourage marriage. Gallagher, a supposed marriage expert, insisted the $21,500 she was paid was only to write brochures and essays for the government, not to tout the policies in her column; but meanwhile, she did so repeatedly—praising Bush as a "genius" and as the nation's all-knowing "daddy" (quick, a Bush-sickness bag!) during a period when he was publicly debating those policies—without disclosing she was being paid by the administration.

McManus praised Bush policies in his syndicated column without acknowledging being paid $10,000 by Health and Human Services (HHS), ostensibly to help train counselors about marriage (problematic in itself—how did this become the government's business, and how much did it have to do with the Bushies' anti-gay agenda?). HHS assistant secretary Wade Horn tried to shift blame and blur the issue by saying the line between journalism, commentary, and consulting had blurred. (Right—and who was doing the blurring?) "Where's the line?" he asked. It seemed clear enough: "Readers have a right to expect that the columns they are reading have not been secretly bought and paid for by the government," wrote journalist and self-described, former "witting cog in the Republican sleaze machine" David Brock.

Regular folks. "I just want to make sure that my daughter has Social Security when she retires as well," said SANDRA JAQUES, a single mom from Iowa, as she sat a few feet from Bush at a White House economic conference in December 2004—

showing how "regular folks," as Ms. Jaques was introduced, were behind Bush's **Social Security** plan. This regular folk, however, also happened to be the Iowa state director of a conservative advocacy group, FreedomWorks, whose founders were former Republican leaders Dick Armey and Jack Kemp, blogger Josh Marshall reported. Jaques also served as a spokeswoman for For Our Grandchildren, a group mounting a nationwide campaign for private savings accounts, the core of Bush's Social Security scheme.

Why not whole halls full of "regular folks"? Such were the "Ask President Bush" town-hall-style meetings held during the 2004 campaign, which were packed with carefully screened Bush supporters but carefully designed so that "unsuspecting viewers" tuning in their local news would think they were "watching a completely open forum," the *New York Daily News* reported. ("Typical question: 'Mr. President, as a child, how can I help you get votes?'")[194]

"Position: Top." For nearly two years, until February 2005, JEFF GANNON was a fully credentialed White House correspondent and "Washington Bureau Chief" for the Web site *Talon News*, and not only attended press conferences daily but was called on for questions with a regularity the *Washington Post* or *New York Times* might envy—questions such as, "How are you [Bush] going to work with people [Senate Democrats] who seem to have divorced themselves from reality?" Gannon turned out to be JAMES GUCKERT, working under an alias for a "news organization" with no circulation or readership, and to have "an apparently promising career as an X-rated $200-per-hour [gay] 'escort'" which he advertised by posing nude on his own

Web sites, such as Hotmilitarystud.com and Militaryescorts
M4M.com, where he described himself as "military, muscular,
masculine and discrete [sic] . . . Position: Top."[195] *Talon* and
GOPUSA, another site that used Gannon's stuff, were
owned by BOBBY EBERLE, a wealthy Texas GOP donor, dele-
gate to the 2000 Republican National Convention, and
member of Texas Christian Coalition and Texas Right to
Life, and staffed mostly by Republican activist volunteers.
Their "news" was often copied, verbatim and without attri-
bution, from GOP and White House press releases;
"Gannon" lifted more than half of the text in at least two of
his articles directly from GOP "fact sheets," according to
Media Matters for America. (He did show some originality
on one occasion, when he reported, "Kerry Could Become
First Gay President." Guckert, wrote Frank Rich, was
apparently "yet another link in the boundless network of
homophobic Republican closet cases.") "Gannon" was real
enough, however, for right-wing radio/TV hosts Rush Limbaugh and Sean Hannity to cite repeatedly as a source; for
Hannity to describe as "a terrific Washington bureau chief
and White House correspondent" and invite onto his show;
and to be invited to the exclusive White House press
Christmas party in 2003 and 2004.

Jihad. The *New York Times*'s Maureen Dowd, who was
denied a White House pass after Bush took over, was mystified
by how "someone with an alias, a tax evasion problem and
[nude] Internet pictures . . . is credentialed to cover a White
House that won a second term by mining homophobia and
preaching family values." How did Guckert/Gannon/hotmili-
tarystud.com get through the normally months-long Secret

Service background check, and retain his pass for two years? Former Reagan and Bush I official Bruce Bartlett was less mystified. "If Gannon was using an alias," he wrote, "the White House staff had to be involved in maintaining his cover."[196]

Dowd wasn't *really* mystified: "With the Bushies, if you're their friend, anything goes. If you're their critic, nothing goes. They're waging a jihad against journalists— buying them off so they'll promote administration programs, trying to put them in jail for doing their jobs and replacing them with ringers . . . Even the Nixon White House didn't do anything this creepy."

Outed: The Bushies are a bunch of po-mos. Rich saw the story's full import: The Bushies' "brilliant strategy," he wrote, was not merely to go over the heads of "the filter," as Bush called the news media, and to lie "directly to the people"; it was, "to blur the boundaries between the fake and the real and thereby demolish the whole notion that there could possibly be an objective and accurate free press." After railing for years against postmodernism and relativism as threats to Western civilization, conservatives "are now welcoming in a brave new world in which it's a given that there can be no empirical reality in news, only the reality you want to hear (or they want you to hear)."

INFORMATION WARFARE. The Bushies' manufacturing of news spread to—or was it from?—the Pentagon, whose "psy-ops" propaganda operations were once aimed only at "enemy" populations.

In 2002, the Pentagon set up an OFFICE OF STRATEGIC INFLUENCE (OSI) to pipe propagandistic news items—

possibly including false ones, officials acknowledged—to foreign news media in order to influence overseas opinion. (To further the struggle against the Islamist extremists, with their myths and lies.) As critics noted, misleading information could easily be picked up and repeated by American news outlets. It was fitting, therefore, that the operation was headed by Under Secretary of Defense DOUGLAS FEITH, whose rogue **intelligence** ops cooked up the Saddam-Osama link used to justify the Iraq invasion and helped spin rosy pictures of post-war Iraq.

News of the OSI became such an embarrassment that it was quickly shut down. But "much of OSI's mission . . . has been assumed by offices through the U.S. government," the *Los Angeles Times* reported in December 2004. The *New York Times* reported that the Pentagon was "debating" how far to go in adapting "the deceptive techniques endorsed for use on the battlefield" to "covert propaganda campaigns aimed at neutral and even allied nations."

(If the administration seemed to be stamping "U.S. Department of Disinformation" in large letters on its propaganda efforts, perhaps the explanation was that, until his resignation in January 2005, the Pentagon's "strategic communications programs" were still being coordinated by Douglas Feith—the guy GEN. TOMMY FRANKS once called "the fucking stupidest guy on the face of the planet."[197])

- In May 2004, U.S. cable and satellite TV subscribers began to receive the Pentagon Channel. As Arianna Huffington remarked, "DoD television execs (there's a new phrase)" promised plenty coverage of speeches by the Joint Chiefs of Staff and Congressional appearances by Rumsfeld. ("Can a **Social Security** Channel be far behind?" Frank Rich wondered.)

THE MOTHER OF ALL White House fake news stories is surely the **Iraq** war: Not just the disinformation campaign preceding it but the leashing or "embedding" of journalists covering it. "We were very happy with the outcome" of the military's effort "to dominate the information environment," the head of media relations for the Marine Corps told a symposium in 2004.[198]

Daring assaults on truth. The army wouldn't even allow a hero and his family the dignity of the truth about his death. CPL. PAT TILLMAN gave up his $3.6 million contract as an NFL football player after 9/11 to join the Army Rangers. After he was killed in Afghanistan by members of his own unit who mistook him for the enemy, the army "spun a phony tale of heroism for his family and the nation, [saying] Corporal Tillman had been killed by enemy fire as he stormed a hill. Soldiers who knew the truth were ordered to keep quiet about the matter," the *New York Times*'s Bob Herbert noted. Tillman's family revealed in May 2005 that they were not told how he really died until after a nationally televised memorial service "that recruiters viewed as a public relations bonanza."[199] Tillman's mother called the cover-up "disgusting."

The Tillman story recalled the Pentagon's fictionalization of the rescue of Army Private JESSICA LYNCH from an Iraqi hospital after she was captured by Iraqi forces in March 2003. Contrary to the Pentagon version—as told in a video given to the media—Lynch had not tried to fight off her captors, had no stab or bullet wounds, and had been given the best treatment available for injuries sustained in the crash of her Humvee. There was no evidence she was interrogated or slapped around. Army Rangers and Navy Seals were told that Iraqi soldiers had already fled before they "stormed" the hospital in a "daring nighttime assault." In fact, two days before the rescue, a doctor had risked *his* life by putting Lynch into an ambulance and having her driven to the U.S. checkpoint. As they approached it, U.S. soldiers opened fire. The ambulance fled just in time back to the hospital. "Some" have suggested the whole rescue raid was a propaganda stunt staged at the behest of the Bush administration. At any rate, as Lynch told ABC TV: "They used me to symbolize all this stuff. It's wrong. I don't know why they filmed it [her rescue], or why they say these things." Well, according to eminent war critic Col. David Hackworth, "Jessica was used right from the first to sell the war to the American people and to encourage their daughters to join up and be heroes." Meanwhile, veterans groups, wrote the *Toronto Star*'s Lynda Hurst, were "outraged that while Lynch is everywhere in the media, there is little coverage of the wounded, maimed and dead of Iraq."

ONE OTHER fake news story must be mentioned—the White House account of Bush's actions on **September 11**. While the administration had no time for any *investigations* of 9/11, it had, Frank Rich noted, "all the time in the world" to assist the production of a TV movie, Showtime's *DC 9/11: Time of Crisis*, which enshrined the official account of Bush's strong and decisive (in reality, utterly confused and incompetent) leadership on the day of the attack.

NASCAR NATION: *CALL US ELITIST, BUT . . .*

The cultural and aesthetic objections to Bushism were summarized well enough for present purposes by Jonathan Miles, writing in the *New York Times Book Review* about the NASCAR stock car racing boom. Noting that "NASCAR dads now get to pick our presidents," Miles observed:

> For a certain segment of the population, NASCAR'S raid on American culture . . . triggers the kind of fearful trembling the citizens of Gaul felt as the Huns came thundering over the hills. To these people, stock-car racing represents all that's unsavory about red-state America: fossil-fuel bingeing; lust for violence; racial segregation; run-away Republicanism; anti-intellectualism . . . the corn-pone memes of God and guns and guts; crass corporatization; Toby Keith anthems; and, of course, exquisitely bad fashion sense . . . [They are] repulsed by the deep-fried spectacle of a Nascar event, with its schizo mix of beery loutishness and Promise Keeper piety.[200]

Not to let the America-hating liberal media elite have the last word, the conservative-elite *National Review* dispatched John Derbyshire to put on his pith helmet and make "One journalist's journey of discovery" to "NASCAR Nation," where he discovered a "noisy and beery" crowd sporting "a lot of tattoos and a lot of Confederate flags"—in short, "a sport in which physical courage is admired, family bonds are treasured, the nation's flag [*which one?*] is honored . . ."

"OWNERSHIP SOCIETY"

During the 2004 election campaign, Bush unrolled his new **economic** theme—his answer to the New Deal and Great Society, which he was busy demolishing. The ostensible aim was a society in which everyone owns something—stocks, bonds, a home, perhaps a little oil company—because "if you own something," Bush declared, "you have a vital stake in the future of America." ("Call me naïve," the *New York Times*'s Paul Krugman wrote, "but I thought all Americans have a vital stake in the nation's future, regardless of how much property they own.")

When Bush invoked the "ownership society," he also talked about private investment accounts within **Social Security**, private Retirement Savings Accounts, Lifetime Savings Accounts, and **Health** Savings Accounts—all of which, surprise, surprise, would principally benefit the wealthy. The amount of income that could be sheltered from taxes under the new savings accounts was far more than households of modest means could afford to save. The new accounts were in fact further tax cuts for the well-to-do. This was not just another empty Bush slogan, wrote *The New Republic*'s Jonathan Chait; this one referred to some weighty proposals that "share one crucial thing with all the domestic policies [Bush] cares about . . . they redistribute wealth upward."

How can such policies be sold politically? Why, by promising that everyone can join the elite! Voilà—the "ownership society." (Conservatives, Krugman noted, misleadingly point out that a majority of American families now own stock. Most have a relatively tiny stake in the market: More than half of corporate profits accrue to the wealthiest 1 percent of taxpayers, while only about 8 percent go to the bottom 60 percent.)

PLAMEGATE AND PRESS FREEDOM

> *The fundamental right of Americans, through our free press, to penetrate and criticize the workings of our government is under attack as never before.*
>
> —Conservative columnist and former Nixon speechwriter
> William Safire, *The New York Times*, 9/29/04

In July 2005, a federal judge ordered *New York Times* reporter Judith Miller jailed to coerce her to reveal who leaked to her the identity of a CIA agent, VALERIE PLAME/WILSON. Plame was first identified publicly as a CIA operative on WMDs in July 2003 by conservative columnist ROBERT NOVAK, who cited "two senior administration officials" as his source. The "outing" was apparently intended to punish and/or discredit Plame's husband, former Ambassador JOSEPH WILSON, for refuting Bush administration claims about Iraqi WMDs. It also ruined Plame's career, endangered other agents, and may have been a federal felony. A grand jury investigation found that the leakers included KARL ROVE and **Dick Cheney's** chief of staff, I. LEWIS ~~"SNITCHER"~~ "SCOOTER" LIBBY. (Law-enforcement officials previously said they had hard evidence of possible criminal misconduct in the case by another Cheney aide, JOHN HANNAH.[201] But "[o]nly a very high-ranking official could have had access to the knowledge" that Plame was on the CIA payroll, "an intelligence source" told *Time*.)

Two years after the leak, however, the only one in jail was Miller, who—unlike Novak—never even wrote about Plame. What ever Miller's reason for refusing to name her source, the fact remained that without assured confidentiality, potential sources would be frightened into silence and, as a *Times* editorial said, "the press would be left largely with only official government pronouncements to report." Also threatened with a jail sentence for refusing to testify in the Plame investigation were *Time* reporter Matt Cooper and several other journalists.

The Plame leak was part of a growing pattern. In January 2004, the White House declassified an off-the-record press briefing by former White House counterterrorism chief RICHARD CLARKE and sent the document to FOX NEWS to broadcast while he was testifying before the 9/11 Commission, hoping it would appear to contradict his testimony and that, henceforth, no government official could talk to a reporter off the record without fear of being "outed" later. (Also see **Free Speech**.)

The Plamegate prosecutors introduced a new practice— asking people suspected of disclosing Plame's identity to sign waiver forms that instruct journalists to reveal once-confidential conversations with them. It would soon be "all the rage" to ask government and corporate employees to sign such waivers to discourage them from talking to reporters, *Times* executive editor Bill Keller predicted.

PRESIDENTIAL POWER, RELENTLESS EXPANSION OF

> *I'm the commander—see, I don't need to explain—I do not*
> *need to explain why I say things . . . That's the interesting*
> *thing about being president.*
>
> —George W. Bush,
> quoted by Bob Woodward in *Bush at War*

Six months into his second term, Bush was at once the least popular president at that point (with a public approval rating of 42 percent) and one of the most powerful ever. Driven by ego, lust for executive power and privilege, partisan fanaticism, and visions of a Pax (or Bellum) Americana, Bush and crew came to office set upon reconstructing the pre-Watergate imperial presidency. (Right down to the symbols: Amid record deficits, the administration spent $2 million to buy back the former presidential yacht *Sequoia*, which had been sold by President Carter in "trying to rid the White House of an imperial image," the *New York Times* noted.) Bush "intends to stretch the powers of his office to their limits [and] is centralizing power in the White House in ways not seen since Richard Nixon," wrote former White House aide David Gergen in the *Times*. The goal was "no less than . . . long-term Republican hegemony over American politics and . . . long-term American hegemony over the world."

Here, "Bush" may really mean **Dick** Cheney, whose thinking, wrote former Nixon counsel John Dean, "was formed during his years in the White House as Ford's chief of staff, in the wake of Vietnam and Watergate, when Congress set about dismantling the imperial presidency. Cheney still seems to resent these moves."

After **September 11**, the White House grabbed "wartime" powers unprecedented in recent times. Secret memos asserted that there were effectively "no limits" on the president's authority to wage war and, *Newsweek* noted, that his powers "were so expansive that he and his surrogates were not bound by congressional laws or international treaties proscribing torture." (See **Human Rights**.) The *Times*'s Linda Greenhouse remarked that the legal arguments the administration made before the Supreme Court for its right to detain, without trial, anyone it deemed an "enemy combatant" were "strikingly similar" to those it made for the **secrecy** of Cheney's **energy** task force. In both cases, the administration put forward "a vision of presidential power . . . as far-reaching as any the court has seen . . . [arguing] for the exercise of presidential authority without judicial interference." What the administration was defending, wrote the *Times*'s Paul Krugman, "is a doctrine that makes the United States a sort of elected dictatorship: a system in which the president, once in office, can do whatever he likes, and isn't obliged to consult or inform either Congress or the public." (See **War Profiteering, Political**.)

"Masters of the universe." In the Bush administration, *The New Republic* commented, "there is really only one crime worthy of internal exile or firing: dissent." Following their "re"election in 2004, Chenrobush (Cheney-Rove-Bush—not to be confused with a *nuclear* disaster) set about eliminating any pockets of dissent by replacing a raft of top officials with White House staff members whose most important qualification was loyalty. The epitome was the replacement of Secretary of State COLIN POWELL, an occasionally dissenting voice on the invasion of Iraq and other **foreign policy** issues, with CONDOLEEZZA RICE, whose appointment, said *The New Republic*, portended "an administration that . . . believes that the biggest problem of the first term was an excessive openness to competing views." With her appointment and those of fellow "team players" PORTER GOSS as Director of Central **Intelligence** (who quickly purged the CIA of non-yes-men), White House counsel ALBERTO GONZALES as attorney general, and domestic policy adviser MARGARET SPELLINGS as education secretary, the pattern was clear. Bush "is acting as if he truly believes that he and his team have a perfect track record [and] that they know best," wrote Gergen. When presidents win their first elections, he added, "they and their teams think they are king of the hill; when they win re-election, they too often think they are masters of the universe."

Dissing Congress. "It is simply a fact that the president has thinly veiled contempt for the Congress," Brookings Institution scholar Thomas Mann told *National Journal* in 2003. "The vice president has the same. The secretary of defense has the same. Basically, members of Congress have been dissed badly by this administration." This despite Congress's being (a) under GOP control and (b) a coequal branch of government under the Constitution—designed, in fact, to be the most powerful branch, and the one empowered to initiate war. That power above all was what the Bush White House wanted to "re"claim.

As tokens of their esteem, the Bushies not only deceived Congress, along with the public, on the supposed threat from **Iraq** but secretly and illegally diverted $700 million (of "your money," as Bush liked to say) appropriated by Congress for the war against Al Qaeda in Afghanistan to preparations for Bush's war. "Some people are gonna look at a document called the Constitution, which says that no money will be drawn from the Treasury unless appropriated by Congress," Bob Woodward, who exposed the diversion, said on CBS's *60 Minutes*.

Cheney's attempt in October 2003 to shut down the Senate Select Committee on Intelligence inquiry into prewar intelligence on Iraq enraged even some Republicans, such as committee member CHUCK HAGEL (R-NE). When asked about Rumsfeld's warning that criticism of U.S. policy in Iraq might embolden terrorists, Hagel, a Vietnam veteran, told *National Journal*, "I find that offensive. I heard that same argument in Vietnam for 11 years: 'Don't dare question. Don't dare probe.'" Administration officials, he added, "should review what happened in Vietnam, and they should review history and review the Constitution. Article I of the Constitution is [on] the legislative branch, not the executive branch." Congress "is the only thing that stands in the way between essentially a modern-day democratic dictatorship and a president who is accountable to the people," Hagel warned, but Congress "could become an adjunct to the executive branch."[202]

In April 2004, *Salon* noted that the Republican chairman of the Senate Foreign Relations Committee, Richard Lugar, had "been granted exactly one meeting in the past year with the president, as though he were a foreign leader." In May 2004, the administration sent a Pentagon report on what was known so far about the prisoner abuses in Iraq to news organizations before it was sent to the Senate Armed Services Committee. "That's quite a commentary," said Sen. John McCain (R-AZ).

Democrats? Fuggedabadit. In November 2003, after congressional Democrats asked for information about how much taxpayer money the White House had spent on Bush's "Mission Accomplished" stunt aboard the USS *Abraham Lincoln*, the White House notified Democratic lawmakers that thenceforth, they would have to submit any questions through the GOP chairmen of the House and Senate Appropriations Committees. "I have not heard of anything like that happening before," Norman Ornstein of the conservative American Enterprise Institute told the *Washington Post*. "This is obviously an excuse to avoid providing information [to Democrats]."

The administration vastly increased the use of regulatory action, exempt from Congressional oversight, instead of legislation to implement far-reaching policy changes in everything from **environmental** and **consumer, health and safety** regulations to public funding of religious groups, the *Progress Report* noted. Repeatedly—20 times in one week in August 2004 alone—Bush ignored the Senate's advise-and-consent role and used RECESS APPOINTMENTS to install, in the dark of night, as it were (and as it often *was*), officials who were too ideologically extreme or conflict-of-interest-laden to win Senate approval. Also see the attack on the Senate FILIBUSTER rule under **Justice and the Judiciary**.

QUAGMIRE (kwag´mir):

Country in Southwest Asia, at the head of the Persian Gulf, coinciding more or less with ancient Mess-o-potamia.

REPUBLICANS AGAINST BUSH

Beneath the famous GOP unity and discipline under Bush, there probably wasn't as much intra-party dissent since Nixon. "Former Republican members of the U.S. Senate and House, governors, ambassadors, [and] aides to GOP Presidents . . . have explicitly endorsed" Kerry, noted *The Nation's* John Nichols in October 2004. For many, it would be their first Democratic vote. We could cite many billions of examples, but the remarks of a few convey the range of their concerns:

"A perilous ride in the wrong direction." Former AMBASSADOR JOHN EISENHOWER, son of the former president, wrote, "The fact is that today's 'Republican' Party is one that I am totally unfamiliar with." Former U.S. SEN. MARLOW COOK (R-KY): "I am frightened to death of George Bush . . . I abhor a government . . . that refuses to tell the country with whom the leaders of our country sat down and determined our energy policy . . . a dangerous leader who flouts the truth [and] takes the country into an undeclared war [and is] taking our country on a perilous ride in the wrong direction." Former Minnesota Governor ELMER ANDERSEN: Bush "has led us into an unjustified war . . . I am more fearful for the state of this nation than I have ever been." Former

Michigan Governor WILLIAM MILLIKEN: "My Republican Party is the party of Theodore Roosevelt . . . This president has pursued policies that will cause irreparable damage to our environmental laws . . ." Former Sen. BOB SMITH (R-NH): "As an environmentalist . . . I know that this administration has turned environmental policy over to lobbyists for the oil, gas and mining interests . . . I believe President Bush has failed our country and my party." Former Rep. PETE McCLOSKEY (R-CA): "Nixon was a prince compared to these guys . . . These people believe God has told them what to do. They've hijacked the Republican Party we once knew." Former Colorado State Senator AL MEIKLEJOHN: The invasion of Iraq "made the entire Muslim world hate us. And for what? For what?" TIM ASHBY, commerce official under Reagan and Bush I: "[It is] a dangerous epoch—made more so by a president who sees the world in stark black and white because simplicity polls better and fits into sound bites." CLYDE PRESTOWITZ, commerce official under Reagan: "[T]he Bush administration might better be called radical or romantic or adventurist than conservative. And that's why real conservatives are leaning toward Kerry." Former Oregon Secretary of State and State Treasurer CLAY MYERS: "Mainstream Republicans believe in fiscal responsibility, internationalism, environmental protection, the rights of women, and putting middle-class families ahead of big business lobbyists." Also see "Military commanders and diplomats against Bush" under **Foreign Policy**.

SCIENCE AND TRUTH, POLITICIZATION OF

In 2004, more than 4,000 scientists—including dozens of Nobel laureates, medical experts, former federal agency directors, and university chairs and presidents—signed a statement accusing the Bush administration of systematically politicizing science and distorting scientific findings on everything from the **environment, health,** and the **economy** to **Iraq** to serve the White House's political goals. The administration, said the statement,[203] has censored and suppressed reports by the government's own scientists (see **Secrecy and Censorship**); filled official posts and scientific advisory committees with unqualified political appointees who often have close industry ties and clear conflicts of interest; disbanded government panels that provided unwanted advice; refused to consult independent experts; misrepresented scientific knowledge, and misled the public about its policies. No previous administration had "engaged in such practices . . . so systematically nor on so wide a front." One of the signatories, RUSSELL TRAIN, who served as EPA administrator under Presidents Nixon and Ford, noted "how radically we have moved away from regulation based on independent findings and professional analysis . . . to regulation controlled by the White House and driven primarily by political considerations." The statement was accompanied by 37 pages of details and examples, such as:

- **To support its decision to do little or nothing about global warming**, the administration "consistently misrepresented," suppressed, and/or censored "the findings of the National Academy of Sciences, government scientists, and the expert community at large."

- **The administration suppressed an EPA study** that found that a bipartisan Senate clean air proposal would yield greater health benefits than the administration's proposed CLEAR SKIES ACT.

- **EPA staffers were told not to undertake the normal scientific and economic studies** when the administration planned to loosen regulations on mercury emissions from power plants in 2003.

- **Highly qualified scientists were dropped from advisory committees** dealing with childhood lead poisoning, environmental and reproductive health, and drug abuse, and replaced by "individuals associated with or working for industries subject to regulation."

- **Censorship of government scientists** also occurred at the Departments of Health and Human Services, Agriculture, and Interior; and the White House disbanded scientific advisory committees to the Department of Energy on nuclear weapons and to the State Department on arms control, when scientific findings have been "in conflict with the administration's policies or with the views of its political supporters."

- **In making invalid claims about Iraq's alleged nuclear weapons program**, "the administration disregarded the contrary assessment by experts at Livermore, Los Alamos and Oak Ridge National Laboratories."

Dumb new world. Judging by polls, the administration appeared to be winning its war on science, truth, and knowledge. Majorities, especially among Bush voters, continued to believe Saddam's regime was involved in 9/11 and that WMDs had been found in Iraq—even after the 9/11 Commission and U.S. weapons inspectors said otherwise. Under Bush—whose stated view was that "the jury is still out" on EVOLUTION—the plurality of Americans who said God created humans in their present form about 10,000 years ago grew to 55 percent, including 67 percent of Bush voters, according to a CBS News poll in November 2004. *Only 40 percent—and 28 percent of Bush voters—believed humans had evolved.* More than two-thirds favored schools teaching creationism along with evolution; 37 percent (45 percent of Bush voters) favored teaching creationism only. These findings set the U.S. apart from all other industrialized nations: Typically, 80 percent or more (in Japan, 96 percent) accept evolution, and very few reject the idea outright—even in socially conservative, predominantly Catholic countries like Poland, the *New York Times* noted: "Indeed, two popes, Pius XII in 1950 and John Paul II in 1996, have endorsed the idea that evolution and religion can coexist." A May 2004 Gallup poll showed that the number of Americans who believe in heaven (81 percent), hell (70 percent), angels (78 percent), and the devil (70 percent) had also risen sharply since the 1990s. These beliefs were "stronger among Republicans, frequent churchgoers, Southerners and those with a high school diploma or less," the Religion News Service reported.

While the national stupidity epidemic clearly preceded Bush's election, the administration returned the favor—by, for example, approving the sale of a book in Grand

Canyon National Park that suggested the canyon was created in six days several thousand years ago. After all,
believers in creationism, angels, etc., were apt to be
believers in Bush as well.

Radical relativists of the right. The administration's
"expert-bashing . . . has deep roots in ideology," wrote
Franklin Foer in *The New Republic*. "Since its inception,
modern American conservatism has harbored a suspicion of
experts." Beginning in the 1960s, conservatives—mirroring
their enemies on the far left—had taken "the radically postmodern view that 'science,' 'objectivity,' and 'truth' are
guises for an ulterior, leftist agenda; that experts are so incapable of dispassionate and disinterested analysis that their
work doesn't even merit a hearing." But if science inevitably
serves an ideological agenda, then let's make sure it's *our*
agenda.

The right's agenda had changed radically since William
Jennings Bryan took up battle against the teaching of evolution around 1920, wrote the *New York Times*'s Maureen
Dowd: "[H]e did it because he despised the social Darwinists
who used the theory to justify the 'survival of the fittest' in
capitalism . . . an economic system that crushed poor
workers and farmers, and [to justify] keeping society
divided and unequal. The new evangelicals challenge science because they've been stirred up to object to social engineering [conducted] on behalf of society's most vulnerable:
the poor, the sick, the sexually different."

But the Bushies' war on science was first and foremost
about advancing **corporate** interests and silencing scientific
critics of their social-Darwinian policies—to wit, survival

(or rather, *subsidy*) of the fattest, the richest and most powerful. And increasingly, the Bushies' approach to attacking regulations opposed by business was to attack the science behind them—because, as one expert told the *Washington Post*, "[t]he argument that it costs too much to protect people does not sell. But what does sell is this idea that the science is not good." Another scientist called this "manufacturing uncertainty." As Bush said about evolution, "the jury is still out." As Cheney said about a Saddam link to 9/11, "we don't know." It was all of a piece.

The "sound" of industry money. Naturally, the Bushies claimed it was *their* policies (such as on climate change) that were based on "SOUND SCIENCE" (i.e., industry-favorable, often *industry-funded* science), not "junk [i.e, *independent*] science." The "sound science" slogan and movement, Foer noted, were pioneered by the tobacco lobby, which in the early 1990s "quietly formed a coalition of industries that would challenge every aspect of government science, from its studies of global warming to auto safety." The so-called ADVANCEMENT OF SOUND SCIENCE COALITION was advised by future Bush Interior Secretary GAIL NORTON. Its approach became the Bushies'. The results, wrote Foer, "have been disastrous."

One small line by a lobbyist, one giant leap for big business. Immediately after Bush's "election" in 2000, a little-known piece of legislation "written by an industry lobbyist [was] slipped into a giant appropriations bill . . . without congressional discussion or debate," the *Washington Post* reported. The so-called "DATA QUALITY ACT" (DQA) was just two sentences ostensibly aimed at ensuring the quality and objectivity of information disseminated by federal agencies. But—as intended—it has been used mainly by industry to challenge scientific data indicating risks to workers or consumers and to demand that any regulations be based on an impossible scientific *certainty*. By 2004, the *Washington Post* reported, it had been used by SUGAR interests to challenge dietary recommendations to limit sugar intake; LOGGING groups to challenge restrictions on timber harvests; the SALT Institute to challenge the government recommendation that people cut back on salt; the NICKEL industry to challenge government warnings about that metal; the CHEMICAL industry to challenge proposed bans on toxic-chemical-treated wood used in playground equipment; even the Association of Home APPLIANCE MANUFACTURERS to challenge the Consumer Product Safety Commission rankings of the safety of clothes dryers.

Science is ever evolving and never 100 percent certain. Recognizing this, the *Washington Post* noted, substances like DDT, vinyl chloride, and asbestos were regulated or banned before their full effects were known. The present regime would no doubt have refused to—siding with the manufacturers and hiding behind the DQA. "It's a tool to clobber every effort to regulate," an environmental law expert said.

To impose political/business control over all science-related matters, the Bushies put the White House OFFICE OF MANAGEMENT AND BUDGET (OMB) in charge of "reviewing the scientific accuracy" of any government-issued warnings related to public heath, safety, and the environment—for which, a former OMB official told *Grist*, "the agency is completely lacking in the personnel, expertise, and knowledge necessary to be that sort of judge and jury . . . It's an extraordinary act of hubris." Unless the purpose was to "review" all science for *political* correctness. Certain governments had done it before.

Doctor Evil. The author of that policy change, and the administration's chief "sound science" flack, was JOHN GRAHAM, the director of the White House's crack regulation-killing unit, the Office of Information and Regulatory Affairs (OIRA). Graham formerly headed the Harvard Center for Risk Analysis, a think tank funded by Dow Chemical, the Chemical Manufacturer's Association, and other industry groups, which promoted the view that the costs of most health and safety regulations outweigh the benefits. Graham also proposed a change that would replace government-funded scientists on peer-review panels with industry-funded scientists—which, according to a Union of Concerned Scientists report, "could ultimately destroy integrity in science as we know it."

Defunding Science. Bush's 2006 budget proposal, released in January 2005, cut the Pentagon's budget for basic science and technology research by 20 percent. Two weeks after the November 2004 election, Bush had signed a $388 billion omnibus spending bill (see **Economic Policy**) that included money for projects like the Alabama Sports Hall of Fame and the Country Music Hall of Fame in Nashville but cut the NATIONAL SCIENCE FOUNDATION budget by $100 million. The NSF "supports technological innovation that is crucial to [America's] economic prosperity," said Rep. Vernon Ehlers (R-MI), a former physics professor who chaired a technology subcommittee. "I am astonished that we would make this decision at a time when other nations continue to surpass our students in math and science and consistently increase their funding of basic research."

Pray for America. Under Bush, the government had, however, provided $2.3 million for research into whether prayer can heal illness. As if *we* needed to be told, a Harvard psychologist called "PRAYER RESEARCH" "a total waste of time and money," noting: "Intercessory prayer presupposes some supernatural intervention that is by definition beyond the reach of science." Not quite: Some researchers attributed prayers' effects not to divine intervention but to "subtle energies," "mind-to-mind communication," or "extra dimensions of space-time," the *New York Times* reported. (Feel better about your tax dollars now?) And yet, Reverend Raymond Lawrence, Jr., pastor of New York-Presbyterian Hospital/Columbia University Medical Center, was of little faith: "This whole exercise cheapens religion, and promotes an infantile theology that God is out there ready to miraculously defy the laws of nature in answer to a prayer," he blasphemed.[204]

U.S. Is Losing Its Dominance in the Sciences," the *New York Times* reported in May 2004. The numbers of scientific patents, prizes, and doctoral degrees awarded to Americans, and of papers by Americans published in major journals, were in sharp decline. "Foreign advances in basic science now often rival or even exceed America's, apparently with little public awareness of the trend or its implications for jobs, industry, national security or the vigor of the nation's intellectual and cultural life," the *Times* noted. All Bush's fault? Well, while China and other countries surged ahead and were poised to profit from advances in medical, energy, environmental, and computer technology, we funded prayer research, banned stem cell research, and discouraged the teaching of evolution (without which biology and medicine cannot be understood), and *de*-funded basic research in favor of missile defense and other cold-war-era fixations. Under Bush, more than half of federal research funding went to military research. "It's as if we have an industrial-age presidency, catering to a pre-industrial ideological base, in a post-industrial era," wrote the *Times*'s Tom Friedman.

Our dirt-road "information superhighway." In Bush's first four and a half years, the U.S. dropped from 4th to 16th place in global rankings of broadband Internet usage— "arguably the result of the Bush administration's failure to make a priority of developing these networks," a former U.S. Foreign Service officer in Japan wrote in *Foreign Affairs*. The U.S., he added, was the only industrialized state without a national policy for promoting broadband. Japan and Korea, which were far ahead—along with China—"will be the first to reap [the] benefits—from increased productivity to stronger platforms for technological innovation; new kinds of jobs, services and content; and rising standards of living," wrote Tom Friedman, adding that the Bush adminis-tration "seems more interested in indulging creationism than spurring creativity." Friedman noted that he was thinking of running for high office on one promise—"that within four years America will have cellphone service as good as Ghana's."

SECRECY, CENSORSHIP, *AND HOW TO DEAL WITH CRITICS AND WHISTLE-BLOWERS*

I live in a transparent country. I live in a country where decisions made by government are wide open and people are able to call people to—me to account.

—George W. Bush, 2/24/05

From day one, the Bushies showed a transparent passion for keeping their employers, the American public, out of their affairs—angering even conservative Republicans who had attacked President Clinton for the same thing. Rep. Dan Burton (R-IN) (who hounded Clinton for years) called the Bushies' obsession with secrecy "dictatorial." After **September 11** especially, the White House accorded itself almost unlimited powers of secrecy in the name of the "war on terrorism." "Patriotic citizens," wrote Paul Krugman, were not to "ask awkward questions." The Bushies record on secrecy "makes Richard Nixon . . . look like a boy scout," wrote Russ Baker in 2002. They "have created the most secretive presidency of my lifetime," far *Worse Than Watergate*, wrote John Dean in his book by that name. (Dean, a reviewer noted, "implies that the culture of secrecy radiates from Bush, who could build a political career only by hiding inconvenient facts about his sketchy business dealings and frat boy past.") There was, as Dean once told Nixon, "a cancer growing on the presidency." Let the biopsy begin:

Fiefdom of Information. In October 2001, AG JOHN ASHCROFT ruled that Justice Department (DOJ) policy should be, whenever possible, *not* to give out information requested under the FREEDOM OF INFORMATION ACT (FOIA). This reversed the Clinton policy that documents should be withheld only when disclosure would cause harm. In one instance, an FOIA request from reporters to obtain a national database of illegal immigrants who had served prison time for felonies was denied on the grounds that it was not a matter of public interest. "What's more in the public interest than to know if a convicted child molester" was deported or released in the U.S.? A journalist wondered.[205]

Asserting personal ownership of history. The PRESIDENTIAL RECORDS ACT of 1978—one of the key post-Watergate reforms—established that a president's White House records "are not his personal property but rather belong to the American people," the *New York Times* noted. A Bush executive order in November 2001 essentially repealed that principle. It declared that a sitting president could block the papers of a predecessor even if the latter had approved their release, and former presidents or vice presidents or their families could block release of documents against the will of a sitting president. Bush and Cheney had given themselves and their families permanent control over their records going back to the beginning of the Reagan administration—including, perhaps, such embarrassing matters as U.S. support for and arming of Saddam Hussein.

- Bush's nominee in 2004 for national archivist, Allen Weinstein, was a historian "infamous among historians for his penchant for secrecy," *Salon*'s Geraldine Sealey noted. The nomination came as the National

Archives prepared the papers of Bush I for scheduled release in January 2005. Critics feared Weinstein would restrict or delay access to those and other important documents.

Classified. Classified. Classified. In 2003, the administration revoked Clinton rules that said information should not be classified "if there is significant doubt" that releasing it would harm national security. The new Bush policy also allowed documents to be kept classified for 25 years without a specific reason, compared to 10 years under the Clinton rule; postponed automatic declassification of documents 25 or more years old; and permitted reclassification of documents that have already been made public. In 2004, the federal government classified a record 15.6 million documents— a 79 percent increase from 2001; classified most of them for longer periods; and declassified the lowest number of documents since 1994.

9/11 failures: Classified. In its final report in July 2004, the 9/11 COMMISSION "sharply criticized the government for classifying too much information. It said the 9/11 attacks might have been postponed if the government had publicized the August 2001 arrest of an alleged Al Qaeda conspirator, ZACARIAS MOUSSAOUI, the *Washington Post* noted. "Three-quarters of what I read that was classified shouldn't have been," said commission chairman Thomas Kean. (And of course, the White House covered up pre-9/11 warnings, obstructed the 9/11 Commission at every step, etc., etc., etc. See **September 11**.)

Stuffing the cat back in the bag. In April 2004, the administration tried to gag a former FBI translator, SIBEL EDMONDS, who charged that she saw information proving senior officials knew of Al Qaeda plans to attack the U.S. with aircraft months before 9/11. The DOJ cited the rarely used "state secrets privilege" to try to prevent Edmonds from testifying in a lawsuit brought by relatives of 9/11 victims. The DOJ also *retroactively classified* information it gave to Congress two years earlier about Edmonds's allegations that the FBI had missed critical pre-9/11 warnings.

The secrecy bacillus and homeland insecurity. A heavily censored Pentagon report released in March 2004—a full two years after its completion—concluded that the U.S. remained woefully ill-prepared to detect and respond to BIOTERRORISM and said one of the gravest problems during the fall 2001 anthrax attacks "was the government's failure 'on all levels' to provide 'timely and accurate information,'" the *New York Times* noted.

Terrorism: Bad news is good news is . . . no news! In 2005, the State Department decided to stop publishing its annual report on international terrorism "after the government's top terrorism center concluded that there were more terrorist attacks in 2004 than in any year since 1985": 625 "significant" terrorist attacks in 2004 versus 175 incidents in 2003, not including attacks on U.S. troops in Iraq, Knight-Ridder reported. The statistics were to be removed even from the report provided to Congress. Perhaps the decision had something to do with the previous year's report, which initially showed a sharp decline in the number of people wounded in terror attacks in 2003 and was cited by the Bushies as "clear evidence that we are prevailing in this fight." They later acknowledged the findings were "inaccurate": Revised figures showed an increase in terror incidents; an 81 percent increase in the number of people wounded in terror attacks, to 3,646; and the highest number of "significant [terrorist] events" since 1982.

Secret law comes to America. You are required to show a government-approved ID before boarding an airplane, but the government won't show you the law that says so. Why? Because it is not required to. Why? Because, the Bush administration asserted, the law is "sensitive security information." And why is that? Sorry, you're not allowed to know that either. Same with the law authorizing passenger pat-downs, and other rules. And when privacy advocate JOHN GILMORE sued to challenge the ID requirement, the DOJ asked the court to keep its arguments secret—even from Gilmore. "We're dealing with the government's review of a secret law that now they want a secret judicial review for," Gilmore's attorney told AP. "This administration's use of a secret law is more dangerous to the security of the nation than any external threat . . . How are people supposed to follow laws if they don't know what they are?" Under the HOMELAND SECURITY ACT of 2002, the government could issue almost unlimited "security directives" free of public scrutiny. This is "a qualitatively new development in U.S. governance," noted the Federation of American Scientists' Project on Government Secrecy. "This is not some dismal Eastern European allegory. It is part of a continuing transformation of American government . . ."

- In 2004, AG ASHCROFT had the Government Printing Office order librarians around the country to destroy their copies of the federal laws on ASSET FORFEITURE and related publications, which the DOJ claimed were not "appropriate for external use." Such as, presumably, their normal use by people who feel the government has improperly seized their assets—a power which Ashcroft's PATRIOT ACT of 2001 expanded. A University of California librarian said she had never heard of the federal government trying to recall copies of legislation.

Secret surveillance and searches: "ACLU's lawsuit over PATRIOT Act was kept secret—per PATRIOT Act," a Reuters story noted. At issue in this 2004 lawsuit was an expansion of the Patriot Act signed by Bush in December 2003, which (a) allowed the FBI and DOJ to secretly seize library, medical, and financial records and businesses' customer records, without having to show a compelling need to a judge; (b) broadened the definition of "financial institutions" which can be subpoenaed to include such businesses as the Postal Service, insurance companies, pawnbrokers, dealers in precious metals, travel agencies, and casinos; (c) barred subpoenaed businesses, under threat of criminal penalties, from revealing to their customers that the FBI sought records of their transactions. "Before the PATRIOT Act, the FBI could use this invasive authority only against suspected terrorists and spies," an ACLU attorney noted. "Now it can . . . obtain information about anyone at all."

Threat to Dissent Censored. *Under* the PATRIOT Act, the ACLU could have been prosecuted for releasing any of the papers in its lawsuit *over* the PATRIOT Act. But the freedom-loving Bushies insisted on blacking out only portions as threats to national security, such as a quote from a 1972 Supreme Court decision: *"The danger to political dissent is acute where the Government attempts to act under so vague a concept as the power to protect 'domestic security.'"* Evidence the DOJ submitted to the court was also kept secret, even from the plaintiffs—a practice both unusual and without case law precedent.[206]

Energy executive privilege. Defying repeated requests from Congress's Government Accountability Office (GAO) and from public interest groups that believed citizens have a right to know who was writing their **energy policy**, the White House refused to release the names of energy industry insiders who took part in closed-door meetings of Cheney's ENERGY TASK FORCE in 2001. No prior administration had ever challenged the GAO's authority in such requests. A lawsuit by the GAO for release of the records was dismissed by a judge appointed by Bush. The White House "argued the courts and Congress have no business making inquiries, even limited ones, into the decision-making power of federal agencies and offices," wrote CNN's Bill Mears. In a lawsuit brought by Judicial Watch and the Sierra Club, the White House claimed the 1972 Federal Advisory Committee Act, which requires that presidential advisory committees must hold their meetings in public, make their records accessible, and have a membership that is "fairly balanced," was unconstitutional—"an extraordinary assertion of executive power and privilege," said Judicial Watch. In May 2005, the conservative and largely senile D.C. Circuit Court of Appeals reversed a lower court and ruled in Cheney's favor.

Subverting open government. On the same pattern as the energy task force, Bush set up a "Commission to Strengthen **Social Security**" which he stocked with various right-wing "experts" and executives of companies that would reap huge profits from his privatization plan, who met behind closed doors under a new Bush rule that supposedly permitted such meetings. Federal statutes clearly required such meetings to be open, a legal expert on open-government rules told the *New York Times*.

See no unfair tax cuts, hear no funding shortage, speak no unemployment.

- In 2001—the year of Bush's first and largest round of Tax Cuts For the Rich—the Treasury Department stopped releasing information about the distribution of tax cuts by income level.
- In 2003, the administration, "under fire for its handling of the economy . . . quietly killed off a Labor Department program that tracked mass layoffs by U.S. companies," the *San Francisco Chronicle* reported.
- In 2003, the administration stopped publishing the annual budget report that showed state governments how much they were, or weren't, getting from Washington.

IRS goes secret. Reversing 20 years of open-records policy, the Internal Revenue Service refused to release statistical tables and other information that had allowed the public, Congress, and tax lawyers to judge how the agency was enforcing the tax laws. "In the past," noted Public Citizen, which joined in a lawsuit in April 2005 charging that with-holding the material was illegal, "researchers used such information to demonstrate, for example, that wealthy tax-payers are much more successful than poor ones when it comes to reducing the amount of taxes and penalties that the IRS initially claimed they owed in enforcement actions." No longer. Release of such information, the government said, would compromise **homeland security**!

The (secret) Administration Millionaires' Secrecy Act. In November 2004, House Republicans quietly moved to repeal the requirements that senior-level officials report their personal financial assets valued at more than $2.5 million and disclose the dates of their stock transactions—"the greatest single safeguard against insider trading by govern-ment officials [and] a first-line defense against corruption," watchdog groups noted. (**Dick** Cheney's Halliburton stock options? No longer the public's business.) The provision was slipped into the 497-page "9/11 Recommendations Imple-mentation Act." (Who wants to vote against a major antiter-rorism bill?) When open government advocates complained about it, the provision was *expanded* to include not just intelligence and national security officials but *all* senior administration officials. Teach *them* to complain.

SILENCING SCIENTISTS, EXPERTS, AND WHISTLE-BLOWERS. This was the story all over the administration. Top Agriculture Department officials concealed "mad cow" and other food safety risks. (See **Consumer**.) In the wake of 9/11, the White House directed the EPA to shut down the public release of information about pipeline safety and pollution problems at chemical plants, and directed the agency to give New Yorkers misleading assurances on the health risk from the debris-laden air after the World Trade Center collapse. In September 2004, an official in EPA's Rocky Mountain region instructed his regional staff: "[S]ince it is two months before election day . . . here is how to handle [media] inquiries for information [on environmental matters] that seem partisan: 'NO COMMENT.'"[207] In October, the head of the EPA's Midwest region ordered all staff to "refrain from answering [press] inquiries directly." This, he explained, "will prevent EPA management from being surprised by news coverage." As it so happened, Bush-Greenwatch reported, "EPA top brass had been unpleasantly 'surprised' a few weeks earlier, when the press got wind of EPA scientist Peter Howe's objections to a plan for a new $2.1 billion coal-fired power plant in Wisconsin. Howe was reprimanded and suspended for two weeks for allowing his opinions to get out into the public sphere."

The same month, the House Committee on Government Reform approved new whistle-blower protection legislation—to which the White House "quickly objected, saying such protections would open the door to gratuitous complaints against its officials."[208]

Meanwhile, government reports, fact sheets, and Web sites on everything from **abortion** and **AIDS** prevention to **global warming** and vehicle safety were deleted, censored, or distorted to conform with right-wing policies and mythologies.

Gagging the Park Service. In 2000, candidate Bush promised to close the $5 billion funding gap for America's national parks. But the parks "have been steadily deteriorating since the President took office," BushGreenwatch reported in 2004. "To deter public awareness" of this reversal, Bush "has imposed a gag rule on park managers to prevent them from disclosing just how underfunded the parks have become." All over the parks system, business reports showing crippling budget shortfalls were withheld or cancelled. According to the House Committee on Government Reform, the chief of the U.S. Park Police was fired after she told the press her agency didn't have adequate funding or personnel to keep parks and monuments in Washington, D.C., safe.

Blacking out the white face of Justice. In October 2003, an internal report that harshly criticized the Justice Department's diversity efforts in the hiring, promotion and retention of minority lawyers "was edited so heavily when it was posted on the department's Web site . . . that half of its 186 pages, including the summary, were blacked out," the *New York Times* reported. After the deleted passages were electronically recovered and circulated by a self-described "information archaeologist," the DOJ pulled the entire report from its Web site.

Warning on ethics ~~violations~~ complaints. In November 2004, as House Majority Leader TOM DELAY's legal and ethics problems mounted, the House Committee on Standards of Official Conduct, in an apparent—no, *trans*parent—attempt to intimidate would-be whistle-blowers, warned that it could take "disciplinary action" if any House member filed an ethics complaint containing "innuendo, speculative assertions, or conclusory statements" about any other member.

The black hole of Iraq. In the lead-up to the war, leading Republican members of Congress—even Senate Armed Services Committee Chairman John Warner (R-VA)—were astounded by the Bushies' refusal to share information justifying military action. "What is the connection between Iraq and Al Qaeda?" asked Sen. Kit Bond (R-MO). White House Chief of Staff Andrew Card: "Don't worry." Truthtellers, meanwhile, were punished:

- When GEN. ERIC SHINSEKI told Congress that postwar Iraq would require a large occupation force, that was the end of his military career.
- As Shinseki was proved right, the administration banned photographs of returning coffins of U.S. troops. As many as 30,000 serious U.S. casualties—so-called 'non-battle' injuries and diseases—were omitted from official, published casualty reports. The army banned the *Denver Post* from Fort Carson, Colorado after the paper ran a story exposing poor treatment of injured troops at the base.[209]
- White House economist Larry Lindsey lost his job in 2002 soon after publicly (and correctly) estimating the war would cost three to four times the Pentagon's estimate.
- After former ambassador JOSEPH WILSON helped expose the Bushies' knowingly false claims about Iraqi efforts to obtain uranium, the White House struck back by revealing that his wife was a CIA operative. (See **Plamegate**.)
- At the end of the first term, the White House dumped the chairman of the President's Foreign Intelligence Advisory Board, BRENT SCOWCROFT, a former national

security adviser under Bush I, who was increasingly critical of the Iraq war. In fact, Scowcroft "and the rest of the board were asked to resign en masse," the *New York Times* reported. Bush replaced Scowcroft with former investment banker and White House economic policy coordinator Stephen Friedman.

A hood over Abu Ghraib. "Those who make allegations of a culture of deception, of intimidation or of cover-up [of prisoner abuses] need to be extremely careful about such accusations," DONALD RUMSFELD intimidated in May 2004. That month, SGT. SAMUEL PROVANCE, a soldier and key witness in the Abu Ghraib investigation who told ABC News he believed the military was covering up the extent of abuse, was stripped of his security clearance, transferred, told he may face prosecution, and officially "flagged"— meaning he could not be promoted or given any awards or honors—because his comments were "not in the national interest." Provance, who served in a military intelligence battalion stationed at Abu Ghraib, said the officer in charge of the investigation had tried to discourage him from speaking out by threatening to take action against him for not speaking out sooner![210] (See **Human Rights**.)

SEPTEMBER 11, NATIONAL SECURITY, AND THE "WAR ON TERROR": *FAILURE, LIES, COVER-UPS*

If the president wants to own Sept. 11 he's entitled. But it does not come alone. Sept. 10 is his, too.

—Columnist Richard Cohen

Bush presided over four of the worst "intelligence failures" in U.S. history, including *the* worst—the failure to prevent 9/11. The other three—the false intelligence about (a) **Iraqi** WMDs and (b) terrorism links, and (c) the underestimation of Iraqi resistance to occupation, with all that *those* "failures" led to— compounded the 9/11 failure. All were at bottom—at the top, rather—*presidential leadership* failures. And no worse ones are imaginable; protecting national security and American lives is a president's primary responsibility.

The 9/11 attacks "were neither unimaginable nor unpreventable," wrote Matthew Yglesias in the *American Prospect*.

> That al-Qaeda was planning attacks was well-known, and that the World Trade Center was the most likely target was conventional wisdom in the counterterrorism community. Field agents from the FBI had in their possession key pieces of information that could have unraveled the plot had leaders in Washington known what to be looking for. And the CIA was trying—hard—to warn the president that the government should be looking for something along the lines

of what did eventually take place. But Bush ignored his Presidential Daily Briefs, no extraordinary action was taken, and key information remained lost in the bowels of the bureaucracy. Thousands of Americans died, and the president's approval rating skyrocketed.[211]

Through revelation after revelation of their negligence, the Bushies insisted they *were* attuned to terrorism before 9/11; that they had no warnings and could have done nothing to prevent the attack; that if anyone was at fault, it was Clinton! Bush was the *hero* of the hour rather than the president on whose watch the U.S. suffered its worst domestic attack ever—while his attention, despite multiple warnings, remained fixed on his thirst for war with Iraq; on missile defense—the Bushies' top military priority from the start; and on tax cuts and favors for big business. Far from taking any responsibility and paying any political price for their failures, Bush and crew exploited and profited hugely from them—thanks to our obsequious news **media**; boredom with any story more than two weeks old and not involving a bedroom; confusion of patriotism with blind loyalty to the president; the Bushies' readiness to *exploit* patriotism and fear (see **War Profiteering, Political**) and to lie; and Democratic leaders' fear of speaking out.

Some Republicans were less timid. Bush, the self-proclaimed "war president," had "done a terrible job on the war against terrorism," said former White House counterterrorism chief RICHARD CLARKE in March 2004. (Within hours of Clarke's saying "the previously unsayable," Paul Krugman noted, "the character assassination began.") Clarke told of an administration uninterested in Al Qaeda, but instead hell-bent from the start on invading Iraq—a story amply supported by other insider accounts. In July 2004, six of the ten members of the Republican-led 9/11 COMMISSION concluded that *9/11 could have been prevented.* The commission reported that Clarke, the CIA, and others *warned the administration as many as 40 times* of the threat posed by bin Laden. But, as journalist Thomas Powers wrote, "that is not what the administration wanted to hear, and it did not hear it." [212]

And as Bush began his second term, bin Laden remained at large, Al Qaeda remained entrenched along the Pak-Afghan border, the Taliban was back in much of Afghanistan, violence in Iraq was escalating, and global hatred of America was at a longtime high. Indeed, according to one expert, Bush's "re"election made a new and more terrible attack on the U.S.—possibly nuclear—inevitable.

***Who* weakened our defenses?** The Bushies' uninterest in terrorism predated not only 9/11 but 12/12 (December 12, 2000—the day the Supreme Court decided *Bush v. Gore*). In January 2000, a 7,000-word article in *Foreign Affairs* by CONDOLEEZZA RICE, candidate Bush's foreign policy adviser, explained his national security policy without a single mention of Osama bin Laden or Al Qaeda, which had already perpetrated several deadly attacks on U.S. facilities.

But go back further. Throughout the 2004 campaign, **Dick Cheney** attacked John Kerry for voting for cutbacks in intelligence and in weapons programs during the 1990s. As defense secretary under Bush I, Cheney bragged of terminating the very same weapons programs, and led the effort to block the very same intelligence reforms the 9/11

Commission said were needed, particularly the creation of a director of national intelligence position, which was established in December 2004 over the Bushies' fierce opposition—especially DONALD RUMSFELD'S, who, like Cheney before him, was seeking to maintain his own power over intelligence agencies and funding.

Rep. PORTER GOSS (R-FL)—soon to be named director of central intelligence by Bush—attacked Kerry for seeking budget cuts Goss said were "devastating to the ability of the CIA to keep America safe." Less than two years after the 1993 World Trade Center attack, Goss called for cutting intelligence personnel by 20 percent—far more than Kerry then proposed. Goss specifically targeted the "human intelligence" resources that were disastrously lacking prior to the 9/11 attacks.

Clinton blown off. As the 9/11 Commission made the Bushies' failures clearer by the day, **Dick** Cheney claimed that during the 1990s there wasn't "any great success in dealing with the terrorist threat." But when Clinton ordered attacks on Al Qaeda bases in Afghanistan in 1998, he was accused by Republicans of "wagging the dog" to distract from his intern-al problems. Nonetheless, the Clinton administration had quite a list of successes, including foiling the millennium plot, an Al Qaeda attempt to dominate Bosnia, and an attack on the U.S. embassy in Albania.

"ALL HAT AND NO CATTLE" ON TERRORISM. In the eight months before 9/11, Bush's national security leadership met formally nearly 100 times. Terrorism was the topic during two of those sessions. The administration, the *Washington Post* noted, "expressed disdain for," and rolled back, the counterterrorist policies it had inherited from Clinton. Counterterrorism itself, it would seem, was just *too Clinton*.

"No attention. Army LT. GEN. DONALD KERRICK, a Clinton holdover in charge of the National Security Council staff, told the *Washington Post* that Clinton's cabinet advisers had met "nearly weekly" on terrorism; under Bush, Kerrick said he didn't detect "any activity but what Clarke and [his Counterterrorism Security Group] were doing." In February 2001, PAUL BREMER, who had chaired the bipartisan National Commission on Terrorism under Clinton, said, *"The new administration seems to be paying no attention to the problem of terrorism.* What they will do is stagger along until there's a major incident and then suddenly say, 'Oh, my God, shouldn't we be organized to deal with this?'" (Emphasis added.)

- In 2004, Bush said that prior to 9/11 "we thought oceans could protect us." The bipartisan HART-RUDMAN COMMISSION, commissioned by Clinton, warned the new administration in its very first days of the likelihood of an attack on the "homeland" and urged specific **homeland security** measures. Bush put the recommendations aside and instead waited five months to create a new task force headed by **Dick**— which never met before 9/11. On September 10, Cheney's office told senators it might be another six months before he would be able to review their draft legislation on counterterrorism and homeland defense, which they had sent him in July.

- In a memo to Rice, the new National Security Director, in January 2001, Clarke described the "urgent need" for a "principals-level review on the al-Qaeda network." The memo belied Rice's claim in 2004 that "No Al Qaeda threat was turned over to the new administration."
- One of the Bushies' first acts was to downgrade Clarke's position from cabinet level to something considerably less.

Could have killed bin Laden? Clarke urged the incoming administration to resume flights of the CIA's PREDATOR unmanned surveillance plane, which had spotted bin Laden as many as three times in late 2000. By February 2001, a missile-armed Predator was ready to go; but Rumsfeld's Defense Department "didn't want the CIA treading on its turf," *Newsweek* reported, and the Predator wasn't flown again over Afghanistan before 9/11 (after which it was deployed within days).

Stood down. The incoming Bush administration abandoned Clinton's deployment of cruise missile submarines and gunships near Afghanistan, which had allowed the option of a quick strike against Al Qaeda's top leaders.

Stood up. Despite urgings by Clarke and others, the administration provided scant support to the tottering anti-Taliban Northern Alliance in Afghanistan.

No follow-through. After twice warning the Taliban it would be held responsible for an Al Qaeda attack—and after concluding by February 2001 that Al Qaeda had carried out the October 2000 attack on the USS *COLE* off of Yemen—the Bush administration still ordered no military action. According to the 9/11 Commission Report, "Bin Ladin's inference may well have been that [such] attacks . . . were risk free."

Subsidizing the Taliban. In May 2001, while cutting counterterrorism funding, the administration gave $43 million in aid to the Taliban—which continued to host and support Al Qaeda—for cracking down on opium growers. This was the same government against which the UN imposed sanctions, at the behest of the U.S., for refusing to turn over bin Laden.

W for wimpy. The administration did not begin a counterterrorism policy review until April 2001, by which time "significant slippage in counterterrorism policy may have taken place," according to the joint Congressional inquiry into 9/11. After 9/11, the administration's story was that it had been developing a more aggressive policy, one that would not merely "roll back" but "destroy" Al Qaeda. Aggressive? According the 9/11 Commission Report, the new plan consisted of "dispatching an envoy to give the Taliban an opportunity to expel bin Laden and his organization," followed, if necessary, by stepped-up diplomatic pressure and support for anti-Taliban forces, over a three-year "timeframe." The new strategy wasn't even discussed at cabinet level until September 4, 2001, and by 9/11 had still not reached Bush's desk.

Defense too FEMAnine? That month, Bush announced a new Office of National Preparedness for terrorism at the Federal Emergency Management Agency—*and* proposed to cut FEMA's budget by $200 million.

"The world of yesterday." On 9/11, RICE was scheduled to give a speech on, in her words, "the threats and problems of today and the day after, not the world of yesterday." The speech, of course, promoted MISSILE DEFENSE—Reagan's 1980s, cold war "Star Wars" fantasy—as "the cornerstone of a new national security strategy," and contained "no mention of al Qaeda, Osama bin Laden or Islamic extremist groups," the *Washington Post* noted. Rice's predecessor, Sandy Berger, was described as "totally preoccupied" with the prospect of a domestic terror attack, and told the incoming Rice she would be "spending more time on this issue" than on any other. As if.

- Setting the tone for his whole administration, Bush never spoke publicly of the dangers of terrorism before 9/11, *except* to promote his missile shield. (The 9/11 hijackers had box cutters and plane tickets, but no intercontinental ballistic missiles whatsoever.)
- When Congress tried to fill gaps in Bush's counterterrorism budget with $600 million diverted from missile defense, RUMSFELD's pet project, Rummy threatened a Bush veto. That was on September 9.

Talk about boobs: Ashcroft's priorities. In spring 2001, Ashcroft laid out his priorities for the FBI to its director, Louis Freeh: "'Basically violent crime and drugs,' recalls one participant. Freeh replied bluntly that those were not his priorities, and began to talk about terror and counterterrorism. 'Ashcroft didn't want to hear about it.'"[213] From May to August 2001, Ashcroft listed top DOJ priorities several times but never included terrorism. Ashcroft, a blogger wrote, "was too busy covering up statues' boobs [see **Values**] and wasting time on other crack-pot right wing obsessions like hookers in New Orleans and hookahs on the Internet."[214] Ashcroft's budget request for fiscal 2003—submitted on September 10, 2001—called for increases in 68 programs, not one of which involved counterterrorism, but cut $65 million from counterterrorism grants to state and local governments and denied FBI requests for $58 million for additional counterterrorism field agents, intelligence analysts, and translators. Ashcroft's attitude "really undermined a lot of effort to change the culture and change the mind-set" of FBI agents, a former FBI official told the *New York Times*.

Number of FBI analysts working on Al Qaeda before 9/11: 2. FBI counterterrorism chief Dale Watson told the 9/11 Commission he wished he'd had 500.

Inaction on terrorist financing. In mid-2001, the *Washington Post* reported, the Bush administration "spent months fending off" the laws and institutions "that are central to the war against al Qaeda's financing." Special panels had been set up at the Organization of Economic Cooperation and Development (OECD) and the Group of Seven to punish rogue banking systems. But three months after they took office, the Bushies—who didn't really go in for regulating powerful industries or rich folks' money, or for international cooperation—

suspended U.S. participation in both panels. Treasury Secretary PAUL O'NEILL wrote that the OECD project to stamp out tax havens whose secrecy protects drug traffickers, tax evaders, and terrorists was "not in line with this administration's tax and economic priorities." In Congress, three rival bills to require identification of foreign owners of certain U.S. bank accounts useful to such bad guys failed to get the administration's support.

"Catastrophic," "pending," "imminent," "spectacular," "very, very, very, very big," and other non-warnings. On 9/11, White House spokesman Ari Fleischer said the administration had received "no warnings." That essentially remained the Bushies' line thereafter. Guess it depended on the definition of "warning," or of "no."

- In April and May 2001, Bush received intelligence reports titled, for example, "Bin Laden network's plans advancing" and "Bin Laden threats are real," and CIA warnings that attacks would be "catastrophic."
- In May, Clarke wrote to Rice and her deputy, Stephen Hadley, "When these attacks occur, as they likely will, we will wonder what more we could have done to stop them."
- A terrorist threat advisory in late June "indicated a high probability of near-term 'spectacular' terrorist attacks," said the 9/11 Commission Report. "On June 25, Clarke warned Rice and Hadley that six separate intelligence reports [warned of] a pending attack . . . The intelligence reporting consistently described the upcoming attacks as occurring on a calamitous level . . . One Al Qaeda intelligence report warned that

something 'very, very, very, very' big was about to happen." One June briefing to top officials was titled, "Bin Ladin Attacks May be Imminent." Another warned of "near-term attacks . . . of catastrophic proportions."

- In July, FBI agents in Phoenix monitoring a large number of Arab suspects who were enrolled in flight schools and asking questions about airport security warned of a possible plot by bin Laden and recommended monitoring flight schools around the country. The PHOENIX MEMO was never transmitted to the CIA or even to senior levels at FBI headquarters. Might the information have been "shaken loose," as Clarke put it, in an administration more concerned with terrorism? (a) Yes.

- That same month, CBS News reported, because of a Justice Department "threat assessment" (which was never made public), ASHCROFT quietly began "traveling exclusively by leased jet aircraft instead of commercial airlines." ("Faith has its limitations," the *Arkansas Times* later commented.)

- In July, CIA Director George Tenet was described as "nearly frantic" over the storm of intelligence warnings, and had delivered so many warnings that "some administration colleagues grew tired of hearing them," the *Washington Post* reported. By the end of July, Tenet later told the 9/11 Commission, "The system was blinking red" and could not "get any worse." Now, at last, Bush swung into action and began the longest presidential vacation in 32 years.

"Nothing about an attack on America." In his pièce de résistance—résistance to taking terror warnings seriously—on August 6, Bush received an intelligence briefing or Presidential Daily Brief (PDB) titled "Bin Laden Determined to Attack Inside the United States," which said "a group of bin Ladin supporters are in the U.S. planning attacks" and warned of "activity in this country consistent with preparations for hijackings or other types of attacks, including recent surveillance of federal buildings in New York." Bush rushed back to Washington—correction: remained on vacation at his ranch for another 27 days, "pick[ing] yard work over his #1 duty to America," one blogger blogged.[215] Well, not quite: After receiving the PDB, Bush "broke off from work early and spent most of that day fishing."[216] The 9/11 Commission found "no indication of any further discussion before September 11 among the President and his top advisers of the possibility of a threat of an al Qaeda attack" in the U.S.

After 9/11, the White House kept the briefing secret. When word of it got out in 2002, Fleischer lied about its title, leaving out the crucial word "Inside." Rice tried to dismiss it as "analytical" and "historical," containing "no new threat information." In fact, it was *so* unimportant, the Bushies refused for the next two years to release the text on the grounds of its "sensitivity"; it contained "the family jewels," said Cheney.

Even after the White House finally relented in April 2004 and the public learned the title of PDB—and that, as the *New York Times* said, it "spelled out the who, hinted at the what and pointed toward the where"—Bush went before the cameras and claimed:

- The PDB "was no indication of a terrorist threat" and "said nothing about an attack on America"!! The memo only said "Osama bin Laden had designs on America," Bush said—"Well, I knew that"—and that "America was hated by Osama bin Laden. That was obvious." Actually, it said bin Laden was planning an imminent attack that might involve hijacking airplanes or target buildings in New York—but why split hairs?

- The memo did not warn of the "hijacking of an airplane *to fly into a building*." But what difference would that have made? Jonathan Chait noted in *The New Republic*. "[W]e wouldn't have let the hijackers take control of the planes and then tried to fortify the World Trade Center against a crash; we would have put the government on high alert against hijackers."

- "Had I had any inkling whatsoever that the people were going to fly airplanes into buildings, we would have moved heaven and earth . . ." Nice to know he cared. Bush had plenty of inkling, including about airplanes, and would have had a lot more if he'd been, you know, *interested*.

- *"There was not a time and place of an attack."* And on another occasion: "Had I known that the enemy was going to use airplanes to kill *on that fateful morning* . . ." And again, "Had my administration had any information that terrorists were going to attack *New York City on September the eleventh* . . ." (Emphasis added.) So his *defense* was that they failed to foil the plot? And bin Laden had not had the courtesy to preannounce the exact time and place . . . so nothing could be done. (Never mind that, as *Newsweek* reported, on September 10, "a group of top Pentagon officials suddenly canceled travel plans for the next morning, apparently because of security concerns.")

No new security measures. During the summer of 2001, the Federal Aviation Administration issued as many as 12 warnings of possible terror attacks to the airlines and airports, at least two of which mentioned the possibility of hijackings—but issued no directives for increased security at checkpoints or on board aircraft. "U.S. airports at least should have been on high alert on September 11," said *Newsweek.* "They weren't. Indeed, the two airlines involved in the hijackings say they were barely aware of the FAA warnings." [217]

Easing entry for terrorists. Five of the 9/11 hijackers entered the U.S. in spring-summer 2001 under the Bush administration's brand new VISA EXPRESS program, which allowed Saudis to obtain visas through their travel agents instead of appearing at a consulate in person. "The issuing officer has no idea whether the person applying for the visa is actually the person in the documents and application," an official later said. The program was canceled immediately after 9/11 . . . right? Well, no, not until July 2002.

9/11, 9:00–11:00 A.M. When told while visiting a Florida elementary school that "America is under attack"—when life-and-death presidential orders were needed—Bush's instinct was to just sit there and continue reading from

My Pet Goat. ("To project strength and calm," the White House sheepishly explained later.) On 9/11, Bush—who was to milk 9/11 politically for the next three years and literally build his image on the ruins of the World Trade Center—failed the most basic test of leadership and judgment.

• The commander of the North American Aerospace Defense Command (NORAD) told the 9/11 Commission that had information about the hijackings been passed along faster from the FAA, which tracked the flights—and *had there been an immediate shootdown order—fighter jets could have intercepted and shot down most or all of the hijacked planes.* Cheney did not issue a shoot-down order until more than an hour after Bush was told a second plane had hit the World Trade Center. "And once the shootdown order was given, it was not communicated to the pilots," said the 9/11 Commission Report.

"I don't think anybody could have predicted that they would try to use . . . a hijacked airplane as a missile," was the May 2002 statement that, more than any other, put CONDOLEEZZA RICE into the Bushitters Hall of Fame. "There was nobody in our government, at least, and I don't think the prior government that could envision flying airplanes into buildings," Bush claimed in April 2004—shortly after the *Wall Street Journal* reported that under Clinton, the federal government had on several occasions "taken elaborate, secret measures [against] just such an attack." Maybe Bush really *didn't* read newspapers. Evidently, the president and his director of national security also didn't know that:

- The CIA warned of such an attack twelve times in the seven years before 9/11. The agency learned in 1995 that an associate of 1993 World Trade Center plotter Ramzi Yousef had talked about crashing a jetliner into CIA headquarters.

- A 1999 intelligence report prepared by the Library of Congress research unit warned that Al Qaeda terrorists could hijack airliners and fly them into government buildings like the Pentagon. Sen. Charles Grassley (R-IA) called the report "one of the most alarming indicators and warning signs of the [9/11] plot."

- The FBI had known since at least 1999 that an unindicted co-conspirator in the 1998 U.S. Embassy bombings in Africa had been sent for pilot training in Oklahoma.

- Prior to attending the G-8 conference in Genoa, Italy (with Rice) in July 2001, Bush was warned that Islamist terrorists might attempt to crash an airliner into the conference site.

- In August, FBI agents in Minneapolis arrested ZACARIAS MOUSSAOUI on immigration charges. They suspected the French-Moroccan flight student was planning a terrorist act involving a large aircraft—possibly even a crash into the World Trade Center. FBI higher-ups in Washington, who knew of Moussaoui's terrorist connections, denied local agents authority to investigate— "action that even then would have seemed routine"[218]—and Moussaoui, who was to be the 20th hijacker, was never linked to the others. The 9/11 Commission said merely publicizing his arrest might have led the plotters to cancel the attack. But the panel "refrained from naming any of the FBI officials involved," which in the mad, conspiratorial view of the World Socialist Web Site, "has a definite significance. Named individuals . . . would be likely to defend themselves by shifting responsibility to those higher up in the chain of command . . . The 9/11 commission sought at all costs to avoid such an outcome."[219]

LET THE ~~INVESTIGATION~~ COVER-UP BEGIN. A congressional inquiry into 9/11 was delayed for months as the administration and its allies claimed it would interfere with the war on terrorism. In January 2002, Bush and Cheney asked congressional leaders to limit any investigation to the intelligence committees—which held closed-door meetings, were chummy with the intelligence agencies, and would not consider the administration's *use* (i.e., nonuse) of intelligence. In February, Cheney phoned Senate Majority Leader Tom Daschle (D-SD) to warn that if he tried to broaden the investigation, administration officials might say they were too busy running the war on terrorism to show up—and Daschle might be accused of interfering with the mission.[220]

The "bipartisan" 9/11 Commission. For nearly a year after it was first proposed in the Senate, the White House tried to block any independent commission. Bush finally gave in in November 2002 and appointed honest, upright, apolitical HENRY KISSINGER to head it. Kissinger resigned a month later over conflicts of interest: His consulting business depended largely on his coziness with the powers that be, not just in Washington but in Riyadh and other capitals where a full exposé of 9/11 might not be welcome. What could Bush have been thinking?

Kissinger's replacement was former New Jersey Governor THOMAS KEAN. The commission, though composed of five Democrats and five Republicans, was chaired by a Republican (Kean) and vice-chaired by a Democrat, LEE HAMILTON, not known for rocking the boat. The commission's executive director, historian PHILIP ZELIKOW, though billed by the Bushies as "one of the foremost experts" on Islamist terrorism, had written only one article on terrorism and none, apparently, on Al Qaeda. He was, however, a close friend and colleague of "Condi" Rice, had worked on Bush's transition team and on the President's Foreign Intelligence Advisory Board, and maintained contacts with White House officials, including KARL ROVE. Better yet, he had "expressed strong support for Bush policies, including the invasion of Iraq," Joe Conason noted in *Salon*. Zelikow proved his qualifications in February 2004 when he learned from Clinton attorney Bruce Lindsey that the White House was withholding 75 percent of some 11,000 pages of Clinton administration documents from the commission; Zelikow didn't tell the commission about this for months, until Lindsey went public about it. Unlike Bush, Clinton wanted *his* record, at least on terrorism, to be known—and could say truthfully, "I never had business relations with that man, Mr. bin Laden, or any of his relatives." (See **Bush's Business Career** in *The Bush-Hater's Handbook*.)

"We are doing everything we can to cooperate with the commission," said the White House. And yet, by February

2004, 9/11 panel members were "fed up with what one calls 'maddening' restrictions" on their access to the intelligence reports Bush received before 9/11, *Newsweek* reported. Without seeing exactly what Bush had been told, Kean and other commissioners said, they couldn't write a report that would "withstand the laugh test."

Bush officials had agreed, after a long battle, to provide the PDBs provided they be allowed to "edit" them and decide which portions were "relevant." The panel asked to see 360 PDBs; then-White House counsel ALBERTO GONZALES let them see just 24, and limited their viewing to four of the panel members, who could then write brief summaries for the others. The White House then objected to the wording of the summaries and refused to let the other commissioners see them. Most galling to some commissioners was the Bushites' claim to be protecting the principles of executive privilege and confidential advice—after they had selectively shared some of the PDBs with BOB WOODWARD for his flattering book *Bush at War*.

- In 2003, the commission told the White House that without an $11 million budget increase it could not complete its investigation. The request was brushed off.
- In January 2004, commission members battled with Congress for a two-month extension they said they needed to finish their work. The White House opposed it, then pretended to be on the commission's side while House Speaker DENNIS HASTERT (R-IL) refused even to allow a vote on it.

"Cheney Wows Sept. 11 Commission by Drinking Glass of Water While Bush Speaks."—The *Onion*. In January 2004, Bush agreed to be questioned by the commission, but only in private; only with the chairman and vice chairman; not under oath; only for one hour (or 1.2 seconds per life lost on 9/11); and only together with Cheney—the better to keep their stories straight, "as there is some doubt about the extent to which Bush was kept in the loop," *The Nation*'s John Nichols observed. The White House also insisted there be no recording or transcript taken. Why? "No Record, No Accountability," as Nichols's story was headed. The lack of any official record would afford Bush and Cheney "an opportunity to deny statements, question interpretations and challenge conclusions," and also saved the administration "the embarrassment of having to explain why, when the commander in chief is asked questions, the vice president answers."

Amneezzia—or, Putting the Con in "Condi." Rice's performance before the 9/11 Commission deserved an Oscar for best supporting actress. The White House refused at first to let her testify publicly, saying the separation of powers prevented presidential advisers from appearing before Congress. As it happened, (a) the 9/11 Commission was not a congressional committee, and (b) many previous presidential advisers had testified before congressional committees.

Rice finally agreed to testify, but in exchange the commission had to agree not to seek testimony from any other White House aides, even if it were critical to the investigation. Some examples of Rice's "testimony":

- "I don't remember the Al Qaeda cells as being something that we were told we needed to do something about." According to the 9/11 Commission Report, starting in January 2001, Richard Clarke told Rice "at least twice that al Qaeda sleeper cells were likely in the United States."
- "I do not remember any reports . . . that planes might be used as a weapon," *and,* "The threat reporting that we received in the spring and summer of 2001 was not specific as to . . . manner of attack," *and,* "I was certainly not aware of [intelligence reports about planes as missiles] at the time that I spoke [in 2002]." By 9/11 there had been 12 separate and explicit warnings about terrorists using planes as weapons.[221]
- Had she known the Immigration and Naturalization Service had cut its internal security enforcement budget by half in the months before 9/11? "I don't remember being made aware of that, no."
- Had she known the Saudis were barring U.S. access to Al Qaeda suspects before 9/11? "I don't remember anything of that kind."
- Why had the Bush administration curtailed air marshals on domestic flights before 9/11? "I was not told that," said the director of national security.

Rice did much better at "remembering" things that *hadn't* happened:

- "The decision that we made was to, first of all, have no drop-off in what the Clinton administration was doing" to fight Al Qaeda. (See page 355–356.)
- "We moved quickly to arm Predator unmanned surveillance vehicles for action against Al Qaeda." To arm them, but not to *fly* them.
- The Bushies' pre-9/11 strategy called for use of "all aspects of our national power," including "military," against Al Qaeda. Gee—Deputy Secretary of State Richard Armitage told the commission military options were added only after 9/11.
- "We bolstered the Treasury Department's activities to track and seize terrorist assets." (See "Inaction on terrorist financing," p.000)
- "We increased funding for counterterrorism activities across several agencies." Hey, even shortly *after* 9/11, the White House cut an emergency request from the FBI for counterterrorism funds by nearly two-thirds.
- "When threat reporting increased during the spring and summer of 2001, we moved the U.S. government at all levels to a high state of alert and activity." Gen. HUGH SHELTON, chairman of the Joint Chiefs of Staff under Clinton and into the early Bush administration, said the Bushies moved terrorism "farther to the back burner" in the summer, even as warnings mounted.
- "The vice president was . . . in May, tasked by the president to put together a group to [review] domestic preparedness." He just never got around to convening it.
- "President Bush is leading the country during this

time of crisis and change [such as] by creating the Department of **Homeland Security**." Which he fought against, t&n.

- "[Bush has] directed the transformation of the FBI into an agency dedicated to fighting terror." Versus: "FBI FAILS TO TRANSFORM ITSELF, PANEL SAYS."—*Washington Post*, June 2005. The bipartisan panel, formed of members of the 9/11 Commission under the same leaders, was "taken aback" by the extent of the failure, citing high turnover, poor training, and continued inability to build a modern computer system.

- "We have created . . . the TTIC [Terrorist Threat Integration Center], which does bring together all of the sources of information from all of the intelligence agencies." Others said it "created more of a moat than a bridge" and "served little more than to give the appearance of progress." (See **Homeland Security**.)

- After 9/11, Bush "put states on notice if they were sponsoring terrorists." If so, he forgot one or two. He continued to call Saudi Arabia "our friend" despite Saudi *government* support for terrorists—even allegedly for the 9/11 hijackers.[222]

Preemptive war on the commission. As the Bushies' efforts to stonewall the commission began to fail, the *Progress Report* noted, "the administration and its allies stepped up their attempts to discredit the Commission, commissioners and witnesses." Right-wing columnists called for shutting the commission down. In a front-page editorial, *New York Post* and FOX NEWS owner RUPERT MURDOCH declared that "it clearly was not a fact that President Bush was warned against possible attacks in this country" and

Blaming the FBI. Bush's August 6 PDB contained "nothing about the threat of attack in the U.S.," Rice, under oath, told the commission—before admitting the PDB was titled "Bin Laden Determined to Attack Inside the United States." She added, "there was no recommendation that we do something about this; the FBI was pursuing it . . . it was the FBI's responsibility." Bush—who had promised to "usher in an era of personal responsibility"—told the commission, "whoever was the acting FBI director [didn't he know?], had they found something, would have said, Mr. President, we have found something that you need to be concerned about . . . That didn't happen." "Condi" likewise told the commission, "The FBI was pursuing it."

accused the Democratic commissioners of slander. An Ashcroft spokesman said they had (unlike Republicans) "political axes to grind." Sen. MITCH McCONNELL (R-KY), a close ally of the White House, decried "the partisan gallery of liberal special interests seeking to bring down the president." (Please, don't get our hopes up.) And as always, TOM DELAY saw the big picture: The "politicization" of the commission, he said, "undermines the war effort [in Iraq] and endangers our troops." Investigation = treason.

No direction, no plan. The acting FBI director in the summer of 2001, THOMAS PICKARD, told the 9/11 Commission that ASHCROFT had shown "little interest" in terrorism. "Pickard told us that after two such briefings Ashcroft told him that he did not want to hear about the threats anymore," the commission's report noted. Ashcroft responded that he "assumed the FBI was doing what it needed to do." Ashcroft's assumption was "dangerous," the commission's final report noted. "He did not ask the FBI what it was doing in response to the threats and did not task it to take any specific action. He also did not direct the INS, then still part of the Department of Justice, to take any specific action . . . In sum, *the domestic agencies never mobilized in response to the threat. They did not have direction, and did not have a plan to institute. The borders were not hardened. Transportation systems were not fortified. Electronic surveillance was not targeted against a domestic threat. State and local law enforcement were not marshaled to augment the FBI's efforts. The public was not warned.*" (Emphasis added.)

Six lost opportunities. THE 9/11 COMMISSION REPORT, published in July 2004, listed around ten opportunities to disrupt the 9/11 plot—four during Clinton's eight years and six in Bush's first eight months. This did not stop the GOP from immediately suggesting the report condemned Clinton. It "covers eight years of the Clinton administration and eight months of the Bush administration," said House Speaker DENNIS HASTERT (R-IL). (The report should not become a "political football," he added, converting the extra point.)

The report cited Bush's failures to (a) watch-list, trail, or share information about two of the future hijackers or link them to the USS *Cole* bombing; (b) link the arrest of Moussaoui to other warning signs; (c) recognize phony passports and visa applications; (d) expand no-fly lists to include names from terrorist watch lists; (e) search airline passengers identified by the computer-based CAPPS screening system; and (f) harden aircraft cockpit doors "or take other measures to prepare for the possibility of suicide hijackings." "Across the government," the report concluded, "there were failures of imagination, policy, capabilities, and management," of which "[t]he most important failure was one of imagination. *We do not believe leaders understood the gravity of the threat . . . Terrorism was not the overriding national security concern for the U.S. government.*" (Emphasis added.)

The report also recommended measures such as improved border and port security and an integrated terrorist "watch list" which, wrote Richard Cohen in the *Washington Post*, "you would have thought would have been implemented on Sept. 12, 2001." Wrote Robert Scheer, Bush's "nearly three years of bragging about his 'war on terror' credentials has been exposed as nothing more than empty posturing."

"Losing the war on terrorism." According to perhaps the world's leading bin Laden expert, Yossef Bodansky, former director of the U.S. Congressional Task Force on Terrorism and Unconventional Warfare, Bush's "re"election made another major Al Qaeda attack on the U.S., possibly using nukes, "virtually inevitable." In November 2004, Bodansky—a well-known conservative—told the *Jerusalem Post* Al Qaeda was likely "tying up the knots" for an attack on the U.S. using WMDs.

After 9/11 a "theological debate" emerged within Al Qaeda and its supporters "over whether the mass killing of innocents is permissible," according to Bodansky. The reelection of Bush, Bodansky said, "was viewed by bin Laden and his cohorts as a decisive answer . . . with Americans now 'choosing' to be the enemies of Islam." Important Islamic religious leaders and members of "the elites of the Arab world" agreed, and gave "the green light" for another major attack and "the kosher stamp" to use nuclear weapons.

America was losing the war on terrorism, Bodansky said, as bin Laden gained support throughout the Muslim world. "In the pre-9/11 world . . . jihadists could count on 250,000 individuals trained and willing to die, and 2.5 million–5 million people willing to help them in one way or another." Newer intelligence estimates "suggest that as many as 500,000–750,000 people are willing and trained to die, 10 million are willing to actively support them . . . while another 50 million are willing to support such a movement financially." [223]

In July 2005, the *Washington Post* described the subway and bus bombings in London that month as "a clear sign that Osama bin Laden and his deputies remain in control of the network" and that "the nerve center of the original al Qaeda network remains alive and well."

SOCIAL SECURITY "REFORM"

> *They want the federal government controlling Social Security like it's some kind of federal program.*
>
> —George W. Bush, November 2000

Social Security "reform" is Bushit for *privatizing* the federal retirement insurance system—turning it into a profit-making industry for financial services corporations; destroying a successful government program that, as such, is hated by the right; and dividing and conquering Democrats into the bargain. Bush's Social Security scheme, which he reintroduced at the start of his second term after it went nowhere in his first, would let some portion of workers' payroll taxes, which fund Social Security, go into private accounts that could be invested in stocks, instead of into the Social Security trust fund, which is invested in Treasury bonds. A worker's future Social Security benefits would be reduced by whatever amount he put into a private account; but the higher returns on stocks would supposedly give him a bigger nest egg and monthly incomes when he retires. Infinitely more certain was that Bush's plan would benefit corporations by vastly expanding the market for their stocks, enrich the financial firms that would market the shares and collect an estimated $10 billion a year in fees on the new accounts, and *create* a Social Security financing crisis where none existed.

Flat-out lie. "The crisis is now," Bush said; the Social Security system had to be drastically restructured, or by 2042 it "will be flat bust, bankrupt." No: Only the Social Security *surplus* or "trust fund" would be depleted (unless the Bushies looted it first, as they were already doing, beginning by denying there was such a thing as a trust fund). True, because of the aging population, benefits paid out were growing faster than Social Security tax revenues coming in. (By law, the Social Security budget is independent of the rest of the government.) But revenues would continue to exceed payouts—enlarging the trust fund—until around 2018. After that, payouts would draw it down. But current benefits were guaranteed until 2042, according to the Social Security trustees—12 years *longer* than they predicted in 1997—or 2052, according to the Congressional Budget Office (CBO). And even after that, enough new money would be coming in to keep paying 81 percent of promised benefits—which, adjusted for inflation and wage growth, would in fact be more than beneficiaries received in 2005. "Social Security is more financially sound today than it has been throughout most of its 69-year history," said the Center for Economic and Policy Research.

To put the "crisis" in another perspective, less than one-fifth of the revenue loss from Bush's tax cuts—in fact, just the portion that goes to people earning over $1,000,000 a year—could keep Social Security solvent for another 75 years. A less than 3 percent reduction in federal spending—or roughly 0.54 percent of GDP, and less than we were spending in Iraq—would accomplish the same thing, the *New York Times*'s Paul Krugman noted. In fact, while Social Security generated surpluses, it was the rest of the federal government—thanks in large part to Bush's war and tax cuts—that was running $400-billion-plus annual federal deficits with no end in sight, and was $7.5 trillion in debt. What about *that* crisis?

Krugman noted the Bushies' "three-card-monte logic." When discussing the Social Security trust fund, they insisted it was meaningless, nonexistent: Social Security revenues were just part of general government revenues—and therefore could be used for non-Social Security purposes, such as paying for tax cuts for the rich or disguising the size of Bush's budget deficits. But when discussing Social Security's future *deficits*, suddenly, that's Social Security's own problem, which can only be remedied by benefit cuts, a Social Security tax increase, getting rid of some old people—whatever. "There's no honest way anyone can hold both these positions," wrote Krugman, "but very little about the privatizers' position is honest. They come to bury Social Security, not to save it. . . . For Social Security is a government program that works."

As *The Nation*'s Matt Biven summarized the plot, "Tax, tax, tax the working and middle class. [Social Security tax is levied only on paychecks, *not* on dividends, capital gains, trust funds, etc.] Assemble a tremendous pile of money doing so. Then give gargantuan tax breaks to the rich. . . . Then cry, 'Hey, there's no money left for working Americans when they retire, the system is in crisis'! And cut benefits. It's a transparent transfer of money" from average people to the rich.

Fraudulent insurance claims. Bush's advertising of his plan's benefits was as phony as the "crisis"; it was based on an almost impossible best-case scenario for stock market returns. Even his own so-called Commission to Strengthen Social Security—though packed with right-wing supporters of privatization and with executives whose companies stood to reap a fortune from it—did not use such crazy assumptions. By its estimates, benefits would be around half the amount Bush claimed, and that was only if one didn't "luck into" a bad period on the stock market—which can last decades. The CBO calculated that the combination of benefits from Social Security and individual accounts was likely to be less than actual benefits under the current system.

Indeed, Krugman noted, none of the privatization schemes could work as promised unless stocks were to yield at least a 6.5 percent rate of return—after inflation, and on top of substantial management fees—for the next 75 years, which is impossible unless the economy grows much faster than anyone expects. But if it does, "it will also yield a bonanza of payroll tax revenue that will keep the current [Social Security] system sound for generations to come"!

"Mathematically certain to fail." A more obvious problem, Krugman noted, was that Social Security is a system in which each generation pays for the previous generation's retirement. If younger workers' payroll taxes were diverted into private accounts, who would pay benefits to older Americans, who spent their working lives paying into the current system? The White House proposed to borrow an estimated $2–$3 *trillion* (by selling Treasury bonds) to replace the diverted funds, and make up for this borrowing by reducing future benefits.

But this whole scheme, the *Los Angeles Times*'s Michael Kinsley pointed out, rested on a very odd assumption coming from believers in the genius of the private sector: Politicians are smart—they know stocks are a much better investment than government bonds; but financial firms are stupid, and will sell stocks to the new private accounts while buying all those new Treasury bonds.

In fact, privatization itself would ensure that bonds outperform stocks in the longer run: The influx of new money chasing stocks would raise their price and lower their subsequent returns while increased government borrowing would raise the interest rates on bonds. Social

Security privatization "is not just unlikely to succeed," Kinsley declared. "It is mathematically certain to fail." Even Bush's handpicked commission apparently realized private accounts wouldn't "save" Social Security but only create a financing crisis.

Or was that the intent? Trillions of dollars in new U.S. debt could drive interest rates so high, the economy, the stock market, the dollar, and federal tax revenues would get whacked. The bond market could refuse to underwrite more debt, bringing the government to the brink of bankruptcy— at which point severely curtailing or even eliminating Social Security (along with the other entitlement programs hated by the right—Medicare and Medicaid) would be presented as the only option.

By January 2005, Republicans in Congress were balking. (Did the Bushies "believe they would be welcomed as liber-ators?" Krugman cracked.) Undaunted, Bush, wrote Krugman, "once again insists that privatization will lead to a 'perma-nently strengthened Social Security system, without changing benefits . . . and without raising payroll taxes on workers.' In other words, $2 - 1 = 4$." Bush, never a very good student, declined to show his arithmetic when Democrats in Congress asked him to include in his 2006 budget proposal an accounting of the money that would be needed for his Social Security plan.

Nor did Bush advertise the fact that Social Security is run very efficiently: Because all the funds are managed together, less than 0.6 cents of every dollar paid out in benefits goes to administration costs. In Britain's retirement system, which adopted privatized accounts, administrative costs consumed 15 cents of every dollar. "Even by the Bush administration's own estimates," the *Progress Report* noted, "in a system of privatized accounts, 5 cents of every dollar would go to administrative costs, more than 8 times the amount spent on administrative costs today."

Heir today . . . Bush "always gets a big round of applause for promising that the money in a private account could be passed on to one's heirs," the *New York Times* remarked. "If those happy clappers only knew the details." Your heirs would only inherit the amount left in your account after you bought an annuity that generated enough monthly income to keep you above the poverty line for life. You would be required to buy the annuity before you could spend any of the money in your account. Those who started out with the smallest accounts— low- and middle-income earners—would have to use the largest share to buy the annuity, and would therefore have the least left over, if anything, for their heirs.[224]

The "progressive" ploy. In spring 2005, the White House floated a new proposal—"progressive price indexing": Low-wage workers' Social Security benefits would be maintained while "higher-wage" workers would face cuts. Behold the new face of Bushism—taking from the rich to give to the poor! Actually, Krugman showed, this was a plan to slash *middle*-class benefits: Middle-income workers would face the largest cuts—10 percent or more—as a percentage of pre-retirement income, while those earning $1 million would see benefit cuts equal to only 1 percent. "In short," wrote Krugman, "this would be a gut punch to the middle class, but a fleabite for the truly wealthy."

Exploiting early death. As each of their rationales for privatization fell apart, the Bushies' came up with new ones. (Sound familiar? **Iraq** your brain.) In January 2005, Bush told African Americans Social Security was a bad deal for them because "African-American males die sooner than other males do" and therefore don't live long enough to collect their fair share of benefits. This was, first of all, false, Paul Krugman noted: Blacks' average life expectancy lags behind whites' mainly because of high death rates early in life; for black men who make it to age 65, life expectancy is close to that of whites. Moreover, since Social Security is progressive and provides proportionally more benefits to lower-income workers, this works to African-Americans' advantage. Bush's use of this false argument, Krugman wrote, "is doubly shameful, because he's exploiting the tragedy of high black mortality for political gain," *and* taking for granted its continuation for the next 40 or 50 years, "instead of treating it as a problem we should solve."[225]

Ready? The *real* agenda. Meanwhile, for millions of workers who diverted much of their payroll taxes into private accounts, the monthly Social Security check would dwindle or disappear; Social Security as we know it would be phased out for the middle class, leaving mainly the poor. Aha! "It's an adage," wrote Krugman, "that programs for the poor always turn into poor programs . . . once a program is *defined as welfare* (emphasis added), it becomes a target for budget cuts." Just as was already happening to Medicaid.

As younger and better-off Democrats no longer saw any "personal payoff" in their Social Security taxes, their support for Social Security, for the Democratic Party, and for any progressive coalition would weaken, and they would learn to identify their interests with the Repubs, argued Charles Tiefer in *Salon*. Privatization might even allow the GOP to sell the idea of a regressive new NATIONAL SALES TAX (see **Economic Policy**) as a way to end Social Security taxes.

On the propaganda front, according to an internal "tactical plan" document revealed in January 2005, Social Security Administration (SSA) managers and employees were instructed by Bush-appointed administrators to disseminate to "all audiences"—through the media, speeches, seminars, public events, even at places like farmers' markets and "big box retail stores"—the message that Social Security faced a financing crisis that needed "to be addressed soon," and to "insert solvency messages in all Social Security publications."[226] A former Social Security commissioner said it was "unusual to use the Civil Service organization to push a political agenda, especially because what they're saying is not true. The program is not going bankrupt." Who paid for all this propaganda? The Social Security trust fund, of course. In March and April 2005 alone, "administration officials participated in a staggering 166 events, conducted 500 radio interviews and placed opinion columns in newspapers with a combined circulation of nearly 8 million readers" to plug Social Security "reform," the *Progress Report* noted. The result? According to a CBS News poll in May, just 26 percent of Americans approved of the way Bush was handling Social Security; only 36 percent thought private accounts were a good idea.

Swift Boat Smear Veterans for Privatization. Meanwhile, the right went to work smearing the 35-million-member, allegedly "liberal" American Association of Retired Persons (AARP), which only opposed private accounts as a *replacement* for Social Security. Compromise? Sorry, the right doesn't speak that language: AARP was "the boulder in the middle of the highway to personal savings accounts. We will be the dynamite that removes them," said CHARLIE JARVIS, a former Reagan and Bush I official and president of USA NEXT, a right-wing lobbying group "fueled by millions of dollars from wealthy donors, trade associations and companies that share its views," the *New York Times* noted. USA Next happily did the smear job on AARP that the White House could not be seen to endorse. The group hired some of the same consultants who helped the so-called SWIFT BOAT VETERANS FOR TRUTH smear John Kerry during the 2004 **election** campaign—where they learned that the more scandalous the lie, the more free media play it got. They came up with an Internet ad showing a soldier with a red X across him, and two gay men kissing at their wedding, with the headline "The *real* AARP Agenda."

"TORT REFORM"

That's Bushit for rolling back the rights of consumers, workers, patients, and other citizens to sue corporations and health-care providers for harm they cause. This had been at the top of Bush's agenda since the start of his political career. By early in his second presidential term, much had been accomplished:

Class-war action. In February 2005, Bush signed a bill sharply restricting CLASS-ACTION LAWSUITS brought against companies for fraud or negligence—"a significant victory for businesses ranging from auto, drug and gun makers to home builders and tobacco companies," the *New York Times* noted. The so-called "Class Action Fairness Act" was of course aimed not at *corporate* plaintiffs or overzealous lawyers in general, but only at the poorer plaintiffs typically represented in class actions. It was designed to funnel these from state courts to more business-friendly federal courts. The measure came after five years and $168 million worth of lobbying by the U.S. Chamber of Commerce, and four years of lobbying by Bush. It was about "creating jobs and growing our economy," Bush explained. In January 2004, an independent study found that the explosion cited by the Bushies in the economic costs of class-action lawsuits was nonexistent.[227]

Bulletproofing gun makers, or, Guns don't kill, Republicans do. In July 2005, the Senate passed a bill—sponsored by National Rifle Association board member and Senator LARRY CRAIG (R-ID)—shielding gun manufacturers, dealers, and importers from lawsuits brought by victims of gun crimes. The House had already passed a similar bill. Senate Majority Leader Bill Frist (R-TN) "yanked similar legislation from debate last year when Democrats successfully attached an extension of the ban on assault-style weapons and the NRA dropped its support," AP noted. Democrats tried and failed to insert provisions in the new bill that would let children and police retain the right to sue. The bill "has one motivation—payback by the Bush administration and the Republican leadership" to the NRA, said Senator Ted Kennedy, who tried and failed to insert a ban on hollow-tipped, so-called "cop killer" bullets. The gun industry gave 88 percent of its campaign contributions to Republicans in the 2004 election cycle.

Pulling the plug on patients' rights. In 2000, candidate Bush promised a patients' bill of rights like the one in Texas, that would allow people to sue their HMO or health insurance company for wrongfully refusing to cover needed treatment. "That's what I've done in Texas," he boasted, "and that's the kind of leadership style I'll bring to Washington." The latter claim, at least, proved true: Bush had *vetoed* the Texas bill, then let it become law without his signature. In 2004, the Justice Department—arguing that the benefits to patients were outweighed by costs to HMOs—asked the Supreme Court "to block lawsuits under the very Texas law Bush touted in 2000," the *Washington Post* reported.

(Presidential) malpractice. Industry lobbyists Bush, Cheney & Associates were unable to discuss the high cost of **health care** without blaming it within 3.6 seconds on "excessive litigation" or "junk" MALPRACTICE SUITS. To protect negligent doctors, hospitals, drug companies, and their insurers, Bush wanted a $250,000 cap on victims' damages for physical and emotional pain and suffering: a week's salary, perhaps, for an insurance or hospital chain CEO for, say, leaving your daughter or husband brain-dead, or removing the wrong organ, or trying to perform heart surgery on a heartless Republican.

Caps on damage awards, though generally much higher caps, had been implemented in many states. Bush's federal cap—which would undercut all state rules—had been repeatedly blocked by Democrats, but was reintroduced by Senate Republicans in February 2005. It was "the main plank of the GOP's health care agenda," noted Robert Levy of the conservative-libertarian Cato Institute, which opposed it on Constitutional grounds; "conservatives are supposed to be champions of states' rights and limited federal government," Levy noted.

Did someone say "class warfare"? The Bush plan would limit only "non-economic" damages, not "economic" losses such as lost wages or earning potential. So a surgeon or, say, an oil executive could still claim millions of dollars in damages whereas a single mother earning $8 an hour, if disabled for life, could never receive enough to cover lifetime support. In California, where pain and suffering (but not "economic") damages were already capped at $250,000, lawyers had been discouraged from taking cases in which the victims are children or retirees because the maximum award would be $250,000; cases can cost that much to bring to trial. "The law has made it impossible for many victims to get access to the court," a lawyer told the *New York Times*. A study showed that caps had "done little more than enrich California malpractice insurers with excessive profits, at the expense of malpractice victims."[228]

Dis"tort"ions of fact. There may indeed have been a *malpractice* crisis in the U.S., but there was no *litigation* crisis:

- Medical errors kill 44,000–98,000 Americans annually—
  more than breast cancer, AIDS, or motor vehicle
  accidents.[229]
- Medical malpractice payouts were *not* on the rise but
  had been "extremely stable and virtually flat since the
  mid-1980s," according to a comprehensive study. The
  vast majority of patients who were harmed by medical errors or negligence never even filed suit.[230]
- According to the CBO, there was "no statistically significant difference" in health care spending between
  states with and without malpractice caps because
  *malpractice costs account for less than 2 percent of
  that spending.* In fact, doctors' insurance premiums
  went up 25 percent less in the states without caps
  than in those with. And while malpractice payouts
  went down between 2001 and 2002, there was no
  corresponding decrease in doctors' premiums
  because the insurance companies pocketed the difference. Rates had risen, "some" said, because
  insurers were gouging physicians to make up for
  stock market losses.[231]
- Contrary to Bushite claims, doctors ordering lots of
  expensive tests "may be motivated less by liability
  concerns than by the income it generates" for them,
  the CBO reported.
- Bush claimed "lawsuits are driving docs out of the
  practice, which means there's less availability": As
  he lamented so memorably, "Too many OB/GYNs
  aren't able to practice their love with women all
  across this country." The GAO found that "reductions in supply . . . could not be substantiated." In

some states supposedly in a full-blown liability crisis, the number of "docs" practicing their love had been steadily rising.

- Working on a contingency basis, medical malpractice lawyers risk their own money to bring cases to trial; far from taking frivolous or "junk" lawsuits, "we do everything we can to weed out cases that are without merit," one lawyer told the *New York Times*.

"The genius of tort reform," said a *Times* editorial, "is that it offends only one big-money lobbying group: trial lawyers, who are important financial supporters of the Democratic Party." Do something to reduce medical errors? Weed out the negligent doctors responsible for generating most of the malpractice awards? Restrict insurance rate increases? Are you kidding? Attack the *victims* of malpractice, and protect the most powerful business lobbies—that's the Bush way.

"UNITER, I'M A"

I'm a uniter, not a divider.

—Bush 2000 campaign slogan

Blue states buzz over secession.

—*Washington Times*, 11/9/04

VALUES, MORAL *VS. BUSHIST*

In widely publicized exit polls on **Election** Day, 2004, 22 percent of voters cited "moral values" as their main concern. Never mind that 78 percent did not: The Republicans jumped all over the stat as proving that America was on their page while the Dems were hopelessly out of touch. The media quickly bought into this as the story of the 2004 election. Many Dems did, too.

The other 78 percent presumably included those less concerned about gay marriage than about honesty on the part of their leaders, protecting the environment, and maintaining the social safety net. *Those* values, most Americans would have agreed—unlike the kind that seek to punish people for their sexual orientation, make the middle class and poor pay for tax cuts for the rich, conjure phony threats to sell politically motivated wars, and obscure it all behind talk about values—were still more or less the Dems' domain.

Focusing on the wrong boob. The 2004 "values vote" story began officially on February 1, when a glimpse of "bare" breast (the all-important nipple was in fact covered) transformed the annual three-hour orgy of violence and sexual titillation known as the Super Bowl into something unwholesome and un-American. Janet Jackson's "wardrobe malfunction" was so shocking that every news channel was obligated, in the service of public morals, to rerun the video (safely pixilated) twice an hour or so for the next month or two. And it became the Bushies' pretext for launching an anti-obscenity campaign (also see **Free Speech**) that would please religious and social conservatives while distracting millions of voters from, for example, the rising body count in Iraq and Bush's plummeting approval ratings.

The decency crusade was just a part of a new election-year tack, Arianna Huffington noted: "It appears KARL ROVE is planning a small rewrite for his candidate: 'I'm a culture war president.'" Within a month of Boobgate, Bush backed AG JOHN ASHCROFT's "efforts to poke around the private medical records of women who've had abortions," doubled spending on anti-sex education programs (see **Abortion** and **AIDS**), and pledged $23 million for schools—for badly needed books or repairs? No, to investigate students for drug use. Bush also hinted again that he would support a constitutional ban on gay marriage. ("You would think," wrote Huffington, "the Christian right has more pressing matters to worry about. America now has 35 million people living in poverty, many of them working poor. Maybe they should take another look at the Bible.")

Bush also found $1.5 billion—including $300 million diverted from welfare funding—for a new program to promote marriage among welfare mothers. Similar programs, critics noted, had failed to promote marriage or help people escape poverty, and only pressured poor women into staying in bad relationships. But those criticisms were admittedly based on experience rather than faith.

"There's barely a speech by President Bush that doesn't cite the glories of human freedom," conservative journalist Andrew Sullivan observed in *Time*. "But there's a strange exception to this Bush doctrine. It ends when you reach America's shores . . . The government, Bush clearly believes, has a right to be involved in many personal decisions you make—punishing some, encouraging others . . ." Other

Holy alliances. Pandering to his fear- and hate-based base, Bush called for a constitutional amendment banning GAY MAR-RIAGE, which would deny gays the legal, financial, and alleged emotional benefits of marriage. Bush "believes that we should not carve out *special privileges* for people on the basis of sexual orientation" (emphasis added), KARL ROVE assured a meeting of the "Christian" Family Research Council, at which FRC founder and board member JAMES DOBSON declared that the "homosexual activist movement" was "the greatest danger" to "the family and indeed to the nation." To his credit, Bush personally seemed not to share this bigotry.

In Ohio, one of the states that passed a gay-marriage-ban ballot measure in November 2004, defense lawyers promptly used it to seek dismissals of DOMESTIC-VIOLENCE charges, "citing the amendment's prohibition against any legal status for unmarried couples that approximates marriage" and noting that

examples: Funneling public money to religious groups for "social work" under Bush's **"faith-based initiative,"** tripling funding for "character education," and sending federal agents to bust users of medical marijuana. "It's the nanny state with more cash," wrote Sullivan. "Your cash, that is. Their morals." On all these issues, Sullivan noted, Bush would let the federal government overrule state laws. STATES' RIGHTS, traditionally sacred to conservatives, "are well and good—as long as the states don't do things that some Republicans disapprove of."

the state's domestic-violence law applied only to a "person living as a spouse," the *Toledo Blade* reported.

Even if unintended, this consequence might be of *little* consequence to the religious right. In November 2004, the *Guardian* reported, representatives of the Mormon church teamed up with Sheikh Yusuf al-Qaradawi, "a controversial Islamic scholar who approves of wife-beating and believes in traditional family values," along with Cardinal Alfonso Trujillo, "who campaigns against condoms on behalf of the Catholic church," and Mahathir Mohamad, the dictatorial former prime minister of Malaysia "who sacked and jailed his deputy for alleged homosexuality," at a conference "to 'defend the family' and fight progressive social policies." The congenial conference setting was Doha, in Qatar, which rejected the international Convention for the Elimination of Discrimination Against Women.[232]

Under all the moralizing, the usual GOP hypocrisy prevailed. The major media companies, *all* headed by Bush supporters, were more eager than ever to satisfy the appetites of Americans, red and blue, for entertainment of all degrees of blueness and X-ness (not to mention violence and imbecility). "If anyone is laughing all the way to the bank this election year," wrote the *New York Times*'s Frank Rich in November 2004, "it must be the undisputed king of the red cultural elite, RUPERT MURDOCH," owner of FOX and its "very blue entertainment portfolio"—which included books like

How to Make Love Like a Porn Star and *How to Have a XXX Sex Life* (both promoted on Fox News). And "you can be certain that a party joined at the hip to much of corporate America . . . will take no action to curtail the blue culture these [red] voters deplore," Rich added. Every election, "Republican politicians promise to stop abortion and force the culture industry 'to clean up its act'—until the votes are counted. Then they return to their higher priorities, like cutting capital gains and estate taxes."[233] *And* rewarding the big-media pornographers with tax breaks and easing of media ownership rules. As long as they keep their campaign contributions coming and their political coverage GOP-friendly.

Psst—want some *real* porn? How about the entire career of House Majority Leader TOM DELAY (R-TX), who—while telling his evangelical Christian brethren that God was using him to promote "a biblical worldview" in U.S. politics—made himself the poster child for GOP corruption, earning four rebukes from the House Ethics Committee over a six-year period during which only five other members of Congress received even one? DeLay, godfather of the protection racket known as the **K Street Project**; serial seller of legislative favors to consumer-gouging energy companies and other corporate special interests; author—with former ENRON CEO KEN LAY—of "the Enron bill," which would have completely deregulated the electricity industry; architect of the infamous, apartheid-style congressional redistricting in Texas in 2003, whose way was paved by corporate money raised by "DeLay, Inc." and illegally used to win state legislative seats, according to a grand jury indictment of three

DeLay associates; DeLay, who, said Norm Ornstein of the conservative American Enterprise Institute, "has taken every norm the Legislature has operated on and shredded it." ("On a scale of 1 to 10, Democrats abused their majority status at about a level 5 or 6," Ornstein told *Salon*. "Republicans today have moved it to about an 11.")

Still horny? How about ~~mobster~~ monster lobbyist and close DeLay associate JACK ABRAMOFF and his sidekick, PR man and former DeLay spokesman MICHAEL SCANLON, who in early 2005 appeared headed for indictment for allegedly bilking at least $80 million out of six newly wealthy Indian tribes for lobbying and PR work most of which the tribes never received? While this went on, the two directed the Indians to donate more than $10 million to GOP politicians and right-wing organizations, and "exchang[ed] gleeful messages mocking tribal leaders as 'morons,' 'troglodytes' and 'monkeys.'" "'I want all their MONEY!!!' Mr. Scanlon exuberantly e-mailed in the midst of one deal."[234]

Abramoff was best known for teaming up with Christian Coalition leader, lobbyist, and GOP bigshot RALPH REED in 2002 to charge a Louisiana tribe millions to organize a "Christian" crusade against gambling in order to shut down a rival tribe's casino—then charging the rival tribe $4.2 million to lobby lawmakers to reopen it! In 2000, money from a Mississippi tribe and a gambling services company, paid through and partly by Abramoff, financed a DeLay golfing vacation with his family in Scotland. (House rules prohibit members from accepting payment for travel costs from a registered lobbyist.) Two months later, DeLay helped kill the Internet Gambling Prohibition Act, which was opposed by the two donors.

They draw the line at cannibalism. Well, actually . . . In the 1990s, conservative pundit David Brooks noted, "folks" like Abramoff and GOP activist GROVER NORQUIST "were talking up the virtues of international sons of liberty like Angola's JONAS SAVIMBI and Congo's dictator MOBUTU SESE SEKO—all while receiving compensation from these upstanding gentlemen . . . Only a reactionary could have been so discomfited by Savimbi's little cannibalism problem as to think this was not a daring contribution to the cause of Reaganism."[235]

WAR PROFITEERING, CORPORATE

"Come on," you protested in March 2003. "After all their other Bushit about **Iraq**, they're going to just give billions of dollars in contracts to their **corporate** cronies without competitive bidding or anything, *and* let them rip off the U.S. government—not to mention the Iraqis—right under everybody's noses? Get outta here." Remember? Well, once again, you misunderestimated (see **Bushisms**) the Bushies' sheer "Yeah? What are you going to do about it?"-ness.

The rule seemed to be, the closer the contractor was to the Bushies and GOP, the worse the abuses—the preeminent example being HALLIBURTON, from which former CEO Dick Cheney continued to receive a $150,000 salary and own stock options. First, read under **Dick** how Halliburton *got* the lion's share of the Iraq contracts—at least $18 billion worth—including a secret, no-bid contract to put out oil fires that turned into an open-ended, $10-billion-plus deal to provide army support services. (Under Bush, half the Pentagon's roughly \$400 billion budget went to private contracts, of which only 40 percent were conducted under "full and open competition," according to the Center for Public Integrity. Three of the top ten contractors collected less than 10 percent of their contract dollars through open bidding.[236]) Then read here how Halliburton's services were so shoddy, corrupt, and possibly criminal, they might have jeopardized the very outcome of the war—and how Halliburton was rewarded with bonuses and more contracts. How the Bushies used Iraq as a laboratory for radical privatization. And how miserably the experiment failed.

Plenty of experience. Halliburton pioneered military-services outsourcing. In 1992, under Defense Secretary Cheney, the Pentagon commissioned Halliburton subsidiary Kellogg Brown & Root (KBR) for a classified study on whether the military should use more private contractors! KBR said, "I will," if you will, and the two were quickly married: KBR got one of the first private army support contracts, outsourcing took off—and in 1995 Cheney, with no business experience, became CEO of a multi-billion-dollar firm. During his five years at Halliburton, the value of its federal contracts doubled.

Several federal investigations in 2004 centered on allegations that on Cheney's watch, the firm was involved in a \$180 million bribery scheme in Nigeria, broke the law by doing business in Iran, and overcharged the army for work in the Balkans. In 2002, Halliburton paid \$2 million to settle charges it inflated costs on a maintenance contract at an army base in California. And in August 2004 it paid a paltry \$7.5 million to settle SEC charges that it defrauded shareholders of billions by inflating revenue while under Cheney's management. With a ~~eri~~ record like that, no wonder Halliburton rocketed under Cheney/Bush from the Pentagon's 37th largest contractor to number one.

- By early 2004, Halliburton was getting around *$1 billion a month* for Iraq work—more than one-fifth of the $4.7 billion a month (or about $157 million per day) the U.S. was spending in Iraq. Halliburton's KBR subsidiary had billed the army $9.6 billion (a sum expected to grow by $6 billion a year) for army support services in Iraq such as food, laundry, and trash collection—for which the army initially estimated and budgeted $3.6 billion. KBR was also supporting operations in Afghanistan, Djibouti, Georgia, Jordan, and Uzbekistan under the same open-ended, "cost-plus" contract.
- A Pentagon review in 2004 concluded Halliburton overcharged the army by $61 million for gasoline for Iraq's civilian market—charging more than twice the going rate to truck fuel to Iraq from Kuwait.
- Congressional and military reviews found the army being billed $100 for each 15-pound load of wash—or $1 million a month in overcharges. KBR employees were housed in five-star, $110 hotel rooms in Kuwait while the troops lived in tents at a cost of $1.39 per day. Taxpayers were billed for empty trucks driven up and down Iraq, and $85,000 vehicles were abandoned for lack of spare tires. Workers were told to "look busy" while doing virtually no work for salaries of $80,000 a year. Halliburton charged the army for

meals it never served to troops (it repaid $36 million and set aside more than $140 million for a possible settlement on that issue). It even fell behind in delivering drinking water to the troops. Privatization = Efficiency!

- The Army Corps of Engineers' chief of contracting alleged in October 2004 that officials had shown favoritism toward the company and had tried to remove her from her contract-monitoring post after she raised questions about Halliburton contracts.
- A third or more of the government property Halliburton was paid to manage for the Coalition Provisional Authority (CPA) in Iraq—including more than $18 million worth of vehicles, generators, and computers—were missing, the CPA inspector general reported in November 2004.

A GAO report in July 2004 said Halliburton overcharged the government by more than $165 million. The same month, Senate Republicans voted down a proposal to impose stiffer penalties on contractors who overbill. In February 2005, the army, ignoring its own auditors' counsel, decided *not* to withhold partial payments to Halliburton while these issues were pending. In fact, that month the administration budgeted an additional $1.5 billion for Halliburton services and awarded the firm $9.4 million in bonus payments. Critics said the administration was "going easy" on the company. Cheney responded, "Halliburton gets unfairly maligned."

EASI money. Halliburton didn't have Iraq *all* to itself. The stock price of ENGINEERED SUPPORT SYSTEMS INC. (on NASDAQ,

EASI) more than doubled in the first six months of the war thanks to contracts to refit military vehicles and build $19 million worth of its protective shelters against Saddam's chemical and biological weapons stockpiles. (No wise-cracks, please.) In January 2005, WILLIAM H. T. BUSH—or "Uncle Bucky," to W.—who sat on EASI's board, cashed out a half-million stock options for a $450,000 profit.[237] Lucky timing, maybe; some of EASI's sole-source contracts, valued at $158 million, were under investigation by the Pentagon.

From the Iraqis' trough, too. Halliburton was also one of the principal beneficiaries of the Iraqi oil money in the Development Fund for Iraq, which was intended to help rebuild the country. As of July 2004, the U.S.-led occupation authorities had spent or earmarked nearly all of the $20 billion in the development fund—most of which went to non-Iraqi firms—but had spent just 2 percent of an $18.4 billion Iraqi aid package approved in October 2003. The withheld funds gave them leverage over Iraqi politicians in demanding military bases, economic "reforms," etc., while the use of Iraqi money allowed the CPA "to bypass U.S. con-tracting rules on competition, oversight and monitoring for controversial projects," the *Washington Post* noted.

- The largest such contract went to Halliburton's KBR subsidiary, which was paid $1.66 billion to truck gaso-line and other fuels into Iraq—a country with the world's second-largest oil reserves.
- HARRIS CORP. of Florida got $48 million from Iraqi oil funds to run Iraq's media network and newspaper, which, the *Post* reported, "have been widely criticized

as mouthpieces for the occupation and symbols of the failures of the reconstruction effort."

- No-bid contracts went to MOTOROLA INC. to supply police radios and to CUSTER BATTLES LLC to provide security for the main U.S. military base in Baghdad. In October 2004, two Custer Battles managers accused the company of defrauding the U.S. government out of tens of millions of dollars by repeatedly inflating prices or billing for nonexistent services. The Justice Department declined to prosecute. Partner (and Fox News commentator) MICHAEL BATTLES "is very active in the Republican Party and speaks to individuals he knows at the White House almost daily," a Pentagon report said.[238]

- In February 2005, four former Custer Battles employees, all military veterans, told NBC News they had quit in disgust, saying company men terrorized and indiscriminately shot down unarmed Iraqis— "local civilians on their way to work. What we saw, I know the American population wouldn't stand for," one of the four said.

- In 2004, while Iraqis faced "massive outbreaks of cholera, diarrhea, nausea and kidney stones" from drinking contaminated water, *The Nation* noted, the State Department took "$184 million earmarked for drinking water projects and moved it to the budget for the lavish new U.S. Embassy in Saddam's former palace."

Iraqi officials were given little say in the use of their own country's money. Iraqi company executives complained they were not even allowed into occupation headquarters to meet with contracting officers, and "that the process was so secretive that they had to bribe CPA translators to get information about what requests for bids were coming up," the *Washington Post* reported. Nearly $100 million in disbursements were completely undocumented. Naturally, the White House stonewalled auditing efforts by the international monitoring board charged with overseeing Iraq's oil revenues—further fueling Iraqis' suspicions that we had come to steal their oil. No wonder the CPA's Program Management Office contracted with a mercenary firm to protect its employees from "assassination, kidnapping, injury and embarrassment"![239]

A playground for right-wing theorists. Iraq was the central front in the crusade to bring the benefits of Bushonomics—that "toxic mix of ideological obsession and cronyism," wrote Paul Krugman—to the world. (See **Foreign Policy**.) By "making Iraq a playground for right-wing economic theorists, an employment agency for friends and family, and a source of lucrative contracts for corporate donors," wrote Krugman, "the administration did terrorist recruiters a very big favor" by "reinforcing the sense of many Iraqis that we came as occupiers, not liberators." What Iraqis saw, wrote Naomi Klein in *The Nation*, was "desperately needed jobs going to Americans, Europeans and South Asians; roads crowded with trucks shipping in supplies produced in foreign plants, while Iraqi factories were not even supplied with emergency generators. As a result, the reconstruction was seen not as a recovery from war but as . . . a foreign invasion of a different sort. And so, as the resistance grew, the reconstruction itself became a prime target." With security costs eating up 25 percent of reconstruction contracts, insurance up to 30 percent, and 20 percent or more lost to corruption—well, wrote Klein, "Don't do the math."

Extreme outsourcing. Iraq's economic planning itself was subcontracted, after "a highly questionable bidding procedure," to a consulting firm with close ties to Jeb Bush. Private firms provided the bodyguards for U.S. officials and guards for U.S. installations. What was next—"Use a WarCorp® army for your next war. WarCorp®. We shock, we awe, we do it all"?

In fact, they already did. U.S. contractors were involved in 16 of the 44 alleged abuses at ABU GHRAIB (see **Human Rights**) where, according to army reports in 2004, contract interrogators and "translators" repeatedly resorted to body language, and encouraged soldiers to abuse prisoners as well. After a private interrogator from CACI INTERNATIONAL was cited for sexual humiliation of prisoners, yet kept his job, the army, declaring itself "satisfied" with CACI, awarded it a no-bid, $23 million contract to continue providing private interrogators in Iraq. A TITAN CORP. interpreter wearing a military uniform allegedly raped a teenage male detainee while a female soldier took pictures.[240] For you investors, those ticker symbols are CAI and TTN.

In July 2004, Senate Republicans defeated an attempt to bar private contractors from interrogating prisoners, while the White House sought immunity from Iraqi prosecution for U.S. contractors. Wrote Klein, "It seems likely that [interim Iraqi Prime Minister Iyad] Allawi will agree, since he is, after all, a kind of U.S. contractor himself: A former CIA spy, he is already threatening to declare martial law, while his Defense Minister says of resistance fighters, 'We will cut off their hands, and we will behead them.'"

Homeland Security, too, offered our corporate carrion birds rich feeding. From 2002 to 2005, BOEING and Integrated Coast Guard Systems (ICGS), a partnership of LOCKHEED MARTIN and NORTHROP GRUMMAN, between them paid more than $250 million to settle charges of defrauding the Pentagon—*and* received nearly $700 million in Department of Homeland Security (DHS) contracts, making them the two largest DHS contractors. In late 2004 DHS's inspector general reported that Boeing overcharged the department $49 million on a contract to install and maintain bomb detection and other screening equipment at U.S. airports, and that a ICGS deal to install new engines in Coast Guard helicopters would take longer and cost more than if the Coast Guard did the work itself.[241]

Past performance has no bearing. In September 2004, the Veterans Affairs Department scrapped a new computer system installed at a VA hospital in Florida by the consulting firm BEARINGPOINT because it didn't work, and the Justice Department launched a criminal inquiry. An independent assessment of the system, which was to have been expanded nationwide, said it could serve "as an exemplary case study in how not to do technology transition." The firm had collected about $117 million for what began as a $750,165 work order. Two months later, a company that could not get a computer system to keep track of rubber gloves got a DHS contract worth up to $229 million "to help consolidate and integrate the agency's vast financial resources and assets," including accounting, grants management, etc. "Every large company has successes and failures, right?" a DHS spokesman said, referring to the VA fiasco. This could be completely irrelevant, but BearingPoint had close ties to Florida governor and future president JEB BUSH and contributed more to the 2000 and 2004 Bush-Cheney campaigns than any other major Iraqi contractor, according to the Center for Responsive Politics. Oh, didn't we mention? In March 2004, a federal investigation found that BearingPoint had been awarded a $240 million USAID contract in Iraq after writing most of the job specifications itself, effectively knocking its competitors out of the running. The contract was to develop "a competitive private sector" in Iraq. The company also had a $64 million USAID contract to help Afghanistan implement "reform measures."[242] As they say in Pashto, *oy vey*.

SAIC and ye shall fleece. In 1990, SCIENCE APPLICATIONS INTERNATIONAL CORP. (SAIC) was fined $1.3 million for falsifying testing of samples from Superfund toxic waste sites. In 1993, it was charged with fraud over a military contract. And in 1995, it paid $125,000 over allegations that it lied about the results of tests on a security system for the Treasury Department. "Lucky for SAIC," the *Progress Report* noted, "it also has close ties to the current [Bush] administration." Three former top executives had become Pentagon or White House officials; one was a key aide to Under Secretary of Defense DOUGLAS FEITH, who was in charge of supervising contracts in Iraq. And SAIC had donated heavily to GOP candidates. Hello: After 9/11, SAIC got the contract to overhaul the FBI's computer system—by December 2003. In February 2005, the FBI announced that the new, $171 million system had a problem: It didn't work. Meanwhile, SAIC got seven no-bid contracts for work in Iraq, including an $82 million deal to run the country's TV/radio network, despite having no media experience, as quickly became apparent.[243]

WAR PROFITEERING, POLITICAL

I've never been able to understand how Republicans have turned this tragedy into a victory.

—David Pototari, co-director,
September 11th Families for Peaceful Tomorrows

It didn't take a Karl Rove to appreciate the political windfall Bush received immediately after **September 11**, when—having failed to prevent the worst terror attack in our history—his popularity skyrocketed.

On September 10, 2001, wrote Matthew Yglesias in the *American Prospect*, Bush "was already heading for failure." His decision "to ignore the message of the 2000 election" and pretend to have a mandate to move far to the right had led to the defection of Senator Jim Jeffords and the GOP loss of Senate control. Bush's approval rating "was low and falling. National-security hawks "were up in arms at the revelation that the Bush tax cuts left no room for upgrading [the] military . . . The Bush domestic agenda was going nowhere fast."

Then came 9/11, thousands died—and Bush's approval rating zoomed to around 90 percent. Support for Republicans in Congress went from 37 percent in August to 67 percent.

Thus, wrote Yglesias, "was born the poisonous dynamic [wherein] Bush's political operatives want people to feel as threatened as possible."

Being rewarded for failure, he noted, is "all backward. Incumbent presidents never campaign on the basis of how bad the economy is doing." But what other president had the nerve or the Rove to so shamelessly exploit a disaster and play on the fear, anger, pride, and patriotism it aroused? While refusing to accept any *responsibility* for 9/11, the Bushies wasted no opportunity to make the images of 9/11® destruction and heroism their own partisan property and to obscenely link political opponents with Saddam and bin Laden. They used the war on terrorism® to blame for the lousy **economy**; justify upper-income tax cuts, rollbacks of **environmental** rules, and **energy** drilling on nature preserves; attack **labor** unions and **abortion** rights supporters; push through right-wing **judicial** nominees; pass, said John Dean, "the most repressive new laws imaginable and [call] it an act of patriotism"; and to resist any investigation of the causes of 9/11 (they had no time for commissions of inquiry—they had a war on terrorism to fight). Bush and Cheney, said John Dean, "have found that when Americans are frightened they can be governed like sheep."

Let's not forget the "hijacking [of] legitimate American outrage and patriotism over 9/11 to conduct a pre-ordained war against Saddam Hussein," in the words of Tom Maertens, who worked in the National Security Council and State Department under Clinton and Bush, and who wrote that "the Bush administration has practiced the most cynical, opportunistic form of politics I witnessed in my 28 years in government."

Above all, the Bushies used fear and war to regain GOP

control of the Senate in 2002 and retain the White House in 2004, neither of which was likely without 9/11 or its illegitimate offspring, the **Iraq** war.

> *Terrorists continue plotting to kill on an ever larger scale, including here in the United States . . . we might lose tens or even hundreds of thousands of lives as the result of a single attack.*
>
> —Cheney speech, 1/14/04

> *Our country is much safer today than it was on September 11.*
>
> —White House spokesman Scott McClellan two days later

TERRORISM ADDICTS. Indeed, wrote Yglesias, "the worse [Bush] handles terrorism, the better he does in the polls." Each of the administration's terror alerts and releases of bin Laden tapes boosted Bush's ratings by providing "a beneficial reminder that the threat is still out there"—and each happened to come at a politically propitious or perilous moment for the White House. The release of a bin Laden tape four days before the 2004 election may even have saved it for Bush. Describing it as "a gift," a "senior GOP strategist" told the *New York Daily News*, "anything that makes people nervous about their personal safety helps Bush."[244] The Republicans, wrote Yglesias, "have become terrorism addicts, with each new warning, tape, attack, or whatever giving them a desperately-needed pick-me-up to get through one more legislative session, one more election, one more week of bad news from Iraq."[245]

Scaring us to distraction: The art of the terror warning. The strangely coincidental timing of the Bushies' terrorism warnings became apparent early in 2002.

- Early March—just as Democrats were beginning to question aspects of the Bush "war on terror"—saw the debut of the administration's color-coded alert system, which did little but alarm the public and provide grist for comedians (and cover for the Bushies' butts in the event of an attack).

- A torrent of warnings followed the revelation, in May, of the terrorism briefing Bush had received on August 6, 2001, which warned of Al Qaeda attacks "inside the U.S.," possibly involving hijacked aircraft and targeting New York City.

- On June 11, 2002, Ashcroft announced that an American citizen named Abdullah al-Muhajir, née JOSE PADILLA, was under arrest on suspicion of plotting a terror attack in the U.S., possibly using a nuclear "dirty bomb." But Padilla had been arrested more than a month earlier and held secretly. Why were public fears of a nuclear attack not allayed then? The announcement, the *American Prospect* noted, "coincided precisely with the moment congressional investigations into the missed warnings before September 11 began to come very close to [Bush] himself," with the testimony of RICHARD CLARKE.

Smoke bomb. As it turned out, Padilla "had no nuclear materials when arrested or any immediate prospect of getting any," and the "plot" consisted of conversations between him and another U.S. prisoner who made threats to interrogators against the Statue of Liberty and Brooklyn Bridge that were reportedly based on memories of the movie *Godzilla*.[246] Three years later, Padilla remained in jail without formal charges. Labeled an ENEMY COMBATANT—a term invented to allow the president to strip legal rights from, and imprison indefinitely, any citizen he chooses—Padilla embodied the Bushies' use of the war on terror to seize dictatorial powers. In his dissent from the Supreme Court's refusal to hear Padilla's case, Justice John Paul Stevens said it posed "a unique and unprecedented threat to the freedom of every American citizen. At stake is nothing less than the essence of a free society."

Bush job-approval: Code Red. The 2004 **election** season brought a fresh series of peculiarly timed terror warnings that lacked new intelligence, details, or guidance on how to respond. On May 16, a Gallup poll showed Bush's job-approval rating had fallen to 46 percent. A few days later, information emerged suggesting that responsibility for **human rights** abuses of Iraqi prisoners went high up in the administration. And on May 26, AG ASHCROFT announced that Al Qaeda was "almost ready to attack the United States" and had the "specific intention to hit [the U.S.] hard." A senior administration official admitted (anonymously) there was "no real new intelligence . . . no significant change that would require us to change the alert level." (Ashcroft asked the public to look out for seven Al Qaeda suspects whose names had already been circulated by the authorities months before, and whom officials anonymously told the *New York Times* they had no reason to believe were in the U.S.) Asked to explain his timing, Ashcroft could only say, "We believe the public, like all of us, needs a reminder." When John Kerry responded by calling for **homeland** security improvements, a Bush spokesman said Kerry "has played politics with homeland security throughout this campaign."

Drowning out Kerry. In July 2004, two days after Kerry grabbed the headlines by picking John Edwards as his running mate, Homeland Security (DHS) Secretary TOM RIDGE grabbed them back by announcing that "Al Qaeda is moving forward with its plans to carry out a large-scale attack in the United States." He did not elaborate on what was new about his statement, nor did he raise the terror alert level.

As Kerry was enjoying a bounce in popularity a few days after the Democratic convention, Ridge, citing "new and unusually specific information about where Al Qaeda would like to attack," announced that he was raising the threat level to "Code Orange" in New York City (which he seemed to forget was already at "orange"), New Jersey, and D.C. In fact, officials soon admitted, the information was at least three years old. Ridge—who had claimed that "we don't do politics in the Department of Homeland Security"—worked a little plug into his announcement: "The kind of information available to us today is the result of the President's leadership in the war against terror." This, *The Nation* noted, "just a few breaths after invoking frightening images" of WMDs.

The Democrat/terrorist Medicare plan. In early August, on the same day that Kerry criticized the administration for blocking a bipartisan plan to give seniors access to lower-priced prescription drugs from Canada, FDA's acting commissioner said terrorist "cues from chatter" led him to believe Al Qaeda might attack Americans by contaminating imported prescription drugs. He wouldn't provide details to back his claims, and a DHS spokesman conceded, "We have no specific information" about "any Al Qaeda threats to our food or drug supply."

"Threat fatigue": Now please continue shopping. In April 2004, a report by the GAO concluded that the lack of specific information and guidance in the administration's terror warnings undermined their credibility and hampered authorities' ability to protect the public. "They didn't say what was new and didn't suggest any additional measures to be taken other than please be a little bit more vigilant and please go about your shopping," a GAO official observed. In a September 2004 poll, 59 percent said they would not evacuate their town immediately if directed to do so by the government.[247] Repeatedly raising the warning level also created huge costs for city and state governments—especially blue New York and Washington, D.C.—"for which [federal] Washington is not paying its share," the *New York Times* noted, concluding that the color-coded threat chart didn't "serve the purpose for which it was invented." Oh, but didn't it?

The master's strategy. In January 2002, Bush promised he had "no ambition whatsoever to use the war as a political issue." That same month, KARL ROVE advised GOP operatives to tell the American people they could "trust the Republican Party to do a better job of . . . protecting America."

- As the 2002 midterm elections neared, "White House political director KEN MEHLMAN developed a secret PowerPoint presentation . . . urging Republican candidates to highlight fears of future terrorist attacks."[248]

- In just the last week of the 2002 campaign, Bush made 17 speeches emphasizing the terrorist threat from Saddam and (oh, right) Al Qaeda and suggesting—four times in two days—that Democrats in the Senate were *"not interested in the security of the American people."* Bush then refused to apologize because, a spokesman said, "there has been no attempt on [Bush's] part to politicize the war"!

- In a successful campaign heavily backed by the White House and RNC and epitomizing GOP moral rot, Georgia Senate candidate SAXBY CHAMBLISS ran ads featuring photos of Saddam Hussein and Osama bin Laden, implying that Democratic incumbent MAX CLELAND helped our enemies by voting "against the president," and saying he "lacked the courage to lead." Chambliss, had avoided service in Vietnam. Cleland was a highly decorated, triple-amputee Vietnam vet.

"Leave No Corpse Unexploited." [249] The tight 2004 election race saw the Bushies take to the low road—to explore strange new strategies . . . to seek out new smears, new deceptions . . . to boldly go where no campaign had gone before!

Kicking it off in his January 2004 State of the Union address, Bush made 40 references to terrorism, 9/11, war, and Saddam Hussein, and referred to "those" who supposedly harbor a "false hope" that "the danger is behind us."

The campaign's first ads featured photos of firefighters carrying flag-draped coffins out of the ruins of the World Trade Center. The ads were pulled after 9/11 victims' outraged families wildly accused the campaign of exploiting the tragedy for political gain. Firefighters, too, were outraged—with good reason: Since 9/11, Bush had been using images of himself with his arm around a firefighter at Ground Zero while at the same time seeking to cut funding and overtime pay for firefighters and other FIRST RESPONDERS. (See **Homeland Security**.)

(Ground) Zero shame. The GOP decided to hold its 2004 nominating convention in New York City in late August and early September, the latest date a convention had ever been held, which ensured that Ground Zero would be their backdrop on the eve of the third anniversary of 9/11. Consideration was given to having Bush give his acceptance speech *at* Ground Zero. "We read that and we were just sick to our stomachs," a representative of 9/11 families told *Salon*. Why, they wondered, would Bush want to shine a spotlight on 9/11 at all? "It's a symbol of [his government's] failure."

Bring us bin L. (July 27 or 28, if poss.) In July, *The New Republic* reported that the Pakistanis were being pressed hard by the Bush administration to announce the capture of high-value terrorist targets (HVTs)—including Osama bin Laden—before the November election, and specifically during the Democratic National Convention. "No timetable[s]" were discussed in 2002 or 2003, a "recently departed intelligence official" told the magazine. But for some reason, 2004 was different. Pakistani officials said they were "told at every level that apprehension or killing of HVTs before [the] election is [an] absolute must" and that a late July deadline was given repeatedly by Bush officials, who specified "it would be best if the arrest or killing of [any] HVT were announced on 26, 27, or 28 July." Those were the first three days of the Democratic convention. A Pakistani general reportedly said, showing off his fluent English, "If we don't find these guys by the election, they are going to stick this whole nuclear [proliferation] mess up our asshole." [250]

And behold—"on July 29, just hours before Kerry's keynote address," *The Nation* noted, Pakistan announced the capture of an Al Qaeda suspect wanted in connection with the 1998 of U.S. embassy bombings in Africa. "Curiously, he had been apprehended five days earlier." Even curiouser, the announcement was made at midnight Pakistani time, when most Pakistanis were asleep, but in time for prime-time news in the U.S.

The Kerry–bin Laden ticket. Throughout the campaign, Bushies and their allies implied—no, *said*—Al Qaeda wanted Kerry to win. In no instance was any evidence offered to back the claim. A.Q. would seem far more likely to favor Bush, given the recruiting boost and green light for more terrorism he gave it by invading Iraq.

House Speaker DENNIS HASTERT said Al Qaeda "would like to influence this election" to help Kerry win. (Hastert was fresh from implying on Fox News that financier and Kerry supporter George Soros might be a drug dealer: "You know, I don't know where [he] gets his money . . . if it comes overseas or from drug groups or where it comes from." "You think he may be getting money from the drug cartel?" "I'm saying we don't know."[251])

Rep. Tom Cole (R-OK) proclaimed that "if George Bush loses the election, Osama bin Laden wins." The claim was echoed by RUSH LIMBAUGH, the *Washington Times* ("the view of Al Qaeda is 'anybody but Bush'"), DICK MORRIS (who penned a *New York Post* column titled "Terrorists for Kerry"), Fox News's OLIVER NORTH ("Every terrorist is hoping John Kerry gets elected") and MONICA CROWLEY, MSNBC anchors AMY ROBACH and CHRIS MATTHEWS, CNN's senior political analyst BILL SCHNEIDER, and others. Deputy Secretary of State RICHARD ARMITAGE claimed Iraqi insurgents had stepped up their attacks because they wanted to "influence the election against President Bush." "State Department officials could not offer any intelligence assessments to back up Armitage's statement," Knight Ridder noted.

In September—just as U.S. deaths in Iraq reached 1,000—CHENEY threatened in a campaign speech that if Americans "make the wrong choice" on Election Day "then the danger is that we'll get hit again" by terrorists "in a way that will be devastating." In other words, *The Nation* paraphrased, "vote for us or you'll die." "The danger might be a bit less if the current administration had chosen to spend less on tax cuts for the wealthy and more on protecting our ports, securing nuclear materials in Russia and establishing an enforceable immigration policy," the *New York Times* noted. A Cheney spokeswoman explained that his comment was—any guesses?—"taken out of context."

"Frightens with Wolves." "With the presidential election just eight days away, the truth has finally emerged: if John Kerry becomes president you will be eaten by wolves." So the *Progress Report* described the Bush TV ad that debuted about a week before the election. Over images of prowling wolves (the terrorists), the voiceover accused Kerry of voting to "slash" intelligence funding "after the first terrorist attack on America," implying that it was after 9/11. In fact the vote took place in 1994; Kerry's proposal amounted to a 3.7 percent cut as part of a larger deficit-reduction proposal; and the following year, Rep. Porter Goss (R-FL)—Bush's pick for CIA director in 2004—sponsored legislation that would have cut **intelligence** personnel by *20* percent. For several years prior to 9/11, Kerry consistently supported *increases* in intelligence spending.

XENOPHOBIA *AND* YAHOOISM

With the Bushies setting the tone (see **Foreign Policy**)— with a president who didn't seem to know Greeks from Grecians, Slovenia from Slovakia, or the Balkans from the Baltic, or that there were blacks in Brazil (see **Bushisms**)— America became a country in which 65 percent supported invading a country that only 15 percent could locate on a map; where french fries were renamed "freedom fries" and their creators were all but officially titled "cheese-eating surrender monkeys"; where failure to display the flag could arouse suspicions of non-patriotism; and where a general who said Muslims worship "an idol" and terrorists "will only be defeated if we come against them in the name of Jesus" was put in charge of military intelligence gathering in the Middle East. (Okay, you suggest a better "X" and "Y.")

ZEALOTRY

When we say "A-to-Z guide," damn it, we mean A to Z—not A to S or A to Q, like so many A-to-Z guides nowadays. Zealotry? See **Abortion and Birth Control, Corporate-Owned Government, Environment, Foreign Policy, Iraq, Justice, Presidential Power, War Profiteering,** and **Xenophobia.**

ENDNOTES

1 "Clarke's Public Service," *Minneapolis Star Tribune*, 3/28/04.

2 Through TownHall.com book service. Only $99.95!

3 "Report: Global Gag Rule Spurring Deaths, Disease," Women's eNews, 9/25/03.

4 "Dr. Hager's Family Values," *Nation*, 5/30/05.

5 "Christian Science?" *Mother Jones*, September/October 2004.

6 "Memo May Have Swayed Plan B Ruling," *Washington Post*, 5/12/05.

7 William A. Smith, "Playing Politics With Compassion," American-Progress.org, 12/1/04.

8 "Some Abstinence Programs Mislead Teens, Report Says," *Washington Post*, 12/2/04.

9 "Study: Abstinence Pledges May Trigger Risky Sexual Behavior," *USA Today*, 3/18/05.

10 "Teen Sex Increased After Abstinence Program," Reuters, 2/1/05.

11 "No Sex, Please—Or We'll Audit You," *Salon.com*, 10/28/03.

12 "Pattern Recognition," CounterPunch.org, 10/2/02.

13 "Well, Ideally," *American Prospect* online, 4/18/04.

14 "Scientist Who Cited Drug's Risks Is Barred from F.D.A. Panel," *New York Times*, 11/13/04.

15 "In a Shift, Bush Moves to Block Medical Suits," *New York Times*, 7/24/04.

16 "Happy New Year for FDA," *Packaging Digest*, January 2002.

17 "Mr. Outside Moves Inside," *US News*, 3/24/03.

18 "The Truth About the Drug Companies," *New York Review of Books*, 8/15/04.

19 "U.S. Scientist Tells of Pressure to Lift Bans on Food Imports," *New York Times*, 2/25/04.

20 "There's Money in Fat," *Natural Life*, May/June 2004.

21 "Out of Spotlight, Bush Overhauls U.S. Regulations," *New York Times*, 8/14/04.

22 "Penalties for Nursing Homes Show a Drop in Last Four Years," *New York Times* 8/6/04.

23 "The Big Squeeze," *American Prospect*, 9/1/04.

24 "Bush Campaign Ads . . . Brought to You by Special Interests," Public Citizen, 3/3/04.

25 Kristen Sykes of Friends of the Earth on PBS's *Now, with Bill Moyers*, 5/30/03.

26 "New Report Finds Unprecedented Special Interest Access Under Bush," BushGreenwatch.org, 5/25/04.

27 "When Advocates Become Regulators," *Denver Post*, 5/23/04.

28 "Lobbying Prohibitions Eased For Former Top Officials," *Washington Post*, 12/5/04.

29 "Pentagon Brass and Military Contractors' Gold," *New York Times*, 6/29/04.

30 "The Greed Factor," *American Prospect* online, 9/1/04.

31 "Tricky Dick," *American Prospect* online, 9/9/04.

32 "Bush-Cheney's Intelligence and National Security Record," AmericanProgress.org, 8/24/04.

33 "Halliburton's Iraq Deals Greater Than Cheney Has Said," *Washington Post*, 6/23/01.

34 "Plenty More to Swear About," *Time*, 6/26/04.

35 "E-Mail Boosts Calls to Probe Halliburton, Cheney," Reuters, 6/1/04.

36 Edward N. Wolff, "Recent Trends in Wealth Ownership, 1983–1998," May 2000.

37 Economic Policy Institute press conference on Bush plan, C-SPAN, 2/10/03.

38 "Corporations and Wealthy Paying Less," AmericanProgress.org, 4/15/04.

39 "It's a Pattern," AmericanProgress.org, 9/20/04.

40 "Deficit Study Disputes Role of Economy," *New York Times*, 3/16/04.

41 "Assessing President Bush's Fiscal Policies," Economy.com, August 2004.

42 "Bush's First Term Scorecard," *Bull and Bear Financial Report*, 10/4/04.

43 "Red States Make a Mockery of Self-Reliance," *Washington Post*, 1/19/05.

44 Robert Hall and Alvin Rabushka, *The Flat Tax*, Hoover Institution Press, 1995.

45 "Administration's Budget Would Cut Heavily Into Many Areas," CBPP, 3/5/04.

46 "Bush's Class-War Budget," *New York Times*, 2/11/05.

47 "Public Would Significantly Alter Administration's Budget," PIPA.org, 3/7/05.

48 "Closing of the Presidential Mind," *New Republic*, 7/5/04.

49 *Lou Dobbs Tonight*, CNN, 6/15/04.

50 "Blaming the Victim," *American Prospect* online, 11/5/04.

51 "Fervent Falsehoods," *Salon*, 4/29/04.

52 "Error of Omission," *New Republic* online, 11/2/04.

53 "The Media Gives Bush a Mandate," *Salon*, 11/10/04.

54 Ibid.

55 "Bush Supporters Still Believe Iraq Had WMD or Major Program, Supported Al Qaeda," PIPA.org, 10/21/04.

56 "Bush's Confused Supporters," TheCarpetbaggerReport.com, 10/22/04.

57 "Misperceptions, the Media, and the Iraq War," PIPA.org, 10/02/03.

58 "Poll: Creationism Trumps Evolution," CBSNews.com, 11/22/04.

59 "A Danger for Dems: A Moral Misstep," *Nation* online, 11/9/04.

60 "Veteran Retracts Criticism of Kerry," *Boston Globe*, 8/6/04.

61 "Moose on the Loose," *Blueprint*, 10/7/04.

62 "The Rambo Coalition," *New York Times*, 8/24/04.

63 "What the NORC Data Will Show," VoterMarch.org, 11/1/01.

64 "Felon Purge Sacrificed Innocent Voters," *Palm Beach Post*, 5/27/01.

65 "What the NORC Data Will Show," VoterMarch.org, 11/1/01.

66 Paul Krugman, "Fear of Fraud," *New York Times*, 7/27/04.

67 "Protect the Vote," *New York Times*, 9/13/04.

68 "Voting Errors Tallied Nationwide," *Boston Globe*, 12/1/04.

69 "A Flood of Voting Problems," *Salon*, 11/2/04.

70 "Preserving Democracy: What Went Wrong in Ohio," 1/5/05.

71 "How a Republican Election Supervisor Manipulated the 2004 Central Ohio Vote, in Black and White," FreePress.org, 11/23/04.

72 "Reform Needed Now," AmericanProgress.org, 1/7/05.

73 "Democracy Inaction," *Salon*, 11/30/04.

74 "How Bush Pushed Gasoline Prices Sky High," YuricaReport.com.

75 "Take $10 Off the Price of Oil," Cato.org, 11/29/04.

76 "Carter Tried To Stop Bush's Energy Disasters—28 Years Ago," CommonDreams.org, 5/3/05.

77 American Council for an Energy-Efficient Economy press brief, 4/9/01.

78 "The ABCs of Hatred," *New York Times*, 6/3/04.

79 "Crossing the Red Line," *New York Review of Books*, 6/10/04.

80 "New Priorities in Environment," *New York Times*, 9/14/04.

81 Robert F. Kennedy, Jr., *Crimes Against Nature*, HarperCollins, 2004.

82 "U. S. Would Allow 720 Snowmobiles Daily at Yellowstone," *New York Times*, 8/20/04.

83 "Bush Administration: There Is No Extinction Crisis," BiologicalDiversity.org.

84 "Craig's List," *Grist*, 4/15/04.

85 "Ex-FBI Agent Charges Feds with Radioactive Coverup at Colorado's Rocky Flats," BushGreenwatch.org, 1/25/05.

86 "The Jeb Bush Friends and Family Plan," WhoseFlorida.com.

87 "Shift on Salmon Reignites Fight on Species Law," *New York Times*, 5/9/04.

88 "Mercury Dangers Downplayed in Favor of Power Industry," BushGreenwatch.org, 10/25/04.

89 "'Clear Skies' Bill Crafted By Polluters, Testimony Reveals," nrdc.org, 2/2/05.

90 "New Bush EPA Rules Change Adds Still More Health Risks," BushGreenwatch.org, 6/2/04.

91 "Why Are These Men Laughing?" *Esquire*, January 2003.

92 "Eight Questions for Condoleezza Rice," AmericanProgress.org, 1/17/05.

93 "Condi Rice: Tsunami Provided 'Wonderful Opportunity' for U.S.," Agence France-Presse, 1/18/05.

94 "Villagers Furious with Christian Missionaries," *Asia News International*, 1/16/05.

95 "Mix of Quake Aid and Preaching Stirs Concern," *New York Times*, 1/22/05.

96 WorldNetDaily.com, 1/31/04.

97 "End of Discussion," *New Republic*, 11/18/04.

98 "The Death of Diplomacy," AmericanProgress.org, 8/16/04.

99 "A Clampdown in China," *New York Times*, 5/17/05.

100 "Nothing But Talk," *American Prospect* online, 9/21/04.

101 "Devil We Know," *New Republic*, 5/30/05.

102 "Pawn Shop: Has America Sold Out The Libyans?" *New Republic*, 8/30/04.

103 "Casualties of War," *Foreign Policy*, September/October 2004.

104 "A Vision and Little Else," *Newsweek*, 9/13/04.

105 "Kerry leads overseas," *Salon*, 10/15/04.

106 "Welcome to Canada!" *Salon*, 11/15/04.

107 "In Italy, Anger at U.S. Tactics Colors Spy Case," *New York Times*, 6/26/05.

108 "Realistpolitik: Finally, Some Foreign-Policy Conservatives Get Fed Up with Bush," *American Prospect*, 5/5/04.

109 "Remaindered: The Decline of Brand America," *New Republic*, 4/11/05.

110 "Colin Powell in Four-Letter Neo-Con 'Crazies' Row," *Observer*, 9/11/04.

111 "Rice's NSC Tenure Complicates New Post," *Washington Post*, 11/16/04.

112 "I Like Lighthearted People. Besides, She's Really Smart!" *Guardian*, 11/17/04.

113 Former State Department Intelligence Analyst Greg Thielmann on *Now, with Bill Moyers*, PBS, 11/19/04.

114 "World Bank—Wolfowitz for President," AmericanProgress.org, 3/1/05.

115 "Legal Observer Details Police Violence," WSWS.org, 12/16/03.

116 "The War on Dissent," *Globe & Mail*, 11/25/03.

117 "Large Volume of FBI Files Alarms U.S. Activist Groups," *New York Times*, 7/18/05.

118 "Ohio Mulls Academic Bill of Rights," AP, 2/13/05.

119 "Academic Freedom Under Attack," AmericanProgress.org, 2/16/05.

120 "Federal Agency Balks at Word 'Gay,'" *Washington Post*, 2/16/05.

121 "Bush Plans Pollution Rules by March, Disappointing Utilities," Bloomberg.com, 1/21/05.

122 "U.S. Pressure Forces Removal of Climate Change Chief," *Financial Times* online, 4/19/02.

123 "NASA Expert Criticizes Bush on Global Warming Policy," *New York Times*, 10/26/04.

124 *"Medicaid May Face Big Cuts,"* Scripps Howard News Service, 12/13/04.

125 "Record Level of Americans Not Insured on Health," *New York Times*, 8/27/04.

126 "Health Care, the Budget and Morality," AmericanProgress.org, 1/25/05.

127 "U.S. Health Care Satisfaction Trails Others," Webmed.com, 10/28/04.

128 "Kerry & Bush Duel Over Medicare Premiums," FactCheck.org, 9/16/04.

129 "And You Thought His First Term Was a Nightmare," *Salon*, 8/25/04.

130 "Up and Away: Bush's Schemes to Fleece the Poor," *New Republic*, 9/13/04.

131 "Our Unnecessary Insecurity," *New York Times*, 2/20/05.

132 "Truth & Consequences," AmericanProgress.org, 4/2/04.

133 "The Bush Record: Homeland Insecurity," Democrats.org.

134 "Truth & Consequences," AmericanProgress.org, 4/2/04.

135 "Hey, Anybody Seen Our Nukes?" AmericanProgress.org, 2/11/05.

136 Josh Marshall, TalkingPointsMemo.com, 12/6/04.

137 "Children Detained By CPA," AmericanProgress.org, 8/5/04.

138 "Army Details Scale of Abuse of Prisoners in an Afghan Jail," *New York Times*, 3/12/05.

139 "More coldblooded than Abu Ghraib," *Salon*, 12/1/04.

140 "Pentagon Investigates New Claims About Guantanamo," AP, 12/21/04.

141 "New F.B.I. Files Describe Abuse of Iraq Inmates," *New York Times*, 12/21/04.

142 "Workers Threatened Over Prison Abuse, Memo Says," AP, 12/7/04.

143 "The Torture Meeting," AmericanProgress.org, 12/20/04.

144 "Hired Guns in Iraq May Have War Crimes Past," PacificNews.org, 5/3/04

145 "Torture by Proxy: How Immigration Threw a Traveler to the Wolves," *San Francisco Chronicle*, 1/4/04.

146 "Rule Change Lets C.I.A. Freely Send Suspects Abroad to Jails," *New York Times*, 3/6/05.

147 Fox Butterfield, "Mistreatment of Prisoners Is Called Routine in U.S.," *New York Times*, 5/8/04.

148 "Mistreatment of Prisoners Is Called Routine in U.S.," *New York Times*, 5/8/04.

149 "Here's the Story of a Hurricane," *Progress Report*, 8/30/05

150 "A Can't-Do Government," *New York Times*, 9/2/05

151 "White House Orders Purge of CIA 'Liberals,' Sources Say," *Newsday*, 11/14/05.

152 "*Fahrenheit 9/11* Interview Outtake of CIA Director Porter Goss," MichaelMoore.com, 8/10/04.

153 "New C.I.A. Chief Tells Workers to Back Administration Policies," *New York Times*, 11/17/04.

154 Rumsfeld Defends General Who Commented on War and Satan," CNN.com, 10/17/03.

155 "More Iraqis Killed by U.S. than by Terror," *Detroit Free Press*, 8/25/04.

156 "War Has killed 100,000 Iraqis: Study," CBC News, 10/29/04.

157 Al Franken Show Blog, "Bush Reject Bad News," AirAmericaRadio. com, 1/5/05.

158 Western States Legal Foundation, Center on Constitutional Rights, and Lawyers' Committee on Nuclear Policy; "Law Groups Say U.S. Invasion Illegal," OneWorld.net, 3/21/03.

159 "The Legality of the Iraq War," eurolegal.org.

160 Ibid.

161 "This War Is Illegal," RobinMiller.com, 3/21/03.

162 "Seven Fallacies of U.S. Plans to Invade Iraq," *Foreign Policy In Focus*, August 2002.

163 "Realistpolitik: Finally, Some Foreign-Policy Conservatives Get Fed Up with Bush," *American Prospect*, 5/5/04.

164 "Bush Wanted To Invade Iraq If Elected in 2000," Guerrilla News Network, 10/27/04.

165 "Congress, administration test limits of rocky relationship," *National Journal*, 10/3/03.

166 "Storm Warnings," *Newsweek*, 3/29/04.

167 Ibid.

168 Ibid.

169 "How Pair's Finding on Terror Led to Clash on Shaping Intelligence," *New York Times*, 4/28/04.

170 "The Case Against George W. Bush," *Esquire*, September 2004.

171 "The Opportunity Costs of the Iraq War," AmericanProgress.org.

172 "How George Bush Bankrupted the War on Terror," *Salon*, 9/11/04.

173 "Terror and Democracy in the Middle East," meforum.org

174 *Machiavelli on Modern Leadership*, St. Martin's Press, 2000.

175 Paraphrased approvingly by Jonah Goldberg, *National Review* online, 4/23/02.

176 "Iraq: The Uncounted," CBSNews.com, 11/21/04.

177 "Report: Iraq to Stop Counting Civilian Dead," AP, 12/10/03.

178 "War Has Killed 100,000 Iraqis: Study," CBC News, 10/29/04.

179 "Iraqi Civilian Casualties Mounting," Knight Ridder, 9/25/04.

180 Pfaw.org, 9/25/02.

181 "Rejected and Renominated," pfaw.org.

182 "Justices Refuse to Consider Law Banning Gay Adoption," *New York Times*, 1/11/05.

183 "Clash on Judicial Nominees Could Spill Into Lawmaking," *New York Times*, 3/7/05.

184 "Imagining America if George Bush Chose the Supreme Court," *New York Times*, 10/18/04.

185 Moveon.org and pfaw.org.

186 "You Can Tell a Republican by His Stripes," *Washington Post*, 12/17/04.

187 "House Majority Whip Exerts Influence by Way of K Street," *Washington Post*, 5/17/05.

188 "Labor Board's Detractors See a Bias Against Workers," *New York Times*, 1/2/05.

189 "Being Dick Cheney," pfaw.org, 5/20/04.

190 "No Room for Progressives on Cable News Inauguration Coverage," MediaMatters.org, 1/21/05.

191 "The [Arianna] Huffington Post" blog, 7/6/05.

192 "Only the Press Has to Tell the Truth . . ." *MotherJones* online, 5/24/05.

193 "In Control," *American Journalism Review*, February/March 2005.

194 "The White House Stages Its 'Daily Show'," *New York Times*, 2/20/05.

195 Ibid.

196 MediaMatters.org, 2/10/05.

197 "Douglas Feith," *Slate*, 5/20/04.

198 "Media Coverage of Iraq Called 'Shameful'," AmericanFreePress.net, 4/12/04.

199 "Truth and Deceit," *New York Times*, 6/2/05.

200 "Nascar Nation," *New York Times Book Review*, 5/22/05.

201 "Cheney's Staff Focus of Probe," UPI.com, 2/5/04.

202 "Congress-s-s-s: That Giant Hissing Sound . . . ," *Washington Post*, 3/14/04.

203 "Restoring Scientific Integrity in Policymaking," Union of Concerned Scientists, 2/18/04.

204 "Can Prayers Heal?" *New York Times*, 10/10/04.

205 "In Control," *American Journalism Review*, February/March 2005.

206 "U.S. Uses Secret Evidence In Secrecy Fight With ACLU," *Washington Post*, 8/20/04.

207 "EPA, Interior Continue to Tighten Public Information," BushGreenwatch.org, 10/15/04.

208 Ibid.

209 AmericanProgress.org, 12/13/04.

210 "U.S. Military Retaliates Against War Crimes Whistleblower," ABC News, 5/21/04.

211 "War Profiteer," *American Prospect* online, 11/1/04.

212 "Secret Intelligence and the 'War on Terror,'" *New York Review of Books*, 12/16/04.

213 "What Went Wrong," *Newsweek*, 5/27/02.

214 MikeHersh.com, 4/15/04.

215 Ibid.

216 "Thanks for the Heads Up," *New York Times*, 5/25/02.

217 "What Went Wrong," *Newsweek*, 5/27/02.

218 "Cover-up and Conspiracy," wsws.org, 5/18/02.

219 "What the 9/11 Commission Report Ignores," wsws.org, 7/24/04.

220 "The Battle Back Home," *Newsweek*, 2/4/02.

221 "Claim vs. Fact: Rice's Q&A Testimony Before the 9/11 Commission," AmericanProgress.org, 4/8/04.

222 "Saudi Government Provided Aid to 9/11 Hijackers, Sources Say," *Los Angeles Times*, 8/2/03.

223 "Terror Expert: Qaida WMD Attack on U.S. Likely Soon," *Jerusalem Post*, 11/29/04.

224 "Some Inheritance," *New York Times*, 2/23/05.

225 "Little Black Lies," *New York Times*, 1/28/05.

226 "Social Security Enlisted to Push Its Own Revision," *New York Times*, 1/16/05.

227 "Study Disputes View of Costly Surge in Class-Action Suits," *New York Times*, 1/14/04.

228 "Dick Cheney, Insurance Salesman," AmericanProgress.org, 7/20/04.

229 "Steps to Prevent Medical Errors Urged," AP, 1/11/05.

230 "Malpractice Mythology," *New York Times*, 1/9/05.

231 Ohio Universal Health Care Action Network fact sheet, 10/28/02.

232 "Fundamental union," *Guardian Unlimited*, 1/25/05.

233 "On 'Moral Values,' It's Blue in a Landslide," *New York Times* 11/14/04.

234 "Sleaze in the Capitol," *New York Times*, 1/1/05.

235 "Masters of Sleaze," *New York Times*, 3/22/05.

236 "Pentagon Awarded $362 billion in Contracts Without Competitive Bidding," Center for Public Integrity, 9/30/04.

237 "If You Can't Find Something Nice to Say," AmericanProgress.org, 2/23/05.

238 "Lawmakers Told About Contract Abuse in Iraq," *Washington Post*, 2/15/05.

239 "Shameless in Iraq," *Nation*, 7/12/04.

240 "Six Employees From CACI International, Titan Referred for Prosecution," *Washington Post*, 8/26/04.

2341 "Homeland Security Business Faulted," AP, 1/3/05.

242 "Sweetheart Deal for Iraq Contract," *Mercury News*, 3/27/04.

243 "It's Enough to Make You SAIC," AmericanProgress.org, 2/21/05.

244 "See tape as boost for Prez," *New York Daily News*, 10/30/04.

245 "War Profiteer," *American Prospect* online, 11/1/04.

246 "DEFCON Artists," *American Prospect* online, 6/12/02.

247 "Vote for Bush or Die," *Nation*, 9/27/04.

248 Ibid.

249 "Rational Security," *American Prospect*, 3/16/04.

250 "July Surprise?" *New Republic*, 7/19/04.

251 *Fox News Sunday*, 8/29/04.

Also by Jack Huberman and available from Granta Books
www.granta.com

THE BUSH-HATERS HANDBOOK

AN A–Z GUIDE TO THE MOST APPALLING PRESIDENCY OF THE PAST 100 YEARS

'Huberman doesn't mince words and part of the book's appeal is the fluency of its invective, both hilarious and, at times, deeply depressing' *Irish Times*

'Bush truly embodies the American dream – that any kid in America who has a former president for a father, plenty of corporate fat-cat buddies and backers, and the biggest campaign war chest in history can become President of the United States.'

And what happens when he lives the dream? This book reveals the truly abysmal record of the 43rd President of the United States. It is a record of deception and hypocrisy, relentless rollbacks of progress of every kind, tireless devotion to the interests of big business and the wealthy, and complicity with the programmes and prejudices of right-wing and religious zealots. All in easy-to-read A-Z format.